Hoards of the Bronze Age in Southern Britain

Analysis and interpretation

Robin J. Taylor

BAR British Series 228

1993

Published in 2019 by
BAR Publishing, Oxford

BAR British Series 228

Hoards of the Bronze Age in Southern Britain

ISBN 9780860547488 paperback
ISBN 9781407318530 e-book

DOI https://doi.org/10.30861/9780860547488

A catalogue record for this book is available from the British Library

This book is available at www.barpublishing.com

BAR Publishing is the trading name of British Archaeological Reports (Oxford) Ltd. British Archaeological Reports was first incorporated in 1974 to publish the BAR Series, International and British. In 1992 Hadrian Books Ltd became part of the BAR group. This volume was originally published by Tempvs Reparatvm in conjunction with British Archaeological Reports (Oxford) Ltd / Hadrian Books Ltd, the Series principal publisher, in 1993. This present volume is published by BAR Publishing, 2019.

BAR titles are available from:

BAR Publishing
122 Banbury Rd, Oxford, OX2 7BP, UK
EMAIL info@barpublishing.com
PHONE +44 (0)1865 310431
FAX +44 (0)1865 316916
www.barpublishing.com

For Ali – who else?

CONTENTS

PREFACE AND ACKNOWLEDGEMENTS

This volume represents publication of my doctorate which was presented to the University of Reading in 1988. Since that time, a number of volumes and papers dealing with deposition, hoards, and related aspects of social archaeology have been published. While these contribute to and reinforce the arguments and theories advanced here, they do not alter the thrust of this research or its conclusions, and I have not attempted to include references to them here.

The study was begun in September 1979 and was funded for three years by a major state studentship from the Department of Education and Science: this invaluable financial support assisted me to lay the firm foundations for the thesis and carry out all the necessary museum visiting. Since the subject areas within prehistory have not yet been narrowed to any great degree, the research produced a large database and consequently provided something of a problem in analysis and presentation: the final writing up of the results into thesis form was much protracted.

Throughout the project and during its translation to book form, much support, both moral and financial, has been afforded me by my wife, Alison. Through her urging, pressure, help, and support, this work has come to a fruitful conclusion: for this I am ever grateful. My children, Matthew and Helen, have also provided a compelling reason to get the whole thing finished, even if their presence has hindered it somewhat at times!

My thanks are due to my employers, English Heritage, who have made it possible for me to continue in archaeology, and who afforded me some time off to complete this work. The University of Reading provided me with every assistance over the years, particularly the Library and its Photographic Department, the Computer Centre, and the Archaeology Department, where much encouragement and advice was offered by Mike Fulford, Grenville Astill, Bob Chapman, Herbert Pike, and Cecil Slade. My tutor, Richard Bradley, afforded me considerable help, advice, and support throughout the work, while guiding my efforts along the right lines and tolerating my slow progress. George Eogan acted as my external examiner and offered kind advice and encouragement towards publication of the thesis.

The libraries of the Ashmolean Museum, the Society of Antiquaries, and the Institute of Archaeology, London provided me with reference material otherwise unavailable – some of it very obscure. Martin Henig kindly introduced me to the Ashmolean Library and continued to give advice and support during the course of my research.

I benefited from discussions with many individuals while carrying out the research, and I must thank Stuart Needham, Andrew Lawson, Roger Thomas, Steve Ford, John Barrett, Brendan O'Connor, Peter Northover, Stephen Cogbill, and Richard Savage. Kristian Kristiansen assisted me in every way during my visit to Copenhagen and discussed his ideas at length with me; I thank him for his continued interest in this project. My brother-in-law, John Ryden, gave some valuable advice on statistics and encouragement generally. Fellow postgraduates Ros Cleal, Julie Gardiner, John Davies, Ann Clark, and Henry Gent shared some of the common problems and solutions presented by the pursuit of research. My parents, brother, and sisters followed the progress of my research with interest, as did my in-laws, particularly my wife's parents, Dick and Elaine Macaulay, who offered every assistance and encouragement over the years.

Lorraine Mepham typed out the first version of the catalogue from a jumble of papers. Charis Burridge managed to transfer my manuscript of the chapters onto word-processor discs, and Annette Hazell word-processed the catalogue, results, and bibliography. I thank them for their efforts. The final editing and rewriting of the thesis were done on the BBC microcomputer, using Wordwise Plus, which made my task easier. Subsequent work towards the publication has been carried out on an Amstrad PC1512.

Finally, I am grateful to the staff of the museums visited during the course of this research for their help in providing information and making the objects available to me for study: without them the thesis could not have any substance! They were as follows: Andrew Sherratt, Ashmolean Museum, Oxford; Mike Farley, Buckinghamshire County Museum, Aylesbury; Stephen Bird, Bath Museums Service; Stuart Needham and Ian Kinnes, Department of Prehistoric and Romano–British Antiquities, British Museum; Elizabeth Owles, Moyses Hall Museum, Bury St Edmunds; Colin Shell, University Museum of Archaeology and Anthropology, Cambridge; Alan Saville, Art Gallery and Museum Service, Cheltenham; Paul Robinson, Devizes Museum; Roger Peers, Dorset County Museum, Dorchester; Elveden Estate Office; Susan Pearce, Rougemont House Museum, Exeter; Malcolm Watkins, City Museum and Art Gallery, Gloucester; Charles Lewis, Elizabethan House Museum, Great Yarmouth; Hilary Ross, Ipswich Museum; David Tomalin, County Archaeologist, Isle of Wight; Robert Trett, The Lynn Museum, Kings Lynn; Tony Higgott, Newbury District Museum; Barbara Green and Bill Milligan, Castle Museum, Norwich; Lynne Williamson and Dennis Britton, Pitt Rivers Museum, Oxford; John Johnston, City of Portsmouth Museums and Art Gallery; Leslie Cram, Reading Museum and Art Gallery; Clare Conybeare, Salisbury and South Wiltshire Museum; Saxon French, Sandringham Estate Office; Mark Brisbane, Gods House Tower, Southampton; Stephen Minnitt, Somerset County Museum, Taunton; Mark Wingate, Winchester City Museums; Rosalinda Hardiman, Wisbech and Fenland Museum.

To all the above people, I am very grateful for their assistance during the course of the study: the faults remain my own.

INTRODUCTION

During the 1960s and 1970s, growing dissatisfaction with the state of the subject of archaeology, with its lack of a cogent theoretical basis, led prehistorians to question many of the basic tenets of the subject: the Bronze Age has been no exception. However, the result has been an increasing difficulty in reconciling material evidence with social models. Metalwork has traditionally been used to formulate chronologies on the basis of typology; the Bronze Age frameworks are the most complex. Radiocarbon dating has altered the picture somewhat, but the lack of associations for much metalwork leaves us with two `hung' dating frameworks, which are not clearly related to one another. In this period of questioning and change, the role of metalwork in the Bronze Age has come under close scrutiny: the subject of this volume stems from that process.

The subject matter under discussion is the hoard material of the Bronze Age in southern Britain. Hoards have been defined as the deposition of two or more metal objects together in the ground with no other archaeological associations. That definition is widely accepted and has been used here in that sense, both in retrieving and discussing information, but it is clear that it is an unsatisfactory one. Single finds with no other associations could be deposited in the same way as hoards; sometimes the hoards are within or adjacent to settlements; they are found with pottery and other artefacts; however, the majority are composed of a collection of bronze objects, found together with no other associations. The value of these collections for typological and chronological comparisons are clear, but this sort of analysis must be dangerous without any other archaeological context. It could be argued in this respect that we have not advanced very far, since the seminal work of Evans on Bronze Age metalwork was published in 1881, although so much more material has become available and has been published.

Thus, the renewed interest in hoards and the questioning approach of modern archaeology have prompted further study. The analytical stance of workers, such as Kristiansen in Denmark, has helped to indicate new ways of examining metalwork: the analysis of wear on the objects, the patterns of deposition, and the use of social frameworks, filled out with other aspects of material culture, have taken us further. The need for new analysis becomes clear, and the Bronze Age hoards form a ready database: the layout of this volume attempts to demonstrate these stages. Broadly, the treatment is in three parts: a survey of attitudes, opinions, and interpretations of hoards and the Bronze Age; then my own analysis of hoards is presented; and finally the work is summarised. In Chapter 1, the material itself, its publication, and analysis by other authors is carefully examined. The cultural and the theoretical backgrounds for the Bronze Age are summarised, examined, and discussed in Chapters 2 and 3. In Chapter 4, the methodology of the new analysis is laid out, explained in application, and the constraints of the material discussed. This is followed by the results of the analysis and an outline of the implications of this data for the interpretation of hoards in Chapter 5. Chapter 6 summarises the previous chapters, and Chapter 7 concludes the work and defines the place of metalwork hoards within the social model of the southern British Bronze Age.

It is clear that this study can only be incomplete: the sheer volume of information for processing precludes further in–depth analysis of many factors of interest; the selection of regional zones straitjackets the overall picture somewhat; the concentration on hoard material, to the exclusion of grave goods, single finds, and settlement material, leads to serious deficiencies in the comparative value of the hoard data; and the inadequate definition and recording of hoard material leads to inconsistency in the patterns recognised. These are not mentioned here as an excuse for incompleteness, but as an indication of areas for further research, because it is clear from this study that more in–depth analysis of metalwork is possible and fruitful, that the objects within hoards carry much valuable additional information that can be analysed, that hoards in isolation can produce patterning in the data, and that these hoards can lend (metaphorical!) weight to our social models of prehistory. It is these questions to which this study has addressed itself, and which it has begun to answer.

PART I

BACKGROUND

CHAPTER 1

PREVIOUS RESEARCH ON BRONZE AGE HOARDS

INTRODUCTION

Much has been written on the nature of Bronze Age metalwork and hoards and a lengthy overview is useful in summarising the range of opinions. This preliminary chapter does this by first considering authors on British material, followed by discussion of the extensive work on European material. This is generally done chronologically, ie early authors first, the latest opinions last, which might tend to lead to repetition and sudden switches in subject, but is probably the best approach to tackling the large amount of information. However, the British and European literature has also been subdivided into 'economic', 'votive', and 'explanation', as a crude way of laying out the range of interpretations. As an adjunct to this, it will be useful to consider some ethnographic and literary parallels for metalworking. All these approaches are by no means separate and are often interdependent in a complex way, but after individual consideration, it should be possible to see the useful lines of enquiry. The intention is to present a reasonably comprehensive overview of opinions and interpretations from which to proceed.

BRITISH MATERIAL

Economic

The majority of authors writing about hoards and metalwork in Britain have tended to view their interpretation in economic terms, placing the emphasis on the 'value' of bronze for transactions and trade. They have followed the seminal work of Evans on British Bronze Age metalwork (1881). Many of his conclusions are still currently followed with minor modifications, and the great mass of information incorporated into his book has remained unsurpassed. The main body of his work was directed towards the definition of types of Bronze Age objects, suggesting uses for them and placing them in a chronological order. He was aided in this by the apparent associations of objects in hoards, which he carefully tabulated, along with a discussion of the nature of hoards (1881, 456–69). To quote Evans *in extenso*, he realised that "these hoards are of more than one character. In certain cases they seem to have been the treasured property of some individual who would appear to have buried his valued tools or weapons during troublous times, and never to have been able to disinter them. In other cases the hoards were probably the property of a trader, as they consist of objects ready for use and in considerable numbers; and in others, again, they appear to have been the stock–in–trade of some bronze–founder of ancient times, as they comprise worn out and broken tools and weapons, lumps of rough metal, and even the moulds in which the accumulation of bronze was destined to be recast... In some other cases, deposits, especially when consisting exclusively of ornaments, may possibly be of a sepulchral character" (1881, 457).

Worsaae had suggested a votive character for some hoards, ie the hoards had a sacred or ritual significance, but Evans did not think that any hoards in this country were of this character (1881, 457). Apart from Worsaae, Evans referred to the work of de Mortillet and Chantre on the French material, who also used similar divisions for hoards (1881, 458): we shall return to these works later. These distinctions were applied to his tables of material contained in hoards by prefixing them with P, M or F, according to whether they could be considered as personal, or belonging to a merchant, or founder; when two letters occurred, these hoards could be considered as either, and some characterised by a P could be sepulchral (1881, 459). It is useful here to remember that Evans was a businessman who had established himself in the family firm (Lee, 1927, 634–7); it may well be that this categorisation of hoards reflects his background and also his keen interest in the study of coins with their arrangement under the rules of evolution (Lee, 1927, 635). This principle was used much more literally by Wilde in arranging the collections of the Royal Irish Academy (1857, 1–4; 1861), works with which Evans would have been familiar. Evans was also able to make certain chronological statements based around the presumed contemporaneity of objects in hoards, although he was not slow to realise that his founder's hoards might contain objects of mixed date (1881, 458). Concluding his work, he justifiably closed the pages "with the consolatory throught that, dry as may be their contents, they may prove of some value as a hoard of collected facts for other seekers after truth" (1881, 488).

Forty years later, the British Museum guide to the Bronze Age collections referred to Evans' threefold system of classification of hoards and presented the chief points from his list of conclusions, based on the examination of their associations, without modification (Smith, 1920, 44–5). Fox echoed this, but separated out founder's hoards as of more importance than personal or merchant's hoards (1923, 51). However, he did recognise that certain of the deposits in the personal and merchant's class could in fact be interpreted as votive offerings, and in both this and the case of founder's hoards, some of the larger hoards might have belonged to chiefs, "following the contemporary Homeric and later Teutonic custom" (1923, 51). The appearance of numerous large hoards was attributed to "the immigrant leaf–sword people" with a different social organisation, who had a weapon–smith attached to their individual retinue: up to this time little manufacture had been carried on in the area of his study (Fox, 1923, 51). When discussing the distribution of finds and hoards, Fox found it significant that several important hoards had a "forest association", this being "doubtless due in part to the need of the craftsmen for charcoal", and that other hoards lay along the line of prehistoric trackways considered to be trade routes (1923, 62–3). Marsh surrounded by forest was felt to be an ideal situation for votive offerings (Fox, 1923, 63). Besides some other comments relating to association and chronology, Fox did not go further into the nature of hoards, although his discussion of distribution had added another dimension to their study.

Childe used the by then standard definitions for hoards: there were 'domestic' hoards, belonging to a householder, 'votive' hoards buried in certain places supposedly sacred to a divinity, 'trader's' hoards with collections of new or unfinished objects, and 'founder's' hoards consisting of large collections of scrap (1930, 43–5). The hoards survived because they had been buried at a time of danger, but never retrieved, while trader's hoards lay along natural routes with the thickest concentrations on the frontier of two cultural provinces (Childe, 1930, 45).

Childe's social interpretation and the consequent implications of these hoards are interesting: the travelling tinker was thought to be an important element in the distribution of metal types, repairing broken tools and collecting scrap metal in times of demand (1930, 44–5). Smiths themselves were the first independent craftsmen and held a privileged position in society, because of the importance of their products. This in turn did away with economic self–sufficiency, as tools had to be purchased from the expert and raw materials had to be obtained "from beyond the communal boundaries" (Childe, 1930, 4–59). These conclusions were virtually paraphrased by Kendrick and Hawkes in their survey of archaeology from 1914 to 1931, especially when they considered the prevalence of founder's hoards in the late Bronze Age (1932, 130–31). Childe went on to develop these themes and the notion of metalworkers as a class apart (1956, 163). The metalworkers were poorly represented in the funerary record and thus could form a distinct, "detribalized" society, enjoying the freedom to travel and find their own markets, as they were producing for an international market, when bronze was the main metal of the industry (Childe, 1956, 163). Founder's hoards now assumed an important aspect in late Bronze Age life: "the merchant artificers must now have travelled the country in veritable caravans collecting scrap metal, doubtless in exchange for new tools", giving "a larger circle of consumers... the advantage of bronze equipment" (Childe, 1956, 174). With the appearance of iron, Childe saw a collapse in this social group: "the new industry, based on ores of relatively common occurrence but still technically unripe for large–scale production, could work with a simpler organization than the bronze industry, requiring the combination of two rather uncommon metals... the bronzesmith had to meet the competition of the blacksmith" (1956, 178). This situation eventually forced the market to contract and destroyed the prosperity and autonomy of theindustry. Now the bronzesmith had to be content with producing tools and weapons for local consumption; having been "politically emancipated from tribal society, he is forced back into it on an inferior status by economic pressure" (Childe, 1956, 180).

Evans' classification was re–iterated by Hodges, but he added a further class to denote the tool–kits of specialised craftsmen (1957, 51). He also noted the possible confusion between large personal and small trader's hoards, and that founder's hoards are almost unknown in Ireland (1957, 52–3). Using the Scottish data for comparison, Hodges postulated a weapon–using class there, but a more even distribution of wealth in the form of bronze objects in Ireland: thus there were fortified structures and a hierarchy in Scotland, but in Ireland metalworking was carried out in settled communities, "the Late Bronze Age population being apparently of the wrong social fabric to engender such a development" (1957, 55–6). If this were the case, the chieftains and social order of Irish legend would have to be later importations or a development without roots in the Late Bronze Age (Hodges, 1957, 57). Coles criticised Hodges' use of the Scottish figures and pointed out that Hodges had used incomplete data both for Scotland and, more seriously, for Ireland, where the change to Hodges' figures brought about by the inclusion of more data could suggest that the reverse was true and that a ruling class did exist (1959–60, 39). Coles did not question the traditional interpretations of hoards, apart from noting that 'votive hoard' is an overworked term, and he felt that complete data were necessary before social organisation could be postulated from hoard composition (1959–60, 37–9).

In dealing with the Welsh metalwork, Savory attributed some of the later hoards there to "a clash between two cultural groups", due to the "warlike" nature of the developing Wilburton complex (1958, 14). The movements of travelling smiths were seen to be curtailed with an increasing development of regional specialisation later in the period; a regionalisation which developed into the four main cultural provinces evident at the time of the Roman Conquest (Savory, 1958, 28 and 49). This 'settling down' of smiths reflects Childe's views (1956, 180; discussed above). Such territorial divisions, coinciding with Roman tribal dispositions, have recently been discussed again by Burgess (1980b, 249). The distributions of metalwork and their related industries have given rise to these 'political' interpretations, but there is no social background to explain why this regionalisation should have developed and have given rise to four separate tribes. However, such indications of political grouping do seem to increase during the Late Bronze Age. Thus Britton, dealing with the Isleham hoard, concluded that we had a combination unprecedented earlier in Britain with "the large–scale production of weapons, the use of horses for traction, a variety of exuberant display in ornament, large and elaborate vessels of bronze" (1960, 282). "For a moment we are given a glimpse behind the curtain: we see the struttings of martial leaders and many of the trappings of a 'heroic age' " (Britton, 1960, 282).

Burgess recognised the problems of categorising hoards along the lines provided by Evans and others (1968b, 25).

This problem of allocating metalwork to a context category, be it hoard or otherwise, has been well illustrated by the detailed scheme evolved for a new 'card index' of Bronze Age metalwork (Needham, Lawson and Green, 1985, v–vii). Burgess also felt that the harsh soil conditions and deterioration of objects since discovery might account for the fragmentary state of some implements (1968b, 25): this is a subject which has been examined more recently by Tylecote (1979, 345–68). Acid soils, apart from peat, do seem to have some corrosive effect on bronzes (Tylecote, 1979, 367). However, this would be unlikely to contribute to the fragmentation of objects. Those which were not already snapped or strained, were probably broken by the post-depositional activities of man. Burgess could not define any of the Wallington hoards as "formal founders' hoards", but he did refer to groups as: those of a personal character; warrior's arms; craftsman's toolkit; and trader's hoard (1968b, 28). Interestingly, he rejected the idea of any scrap survivals and was thus able to see all the objects as being from a contemporary tradition (1968b, 28). Traditional terminologies were again used when dealing with the whole of the later Bronze Age of the British Isles (Burgess, 1968a, 19). Weapon and domestic hoards were also defined (Burgess, 1968a, 19–21). Burgess also suggested that Hallstatt incursions could have given rise to increased hoard deposition in the lower Thames basin, because of the supposed threat (1968a, 28).

Coombs understood the problems of studying hoards, but he felt that hoards must reflect certain aspects of Bronze Age society: the organisation of the metal industry, a preference for certain objects, and the possible existence of a ruling elite, with the contents themselves reflecting supply, demand, and use at the time (1971, 411). Coombs found that hoards in southern England were dominated by socketed axes, unlike those in Scotland and Ireland, which also tended to be smaller and contained few fragmentary objects (1971, 413–5). He pointed out that interpretation depended on the model accounting for the collection of the objects in the first place; and there are a number of objections to the traditional interpretations (1971, 415–6). Objects may have been collected by smiths, either directly, or through middlemen, or acquired in exchange for new tools – all of which could imply an itinerant smith, for which there is no proof either way; indeed, the distribution of objects could suggest the opposite with the sedentary smith working for a master (Coombs, 1971, 416–7). Wilburton and Broadward hoards, with their emphasis on weaponry, could represent a warrior society with a mounted, sword-bearing aristocracy and spear-carrying tribesmen (Coombs, 1971, 419). Aside from these observations and the close study of the objects themselves, Coombs applied the material to the definition of industrial traditions, although he did recognise the problems of non-contemporaneity of objects in hoards and the probable bias of the original collector (1971, 421).

Coombs dealt with weapon hoards specifically in a separate paper, concentrating "on hoard content, reasons for deposition and the social significance of the hoards and their metalwork" (1975, 49). He noted the problems of applying Evans' definitions to material from the south of England (1975, 66–8). Coombs further recognised the difficulty in giving reasons for deposition and non-retrieval with no glimpse of explanation from ethnographic sources: "During the whole span of the Bronze Age there must have been many different reasons for hoard deposition" (1975, 68). As to the idea of burying hoards in times of trouble, he was rightly suspicious of such a motive for people in this situation; instead he favoured a ritual or religious explanation (1975, 68). It is difficult to see why such collections of metalwork were made, and Coombs evisaged the possibility that smiths attached to a ruling minority were re-making weapons after battles (Coombs, 1975, 69–70). The ritual interpretation was taken up with observations such as the location of many groups of material in watery places, the non-functional aspect of many of the weapons, and the prestigous nature of some objects, especially swords (Coombs, 1975, 70–2). The presence of cauldrons during the later Bronze Age is seen to epitomise the chief and his power to redistribute wealth in the form of food. The sum of the equipment would then represent a "privileged minority with a body of retainers" (Coombs, 1975, 72–4).

The tool hoards suggest subsistence activities and the presence of other classes of society (Coombs, 1975, 74): would these lower ranks have had access to the privileges of ritual offering? Deposition in these cases might be explained as collections of material to be worked on by the smiths (Coombs, 1975, 69). The weapon hoards represent a continuation of the warrior society apparent in Early Bronze Age Wessex (Coombs, 1975, 76): a view which needs modification in the light of more recent work on the nature of society in that area. Coombs recognised the speculative nature of such social interpretation for hoards, but felt that it had more to offer than plain studies of technology (1975, 77). This is the true value of this work: it helps us to draw away from the typological and chronological arguments and to ask questions about the underlying processes that gave rise to such deposits. Some of the traditional notions re-appear thinly disguised, as they do in his references to scrap and domestic hoards. Nevertheless, we are moving towards closer examination of interpretations.

Rowlands' thesis on the organisation of Middle Bronze Age metalworking was published in 1976. Rowlands found the application of traditional schemes of hoard definition difficult for the Middle Bronze Age, since most of these had been evolved through research on the Late Bronze Age, "where large hoards of varying content are a significant feature" (1976, 100). An alternative classification based on content was felt to be more practicable and the metalwork was grouped according to three main categories: tools, weapons, and ornaments, in seven possible combinations (Rowlands, 1976, 100). This method only makes assumptions about the nature of the objects themselves, and not about their contexts and associations. The aim was "to treat hoard material as a reflection of industrial activity" and to distinguish clusters of hoards with similar content, which may fall into regional concentrations. Rowlands was forced to focus his attention on tool hoards, since these were best represented in the record and exhibited the greatest regional differences (1976, 103). Even reduced to such narrow levels of expectation, problems are encountered due to the possibility of hoard composition being either random or non-random, to the variation in hoard size, and to the efficiency of recovery on discovery (which does not take into account the fact that some pieces from a group may have been recovered previously) (Rowlands, 1976, 105). Nevertheless, Rowlands was able to distinguish five clusters of hoards containing palstaves; clusters which suggested localised groups, without distinct boundaries, but overlapping with each other (1976, 108). This exercise was repeated for ornaments, and two clusters were distinguished, weapon hoards being left out due to poor evidence (Rowlands, 1976, 109–10).

The hoard evidence was combined with information from the objects themselves and with the distribution of single finds to suggest regional industries (Rowlands, 1976, 117). The organisation of this production could then be discussed (Rowlands, 1976, 164). Rowlands suggested a pattern of seasonal production, in which the smith would produce a stock of implements and then visit settlements to distribute the material; the production being carried out at certain times of the year to fit in with other periods of intense activity associated with the agricultural cycle (1976, 164–5). This would apparently explain the finished or part–finished natures of the objects in the hoards, the absence of metalworking tools and debris, the variety of sub–types in the same hoard, and the generally small size of the hoards (Rowlands, 1976, 164–5). These suggestions are covered in more detail by Rowlands in another paper (1971), which will be examined later as part of the survey of ethnographic evidence for hoards.

However, this scheme does not work for the Middle Bronze Age areas north of the Thames Valley: the material here is more often in the form of single finds, and for these Rowlands suggested a pattern of production on demand by the smith for a single customer, with the objects reaching the archaeological record through use and loss (1976, 165). This pattern was later replaced by a more organised and efficient system of production, such as is seen in central and western Europe. This led to the wider availability of metalwork characteristic of the Late Bronze Age (Rowlands, 1976, 165–6). The circulation and re–use of scrap metal in the Late Bronze Age was seen to be part of a closed process, where the smith not only produced the objects, but also obtained the raw material himself: a different situation to that of the Middle Bronze Age, where the client either provided the raw material, or its accumulation was controlled at a higher political level (Rowlands, 1976, 166–7). This general picture is supplemented by the existence of more specialised weapon smiths operating in a different economic environment throughout the Middle and Late Bronze Age (Rowlands, 1976, 168).

Rowlands was also able to recognise the importance of close individual study of the object themselves: "Palstaves, for example, often display broad crescentic blade edges where repeated re–sharpening has changed the triangular shape of the original cast blade... This emphasises the importance of recognising the stage of development of an artifact at the time it was lost, discarded or collected" (1976, 185). Rowlands' various observations are among the most useful made in recent works about hoard material and related metalwork.

Moving rapidly towards the present state of the literature on hoards, Burgess and Coombs produced a whole volume devoted to the subject (1979). It would be unfair to criticise this volume for failing to come to grips with the implications and interpretation of hoards, since it is more "a contribution to reducing the backlog of unpublished hoards" (Burgess and Coombs, 1979, ii). However, it is a pity that there is not more appraisal of traditional explanations, and indications for future trends in the book. In their introduction, Burgess and Coombs listed four reasons for deposition, with which they think most people would agree: "1. concealment in the ground for security reasons, in an age without safes or other secure alternatives; 2. deposits not recovered for one reason or another from their everyday place of storage, in a house or workshop for example; 3. votive offering; 4. accidental loss, whether shipwreck or a bag of metal goods slipping undetected from a belt or pack–horse" (1979, iv). These reflect the traditional explanations, except that normally we would not interpret the contents of a shipwreck as a hoard. Moreover, the loss of a bag of metal – something which could be easily recovered even in wet ground – must be of minimal importance in accounting for deposition. They go on to note that all these factors would remain constant across time, apart from votive offering, which could be expected to fluctuate with religious beliefs, but, as they rightly recognise, this is not the case, as there are "peaks and troughs of hoard deposition" with regional imbalances in distribution (1979, iv). The distribution of fieldworkers and museums accounts for some of the regional distortion, but Wessex, a well–researched area, is poor in hoards (Burgess and Coombs, 1979, iv–v). They suggest that most of the hoards can be seen to bunch at the end of each metalworking stage in which they occur, representing a response to serious disturbances, which can be explained by other archaeological material. One such example is the Penard period with its increasingly martial equipment (1979, v–vi). The dumping of bronze came to an end with the Iron Age, as recovery was now profitless (Burgess and Coombs, 1979, vi), although one would expect some use for bronze in the Iron Age because of all the decorative fittings present later in the period. Of course, we have no idea of the amount of bronze recovered in antiquity, but it is very likely that this did happen; for example, we get early objects in late hoards, objects which may have been re–discovered and subsequently re–deposited. The varying regional character of hoards is noted by Burgess and Coombs and thought to have social implications: "They are worthy of much fuller investigation", and they have much to tell us, not least "because misconceptions about hoard deposition may have distorted our understanding of the development of Bronze Age metalworking" (1979, vi).

The individual papers in this volume put forward some ideas for interpretation as well. Needham, in dealing with a hoard of two Early Bronze Age spearheads, suggested deliberate deposition, either for security or votive purposes "to ensure a good game supply", and that, as the objects were from two geographically distinct industries, they could have been "the personal possessions of a warrior/hunter, who, perhaps to keep abreast of the times, sought to patronise two rival metalworking traditions" (1979, 18). Farley highlighted some problems of interpretation, when dealing with what would normally be called a 'founder's hoard': he pointed out that the hoard contained some axes only worn to a degree, and it would seem to be folly to discard serviceable implements (1979a, 140). He advanced the explanation that the types of the objects became redundant when traditions changed, and that they had their value only in their original form; they would subsequently be re–made into objects in a new tradition (Farley, 1979a, 140).

The hoard from Danebury was interpreted by Cunliffe and O'Connor as either "the stock–in–trade of an itinerant bronze founder....buried on a lonely, isolated hill top", or as evidence for metalworking on the site associated with an early occupation not clearly defined by the excavations (1979, 242). Further excavation did not resolve the problem of early occupation and the potential association of this material with it (Cunliffe, 1984, 12, 149, 335–40), but this explanation is made more likely by other similar finds and by the presence in the group of two razors, which are often associated with settlement material (Coombs, 1971, 410).

Burgess explained the presence of Hallstatt C metalwork in Britain, not in the traditional terms of raiders, but as a result of "normal culture contact" with peoples bordering the Hallstatt territories, and brought via other communities to Britain (1979, 274–5). The appearance of new types of swords was seen as due to the presence of foreign metalworkers, who travelled to Britain and Ireland to produce their products "entirely alien, in concept and execution, to Irish–British traditions" (Burgess, 1979, 275). These metalworkers also introduced iron–working, which apparently shattered the British bronze market and resulted in the large–scale dumping of Ewart Park phase hoards, because of the amount of surplus bronze on the market; "the only sensible thing for a bronze–worker to do with his stock would be to bury it until it was needed or demand picked up" (Burgess, 1979, 275). As noted before, would bronzesmiths have had such a feeling for economic concepts such as these, and surely bronze would still be a useful commodity? This also means that the smiths, rather than the customers, were holding vast stocks of objects, presumably for their scrap, not their functional value, since many of the objects can be seen to have been still useful at their deposition. Iron, because of its different properties, would not be hoarded, and deposition in this form ceased (Burgess, 1979, 276): presumably the later currency bars reflect a different attitude to the burial of material. Burgess also saw some bronze objects, such as axes and spearheads, as having to compete with superior iron examples (1979, 276), but there is no reason why the bronze examples should not have retained a use of their own; perhaps fashion dictated the need for change, just as it had for the various stages of bronze technology. As for bronze swords, these apparently may have become display or votive items with a high concentration of finds from rivers, where they supposedly ended up as offerings: "For craftsmen struggling to cope with the collapse of the bronze market, this would have been one way of staying in business and using some of their massive bronze surplus" (Burgess, 1979, 277–8). Perhaps they were trying to propitiate the stock exchange! The find from Boyton, the immediate subject of Burgess' article, was thought to be part of the dumping of "vast holdings of redundant bronze", after which the character of the metalworking industries was entirely different (1979, 278). This assumes that the two objects of the find are only a tiny part of a much larger lost sample. Nevertheless, Burgess' article is thought–provoking, and really the only one in the hoard volume to come to terms with the central problem of deposition or to attempt some explanations.

O'Connor briefly discussed hoards and deposition in his study on cross–Channel relations in the Bronze Age (1980). He reviewed the evidence and arguments for and against itinerant smiths and tended to favour local centres of production, as indicated by the distribution of types (1980, 303–4). In examining the literature on hoards and deposition, O'Connor rightly pointed out that few hoards have been found under controlled conditions, so that we have few details of their contexts (1980, 307). He also referred to the interpretation of Romano–British coin hoards (1980, 307): a factor which may have influenced Evans' interpretation of Bronze Age hoards. Over 1400 examples of Romano–British coin hoards are known, and they seem to have been buried in times of stress or danger away from the house, but in a safe place often near some landmark; these hoards, then, were presumably intended for recovery (Robertson, 1974, 12–14). They were always arranged to be as safe as possible, but under such unsettled conditions many were obviously lost (Robertson, 1974, 28–31). Of course, we are dealing here with a different social situation, so we can hardly apply these ideas to the Bronze Age material directly. O'Connor went on to discuss European finds and literature, where votive deposition finds most support, and concluded that we must accept this idea for those deposits in wet places for both sides of the Channel; on the other hand, he felt that these deposits were not substitutes for grave goods (1980, 307–9). He noted the similarity in the forms of deposition between southern Britain and north eastern France during most of the later Bronze Age: "axe hoards in MBA2, few hoards in LBA1, scrap hoards in LBA2, more mixed hoards in LBA3" (O'Connor, 1980, 316). This suggests some widespread underlying link beyond the chance factors of casual loss or deposition in troubled times.

More specific to the British Later Bronze Age, some of the essays in the volume edited by Barrett and Bradley (1980) examined hoards and related forms of deposition or made mention of them. Manby pointed out the distributional bias for Bronze Age implements on the Yorkshire Wolds, including their retrieval for scrap by medieval peasants and for sale to nineteenth century collectors (1980, 331); a careful consideration of activities subsequent to the Bronze Age is a useful correlate for any distributional study. Votive deposits recurred again in Chowne's study: here he referred to Davey's 1971 paper (discussed below), but thought that such bronze deposits in Lincolnshire could be explained as settlements buried by later peat growth (1980, 300). Lawson observed Rowlands' identification of an East Anglian metalworking centre in the Middle Bronze Age, with activity being more intense in the west of the county; in the Late Bronze Age, however, the distribution is more even and may indicate "a more widespread population or, of a more even cover by itinerant smiths amongst a widespread population" (1980c, 279–81). Lawson also showed that some hoards do occur in close proximity to undated enclosures known from aerial photographs, suggesting that hoards may have been deliberately concealed close to settlements (1980c, 281). Johnson also thought that the distribution of later Bronze Age metalwork in Devon reflected the fuller extent of the settlement pattern and might reflect "greater exploitation of alluvial tin which is widely found along the river valleys originating on the tin bearing rocks" (1980, 153).

Needham and Burgess admitted "that the study of hoards is very much in its infancy", while accepting that we have to rely on often poor records of accidental discoveries (1980, 438). Explanations were similar to those proposed in the volume on hoards (Burgess and Coombs, 1979): accidental or deliberate deposition with "major episodes" of deposition, and included the observation that "many hoards are random agglomerations in the sense that they represent the 'freezing' of dynamic assemblages, which had changed continually in their composition up to the moment of final abandonment" (Needham and Burgess, 1980, 437–8). Needham and Burgess noted that alongside these hoards of random, unrepresentative pieces, there are those made up of carefully selected items (1980, 438). They also made reference to river and stray finds: with river finds the problems of secondary contexts and other uncertainties were discussed, and stray finds were seen as finds without context, often resulting from accidental loss (1980, 438–9). The hoard from Petters Sports Field is quoted as a typical example of a founder's hoard, which was recovered in excavation from a context sealed by a layer with Late Bronze Age/Early Iron Age pottery (Needham and Burgess, 1980, 441); here we have a hoard which was deposited and not touched again, despite later activity at the site. Needham and Burgess went on to remark on the composition of founder's hoards and the poor representation in them of certain items from the metalwork assemblage: they thought that this was because the founder only collected large objects with good 'scrap value' and did not bother with the smaller ones (1980, 441–2). Yet this is contrary to such assemblages as Isleham, full of the most scrupulously collected small pieces, although admittedly it is a deposit of exceptional nature. Having reviewed the arguments for the explanation of river finds, they came down in favour of votive deposition, since, in their opinion, this is a simpler explanation and needs no "special pleading" (1980, 442–9). Continental immigrants are also postulated to account for the changes in the area during the Penard period (Needham and Burgess, 1980, 456). The authors continued with observations on the distribution of finds, noting the correlation between high densities of metalwork and good soils, and went on to re–examine the nature of these groups, most of which are founder's hoards (1980, 458–60). Founder's hoards were explained as "stocks of metal and scrap deposited by bronze smiths or tinkers", and it was assumed that the distribution of these related to metalworking foci, whose locations were determined by access to a market, to locally available raw materials and to foreign supplies of metal (Needham and Burgess, 1980, 460). Having discussed the social implications of the distribution of finds, Needham and Burgess mentioned the Yattendon hoard with its Early and Middle Bronze Age pieces, suggesting that this was due to a more complete recycling, perhaps because of a local scarcity of metal (1980, 463).

In emphasising the important role of the Thames Valley during the Bronze Age, Needham and Burgess concluded that "the range and distribution of metalwork in the valley is thus related to the region's position within long–distance exchange networks, the varying patterns of settlement and status maintained by agricultural production within the valley and, most dramatically, to the flamboyant destruction of wealth through the surrender of metalwork to the Thames and its tributaries" (1980, 466). Riverside settlement receives support from the article by Needham and Longley on the site at Runnymede Bridge (1980). This important site, situated right on the bank of the river, may have been part of an organisation directed towards control of the river traffic, at a time when access to the raw materials of wealth may have become important (Needham and Longley, 1980, 429). Our observations on metalwork are now becoming more directed towards a social explanation of distributions and deposition.

Gardiner worked on the metal finds from Lincolnshire, in an attempt to relate distributions to land quality (1980). A land classification which could be related to the Bronze Age situation was evolved, and the distribution of finds tested against it statistically (Gardiner, 1980, 102–5). She suggested a correlation between weapons and land of good quality in the Middle Bronze Age, which changed in the Late Bronze Age into a relationship between prestigious artefacts and access to the river system (Gardiner, 1980, 113). A number of factors may influence distribution, however, and there are too many uncertainties in such a small sample of material to give confidence in these apparently significant correlations. Problems with the use of the chi–squared test occur (referred to below), and the significance of the distribution may have been affected by factors otherwise poorly represented. Nevertheless, we again have an attempt to derive more from our data than pure typologies and thus a valid exercise.

Barrett and Bradley's paper on the Thames Valley envisaged an earlier Bronze Age core area in the Upper Thames and a buffer zone in its lower reaches, both of which affected later Bronze Age activity (1980a, 249). They noted the hoard distribution in this area, biased to the edge of the floodplain and in areas of high concentration of settlement, and felt that this might reflect efficiency in the accumulation, smelting, and exchange of these deposits (1980a, 259). The maintenance of a bronze industry was seen to be part of the mechanism of exchange for access to wealth and status. Barrett and Bradley suggested that "the accumulation and deposition of bronzes may take place at a number of points in the history of production and exchange" (1980a, 260). They indicated various examples where this could be the case, but noted that, before proceeding further, we need to know more about regularities in hoards, such as composition and weight (1980a, 260). The location of hoards close to the river was interpreted as the stockpiling of material for transport in and out of the valley, and this led to a discussion of finds from the river itself: the view advanced was that these were a result of deliberate deposition, "with an attendant embargo on salvage", or in other words a "conspicuous consumption of wealth" similar to earlier grave goods (Barrett and Bradley, 1980a, 261–3). Thus, the pattern was explained as part of a social model involving the intensification of agriculture and the exploitation of long–distance trade between the valley and its hinterland (Barrett and Bradley, 1980a, 263–5).

These two authors discussed the situation in Wessex, which appears to have been an area in decline in the later Bronze Age: the material wealth had moved to areas of more productive soil and those with potential for long–distance communication, such as the Thames Valley (1980b, 202). They also pointed out that when bronze was more efficiently recycled and redistributed, less would be available for hoarding, and the increase in deposition could be an attempt to maintain the exchange value of bronze (1980b, 202–3). It may also have been an attempt to withhold certain material from exchange.

Barrett and Bradley also contributed separate papers to the discussion in this volume. Barrett stressed that we should advance our knowledge of bronze industries by examining regional exchange systems, as an important part of the production and distribution of these objects (1980a, 86). He also recognised the problems inherent in the data: "It is clear that our view of the metal industries through hoard and stray finds is grossly biased, for the more efficient the processes of recycling the less metalwork will be represented archaeologically" (1980a, 95). However, he was able to suggest a change in the later Bronze Age to a social system based on access to wealth and exchange, in contrast to the earlier Bronze Age where rank was based on "symbolic trappings" (1980a, 95). Bradley also stressed the need for further research into the nature of the deposition of metalwork and observed that some Wessex daggers are in a poor condition compared to others: a possible difference in their respective circulation times (1980, 62).

River metalwork was discussed again for the Thames Valley. Three alternatives were suggested: riverside settlements, funerary ritual and discard in a display of wealth (Bradley, 1980, 66). The concentration of more impressive weaponry closer to the river was also noted, correlating with the mould finds from outside this area of distribution (Bradley, 1980, 67). Bradley went on to suggest that apparent differences in food production might be "related to peaks in the abandonment of wealth" (1980, 68). The appearance of iron may have resulted from the reduction in social value of the prestige material, bronze, and the consequent need for an innovation (Bradley, 1980, 70). The widespread availability of iron, however, led to a collapse of the social order and the dropping of long–distance trade networks: Britain went into a period of isolation with strong individual, agricultural communities (Bradley, 1980, 70–71).

Muckelroy considered the role of overseas trade in relation to native Middle Bronze Age industries (1981). In dealing with the Langdon Bay wreck, he observed that the objects in it were at the very margins of their distributions, suggesting that they had lost their symbolic status and associations, or gone out of fashion; now they were only valued as raw material (1981, 290). Obviously, this would be an interesting point in relation to land hoards: do 'scrap' hoards contain objects outside their normal distribution? This does find some reflection in the ethnographic work of Rowlands (1971) and Hodder (1982). In the case of the Moor Sand wreck, Muckelroy argued that a fine sword in almost perfect condition had also been intended as scrap (1981, 291); however, such a fine item could have been traded and may even have been a personal possession. Muckelroy postulated a local surplus in supply, so that objects might travel great distances before being melted down (1981, 292). Perhaps the objects would then have been converted to locally acceptable forms (Muckelroy, 1981, 293–4). Muckelroy suggested that the initiative would have come from the English side of the Channel, requesting a load of 'scrap' from France, which in the case of the Langdon Bay wreck never reached them (1981, 295). This shows how new elements can be introduced into the argument with the appearance of just two new finds; it also introduces the complex question of cross–Channel relations and trade.

Needham recognised the problem of the loss of archaeological material before recovery both for stone moulds and bronze products (1981, Figure 11). This introduces a bias, awkward to determine, into our distribution maps and our considerations of the relative proportions of material. The presence of some axes and a mould otherwise unknown in the Lower Thames Valley at Petters Sports Field suggested to Needham that the smiths in this tradition perhaps enjoyed greater mobility than was usual, or that they were drawn to the site, because it represented such a special market (1981, 52). As for the actual production from Bulford–Helsbury moulds, the evidence implies that this was carried out on or close to contemporary settlements (Needham, 1981, 53–4); a somewhat different situation to other known manufacturing sites, for example Dainton, Devon (Silvester, 1980). It could be argued that the remains at Dainton resulted from "the short–term activity of an itinerant, perhaps highly mobile, smith", but on the other hand it could represent the residue of much larger production (Needham, 1980, 211). Needham concluded that the weapon assemblage represented by the mould fragments was a result of specialist production for a local nobility, involving the possibility of production on demand or as need arose, rather than stock piling (1980, 212–3). Again, we have a problem which is hard to resolve, although each new bit of evidence adds a piece to the jigsaw (even if it does appear to have been assembled wrongly!).

Pearce did not use the term 'hoard' in her study of south–western Bronze Age metalwork, as she felt it to be too imprecise, favouring instead the wider terms of 'association', which could apply to two or more pieces together, or to a single object found within an archaeological context. Sometimes she referred to 'multiple finds' for metalwork groups (1983, 2). She thereby avoided the full implications of deposition, and the potential use of scrap metal in re–cycling objects bypassed the problems of metal circulation (1983, 10–11). Nevertheless, Pearce recognised the social context and the potential of the metalwork for making statements about past behaviour: "It is likely to have been a most important form of regulating and expressing human relationships within the system of behaviour patterns, and it is likely to have been a part of man's expression of his relationship to the supernatural powers" (1983, 12). Pearce was able to use the study of metalwork and to relate it to other finds and sites, producing a model of territories based on central places (1983, 311–12), which could be a feasible pattern of organisation in the south–western peninsula. Her summary of the metalwork and related data is of great use in the study of material from this area.

Votive

Votive interpretations have already been touched on, but under this heading can be assembled a number of viewpoints derived from British authors, which can be seen to represent the use of 'votive' forms of explanation for Bronze Age metalwork.

In dealing with Early Bronze Age material from Scotland, Coles noted that some axes seemed to be deliberately snapped in two, particularly the examples from hoards, and he reflected that: "it is tempting to think either of ritual killing of these objects before their deposition, or the ostentatious deliberate destruction of valuable objects, akin perhaps to potlatch" (1968–9, 33). We shall return to ethnographic interpretations later.

In his review of Bronze Age metalwork in Ireland, Eogan distinguished workshop, founder's, craftsman's, merchant's, and personal hoards (1964, 311). Workshop hoards seem to subsume founder's or merchant's hoards to a certain extent, and craftsman's hoards consist of tools only; all other hoards which do not fit these headings were classed as personal (Eogan, 1964, 311). Eogan distinguished these classes, "following conservative practice", recognising that they are based on the assumption of their owners belonging to a certain category of society, but that "rigid application of such a classification can limit or hinder interpretation" (1964, 310). Eogan further reviewed the literature and interpretations of hoards, when presenting his catalogue of Irish later Bronze Age hoards (1983). He rightly pointed out the unsatisfactory usage of the term 'hoard', noting that it has been equally applied to collections of objects, which could hardly have been closed deposits, as well as to closed groups (1983, 1). He also drew attention to the difficulty of assigning hoards to interpretative classifications, when their content or location could make them eligible for several allocations (1983, 3). Until the hoard material for the whole of Europe has been systematically studied, our efforts at interpretation must be patchy and misleading: we need to understand the complex social and cultural interrelationships that lay behind these deposits (Eogan, 1983, 4). Interpretations of deposition have tended to fall into 'catastrophe' or 'security' hoards (ie those buried at times of unrest), an explanation favoured in countries south of the Alps; and 'votive' offerings, buried for some religious purpose, which is an explanation favoured in northern Europe (Eogan, 1983, 4). Eogan felt that some hoards could be deposited as part of some mystical act, and scrap hoards may actually be objects deliberately broken up as part of such an act before they were deposited (1964, 311). His source for such 'religious' customs was the work of Hundt on hoards in northern Europe, which is discussed later; but from this, and an apparent concentration of North European types in the province of Munster, he postulated the existence of a local cult, perhaps of intrusive origin. The enormous collection of material from the 'Golden Bog of Cullen' may have been a sacrificial or votive deposit, or even an offering place (Eogan, 1964, 311–14). The Irish hoards can generally be split into 'wet' and 'dry' locations, with the proportions varying for each phase of the later Bronze Age, but the majority of recorded locations can be regarded as 'wet' (Eogan, 1983, 5); this was especially the case for hoards of the final, Dowris phase of the Bronze Age, when water seems to have been specially selected for deposition (Eogan, 1983, 7–8). In dealing with earlier hoards of his Bishopsland phase, Eogan noted that the Nordic prototypes of the ornaments and tools are found in graves and we may in fact be dealing with "a new form of ritual practice possibly centred on a cult of the dead" (1964, 285). The Roscommon Phase contains many Wilburton types and consequently belongs to the same date range as the massive Isleham hoard. Curiously, this phase is poorly represented in Ireland, and it seems to be a rather unsatisfactory indicator of the presumed period of increased aristocratic representation in the archaeological record (Eogan, 1964, 292–3): a far call from the later heroic tales. The association of hoards with bogs, particularly in the case of the two largest 'hoards' of the late phase of the Bronze Age, would strongly suggest a ritual function for many of these finds, but decisive evidence is lacking. Eogan concluded: "While it is not possible to offer a satisfactory interpretation for the deposition of all hoards, nevertheless, it is clear that they are an important aspect of Later Bronze Age society and their study does much to illuminate it" (1983, 12).

Burgess *et al* have studied the barbed spearheads from British hoards and those known as single finds; these seem to have a riverine or water distribution and may have possessed a ritual or votive purpose (1972, 228). These objects may have also served as ceremonial weapons, due to the nature of their construction and shape (Burgess *et al*, 1972, 227–8). Conventional interpretation plays its part again, but with an emphasis on the votive aspect, which is more of a European phenomenon. However, Burgess *et al* were able to discern several regional types of hoard, the differences between them suggesting "all manner of social, cultural, technological and political variations, the nature of which can hardly be guessed at" (1972, 229). These could be classed as warrior hoards, over a wide area in which warriors with spears were dominant, and in the north the evidence would suggest warriors with swords. However, the writers recognised that "a region's hoards do not always reveal its political state", and that "the hoard pattern is obviously significant, but one must be careful in interpreting this significance" (Burgess *et al*, 1972, 229–30). Some of this information was worked up from Coombs' thesis (1971), dealt with above.

The notion of ritual deposition would seem to be proved by Davey's study of bronzes and their distribution in Lincolnshire (1971). He noted a dense concentration of finds in the river valleys, with some of the material coming from the river itself, and recognised the problems of interpreting this material (1971, 100). He explained the loss of such apparently valuable items as deposition "in response to some cultic or religious activity" (Davey, 1971, 105). The distribution of bronzes across Lincolnshire as a whole was felt to reflect the true Later Bronze Age situation, although no function could be assigned to these particular scatters (Davey, 1971, 105). This picture of Later Bronze Age metalwork distributions would have been distorted if based on hoards alone (Davey, 1971, 107): an important fact to remember when studying hoards in isolation. Davey used the chi-squared test to show that natural features were important in the distribution of bronzes, the null hypothesis being that there was no significant difference between regions (1971, 96–7). Davey seems to have applied the statistic incorrectly, and part of the problem with this must be that we are dealing with an archaeological sample: in other words, do we have the complete data set represented? The nature of discovery of most items of Bronze Age metalwork would suggest bias. Also, with this particular statistic or any involving the null hypothesis, the null hypothesis of randomness is unrealistic: "Almost any null hypothesis is obviously false in reality" (Doran and Hodson, 1975, 58). This is because archaeological evidence is highly unlikely to have been located at random in the available area: particular zones may have been favoured for particular activities, which was, after all, the basis of Davey's suggestions (1971). However, this method cannot be used to prove them. Water cults have been rather overworked as a model of explanation in recent years.

Burgess postulated a climatic deterioration in the Middle Bronze Age, which gave rise to profound changes in the social and religious order and somehow propagated a water-religion (1974, 195–6). The apparent increase in deposition of hoards in the Ewart Park phase were seen to be "very much a sign of the times, reflecting both the security motive in troubled times and also votive deposition, the two probably linked" (Burgess, 1974, 209). This was also attributed to the unsettled conditions brought on by climatic deterioration and "the rise of Hallstatt power in central Europe" (Burgess, 1974, 209). The scrap trade was seen to be important in the south east, where founder's hoards abound, contrasting with the trader's hoards from Lincolnshire and east Yorkshire, and the Irish personal hoards (Burgess, 1974, 210). However, Burgess also recognised that hoards could represent other things, such as the Broadward weapon hoards which were seen as the property of spear-bearing warriors "much given to ceremonial, and devotees of the water cult", or swordsmen's hoards in the area from Yorkshire to Aberdeen. Both areas also contain tool hoards, representing the "less martial elements in the community" (1974, 210–211). A possible explanation can be provided by invasion, so in Burgess' terms a seventh century Hallstatt incursion occurred in the form of adventurers, traders, and smiths "untrammelled by women and all the cultural paraphernalia", which would make full-scale invasion more noticeable (1974, 213). Thus, we may have recourse to traditional terms of explanations, even if these are covered by qualifications.

Pryor is well-placed to draw our attention to the problem of "wet places" and votive deposition: he pointed out that the Fens have not always been entirely waterlogged and furthermore that, because of peat shrinkage, we have lost the vertical context of most finds (1980, 489–90). "I therefore suggest that much of the Bronze Age metalwork from the Fens was not deposited in watery meres during ritual observances ..., but instead represents settlement material in its horizontal, but not its vertical context" (Pryor, 1980, 490). This point has been made by Lawson, who noted that marine transgression and the location of certain soils had more to do with the distribution of metalwork in the Fens, than ritual deposition in wet places (1979a, 56). River deposition received short shrift from Pryor too, as he showed that rivers in the past could be uncontrollable in spate during the winter months and sufficiently violent to erode any settlement material into them (1980, 489).

We turn to the book by Burgess, which covered the late Neolithic and part of the Bronze Age, and which he stated was aimed at "the interested general reader" (1980a, 12). Burgess examined the organisation of primitive metalworking and noted that there was no ethnographic evidence for the itinerant smith; instead, much metalwork may have been produced by part-time specialists and by smiths attached to chiefs, who concentrated on weapon production (1980a, 274–5). He went on to note that when objects can be paired with their moulds, or appear to originate from the same mould, they often occur within a given radius; the more long-distance links, of which there are several examples, probably represent successive exchanges of the objects (1980a, 275). The supply of metal is something of a problem, and Burgess relied on the idea of recycling. However, he also made the point that "the demands of the scrap trade would have led to a misleading flow of metalwork within the region and attracted undue amounts of exotica from the outside world" (1980a, 276). Later, he went over the arguments for water cults and associated deposition, tying them in with pomp and display (1980a, 350–2). The great quantity of fine metalwork from rivers is related to increased rainfall and waterlogging after 1500 BC (Burgess, 1980a, 351). Burgess cited the example of shields, too flimsy for combat, deposited in wet places; some have holes and cuts, which, it is suggested, represent 'ritual killing' before deposition (1980a, 351). How do we know whether this was so? Some may equally have been damaged in use: several shields have holes which neatly fit sword blades or spearheads. It is unlikely that the arguments for a change in religious practice, centred around a change in climate, will ever be resolved.

Explanation

Finally, in our survey of literature on British hoards and metalwork, there are a number of works aimed at more explanatory models for the Bronze Age, which will be of use in discussion. Rowlands attempted, in his own words, "to contribute to our general understanding of the nature of European Bronze Age society", but "it would be rather foolish to assume some general kind of pan–European social form at this time" (1980, 15). He outlined a system of general principles, which could be applied to later European prehistory, showing how a change from an elementary structure, with its claims to founding ancestors, to a transitional structure, with wealth distinctions, could have come about (1980, 20–21). This was first applied to the Homeric texts and to the Greece of their time as an illustration of this transition, and then to events in central Europe (Rowlands, 1980, 21–31). Southern Britain in the later Bronze Age was examined as part of the wider Atlantic Bronze Age regional economy: bronze represented access to wealth, with the weaponry from rivers resulting from status competition (Rowlands, 1980, 32–45). Hoards were mentioned directly in relation to the collapse of this regional economy. Armorican hoards were seen to mark overproduction of variable quality bronzes and were buried to maintain their value (Rowlands, 1980, 46). This argument has been mentioned already. Perhaps the presence of these 'as cast' implements in other areas resulted from a redirection of trade in an attempt to maintain local production. Rowlands felt that the important aspect of these patterns was not the control of production, but "the manipulation of relations of circulation and exchange" (1980, 46). The forms of circulation and exchange are interrelated but separate, so that wealth from one, for example the exchange of weapons, cannot be converted into prestige in the other, which may depend on food production and surplus (Rowlands, 1980, 46). Furthermore, Rowlands recognised that kinship alliances did not form the link between groups, as traditionally supposed, but made a base for local leaders to compete on: succession to title and the distribution of prestige items, encoding these titles, forming the main focus (1980, 47). "The 'exchange' networks that result from these processes are essentially expansionist and can extend over vast areas. Since the exchanges involved have potentially ritual, political and economic functions attached to them, they form total social networks, rather than being economic in character" (Rowlands, 1980, 47). These systems operated on the periphery of the Mediterranean state systems and were part of a cycle of expansion and contraction in political and economic growth (Rowlands, 1980, 47–8). As Rowlands recognised (1980, 48), these complex patterns of social change and links now need to be examined archaeologically. It is hoped that the examination of artefacts can be a contribution to this.

To conclude this survey of authors on British material, we should refer to a paper by Bradley, which covers some European material as well (1982). He reviewed the usual interpretations for hoards, pointing out that they conform to three categories: economic, social, and religious (1982, 109–11). Several examples showed how hoards and the other categories of deposit, such as grave goods and river finds, could in fact be complementary parts of a single pattern (Bradley, 1982, 112–16). Bradley contended that it was necessary to move the problem away from the processes of deposition to those of consumption: a function tied in with the ability of certain groups to produce a surplus from agriculture or other activities (1982, 116–17). Deposition would seem to be related to patterns of change and social stress, giving rise to the need to express rank: here distribution of wealth could come into its own, legitimising the individual's claim (Bradley, 1982, 118–20). This provides another avenue for research, but the case is hardly proven. These points are considered again in the following chapters (2 and 3).

So, we have had a hundred years of hypothesis and speculation concerned with the objects, their circumstances of deposition, and their associations. This survey of British authors has shown the wide range of interpretations that can be built up on the basis of the Bronze Age metalwork. Much could be done if the data base were more freely available, and more consistently and accessibly published; however, this point illustrates precisely the procedure to be followed. The objects and hoards themselves obviously contain a great store of information. We have to look at those objects themselves in order to gain this extra knowledge. Before we move to the objects themselves, however, we must examine some of the ideas about metalwork, and about hoards in particular, put forward by European authors, often working on much better researched and published data.

EUROPEAN MATERIAL

Votive

Evans was aware of the work of Worsaae on 'votive' hoards, and this is a good point at which to begin the discussion of authors on European material. Worsaae carefully laid out his arguments for interpreting hoards as votive deposits, based on a re–examination of some of the Danish material; the objects had always been thought of as lost, or deposited by thieves, or by people in troubled times, but he observed that, if finds had been intended for recovery, it was difficult to explain the trumpets deposited in some numbers and quite often broken (1866–71, 61–2). The broken nature of the material often matched that from burials too; other hoards contained new material (Worsaae, 1866–71, 63–5). On the basis of the Iron Age evidence for water cults, Worsaae suggested that similar practices occurred in the Bronze Age, resulting in hoards or deposits of other material including animal bones. What had often been regarded as foundry debris could also be explained as the offering by bronze founders to some divinity. Similarly, finds from the Swiss lake villages could have been from temples there (1866–71, 71–3). Even if the analogy does seem rather overdrawn, it was to provide inspiration and discussion for the next century or so.

Müller expanded the votive hypothesis in Denmark and saw it as covering the Neolithic as well as the Bronze Age (1884–9). He thought it very unlikely that all the finds from bogs were objects which had been lost; however, deliberate concealment for security purposes would be natural (1884–9,

241). Where large stones covered hoards, they would both protect and mark the place; he also observed the variable quality of the material in the hoards, including broken pieces: he doubted whether these were destined for recasting (1884–9, 242–4). Thus, these finds could be seen as offerings by immersion: a custom known among ancient peoples and 'savage' tribes, equipment often being offered for use in the 'after-life' (Müller, 1884–9, 244–5). Objects on dry land were interpreted by the same idea that the object was being given to the gods or spirits (Müller, 1884–9, 246). Thus, he emphasised the gift, rather than the location, concluding that its importance might have depended on the size of the offering. Where the objects were in a poor state, they served as an *ex-voto*, fulfilling the intention of the ceremony without actually giving away too much – and incidentally tricking the gods in the process! (1884–9, 274–8). The offerings may have had set numbers of objects, but where the quantity of objects was large, this was hard to explain and burial for other motives must be envisaged (Müller, 1884–9, 249–50). The idea of substitute objects representing the intention without the reality recurs in the work of Kristiansen (1979), when dealing with circulation time (discussed below).

Moving rapidly to more recent works, Hundt attempted an explanation of hoards in the Nordic Late Bronze Age (1955). Using the Mecklenburg region, he noted that many of the hoards came from bogs, wet land, and open water and found it hard to believe that valuable equipment could be lost in such areas and not recovered (1955, 95–6). Arguing against hoards as treasure stores, he remarked that all their owners must have gone away and died. He also doubted whether weapons would be buried in times of threat (1955, 97–8). Therefore, he argued for hoards as votive, with 'founder's hoards' representing offerings from smiths, and suggesting that the idea of offering places in early Christian times had prehistoric antecedents (1955, 99–100). The reasons for the offerings then came under scrutiny, and Hundt was able to suggest a variety of explanations: offerings for a future life with a strong cult of the dead; sun cults; fertility cults; with offerings related to men, women, and also wizards and shamans (1955, 107–22). This last suggestion was tied in with the practices of north Asian shamans, where their equipment, when not passed down to a successor, would be disposed of as an offering (Hundt, 1955, 123). However, Hundt interpreted the majority of Late Bronze Age hoards in his study area as grave goods, while stressing the important religious or ritual nature of the finds (1955, 123).

Hundt's article came at a time when hoards were back under discussion (Müller–Karpe, 1958, 32). Müller–Karpe saw possibilities in the explanation of hoards as votive or sacrificial offerings, instead of their usual interpretation as 'founder's' stores or 'household treasure' (1958, 32). Using the Urnfield finds from Bavaria, he suggested that, although the scrap hoards would have had a value for re-smelting, they could be compared with the broken and burnt objects in cremation burials, where objects were first broken up and then placed on the pyre with the body (1958, 32–4). This was comparable to the offerings of Greek and Italian religions; other deposits containing burnt pottery, bones, and charcoal could be the complementary part of the offerings, and the whole could form a part of Urnfield religion (Müller–Karpe, 1958, 34). Thus, hoards would again be connected with death offerings and with a cult of the dead associated with burning. Bog finds as a group were examined by Jankuhn (1958). These were regarded as offerings, which were precluded from recovery by their very nature. Often they were only distinguished from dry land finds because of their distinctive location. Bog finds could even include barrels of butter, hazelnuts, or animal bones (Jankuhn, 1958, 246–50). Offerings of wooden figures, perhaps representing deities, bog corpses used in some ritual, and also single pieces of bodies were common (Jankuhn, 1958, 252–4). Torbrugge extended the same arguments from wet places to open rivers (1960). He discussed the various ways of accounting for river finds, but thought that catastrophic floods would be unlikely, while finds made at crossings would be difficult to distinguish from other material. He noted the long history of water as a sacred thing (1960, 30–41). He went on to make the point that the sacrifice of a sword to the river must have served a positive purpose, which could not be equalled by the sacrifice of a pin (1960, 42). This work foreshadowed his later, more lengthy contribution on river finds (1970–71), detailed below.

Baudou used the material from the Nordic area and noted the discussion about the meaning of hoards (1960, 122). The hoards were divided up into two main groups with a third, smaller group: "Opferfunde", "Schatzfunde", and "technische Funde" (Baudou, 1960, 127). "Opferfunde" were defined as hoards found in bogs or in association with water, and often the equipment of one person; he cited Hundt on the strange loss of weapons and tools in bogs, although he stressed the need for understanding the local conditions at the time of deposition (Baudou, 1960, 122–3). He criticised Hundt's suggestion that some finds were 'funeral offerings', as these could easily be made for other purposes. Baudou concluded: "Wir müssen uns damit begnugen, von Opferfunden zu sprechen, ohne darauf einzugehen, wem and zu welchem Zweck die Gegenstände geopfert wurden" (1960, 123–4). "Schatzfunde" were buried in times of unrest for security; they also represented material from settlements ready for re-casting, objects belonging to travelling smiths, and some hoards of merchant's stock, full of imports (Baudou, 1960, 124–6). "Technische Funde" formed a small group of finds, including founder's hoards (Baudou, 1960, 127). In this way, Baudou covered various possible interpretations without actually expressing a particular preference for an overall explanation.

The rather uncritical application of terms like 'ritual' and 'offering' by various authors gives rise to various difficulties, as Stjernquist has noted at some length (1962–3). She criticised the assumptions underlying the application of such terminology, noting that 'offering' has two meanings in the literature: either being applied to a single act of deposition or to a whole group of finds and the place where they were deposited (1962–3, 5–8). Having reviewed the literature, she concluded: "Es ist daher unlogisch – wie das oft in der Fachliteratur der Fall ist – den Terminus Depotfund im Gegensatz zu einem Begriff wie Opferfund zu stellen" (1962–3, 19). The deposition of hoards for security purposes came under criticism too: this notion was seen to result from our own modern attitudes (Stjernquist, 1962–3, 24). Stjernquist doubted whether we could easily define an offering without recourse to the lives and social structure of prehistoric peoples, but the work of anthropologists would seem to suggest that fertility cults were important (1962–3, 28–31). In order to test some of her ideas and conclusions, she excavated a possible offering place near a spring at Roekilloma; the site was located in the middle of the best agricultural land and produced large numbers of bones and tools from Neolithic to Roman times (1962–3, 41–9). Stjernquist concluded from this that fertility cults, offerings for life after death, and an axe cult were all important features of the rituals at this time (1962–3, 55–60). In another article, Stjernquist reported on excavations at this site and at a similar site at Gardlösa and concluded that there was an important link between religion and everyday life (1964, 180–4). Although she felt that insights could be gained into actual thought processes through these excavations, she did note that: "The spiritual and mental processes of prehistoric man are not easily comprehended on the basis of archaeological investigation. The 'fossils' of human reactions and social intercourse do not survive in the same way as tools and ornaments" (1964, 180–1). A question mark remains.

Kolling collated Late Bronze Age material from the area around the Saar and Mosel (1968). A section of this work was devoted to deposition, where the old ideas such as 'travelling smiths' and 'times of unrest' were enumerated (1968, 110–1). Kolling made some interesting observations on hoards in this area, noting that some are situated in areas of optimal agricultural potential and could reflect the increased settlement of these areas (1968, 112). No hoards were deposited in bogs or water here, and only a few were under a stone, so the profane or religious distinction could not be applied (Kolling, 1968, 112). However, the study area did include the find from St. Kanzian, where broken and melted objects were dropped into a natural fissure and were thus irrecoverable (Kolling, 1968, 112). Kolling interpreted this as a form of offering and noted that the particular characteristics of this group of material were present in other hoards, concluding that some hoards on dry ground were also offerings, but lacked the unusual association (1968, 112–13). Broken objects would not indicate offerings directly, but melted objects and specific assortments of objects could do so; perhaps votive objects had to be destroyed to prevent re-use (Kolling, 1968, 113–14). Kolling noticed that this material is also in a similar state to that from graves, where the objects could have been destroyed before deposition in the burial (1968, 114). In conclusion, it was shown that not every hoard had a cultic origin: there were a variety of reasons for hoarding in every period. Deposition in this form subsequently came to an end, and the material was then used in other ways in the princely graves and settlements (1968, 116).

Von Brunn collated the hoards from central Germany for the Late Bronze Age and reviewed previous research on them (1968, 230–1). He noted that opinions seemed to switch back and forth between authors, giving hoards economic or religious emphasis, and even classing hoards as 'profane' in the Danube area and 'sacred' in Northern Europe, when we are actually dealing with the same sort of source material (1968, 231–2). von Brunn argued that the whole of the material across Europe should be taken into account – a vast amount of information – which would probably show differences in deposition and different reasons for deposition in various areas (1968, 234–7). Although many characteristics of cults and offerings are known to us, he quite rightly indicated that we have no real ethnographic parallels for the burial of offerings: the whole question had to remain open (1968, 238–9).

Despite the doubts expressed by these writers, authors go on accepting this form of explanation. Zimmermann treated the finds from rivers, bogs, springs, and wells in south-west Germany as offerings (1970). He felt that finds from rivers were the same as offerings in bogs and advanced a series of ways in which the objects could have been deposited in the river: dropping the objects from a boat, throwing them from the bank, depositions on crossing the river, deposition in an old river channel, eroded graves, settlements, and single finds, or accidentally lost pieces (1970, 66–7). These would be individual or group activities with some stretches of river receiving repeated depositions (Zimmermann, 1970, 67).

Torbrügge treated the river finds more thoroughly and thought that they resulted from deliberate deposition (1970–71, 3). He believed that river finds were equivalent to hoards and were buried for the same reasons (1970–71, 87). Although he could establish their deliberate deposition, explanation was more difficult, for when we deal with these finds, we are concerned with "die Ideenwelt des vorzeitlichen Menschen" (1970–71, 123). Torbrügge urged treating the river as both a real natural feature and a mythical place: "Erst dann werden die Dinge zu stummen Spiegelbildern menschlicher Handlungen und Ideen" (1970–71, 123).

Mandera criticised various aspects of the explanation of hoards and combined some of these interpretations (1972). The presence of bones and ashes in some hoards could be mentioned in support of the votive explanation, while ignoring the presence of foundry waste and dross, which could suggest a smithing site (Mandera, 1972, 100). Mandera also asked why the hoards were not dug up again, if they had been buried in times of danger. By the same token, pieces collected together for use as votive offerings could have been quickly buried to save the objects from an enemy (1972, 102). On balance, Mandera accepted that votive explanation applied for the earlier deposits, but felt that political factors later in the Bronze Age led to hoarding for the concealment of valuables (1972, 102).

Jensen also considered the votive character of finds, in his study of a newly-found Hallstatt sword from Denmark (1972). By comparing various objects which occur as single finds, Jensen was able to show how particular types became more or less important in the pattern of deposition across time (1972, 142, Figure 23). He argued again that it was unlikely for so much material to be lost in bogs, and that these finds should be considered as votive offerings (1972, 145). However, he recognised the problems of treating the material: "Die bronzezeitliche Forschung steht hiermit vor einer anscheinend unlösbaren Aufgabe"; but even so, he considered that archaeology could be used in more than a simple culture–historical way. By thinking about religion in the Bronze Age, we might begin to understand how prehistoric peoples oriented themselves in relation to their surroundings (1972, 146–9). There is sometimes the feeling that finds come from watery places in areas such as Denmark, because large parts of the country were aquatic by nature.

Maringer considered water from the point of view of prehistoric religion, using so–called votive finds and sites (1973). He saw water as one of the most sacred elements of religion right back to Palaeolithic times, next to fire (1973, 705–6). In the Bronze Age, Maringer envisaged a great expansion in this belief in, and veneration of, water (1973, 722). Some hoards may have been hidden away in troubled times and were not disturbed, because they were believed to be untouchable offerings to spirits; there was still scope for founder's and merchant's hoards (1973, 722–5). He quoted only one example of an offering known to him from England: Hogmoor with its heavily worn and broken pieces found in a wet situation which was regarded as a battle offering (1973, 727). Presumably he was here referring to the Blackmoor hoard, treated by Colquhoun (1979). Other examples demonstrated the long life of this belief: a belief revolving around water as the residence of higher powers and as a life–giving drink, or as the source of fertility for fields or humans (Maringer, 1973, 760). He stressed the mantic and legal strength of water in ordeals and summarised his argument as follows: "Das Wasser ist so eines der Ursymbole der Menschheit, ein theophores Element, aus dem in später vorgeschichtlicher Zeit Götter und Nymphen hervortreten; es erweist sich jedenfalls in existenzieller Weise dem Göttlichen verwandt; es ist das bevorzugte Element göttlicher Epiphanien" (1973, 760). Perhaps ethnography and anthropology could provide us with suitable models for beliefs and customs, but would they be archaeologically testable? Can we use such peripheral evidence in this way?

Schauer attempted to interpret the Urnfield hoard from Dolina, using the various models discussed above (1974). He found the interpretations hard to apply in this case. Following von Brunn, he considered the circumstances of deposition, but this was inconclusive: the composition of the hoard would indicate a founder's collection of scrap, unlikely to have been buried for security, because of the limited value of most of the material (1974, 121–3). In the end, he followed Hundt in suggesting that the hoard was a collection of material from a workshop offered by the smith for life 'on the other side' (Schauer, 1974, 124). This exposition seems rather an extreme view, drawing heavily on the association and contents of the hoard, but without a wider appreciation of how the evidence can be interpreted.

Randsborg set a new trend with his treatment of Early Bronze Age material in Denmark (1974). He concentrated on the grave material in particular and felt that it reflected a degree of social stratification (1974, 47). He also correlated population size with land quality, noting a general trend for Bronze Age societies to choose poorer soils, while working them to their best advantage, and later to move to more productive land (1974, 41–5). Randsborg demonstrated how various degrees of wealth and social standing could be derived from the contents of graves (1974, 52). In his view, it was increased population size that gave rise to social stratification (1974, 54). Related to this were the hoards and 'offering finds': "From a purely economic point of view the disposal of valuables in the ground is 'waste', but involving social acts like the burial ritual, these processes should be considered functional" (Randsborg, 1974, 58). Randsborg envisaged the ritual burial of objects, because he felt that burial in times of unrest would be unlikely, particularly since this would mean 800 years of warfare in the Eastern part of Denmark, while the Western part remained untouched (1974, 58). Plotting of hoards against grave finds demonstrated an inverse relationship between these two factors: thus in Denmark, the Western zones stressed status through burial practices, while the Eastern zones relied more heavily on the "squandering" of wealth (Randsborg, 1974, 59–60). Randsborg thereby demonstrated the potential of more in–depth studies of the material and noted that hoards were not easily interpreted, although they were related to what he called the "social dimension" (1974, 60). It was to these problems that Kristiansen later addressed himself (1979).

Stein also questioned the traditional interpretations and attempted a more critical analysis of the hoards (1976). 'Security finds' were intended for recovery, whilst 'offering finds' were sunk for eternity or simply offered at a holy place: these were the usual explanations of hoards in the past (Stein, 1976, 18). Hoards could be classified on the basis of composition and find circumstances, and thus Stein distinguished three major categories (with subdivisions): hoards containing raw material, those containing finished products, and those made up of scrap (1976, 19). Stein doubted whether hoards buried for security were a particularly widespread phenomenon and argued that they should be treated as sacred offerings. This might also apply to the deposition of single finds, which would hardly have been worth burying in times of unrest (1976, 110–11).

The same distinction between burial in times of unrest and burial for religious motives was highlighted by Sasse, who introduced a new element into the analysis of hoards: statistics and computing (1977). Using combination statistics on the contents and association of hoards, she was able to define three broad groups of finds: those which consisted only of one ornament, weapon, or tool type; those which apparently contained the equipment of one or several individuals; and those consisting of scrap (1977, 64–5). The data were then subjected to single–link cluster analysis (Sasse, 1977, 65–7). The resultant dendrogram showed various groupings, which also had a regional significance (Sasse, 1977, 70–71). Sasse concluded that the method was useful for highlighting regional differences in hoard deposition, in itself a significant factor, but she still retained the traditional explanations for deposition, favouring the 'sacred' over the 'profane' (1977, 75–6). This was a significant development in providing a working method for the analysis of such groups of finds.

Sasse (1977, 76) drew attention to finds of hoards from settlements, an example of which comes from Wallwitz (Stahlhofen, 1977). Here, a bronze hoard was found beneath the former wall of a house, the foundation having been broken at this point to accommodate this material (Stahlhofen, 1977, 211). The hoard had been carefully placed and was protected by the surrounding structures; it was interpreted as a dedicatory or foundation offering (Stahlhofen, 1977, 211–13). Stahlhofen thought that the presence of male and female equipment could indicate a joint offering of the householder to the household gods, although the possibility of it being material belonging to a craftsman could not be ruled out (1977, 213). It may be worth noting here that the photograph shows the objects to have been quite worn before deposition (Stahlhofen, 1977, Plate 35).

In examining a specific find group – pins – Kubach also made some observations on deposition (1977, 565ff). Most of the deposits seemed to have been in water, which was specifically sought out for the purpose; possibly these finds represent votive offerings to a mother goddess (Kubach, 1977, 575). Kubach found it hard to accept a profane interpretation for hoards and favoured the votive explanation, pointing out that water finds and hoards both increase in number during the early Urnfield period. Moreover, the pins were often deliberately broken prior to deposition, in order to prevent their re-use in profane ways (1977, 578–81). Kubach developed some of these points in a paper on bog deposition (1978–9). He pointed out an increase in deposition from the Neolithic to the Bronze Age, possibly due to a change to wetter conditions at the time (1978–9, 255). Votive offerings in wet places and water represented sacrifices. Although the associations of the offering places are no longer evident to us, Kubach pointed to the historical link between water, evil spirits, and the road to hell (1978–9, 259–60). Kubach thought that women made the offerings of pins and men perhaps those of axes. Through these offerings, people were responding to political unrest in the area (Kubach, 1978–9, 266–8). This may be taking things to an extreme, but it reminds us of the differential distribution of objects and types of hoards in various parts of Europe.

Coles and Harding also found the suggestion that hoards were all votive offerings extreme, when discussing the material from Northern Europe (1979, 517). They pointed out that this is a hard practice to understand, because all the materials had to be imported into the region, but this might equally supply the explanation: the objects were highly valued (1979, 517). Nevertheless, a number of objects and their find circumstances do suggest connections with ritual and would be hard to explain otherwise, for example the 'lurer' and small figurines (Coles and Harding, 1979, 518–19). Apparently much of this changed towards the end of the Bronze Age: Coles and Harding suggested that the adoption of iron, and even a change in the climate, demanded the breakage or burial of ceremonial objects (1979, 523). Perhaps objects fell out of use and had to be disposed of in a way that would accord with their original associations; again, we speculate.

Ultimately, Continental scholars remain as divided as ever on the merits of votive interpretations of this material. The situation is summed up by Rittershofer in his interpretation of the Bühl hoard: "Was die Menschen bewegte, die diese Horte niederlegten, bleibt ohne Antwort; die Gedanken und Wünsche, Hoffnungen oder Befürchtungen, die sie mit ihrem Tun verbanden, werden uns für immer verschlossen bleiben" (1983, 352).

Economic

In France, Chantre divided bronze metalwork by more economic notions: in the Full Bronze Age he distinguished "trésors", or the stock of a travelling merchant; "fonderies", or collections of old bronzes for recasting; and "stations", which were seen to be indications of settlement and lake dwellings (1875–6, 68). Evans had also frequently referred to Chantre in his work (1881). Chantre went on to give clear definitions of his terms, with 'tresors' containing new objects, often of the same form and in large numbers, and without any associated traces of activity, metallurgical or otherwise (1875–6, 71). 'Fonderies' were characterised by material broken, deformed or used: "ce sont des ustensiles, des armes et des ornements hors de service"; again, no traces of habitation nearby could be detected, and foundry material was common in these finds (Chantre, 1875–6, 89). He distinguished two types of founder's deposit: those which were objects for recasting, and those which represented the actual material from workshops (1875–6, 89). He also noted that some of these founder's deposits would suggest a partly sedentary existence, while others, standing in isolation, seemed to have belonged to true nomads (1875–6, 157). Habitation sites could be confused with merchant's hoards, because bronzes from them were often unassociated (Chantre, 1875–6, 158). This more economic approach to hoards in France has lasted up to the present and is akin to the British approach.

de Mortillet collected together a number of hoards in France and provided descriptions (1894). From this he was able to make a number of observations about the hoards themselves, and the weight and number of objects contained in them (1894, 334–5). He also noted special characteristics of particular deposits and observed that axes made up the majority of the contents of special hoards (1894, 336–7). de Mortillet accepted the standard names for hoards: broken objects and debris made up "fonderies", or more accurately "cachette de fondeur", because these hoards are hardly ever associated with furnaces (1894, 338). Collections of new objects or those in good condition made up merchant's hoards; and mixed hoards with both new and old objects were felt to be rare (de Mortillet, 1894, 338). He was also able to show the irregular distribution of hoards, some coming from localities with many examples, while other areas completely lacked any hoards (1894, 339–40). These straightforward results were obtained by a thorough survey of the available evidence: an important prerequisite for any speculation.

The second edition of Déchelette's *Manuel* capably summed up the arguments about hoards at that time and has not really been superseded (1924). The greatest number of Bronze Age objects were seen to come from finds called "dépôts", also known as "trésors" or "cachettes", which were described in the following way: "Un dépôt se compose d'objets n'appartenant pas à une sépulture, mais dont le groupement dans un espace restreint résulte cependant d'un même enfouissement intentionnel" (Déchelette, 1924, 163). However, the difficulty of distinguishing some hoards from grave goods was noted. The regular grouping of objects was commented on, as were the find spots, ranging from those buried in the ground with no association, to material discovered underneath stones, and the most frequent occurrence of axes, some of which, he considered, may have been treated like money (Déchelette, 1924, 164). Déchelette recognised the problems of defining and explaining hoards, preferring two divisions: founder's hoards and simple hoards, "ces derniers comprenant sans doute tout à la fois des offrandes votives ou religieuses, probablement très nombreuses, et des cachettes ou trésors" (1924, 165). Hoards of new, unused objects were not all seen as merchant's hoards, but as a result of the burying of objects for safety reasons; this, he felt, happened because the dwellings of the period were not secure. He cited several examples of hoards in containers found adjacent to other, empty containers (Déchelette, 1924, 165–6). He also supported the idea of water cults extending back into the Bronze Age and accepted the religious nature of some deposits, although the cult places were so ephemeral that votive finds were often hard to distinguish from material that had been hidden (1924, 166). More speculatively, Déchelette wrote about the cult of the axe, the deposition of axes in circles presumably representing the sun symbol, and the possibly votive nature of miniature Armorican axes (1924, 479–84); but, as he remarked himself, "il serait chimérique, dans bien des cas, de prétendre déterminer exactement les conditions de l'enfouissement et la véritable origine du dépôt" (1924, 166).

Briard only used hoard material in a direct way and did not really concern himself with interpretation in his work of synthesis (1965). He was able to define 'complexes' of metalwork on the basis of associations and, on hoards themselves, he remarked that close study could illuminate whether they were imported or locally made (1965, 284–5). In another article, he commented on the presence of swords in the rivers of Brittany and pointed to the importance of fords for ritual combat in the early Irish literature, as in the Cattle Raid of Cooley; thus, he felt that rivers could also mark tribal frontiers (1971, 57–8).

A fairly straightforward use of statistical tests recurred in the analysis of hoards by Verron (1973), in a way similar to Davey's work on Lincolnshire material (1971; discussed above), and the more complex work of Sasse (1977; also discussed above). Verron noted the traditional explanations of hoards and the mainly chronological stance of most work on them (1973, 610–11). He decided to test the data using statistical methods comparable to those used by Bordes in his analysis of Palaeolithic material, and outlined how it could be used on Bronze Age material (1973, 612–13). This was done by listing the hoards according to their contents and then working out the proportions of these contents to the total, making allowances for fragments and checking the significance of any patterning using the chi-squared distribution (Verron, 1973, 614–15). It is interesting to note here that Verron considered it useful to be able to study the 'use state' of the objects, ie at what stage of their life they had been deposited, and whether breaks were deliberate or accidental – but in practice he could not apply this (1973, 616). He tried the method out on some well-known Breton and French hoards and was able to demonstrate significant elements in their composition, even when separated in time and space, which either differentiated the hoards or, in the case of some ornament hoards, demonstrated their similarity (1973, 616–20). Verron thought that this would be an interesting exercise for other ornament 'groups' across Europe, such as the Ornament Horizon in Britain, and concluded that this simple technique was useful "à débrouiller un peu les problèmes posés par les cachettes de l'Age du Bronze" (1973, 620).

Mohen collected together a large amount of material in his catalogue of finds from the Paris area (1977). He advanced a variety of explanations for river finds: objects perhaps fell from boats or resulted from naval battles; there were settlements alongside the rivers, which could be the source for some of the material; and there could be offerings, perhaps to a war–like god, because of the preponderance of weapons (1977, 200–201). Discussing hoards themselves, Mohen also preferred more economic interpretations, such as 'treasures', 'merchant's hoards', or 'founder's hoards', which could be easily distinguished because of the presence in them of complete or incomplete objects (1977, 202). He observed that certain areas had large concentrations of hoards, which would appear to represent zones of production, but that different hoards suggest different things: "D'autre part, les dépôts répresentent des phénomènes culturels divers que nous ne pouvons comparer qu'avec prudence" (1977, 202).

We must refer to two other papers here, which deal with related concepts. Randsborg mentioned hoards in passing in his book on the Viking Age in Denmark. They were seen as a means of disposal for valuable objects in the Bronze Age, and as a way of underlining personal status, a practice which became redundant in the Iron Age (1980, 49). Later, he referred to historic hoards and saw them as a result of raiding, and therefore of hoarding for security: "historical sources from the seventeenth century tell us of people hiding their silverware in a bag, tied to a tree, and then dropping it into a lake or bog" (1980, 139). Wells also highlighted this change from Bronze to Iron Age. In discussing the hoards of the Late Bronze Age in the Eastern Alpine region, he felt that they indicated a metal shortage and were scrap objects collected together for recasting (1981, 123). That they were not all used up in recasting suggests that iron intervened and became more popular. Smiths now became part of the community, replacing the itinerant bronzeworkers who had previously provided the objects (Wells, 1981, 124). Ironically, it was the introduction of iron which probably gave rise to the re–alignment of trading arrangements and the again free availability of bronze for fine metalwork (Wells, 1981, 125). This increased productivity in the Early Iron Age also led to increased deposition in graves, basically to maintain the level of production (Wells, 1981, 127 and

Figure XXXIII). Therefore, bronze and hoarding are firmly rooted in an economic tradition, involving production and supply.

The range of 'economic' explanations for hoarding used by authors on European material have been laid out here, with some other examples of the ways in which hoarding can be viewed, and can be contrasted to the usual interpretation of hoards in Europe as a result of 'votive' acts. To move beyond this deadlock in interpretation, we can examine some further innovative papers.

Explanation

Perhaps more in the line of speculation, we move to the work of Kristiansen and Levy on Danish Bronze Age material. As a preliminary to a detailed study of the hoards, Kristiansen published the results of a 'source–critical analysis' of Bronze Age hoards (1974). In this he examined the date of recovery of hoard finds by various factors such as agriculture, peat cutting, or industrial development, from the beginning of reliable records (1974, 155–60). As Kristiansen rightly recognised, all these things could influence our notion of distributions and the certainty of obtaining closed groups (1974, 152). However, his graphs demonstrated that, although these agencies operated at different rates in different areas, all had now arrived at the same point of very low recovery rates, showing that the actual amount of material available to us for study should be archaeologically representative of what was originally deposited and thus of its original distribution (1974, 160). Therefore, Kristiansen felt that he could rightly proceed, using the museum material as the representative basis of past distributions and situations (1974, 160).

We now turn to a more recent paper by Kristiansen (1979). Kristiansen was concerned to explain "the dynamics of economic processes in tribal societies" and used bronzes as a measure of the circulation and consumption of valuables in these societies (1979, 158). This was done by observing the degree of wear on full–hilted swords and decorated ornaments, with preserved original surfaces, from graves and hoards (Kristiansen, 1979, 158–9). Kristiansen was able to show a change in wear patterns, and by implication circulation time, across different zones and periods in Bronze Age Denmark (1979, 160–64). He went on to evaluate the role of trade and exchange. The raw materials had to be imported, and this was found to be affected by agricultural production and local population levels (1979, 167–75). He considered the relationship between these different factors throughout the sequence in his study area and suggested a basically devolutionary process at work in the tribal structure, leading to a "prefeudal mode of production" (Kristiansen, 1979, 182).

Kristiansen developed these ideas in other papers, using the same material (1980; 1981; 1985). The first of these is essentially the same as his 1979 paper, but in the conclusion he did provide a graph summing up the various relationships considered in the study (1980, Abb. 12). This showed how agricultural production at first exceeded population density in the Bronze Age, but then was overtaken by it, until the social system broke down at the end of the late Bronze Age (Kristiansen, 1980, 32–3). This model is based on one used by Friedman in his work analysing Asiatic social formations (1979; here further referred to in Chapter 3). Kristiansen then set his work against the background of earlier studies of the Bronze Age in Denmark (1981, 243–4). In this paper, Kristiansen also defined his studies more clearly, by stating that: "...the consumption of wealth...was closely linked to the reproduction of rank and political control through the deposition of ornaments and weapons in graves and hoards according to sex, age and rank" (1981, 245). He went on: "By removing scarce and prestigious goods from circulation their value could be regulated and controlled, just as the ritual framework of such consumption sustained religious order and ultimately political control" (1981, 245). The method used in his analysis of circulation time was the same as in his 1979 paper, but placed greater weight on economic factors (Kristiansen, 1981, 253–4). Relating exchange to the production of bronze in Europe, Kristiansen made several significant points about the hoards: increased hoard frequency in Europe may reflect the destruction or storage of bronze to protect its value in periods of over–production; localised stagnation in Scandinavia may have meant that the economy could not meet the demands of alliance and exchange partners; expansion in agricultural production in central Europe may have increased the demand for tools, redirecting production to internal rather than external needs (1981, 260–61). All of these alternatives would fit the changing circulation and land–use patterns apparent in Denmark, which seem to have resulted in a decreased provision of grave goods and an emphasis on special, 'ritual' hoards (Kristiansen, 1981, 261). Kristiansen concluded this paper with a comment on the legitimacy of his applications and techniques: "Archaeologically representative and well published, it [the Nordic Bronze Age] represents a laboratory for testing a wide range of hypotheses on a still badly understood epoch in European prehistory" (1981, 262). Kristiansen's observations on wear, typology, and chronology, published in 1978, have been translated into English (1985). His argument in this paper was that objects could have circulated for different periods of time in different areas, with the result that they may have overlapped in their use–life, although they were not made at the same time (1985, 254–5). Thus, Kristiansen showed that a knowledge of the social context of objects was necessary for us to be able to place them securely in a chronological context (1985, 260). The potential of all this work is clear, but the methods are not. Obviously, first–hand examination of the material would help here and in the work of Levy, discussed next. This point is taken up later, as is a further analysis of Kristiansen's theoretical stance.

A somewhat different approach to some of the same material was taken by Levy (1977; 1979; 1982a; 1982b). Levy was concerned to show how certain sets of ornaments reflected social ranking and thus indicated the presence of a chiefdom society in Bronze Age Denmark (1979, 49–53). She did this by deciding which hoards represented the remains of ritual activity, on the basis of criteria drawn from the ethnographic record, such as association with wet places, arrangement of the objects, and predominance of personal weapons or ornaments (1979, 51). Levy was then able to define 20 "set types", consisting of particular combinations of ornaments in differing quantities. These, she felt, reflected the existence of a ranked society with several levels, above which could be placed hoards of more exotic items, available only to chiefs (1979, 53–6). Levy accepted that some hoards were unlikely to be of ritual significance and suggested their burial in times of unrest, but this applied only to a minority of the material (1982b, 38). She also noted the presence of wear on many items (1982b, 39). This apparent wastage of wealth was compared to the cargo cults of Mesoamerica, a system whereby an individual demonstrated his elite status by massive spending (Levy, 1982b, 45). These points are expanded in Levy's thesis (1977), which was later published with slightly less emphasis on social change (1982a, Preface). Levy's use of ethnographic analogy would seem to reinforce the traditional ritual/non-ritual definitions of hoards (1977, Chapter 4). A potential problem is the use of food rather than material wealth as ritual offerings by some of the sample societies: this contrast with the evidence from Denmark suggested to Levy that a highly stratified society existed during the Bronze Age, rather than a less stratified, or tribal form of social organisation (1977, 114–16). The actual question of change across time within this society remained an open one (Levy, 1977, 125). Levy interpreted these hoard finds in Binford's terms: "These metal resources were mainly used in the socio-technic sphere, mediating relations between individuals and groups, rather than in the technomic sphere, directly mediating relations between people and the environment" (1982a, 1). In other words, objects from ritual hoards were not directly involved in subsistence activities. However, a whole range of criteria were developed to define the ritual hoards and careful selection of the data was implicit (Levy, 1982a, 24–5). Levy concluded that these data were useful in understanding wider social organisations, especially in non-state societies, where religion helps to establish order (1982a, 117–18). This provides another example of the way in which hoard data can be used, along with other information, to go beyond simple economic interpretation.

A session on hoards at a conference on the Bronze Age in Regensburg looked at the ways in which the material has been studied, analysed, and interpreted (Kubach, 1985; Mandera, 1985; Pauli, 1985; Torbrügge, 1985; zu Ehrbach-Schönberg, 1985). Kubach pointed out that there were no good reasons for treating hoards of multiple finds and single finds as separate categories of information; massive hoards of many broken pieces differ more sharply from the contents of a small hoard (1985, 179). Patterns of deposition for single finds could change with time and in relation to patterns of deposition for hoards (Kubach, 1985, 180–83). Mandera recognised the problem of ascribing an interpretation to hoards, when we know so little about the people who deposited them: an uncertainty that has to remain. He commented on the divisions of opinion in current interpretation. The contrast between ritual and political activity may be unreal: Islam is an example of the thin divide between religion and politics (1985, 187–91). Torbrügge also reviewed arguments about hoards and their interpretation, noting that the range of explanations grows with the number of discoveries and their study (1985, 19). zu Ehrbach-Schönberg was able to show how deposition in graves, hoards, river finds, and single finds varied across time and region in Austria, and how various objects were favoured for a particular kind of deposit; for instance, knives, arrowheads, and pins all come from graves (1985, 163–7). Finally, Pauli questioned the simple acceptance of an explanation for one group of material, and another explanation for a different group, by showing that further factors, such as are known from historical examples, could equally explain 'sacrificial' or 'security' deposits. At this distance in time, however, these factors are too complicated to unravel (1985, 197–200). He went on to argue that hoards could be seen as deposits of 'money', in that their contents might have been used in exchange transactions. If so, they may have lost their value at the end of the Bronze Age with the introduction of widely-available iron; other, organic items could have had an exchange value, but would be invisible in the archaeological record (1985, 200–201). Pauli argued for a broadening of the field of study for hoards, so that research does not become self-defeating (1985, 202). His opening sentence summed up the problem facing European researchers: "Es ist mir ein Rätsel, warum das Problem der Hortfunde so dogmatisch behandelt werden muss" (1985,195).

Larsson has used an approach similar to that of Kristiansen to deal with Bronze Age metalwork in Sweden (1984). He visualised two major functional spheres in society – the symbolic and the practical – to explain every activity; the symbolic dimension is a form of social communication with the symbols containing coded information about society itself (1984, 63–5). The circulation of bronze was taking place far away from the metal sources, and the objects may have circulated within three partly-separated levels defined by different types of artefact. Thus, axes were practical objects with many sub-types, while swords were symbolic objects with few sub-types and could be visualised as 'words' in a highly symbolic language developed between different tribes and regions (Larsson, 1984, 69–75). The patterns of distribution re-inforced this approach, with the same types of weapon circulating in areas where the axe types were quite different from one another. Other areas with closely related types of axe were differentiated at the weapon level. Larsson saw this as a multi-level exchange system, reflecting a society composed of local, hierarchically organised structures (1984, 77–9). Larsson noted that his approach would eventually have to take monuments into account and concluded that "the total summary of such a multi-structural approach can only be evaluated in connection to a defined theory of the dialectics of social formations" (1984, 80).

More recently, Larsson has shown through the publication of his doctoral thesis how metalwork can be fitted to the social theory (1986). Apart from the detailed exposition of the metalwork data in southern Sweden, he has laid out how a theoretical framework should be applied, in order to gain insights into the Bronze Age societies of the area (1986, Chap. 2–5). Discussion and analysis followed the detailed presentation of the data, including an in-depth analysis of three regions within southern Sweden, and an analysis of hoard finds; Larsson argued that all hoards should be viewed as equal, in the sense that they are deliberate deposits or statements of a society, and should not be classified separately as 'ritual' or 'functional' (1986, Chap. 6). Larsson sees the mode of production and reproduction, kinship principles, exchange, and core/periphery relationships as fundamental to an understanding of the archaeological data (1986, 183). In their application to the metalwork from southern Sweden, he presents an exciting analysis of social systems in action (1986, Chap. 7).

This lengthy resume has drawn together the ways in which the hoard material has been treated by European writers. What is clear is that the traditional dichotomy remains uppermost: are hoards a result of ritual or secular practices? The emphasis would appear to be in favour of ritual, but the issue remains largely unresolved. This review, however, does highlight some of the more promising approaches to the material within Europe. In particular, the work of Kristiansen and Larsson, although based on traditional ideas, may represent a largely new departure in the interpretation of bronze deposits. It will be taken further in later chapters. Before we can embark on our own analysis, however, we must also give some attention to ethnographic models which can assist in our analysis.

OTHER THEORIES OF DEPOSITION

We have already seen the kind of contribution that anthropology and ethnography can make in supplementing our archaeological interpretations: indeed, it might seem that every case provided a contradiction. Just as in other sciences, we can only suggest the likelihood of something being the case: we can never be certain that it is true. In archaeology the margin of doubt must be wider, because of the nature of our data. Ethnography may help to narrow that gap.

Binford outlined well the problems of dealing with artefacts (1972). He pointed out that the variations in attributes measured in artefacts were often products of subsystems working within the culture that produced them (1972, 94). Binford was showing that the different ideological associations attached to the objects by their makers would affect that object in its method of manufacture and its subsequent uses. Thus, we could visualise artefacts in three terms – the technomic, the sociotechnic, and the ideotechnic (1972, 95–6). Stylistic patterns reinforced the separate groupings, even though the artefacts may have been present in the three different spheres (Binford, 1972, 96). Binford provided an example of the way in which sociotechnic artefacts would be used to exhibit status, which could not be inherited through the objects, thereby necessitating their destruction (1972, 99). It might seem from this that any ethnography could provide the necessary answers about the role of artefacts in society, but of course, archaeology has the necessary time–depth to observe patterns of change (Binford, 1972, 96). Binford felt that archaeology had much to offer anthropology by its studies of material culture, and as it provides the time–depth unavailable in ethnography, "we cannot afford to keep our theoretical heads buried in the sand" (1972, 101). This article was originally published in 1962, and it seems that some 30 years later, we are still trying to come to terms with many of its suggestions. Possibly we have attempted to rush ahead into theory and explanation without giving much thought to the quality of our data: an observation that applies to much of archaeology, but particularly to the uses of ethnography. However, we should still consider some other works relating archaeology to ethnography.

Rowlands' paper on metalworking summed up many of the observations to be made in this field (1971). He observed that in many cases the customer organised the production of the desired object, while the smith only provided the expertise: an example which could be used to explain large scrap metal hoards, where the objects would be collected together for remaking at one time (1971, 211–12). In this case, the smith need not be a full–time specialist, but could work on his own land too (Rowlands, 1971, 213). This highlighted the problem of the itinerant metalworker, so often suggested by prehistorians: there are hardly any ethnographic examples of these, and it is an unlikely mode of diffusion for ideas (Rowlands, 1971, 214–15). Another archaeological assumption that can be shown to be unfounded is the notion that the smith was of high status – indeed the opposite could often be the case (Rowlands, 1971, 216–17). In fact, several common assumptions about the nature of prehistoric metalworking could be shown to be erroneous, and Rowlands emphasised the need to interpret metalwork and its production only in the light of other information, such as "subsistence economy, settlement pattern, technology, sources of raw material and trade" (1971, 221). What is obvious is that Rowlands drew on a number of examples which demonstrated the different nature of metalworking in each of the societies which were described: a factor which should be borne in mind, when making generalisations applied to a variety of material. This tendency is apparent in some of the articles discussed below.

Howard used ethnographic parallels – some of her examples contradicting those of Rowlands – as an adjunct to her thesis on the bronze casting industry in southern Britain (1983). She argued that bronze production was stimulated by demand for the product, and that this in turn was governed by the social, economic, and ritual organisation of the group producing the object (1983, 8–9). Howard brought together various accounts of metalworking in primitive societies that contained blacksmiths, as there are no direct equivalents to bronze workers extant, and looked at the social attitudes to smiths and the organisation of their craft (1983, 17–23). She found that smiths were always regarded as 'set apart' from ordinary people, either as a revered or a reviled group, and sometimes as a combination of both (1983, 25). The industry could be divided into three forms of specialisation: by metal, by activity, and by product; so, bronze or copper working could be carried out alongside ironworking, but could be of higher or lower status, while the extraction of raw materials would often be separate from their use in production. Similarly, the end products could be manufactured using different levels of skill, eg the master smith making the ceremonial ornaments (Howard, 1983, 33–9). Itinerant smiths, as well as sedentary smiths, seem to be well attested, some travelling great distances to manufacture objects, with the work often being part-time and the smith involved in various subsistence activities (Howard, 1983, 40–46). Howard also remarked how metal in ingot or scrap form is always highly valued and often carefully hoarded for future re-working (1983, 49). Products were often made on demand for a customer, but could be made for trade in the larger population centres; even the smith could sometimes be traded himself as a diplomatic item (Howard, 1983, 54–7).

On the basis of these ethnographic observations, and observations made from an analysis of refractory debris from Bronze Age sites in southern Britain, Howard was able to propose three classes of casting organisation during the later Bronze Age in southern Britain: 1. Resident smith producing prestige objects in a fixed workshop patronised by an elite; 2. Smiths locally itinerant and producing tools in bronze moulds, which could be carried around and re-made at a central source when necessary; 3. Smiths producing axes in stone moulds in a long-distance, probably annual, itinerant cycle, perhaps for an elite, because of the problems of casting in stone (1983, 511–12). She was then able to relate these three classes to the archaeological record, both in terms of production and product, although much had to remain speculative. This organisation devolved into prestige production for elite groups in the Iron Age (1983, 525–46). Direct ethnographic parallels indicated ways in which metalworking could be organised in the Bronze Age, but the complexity of the systems that provided these ethnographic parallels could not be examined, and it is uncertain whether their social processes could be truly compared with the hypothetical ones of the Bronze Age.

Welbourn highlighted the ways in which material objects can attain a ritual purpose, when discussing the blacksmiths of the Marakwet in Kenya (1981, 34–5). Particular attitudes and rules applied to these smiths (Welbourn, 1981, 36–8). This is claimed to be archaeology in an extended way, even though it is more clearly ethnography, in that it discusses attitudes towards objects and not the objects themselves. A fuller description of this kind of approach was given by Hodder (1982). In his book, Hodder discussed various aspects of material culture within several African tribes, including metal production (1982, 59ff). He doubted whether stylistic patterning in the metalwork simply reflected human behaviour or represented the nature of industries, and more specifically, whether hoards could arise from seasonal production, being more likely to result from bursts of activity at any time (1982, 59–62). Later, Hodder discussed attitudes to death among the Nuba, who distinguish strongly between purity and impurity and frequently break the personal items of the dead, since these 'are' the deceased; he also described a similar practice among Gypsies (1982, 199–200). The Gypsies believe that the personal possessions of the deceased are a magnet for the *mulo* or ghost, and as a consequence these must be destroyed by breaking and burning them on the perimeters of the camp; some are buried a distance away or dropped in deep water (Okeley, 1979, 88).

Hodder concluded from his studies that we, as archaeologists, have to consider the part played by the symbolism of material culture in the development of ideologies (1982, 210). He also challenged structural-Marxist theories that discuss only the material correlates and "the reflective nature of material culture", without examining "the ideology under which the domination and monopoly of prestige goods are accepted and negotiated" (1982, 210). Hodder's approach has been criticised by Binford: "Hodder seeks to draw the field off into subjectivism and idealism" (1982, 163); a charge which is hard to refute.

General anthropological processes could also be used in the explanation of hoarding: we have already seen how this was applied by Bradley amongst others (1982; discussed above), and this approach will be treated in more detail in Chapter 3. Hoarding could reflect the removal from circulation or destruction of wealth for a variety of social reasons. Meillassoux has discussed *potlatch*, which could be seen to be an example of this. The original report on this practice by Boas contained all sorts of economic terms appropriate to the capitalist society, but not to the society which he was studying (Meillassoux, 1977, 160–61): an attitude perhaps analogous to Evans' treatment of hoards in strictly modern economic terms (discussed above). The purpose of the *potlatch* seems to have been to establish an individual's status in relation to another individual by competitive exchange (Meillassoux, 1977, 162–3). Actually to achieve a dominant position, it is necessary not only to amass such objects, but also to destroy them (Meillassoux, 1977, 165). Thus, the objects used in this way have no productive value (Meillassoux, 1977, 165). This activity could be explained in various other ways. Dupré and Rey visualised an institutionalised destruction of elite goods to help alleviate over-accumulation of such objects, since they could not be consumed in any other way (1978, 193–4).

Gregory distinguished between 'gifts to men' and 'gifts to god' in the *potlatch* system (1980). Essentially the purpose of gifts between men was to accumulate gift-credit, using property which was inalienable: in other words, one expected a return for it (Gregory, 1980, 638–41), whereas the 'gifts to god' achieved "the *alienation of the inalienable*", because one would not expect an actual gift in return (Gregory, 1980, 645). This system would enable a big man to withdraw some of the stock of gifts from circulation by their destruction, and thus prevent the repayment of the gift-credit owed by his opponent (Gregory, 1980, 646). This highlights the differences of opinion as to what constitutes the practice of the *potlatch*, although all the authors indicate that the gifts are non-productive items used as symbols of rank. However, one could argue that this would hardly be the case for many hoards of the Bronze Age, where we are dealing with large collections of tools and weapons, all of which served a purpose and would have been easily re-made into functional items.

O'Shea attempted another area of explanation with the concept of social storage, where societies use storage to combat resource scarcity (1981, 167). This can either be of the direct kind, where food itself is stored, or an indirect form, where food value can be stored through exchange (O'Shea, 1981, 171). The exchange network can either move goods from areas of abundance to those of scarcity, or have the goods available to all: such systems are termed 'complementary' and 'redundant' systems respectively (O'Shea, 1981, 173). This transfer of food value to tokens makes the unequal accumulation of wealth possible, and this, O'Shea considered, would give rise to inflationary tendencies. If so, they might be offset by the destruction of wealth, or by placing it beyond reach in burials, hoards, or river–offerings; alternatively, it could be exchanged outside the regional network (1981, 178–9). This approach was criticised by Binford as being an idea derived from western economics, and which he called a "near Hobbesian contract" (1982, 163). Again, we have the evidence of the 'storage', but not the 'system'.

As an adjunct to ethnographic parallels, literary parallels are sometimes given, as they are by Rowlands (1971). Some of the Early Celtic literature has been summarised by Gillies (1981). Gillies found that the subject divided into two parts: one, where there were direct references to the craftsman and his work, and the other, where there were incidental references to them (1981, 71). Several observations arose from this study, including the position of respect afforded to the smith, both because of his products and his healing powers, and because of the status of other craftsmen in society (Gillies, 1981, 75–6). However, other questions remained: whether smiths travelled round, practising their craft or directing others, and whether the crafts were hereditary and the 'trade secrets' were protected. Nor de we know whether craftsmen remained attached to one patron or not (Gillies, 1981, 77). Gillies concluded with a warning against the careless use of this early literature by archaeologists, bearing in mind the nature of the sources, and the intractability of some of the texts (1981, 81–2).

What has been attempted in this brief outline is to show how ethnographic studies might also aid us in our reconstructions of past activities. The problems of direct application are manifest, for example, many of the studies deal with blacksmiths, who, as Childe observed (1956, 178), may operate in a different social context from bronzesmiths. Also, many of the theories conflict, although they are dealing with the same material. This can be taken as an indication of a healthy state of affairs for the theoretical side of our subject, but it means that ethnography cannot be solely relied upon to provide the analogies. Much depends on our attitude to the artefacts under study (Foxon, 1982), and what we feel it is justifiable to draw from them before we resort to ethnographic parallels. It is clear that this is an area which is open to a more detailed enquiry, but ethnographic parallels can still provide us with useful ideas.

CONCLUSION

This survey has attempted to show some of the richness of the literature relating, directly or indirectly, to hoards. The division between explanations into 'votive' and 'economic' showed the range of possible interpretations, although there are obviously cross–overs between these groupings; the 'explanation' sections were intended to show how a new direction for hoard interpretation could be developed through the use of 'social' archaeology. This second avenue will now be pursued. 'New' explanations seem to have been rejected as readily as 'traditional' ones. Perhaps this is symptomatic of the interregnum in which archaeology now finds itself, where simplistic studies founded in our own ethnocentricity will no longer do, but also where complex studies founded on other disciplines are equally hard to accept. It is within this context that a study of the primary data will be attempted: by first providing an archaeological background and then a social model through which to structure the data. By necessity, this will involve recapitulation of some of the ground already covered; previous research into hoards, metalwork, and the nature of deposition have provided a solid foundation for further study.

CHAPTER 2

THE BRONZE AGE

INTRODUCTION

Having reviewed previous research into Bronze Age metalwork and hoarding, it is necessary to provide a brief outline of the literature on the Bronze Age in general, in order to give the metalwork a physical and cultural background in Britain set against its wider European setting. This picture involves the pottery, settlements, and burials of this period, and all of these can be used alongside the results of our analyses to build up a view of deposition during the Bronze Age. First, we can outline the chronology to be used throughout this work. Second, we will examine the detail for four regions, selected for more detailed analysis (cf Chaps. 4 and 5), and consider their pottery, settlement, burial, and landscape evidence. Third, we can set these regions in their British context and comment on their environment and social setting. Finally, we can view the British Bronze Age in its European context. By necessity, this is done by summarising other authors and their divergent opinions on an obscure period, but it is hoped that enough points of agreement can be identified to provide a useful background.

CHRONOLOGY

No preconceived chronology was used in the actual examination of the hoards and objects themselves: simple descriptions were made of the objects in accordance with accepted terminologies. However, it is necessary to place the material within a stricter chronology than Early, Middle, and Late Bronze Age: this is made simpler because most chronology for the Bronze Age is based on metalwork typology in the first place. The looser terminology of Early, Middle, and Late is retained for the description of other artefactual material and settlements, because of the general lack of precision in these areas.

A convenient phasing to use is that of O'Connor (1980): this adds an appropriate number to the conventional Early, Middle, Late divisions and can be paralleled by most other chronologies (eg Burgess, 1979; 1980a). The greatest difference is the placing of the last Middle Bronze Age phase, or Penard period, in the first phase of the Late Bronze Age in O'Connor's chronology, because abrupt changes at the start of this period suggest a closer affinity with Late Bronze Age industries (1980, 95). This has been criticised by Burgess, in a review, because of its similarity to the Hawkes chronology (never actually published by its author) (1982, 548). However, the implications of O'Connor's chronology are clear and are accepted here.

The table shows a correlation of these periods and phases (on the left; Table 1), with equivalent Hawkes phases, Burgess periods, and metalwork stages. Absolute dates are given in years BC, as standard, and bc derived from Burgess (1980a);

Table 1: Table of chronology

1	2	3	4	5	6	7	8
EBA1	EB1	Overton	2000–1700	1700–1500	V Ballyvalley VI Falkland	A2	
EBA2	EB2	Bedd	1700–1600	1500–1200	VII Arreton	A3	
MBA1	MB1	Branwen	1600–1400		VIII Acton Park 1/2	B	Late MI
MBA2	MB2	Knighton	1400–1200	1200–1050	IX Taunton	C	MII
LBA1	MB3	Penard	1200–1000	1050–850	X Penard 1/2	D–Ha A2	MIII
LBA2	LB1	Isleham	1000–900	850–550	XI Wilburton	Ha B1	MIV
LBA3	LB2		900–700		XII Ewart Park	Ha B3	MV
LBA4	LB3	Llynfawr	700–600	550–450	XIII Llynfawr	Ha C	MVI
EIA1	IA		600–400			Ha D	

Key: 1. Period number (after O'Connor) 2. Old period number (after Burgess) 3. Burgess period 4. Date span BC 5. Date span bc 6. Metalwork stages 7. Central European phase 8. Northern European phase.

correlations with central and northern Europe are provided, based on the works cited and Butler (1981): the complexities of these systems will not be further argued here (cf Burgess, 1982, 547). Brown has recently suggested that Wilburton and Ewart Park have mistakenly come to represent two successive phases of the Bronze Age on the basis of a study of their swords (1982, 2). She suggests that the Ewart Park sword could be a collateral of the Wilburton type (1982, 32).

However, there is enough material other than swords to retain the chronology: an argument in favour of the new terminology. No attempt has been made in this thesis to implement the terminology of 'Cal BC' for calibrated dates, and 'BC' for uncalibrated dates, because the dates derived from the metalwork are based on links to a historical chronology. Radiocarbon dates are given uncalibrated in the old form 'bc'.

Beyond the technical arguments, Rowlands has highlighted the desirability or otherwise of such rigid chronologies: "If it is possible to envisage a pattern of variable industrial content and organisation in Southern Britain even by the 8th–7th centuries BC ..., it must throw some doubt on the efficacy of establishing strictly defined chronological periods on metalwork alone and consequently even divisions based on total cultural assemblages must be given a due sense of proportion if it is not intended merely to impose artificial chronological divisions for convenience's sake" (1976, 161). Rowlands also warns of the problems of using hoards alone for analysis: the way in which objects were selected for the hoard introduces an obvious bias, and closed finds will inevitably produce a sequence of chronological stages (1976, 99). This can be clearly seen in my own results (detailed in Chapter 5), where certain phases of the Bronze Age (eg EBA1) are totally, or almost totally, unrepresented in the hoard record – at least for southern Britain; phases during which the preceding industries may have continued to produce the same range of items. Therefore, it must be borne in mind that the hoards have either been dated to a phase because their contents are typical of that phase, or because the latest object in that hoard predicates the earliest date for deposition: the phase dating does not necessarily indicate the date of deposition. Burgess and Coombs have suggested that hoards typical of a phase were deposited at the end of it, and at the transition to the next (1979, v), yet this must be contrary to the conventional idea of traders' hoards as stores of new items for distribution – and why not at the beginning of the next phase or even at the end of the next, when everyone may have been really tired of all that old–fashioned metalwork? Complexities abound: we should be wary of reading too much into this approach.

REGIONAL FRAMEWORKS

Thames Valley

The evidence for the Thames Valley has been summarised by Barrett and Bradley (1980a), and by Bradley (1984, 106–24). Barrett and Bradley rightly pointed out "the false dichotomy between artefact and settlement studies" (1980a, 247), and it is hard to reconcile these two approaches. The evidence seemed to suggest a concentration of activities in the Early Bronze Age in the Upper Thames area, with a shift to the Lower Thames in the Middle and Late Bronze Ages: this, it was suggested, mirrored the importance of a 'Wessex core area' and the extension of settlement and burial in the Early Bronze Age from Wessex into the Valley (Barrett and Bradley, 1980a, 249). The metalwork evidence was scant for the Early Bronze Age in the Upper Thames, on the other hand, in contrast to the poor burial record of the Lower Thames, but with time much more metal was found (Barrett and Bradley, 1980a, 250). Extensive Deverel–Rimbury cremation cemeteries then appeared in the Lower Thames valley with better settlement associations (Barrett and Bradley, 1980a, 251–2). The situation was summarised for the Early Bronze Age suggesting that the Lower Thames formed the 'buffer zone' and supplied surplus agricultural produce to an Upper Thames 'core area', with links in Wessex. The Upper Thames initially maintained its dominance, but later failed as the buffer zone realised its own potential. This argument explained the locational shift of activity in the Later Bronze Age (Barrett and Bradley, 1980a, 252–4).

The Lower Thames then assumed more importance in the Later Bronze Age, because of its greater productive capabilities and its ready access to long–distance exchange (Barrett and Bradley, 1980a, 255). This was associated with a phase of expansion and increasing cultivation as evidenced by clearance horizons and by the pollen record which suggested a more open environment (Barrett and Bradley, 1980a, 255). Settlements were more low–lying and concentrated on the lower terraces or floodplain, as at Aldermaston and Knight's Farm (Bradley *et al*, 1980), or right on the river itself, as at Runnymede Bridge (Needham and Longley, 1980). Bradley related the density of settlement in the area of Knight's Farm, to attempts to gain social prestige through production of a surplus; in the Late Bronze Age this pattern did not coincide with that apparent from the metalwork, but there may have been a shift of emphasis towards the river (Bradley *et al*, 1980, 292–3). Runnymede Bridge probably had a contrasting role to these upriver settlements, with a siting intended to exploit the potential of the metal trade (Needham and Longley, 1980, 428–30). Barrett and Bradley then tied in the evidence from metalwork with that of settlement, reinforcing the distinction between those sites concerned with producing an agricultural surplus and those others handling the bronze trade (1980a, 263). This Late Bronze Age pattern changed again, when Wessex re–asserted its importance in the Iron Age (Barrett and Bradley, 1980a, 265). Needham and Burgess dealt with the metalwork in its setting for the Lower Thames in more detail, but also found problems in relating metal finds and settlement, at least directly (1980, 460–1). They pointed out that one area had plenty of finds, whereas another, equally productive in the agricultural sense, had hardly any (1980, 461). However, they felt that long–distance exchange and agricultural production maintained the status of settlements and governed the distribution of metalwork (1980, 466).

In sum, the picture offered by archaeological material other than metalwork is of an area which played a subordinate role during the Early Bronze Age, but rose to a dominant position in the Middle and Late Bronze Age. This is reflected in the siting of settlements, the expansion of agriculture, and the use of long–distance exchange. This patterning can be linked and compared with the neighbouring (and overlapping) Wessex region.

Wessex

Barrett and Bradley pointed out that this region is made up of four zones: chalk downland, rich loam soils along the coast of south Hampshire, the productive river valleys of the Avon, Stour, Hamble and Itchen, and the heathlands (1980b, 181). These zones have different levels of archaeological record: our attention is first turned to the well-known barrows of the Wessex culture.

Piggott first drew together this material (1938), which has always been the subject of much interpretation and explanation (Fleming, 1973). Fleming envisaged a pastoralist economy as the basis of the wealth seen in the burial record; pastoralism was also the main basis of social stratification (1973, 580–1). Gerloff took a somewhat different view in drawing together the strands of cultural evidence apparent in the burial goods: she saw the Wessex Culture as arising from the settlement of immigrant Breton tin merchants, who established themselves as a social elite (1975, 244). In due course, contacts with other parts of Europe changed the character of their material culture, as we see in the Wessex II or Camerton–Snowshill phase. Gerloff postulated strong social upheavals at this transition from Early to Middle Bronze Age in Europe and greater evidence of defended settlements and hoarding (1975, 244–5). The movement of people, in her opinion, may have helped to introduce spears, rapiers, and swords to Britain at the end of this period, such metal forms becoming apparent in the Arreton hoards (Gerloff, 1975, 245). However, she produced little evidence that the movement of people resulted in such fundamental changes in the British Bronze Age. Nor does Gerloff explain why much of the Arreton metalwork, particularly the hoards, was peripheral to the main area of the Wessex Culture.

It is against this background that the hoards of the Early Bronze Age were deposited, but other aspects of the archaeological record became increasingly prominent: the Deverel–Rimbury settlements and cemeteries (Barrett and Bradley, 1980b). Settlement can only be hinted at in some zones, like the coastal region and river valleys, where there was a wealth of bronze, a concentration of cemeteries on productive soils, an emphasis on harbours and river estuaries with their possibilities for cross–Channel trade, and a high proportion of imported metalwork (Barrett and Bradley, 1980b, 187–8). The heathlands have numerous barrows, but less evidence of settlement: the barrows appeared in the Early Bronze Age, but continued in use during the first millennium bc (Barrett and Bradley, 1980b, 188). The chalkland continued to dominate the picture of burial and settlement for the Deverel–Rimbury phase, but Barrett and Bradley pointed out that the settlements tended to cluster peripherally to the richest clusters of Wessex burial mounds (1980b, 189). The Deverel–Rimbury settlements, however, seemed to have their own nearby cemeteries (Barrett and Bradley, 1980b, 195). It is clear that there was a degree of overlap between the Wessex burials and Deverel–Rimbury settlements and cemeteries. Their chronologies overlap and they probably existed alongside each other in different parts of the Wessex region. The Deverel–Rimbury tradition was particularly well established in the coastal zone, but later it was able to extend over the areas with the main 'Wessex Culture' (Barrett and Bradley, 1980b, 197–9).

The archaeological record becomes less substantial in the Late Bronze Age (Barrett and Bradley, 1980b, 199–200). Whereas downland sites became scarce, those on the coastal zone seem to indicate much more continuity, and here metalwork was also more frequent (Barrett and Bradley, 1980b, 200). Finally, there was a resurgence of settlement on the downs, coinciding with early hillfort construction (Barrett and Bradley, 1980b, 201). This change accompanied the appearance of iron. Downland sites may have helped to manipulate the supply of this material from neighbouring areas (Barrett and Bradley, 1980b, 203–4). The scale of the deposits at the midden site at Potterne, Wiltshire, contradict this view of Late Bronze Age decline in Wessex (Lawson, pers. comm.), but, interestingly, this site is peripheral to the downland itself.

To summarise, the early richness of the Wessex Culture was soon eclipsed by its inability to dominate the whole region, especially the coastal zone and the Thames Valley. The shift of settlement reflected changes in access to wealth and agricultural supplies. The dominant position of the coastal zone and river valleys was only upset by the appearance of an iron technology. At this stage, the Wessex downland with its early hillforts increased its importance. General discussions of the Bronze Age (below) will touch on these points again.

The South West

Johnson provided a survey of settlements in the South West, although this covered Devon, Cornwall, and the Isles of Scilly (1980, 142), and thus went farther westward than the area under consideration here (see below, Chapter 4), and did not cover the other counties to the east, ie Somerset and Avon. However, Pearce has covered the whole of this area in some detail, while considering the relationship of metalwork and the landscape (1983, Part 4).

Early Bronze Age sites concentrated on the uplands, as on Dartmoor, whereas the metalwork seemed to occur in the coastal lowlands and river valleys, when it was not associated with burials (Johnson, 1980, 145). These were felt to result from "Irish–Continental trading contact" (Johnson, 1980, 145). Early occupation sites in Devon reflected this coastal and upland distribution, but burial and ritual sites were separate from the settlement areas (Johnson, 1980, 146). An area of Central Devon, made up of the Culm measures, was an archaeological blank in the whole of the Bronze Age as it was in the Iron Age, perhaps reflecting the unattractiveness of the land for agriculture. Otherwise, the remaining areas continued the pattern of burials and settlements of the Early Bronze Age into the later Bronze Age (Johnson, 1980, 151). Johnson saw settlement expanding from the coastal regions in the Early Bronze Age inland into formerly unoccupied lowlands with the Later Bronze Age: overall an expansion of existing settlement patterns, rather than a locational shift (1980, 153). These sites survived where conditions in the lowlands and uplands were favourable, but more marginal areas of settlement were later abandoned (Johnson, 1980, 155). Johnson explained the large land divisions of the reaves as involving some organisation, but a deterioration in the weather did not cause a sudden shift of population to the lowlands, and the more marginal upland areas were efficiently managed for several centuries more, although by a relatively small number of people (1980, 172). This meant that settlement, in the lowlands at least, continued on into the Iron Age and may well have continued in more favoured upland locations (Johnson, 1980, 172–3). Mercer, however, linked the evidence from Dartmoor and the Somerset Levels to suggest that deteriorating weather conditions and peat growth, around the turn of the first millennium, brought an end to intensive farming of the uplands for several centuries (1975, 39–40).

The Dartmoor reaves have been exhaustively dealt with by Fleming (1978; 1983); he saw these boundaries as being laid out at one time around 1300 bc, "as part of one grand plan" (1983, 223). Fleming proposed a tripartite land division for South Dartmoor between upland commons, enclosed land, and settled valley zones; on East and North East Dartmoor the pattern was slightly different, lacking the valley zones (1983, 224). He went on to suggest that the decision to build reaves was taken at a regional level, while the communities on the ground built the reaves and divided themselves from each other, but not in areas where the actual land users might have felt it to be unnecessary (1983, 225). Earlier, Fleming had suggested the social groupings who instigated this system: 'communities' inhabited the large parallel reave systems bordering upland pasture, and these were composed of smaller component groups or "neighbourhood groups", reflected archaeologically by the numerous clusters of stone–built houses (1983, 197). Thus, for this part of the South West, we can see large–scale land organisation and the planned settlement of a large area of upland, making it economically useful, even if only as seasonal pasture. A similar process may have taken place in another part of the South West: the Somerset Levels (Fleming, 1978, 112).

Coles has described the Somerset Levels as a concave landscape, where a combination of settlement and subsistence activities could be carried on to great advantage (1978a, 147–8). Thus, upland areas surrounding the Levels could be used for grazing and agriculture, the slopes could be used for restricted arable agriculture and settlement, and the low–lying ground would have been rich seasonal meadows, although the wetter conditions of the second millennium may have created problems for this arrangement (Coles, 1978a, 148). However, settlement would also have been possible in the centre of the Levels on low islands, which were also notable for their productive grazing (Coles and Hibbert, 1975, 16). Coles and Hibbert have shown that between 2200 bc and 900 bc raised bog dominated the landscape, and that only towards the end of the period did renewed flooding alter the ecological balance of this rather marginal environment (1975, 19). This also made it more difficult to communicate between the higher ground by building wooden trackways, but efforts to do so were renewed towards the end of this period (Coles and Orme, 1980, 42). From 1100 BC, the periods of flooding meant that major trackways were no longer built, probably because it was simpler to move around by boat. By contrast, around 400 BC the permanent settlements in the marsh at Glastonbury and Meare were established (Coles and Orme, 1980, 51). The concentration of prehistoric man on this watery environment has been convincingly interpreted in terms of the prevailing economy, ie the need for fish and fowl as a dietary supplement, the need for wood in many activities (including bronze working), and the need for pasture (Coles, 1978b, 88–9). There is no mention of bronze offerings to water deities (partly because bronze finds are not all that numerous), although in theory at least this would have been an ideal area for such observances. Thus, in the Somerset Levels we are dealing with a primary adaptive response to a localised environment, turning conditions to best advantage, when settlement or activities were not made completely impossible by climatic factors.

As already noted (above), Pearce has attempted to place the metalwork within the landscape of the South West (1983, 125ff). For the earliest period of metal use in the South West, Pearce saw continuity from the Neolithic period and an association with henge monuments, although these complexes did not develop in the far west, suggesting that "powerful political and economic territories did not develop here either" (1983, 131). She pointed to a pattern of cultivation on lower ground with movement onto the uplands for the summer season of grazing and ritual at this period; certain areas of settlement were not well–defined and were without major monuments, as in East Devon and West Somerset. This was seen as evidence of a less co–ordinated community organisation (1983, 138–9). In the Wessex II phase (EBA2), barrow building became the norm, as elsewhere in Southern Britain, with the siting of the principal barrow clusters suggesting a continuance of lowland agriculture and upland grazing (Pearce, 1983, 140). Thus, Pearce concluded that towards the end of the Early Bronze Age already established communities had undergone some social change, with newly mature communities appearing with their barrows and metalwork. At the same time, metal production increased (1983, 146).

In the Middle Bronze Age, Pearce saw an expansion of organised field systems and a peak in cultivation on the granite, after which the area of arable land shrank (1983, 148). The associated settlements take the form of farmsteads, as at Trevisker, unenclosed or enclosed, depending on the rank of the occupants (Pearce, 1983, 148–9). Pearce reinforced the points already examined (above) for Dartmoor and the Somerset Levels; she noted a scatter of bronze finds from the Levels at this time and interpreted them as part of settlement–based wealth (1983, 155–9). She contrasted this pattern of fields, settlements, and bronze finds with the earlier phase, where the emphasis was on the higher ground with the ceremonial sites and ritual (1983, 163). In the first part of the Late Bronze Age (LBA1 and 2), the onset of wetter, colder conditions and the growth of peat bogs apparently affected the stable system of agriculture, as did local soil exhaustion (Pearce, 1983, 165–6). The balance between pasture and arable was upset: areas of pasture were now ploughed, as pressure on the other land led to its abandonment. The emphasis of settlement also changed with greater use of defended hilltop sites (Pearce, 1983, 166–8). In the last phases of the Bronze Age and the beginning of the Iron Age (LBA3, LBA4, and EIA1), the enclosed settlements continued to develop, sometimes on the sites of earlier open settlements. Perhaps this process was linked with colonisation of more land (Pearce, 1983, 172). Related to these sites were finds of Late Bronze Age metalwork from sites which were later to be used as hillforts (Pearce, 1983, 175). Pearce suggested that these changes in the landscape resulted from an increase in Late Bronze Age population and led to a more profound social change; she pointed to the need for a centralised authority to control the agriculture, store surpluses, and exert power over the developing peasant class (1983, 177). These developments were reflected in the prestigious bronze finds. She suggested that the occupants of the hilltop settlement held sway over a number of smaller settlements within some sort of territory, although the boundaries of such territories probably changed frequently, until more stable conditions were achieved during the Iron Age (Pearce, 1983, 177–82).

In conclusion, we have seen from the general surveys of the South West, as well as from the more specific studies of Dartmoor and the Somerset Levels, a developing Bronze Age landscape relying on an agricultural basis. In the early phases, this was based around exploitation of the uplands for grazing and some arable cultivation in the lowlands, but in time this became more organised and led to the large–scale land divisions, that we find on Dartmoor. However, the balance of this economic system seems to have been affected by a change in climate and the loss of arable land through over–exploitation and soil exhaustion. This set the scene for social changes, which are evidenced by early defended or defensible sites. The metalwork is seen to fit in with these patterns of settlement and land–use, re–inforcing the picture of a stratified society in the later phases, while indicating a certain elite in the earlier periods with their rich grave goods. Much of this picture remains hypothetical and relies heavily on comparison with the more rounded picture available in Wessex, with its well–preserved downland monuments. However, the specialised landscapes of Dartmoor and the Somerset levels indicate an adaptive strategy capable of utilising more difficult landscapes to advantage.

East Anglia

The other three regions of Southern Britain dealt with above have been fairly closely linked and overlap with each other in the archaeological as well as the physical sense. The region of East Anglia is more physically separate, but has many of the archaeological and landscape features already explored. In terms of metalwork, however, it has assumed greater importance, simply because of the sheer quantities of material from this region. Again, it is necessary to look at barrows, settlements, and other features of the environment.

Lawson has reviewed the evidence of the later Bronze Age in Norfolk: he was unable to indicate many examples of pottery from this period, or traces of settlement, but he could suggest a continuity of activity in the densest areas of earlier Bronze Age barrow distribution, mainly in the west bordering on the fenland (1980c, 271–9). He was also able to suggest that several cropmark enclosures might be of Late Bronze Age date, particularly those near to known hoard sites (1980c, 281). Widespread activity was also implied by the density of Late Bronze Age metalwork, but little is known of the settlements in an area so subject to agricultural damage (Lawson, 1980c, 285). Pryor also pointed to the problem of peat shrinkage in the Fenlands and showed how the finds there may exist in a horizontal, but not a vertical, context; prior to the Late Bronze Age, much of the Fenlands would have been dry and passable and suitable for seasonal settlement (1980, 489–90). He went on to suggest that fairly severe flooding around 1000 bc changed the economic emphasis to mixed farming from summer grazing and a mainly pastoral economy (1980, 492; see below).

Lawson has suggested that barrows were sited on the poorest, lightest soil in Norfolk and on slightly higher ground, probably because these factors dictated the available choice of agricultural land in the earlier Bronze Age (1981, 62). Thus, the barrows would be placed in small clearances made for agricultural purposes, possibly to avoid encroachment on usable arable land (Lawson, 1981, 63). Martin observed this distinction for barrows in Suffolk too, where the distribution of mounds was split between the south–east and north–west of the county, probably due to the existence of woodlands on the intervening boulder clay areas (1981, 77–8). The actual siting of barrows in this area again seemed to coincide with lighter soils, and there did not seem to be any near the Fen edge, whereas there was settlement, at least seasonal, here; this may have been due to placing of barrows on the edges of arable or on pastoral land, and perhaps closer to more permanent settlements (Martin, 1981, 82). In Cambridgeshire, barrow distribution was the same again: sited on the lighter soils and the fen–edge and fen islands, which would have been the favoured locations for settlement and agriculture (Taylor, A, 1981, 119–20).

Lying on the other side of the Fens, as it were, is the site of Fengate near Peterborough, which has afforded us some insights into Bronze Age settlement in East Anglia (Pryor, 1982; 1976). An episode of flooding had reduced the area of settlement and exploitation available in the Neolithic, leading to some pressure on land. This may explain the building of ditched enclosures at the beginning of the Bronze Age, although by this time the fens were beginning to be passable again (Pryor, 1982, 23). Pryor suggested that pasturing of herds was important, moving between summer fen pastures and the fen–edge in winter, with cereals coming from higher land to the west; this system expanded until about 1000 BC, when the whole system was abandoned (1982, 24). The evidence at Fengate suggested a complex management of the landscape in the Early Bronze Age, until large areas of the land enclosed by ditches were inundated around 1000 BC. At this stage, the fen pastures were no longer viable and more emphasis was placed on mixed farming on the upland and higher parts of the fen–edge (Pryor, 1982, 30–32). The associated settlements were spread in small units through the enclosure system; this led Pryor to suggest that the landscape was divided up by local agreement, whilst the settlements themselves were constructed as single–family house units (1982, 36). This was in contrast to later periods after 1000 BC, when settlements became more nucleated, especially in the Iron Age (Pryor, 1982, 37). This pattern has been reflected in recent work at Flag Fen, where a Late Bronze Age timber platform has been discovered; this was constructed in a defensive location, using large numbers of timbers, which could have been procured as part of a network of social obligations (Pryor *et al*, 1986, 22–3). Pryor has ascribed this rather sudden change in the later Bronze Age to population expansion as well as the development of a wetter environment. Increasing pressure was placed on the pasture, as more land was needed for arable. Finally, the fen–edge enclosures were abandoned and the whole area was re–organised (Pryor, 1976, 46–7). Pryor has also lent a different social emphasis to these patterns: despite the intensive land–use of the second millennium, the dispersed settlement pattern argued against increased social stratification (1984, 225). As an immediate adaptive response to environmental changes, leading to the abandonment of the ditched field systems, nucleated settlement could be suggested, but it is not in fact proven: it seems more likely that settlement continued in parts of Fengate, even when at its wettest (Pryor, 1984, 225). Pryor suggested that, as wetter conditions restricted the grazing areas, groups would concentrate on the higher ground and turn to mixed farming; increasing social stratification eventually led to nucleated settlement as early as the fifth century BC (1984, 226).

In conclusion, this somewhat disparate evidence from East Anglia indicates a varied response to environment: as in the Somerset Levels, man was able to exploit the fen–edge in an extensive and profitable way, with a pastoral economy in the earlier Bronze Age, which was eventually replaced by more mixed farming, as climatic change combined with population pressure put the system under strain. Away from this specialised environment, the limited evidence suggests mixed farming through the Bronze Age on lighter soils, where the barrows were sited, and nearby settlements; constraints on land–use in the areas of heavy clay were probably too much to induce forest clearance in these parts. This somewhat disappointing picture provides little context for the metalwork. This is especially unfortunate, since it is of such exceptional quantity (and often quality) in this region.

Summary

These outline sketches of the Bronze Age in each of these four regions have dealt with common themes: pastoralism and wealth displays through round barrows and rich burials, climatic deterioration in the later Bronze Age, and a change to mixed agriculture and more nucleated settlements. Little has been achieved to remedy the "false dichotomy" between our metalwork and other classes of archaeological evidence. Broadly, the metalwork reflects the trends apparent in the changing landscape, both natural and man–made, although we should stress here man's adaptive capabilities in relation to his environment. There is a danger of environmental determinism. The broad trends described above have many common factors, and all contribute to our overall picture of the Bronze Age in southern Britain.

THE BRONZE AGE IN SOUTHERN BRITAIN

It is uncertain whether it is easier to deal with broad particulars at a regional level or sweeping generalisations countrywide, but the intention here is to contrast some of the opinions regarding the Bronze Age on a wider plane. Again, this relies on the evidence of pottery, burials, settlements, and metalwork, along with some further indications of the contemporary environment.

Environment

Mention has already been made of general environmental factors in the discussion of the regional developments of the Bronze Age: a recent survey has brought together the available evidence for this period (Tinsley, 1981), although the level of archaeological interpretation should make us wary of accepting the environmentalist's conclusions without reservation (Tinsley, 1981, cf especially p 210). However, this is a useful starting point and the evidence was presented for climate, sea levels, fauna, and vegetation. Tinsley observed that the Bronze Age seemed to start warm – probably warmer than average temperatures today – but that towards the end of the period, between 800 and 500 bc, a climatic deterioration set in (1981, 210–12), which continued well into the Iron Age (Turner, 1981, 256–61). Deterioration had probably started earlier, perhaps around 2400 bc, but it became very rapid in the first part of the first millennium, although probably it proceeded at different rates in various parts of the country (Tinsley, 1981, 216–7). Sea level changes on the other hand made areas like the Somerset Levels and the Fenland drier and more suitable for settlement during the Bronze Age, until the climatic deterioration finally led to flooding at the beginning of the Iron Age (Tinsley, 1981, 217). Turner placed the deterioration at around 1250 bc, with more rapid deterioration after 850 bc, causing trackways to be built in the Somerset Levels. The wettest phase was reached around 650 bc and subsequently peat grew over the dried–out bogs (Turner, 1981, 260–1). Tinsley suggested that faunal changes resulted from extensive forest clearance, and that there was more reliance on wool than furs for clothing; for this reason, the proportion of domesticates grew in relation to that of wild animals. As the Bronze Age progressed, there was also a change in emphasis from pigs to sheep (Tinsley, 1981, 224–5). She showed that the tree cover was thin on the uplands at the start of the Bronze Age, while other areas had been completely cleared in the Neolithic period, but some lowland areas were still forested and subject to short–lived clearance phases (1981, 231–4). Extensive clearance of the uplands, as on Dartmoor, occurred during the Bronze Age, at first associated with pastoralism, but later with cereal agriculture, and was superseded by heathland due to the effects of over–grazing (Tinsley, 1981,

243–5). Finally, Tinsley ascribed the decline of soil fertility and erosion during the Bronze Age to the introduction of metal technology, "since the bronze axe was a far more potent instrument of woodland destruction than its polished stone predecessor"; worsening climate helped to reduce upland grazing to heath and bog, while lowland areas, apart from the chalklands, were only well cleared during the Iron Age (1981, 248–9), a view endorsed by Turner (1981, 280). Evans also touched on many of these points – climatic change, soil erosion, and forest clearance – ascribing large-scale forest clearance to the introduction of iron tools (1975,134–151).

The general evidence would suggest that the environment during the Bronze Age in southern Britain had some influence on the siting of settlement, particularly in the more marginal areas, either upland or wetlands. Much of central southern England was already well cultivated by this time, and the uplands were cleared for use during a period of favourable climate; all seem agreed on a general deterioration in conditions during the Late Bronze Age with loss of uplands and wetlands due to renewal of bog growth and heathland. Clearance was more effective in the Iron Age and was later encouraged by improved weather conditions.

The archaeological context: earlier Bronze Age

These landscape developments can be correlated in different ways with the artefactual and settlement evidence. The earlier Bronze Age follows on naturally from the later Neolithic and, as Bradley pointed out, it would be naive to assume that major forest clearance took place simply because of the advent of the flat axe (1978, 110). Bradley went on to suggest that, just as there were distinct classes of Beaker burials, so there may have been a class of pastoralists to be associated with Wessex graves (1978, 112–13; above). These were part of a hierarchy, which attained a surplus in the economy, and put it to use in a widespread organisation of the landscape with carefully sited henges, stone circles, and barrow groups (Bradley, 1978, 113). In time, the system had expanded outwards onto more marginal lands, through a series of clearings, less able to support the pressure of use, and there was consequent soil loss through erosion and over-grazing (Bradley, 1978, 114–15). The problem of the influence of climatic change on this situation has been over-stated, according to Bradley, and he explained the retreat from the uplands and the more restricted use of marginal lands by soil deterioration rather than climatic change (1978, 114–15). The response to this was to lay out large field systems on the landscape to gain a more permanent hold on suitable farming land, with examples in Wessex, at Fengate, and on Dartmoor (Bradley, 1978, 116). The establishment of boundaries led to increased territoriality and the development of "domestic compounds", with grain storage pits; wealth and power were now beginning to be concentrated in lowland areas, such as the Thames Valley. The stage was set for the developments of the later Bronze Age (Bradley, 1978, 117–18).

To set against these views of social development in the earlier Bronze Age, Burgess initially saw the change from Neolithic to Bronze Age as being brought about by Continental migrants: the 'Beaker folk' (1974, 165). This sweeping statement – reflecting traditionally held views – was tempered somewhat by an appraisal of the evidence associated with Beakers, with sparse settlement evidence and continuity of other forms of local culture suggesting the assimilation of Beaker 'people' after some time (Burgess, 1974, 173). Burgess subsequently argued against a Beaker folk movement and referred instead to the Beaker 'tradition', which spread across Europe into Britain possibly under the influence of specialist potters or 'cult masters', introducing it as part of a Beaker 'cult package' (1980a, 62–3). He pointed to the lack of evidence for a folk movement and noted that Beakers were accommodated within local traditions, soon being made in Britain (1980a, 64). The use of Beakers began to fade away with sudden changes around 1700 bc, when burials assumed the forms common to the Bronze Age, and the Wessex culture began to emerge (Burgess, 1980a, 80–81).

Pottery provided the framework for defining communities and their distribution in the Early Bronze Age, but had its own attendant difficulties, particularly where distributions overlapped (Burgess, 1974, 178–9). However, Burgess pointed out the problem of identifying the Wessex 'Culture', when the defining characteristics were restricted to a few graves in the Wessex area; instead, we could envisage a development out of the local late Neolithic, when Wessex was already rich, with strong social stratification existing amongst the groups, although he saw this as inspired by 'new arrivals' from Brittany (1974, 186–7). The whole range of Bronze Age pottery types appeared at this time, often in funerary contexts with privileged and prestigious burials, but sometimes in domestic contexts, as is the case for Deverel–Rimbury pots, which "epitomize the more stolid majority in the population" (Burgess, 1980a, 84–5). The more flamboyant element of the population was reflected by the Wessex burials: these were now seen to be local developments, burials at the head of a hierarchy of ranked burials, encouraged by access to Continental sources and ideas (Burgess, 1980a, 100–104). With time these began to be supplanted by cremation cemeteries associated with Deverel–Rimbury pottery and settlement sites, some of them enclosed, with round houses (Burgess, 1980a, 116–8). The exploitation of highland areas was seen to reach its maximum extent at this time too (Burgess, 1980a, 116–8). This later led to an agricultural crisis as upland soils failed to stand up to pressure. These difficulties were exacerbated by climatic change, until the "old dynasties" lost control and were replaced by "new elites", centred on new regions, such as the Thames Valley and the Fens, where metallurgy and water–based religion re–inforced their power base (Burgess, 1980a, 129–31). Deverel–Rimbury communities now dominated the stage, but may have formed just one element in a two–tier system, with prestigious burials of the pastoral groups dominating the chalk downs and cremations of sedentary cultivators on the lower ground (Burgess, 1980a, 137–8). All this came to an end around 1200 BC, when Burgess envisaged catastrophic changes affecting the whole settlement and cultural pattern; this was attributed to much worse climatic conditions and soil exhaustion, leading to a drastic re-organisation of the landscape and the building of 'ranch boundaries' on the downland (1980a, 157). His 'Age of Stonehenge' was succeeded by the 'Age of Hillforts' (1980a, 158).

Some of these points, regarding change and reasons for change, were taken up by Bradley. He doubted the evidence of immigration at this time, and disliked the untestable hypotheses behind climatic catastrophe. He looked instead at society (1980, 59). The Wessex culture came to an end, because it was unable to maintain a dominant position as a 'core area', deriving its products from a 'buffer zone', which took off at the expense of the patron. Also, the Wessex area was not particularly productive, and added pressure on the land would only mean that the chief began to accumulate more of a decreasingly available surplus (Bradley, 1980, 61–3). These points were also taken up by Barrett (1980a). He visualised a chain of "generalised exchange" with goods flowing in payment of brideprice; the 'Beaker package' was one part of "the extensive patterns of communication established by these open social systems" (1980a, 78–80). The 'core areas' developed a system of short land-use on marginal soils with little investment of community effort. Barrows were sited on the periphery of utilised land, so as to be easily visible to the communities: "a physical manifestation of the external relationships by which these societies survived" (Barrett, 1980a, 80–81). Barrett went on to point out that our notions of the Early Bronze Age are traditionally focused on the Wessex Culture and its barrows, without taking into account the archaeology of areas such as the middle and lower Thames Valley, the southern coastal plain, the central plain, and the fen-margins of East Anglia (1980a, 80–81). The importance of Deverel-Rimbury material was now apparent: it formed a complementary assemblage with its main focus outside the distribution of Wessex Culture burials and was thus part of the material culture of the 'buffer zone' (Barrett, 1980a, 81–4). It may be that methods of burial indicated a different attitude to the land too: these were closely tied to land inheritance and establishment of rights over that land by burying near to enclosures. Religious ideas may have been the factor which maintained the dominance of the core areas for so long (Barrett, 1980a, 84–5). However, the core areas with their ceremonial enclosures were diminishing their stock of land to such an extent that reciprocal exchange relations could no longer be maintained, while the buffer zones were building up their power and wealth through access to metal resources. Eventually, this led to the communities of the buffer zones colonising parts of the core areas, and a change in the social system that set the pattern for the later Bronze Age (Barrett, 1980a, 85–90).

These patterns and ideas have been reiterated by Bradley (1984). He also made the link with the collapse of Mediterranean societies, so often used in explaining the rise and fall of Bronze Age society in Britain: if we visualise this as a severing of exchange links, we can see this as part of a larger social breakdown already under way and not as a causal factor (1984, 92–4). In Wessex, there were attempts at a re-organisation of farming practices and the building of a few elaborate barrows, after the traditional practices were obsolete. This period also saw attempts to reconstruct Stonehenge, but these came too late and the social system had changed (Bradley, 1984, 94–5).

The archaeological context: later Bronze Age

The complex arguments outlined above have indicated the disparate nature of the evidence, and the ways in which it can be interpreted. We have moved away from simpler causal explanations of change, like invasion, climatic change, or other catastrophe, to see a complicated pattern of social relationships intimately related to agricultural production, religious symbolism, economic potential, and exchange networks. We have seen how Wessex society brought about its own downfall, making way for the patterns of the later Bronze Age. We can now examine how the archaeological material of this later period has been put into context.

This is the period characterised by "the oldest industry and trade of Britain" (Childe, 1956): a complex of metal products. Childe saw this as offering economic and social freedom to those engaged in their manufacture, brought to an end only by the more widely available iron (1956, 178). The emphasis on metalwork is in part a product of the archaeological record: many bronzes, few burials and settlements (Burgess, 1974, 198). Burgess explained the changes in the later part of this period in terms of invasion by Hallstatt raiders and traders, but he was unable to integrate the settlement evidence with the evidence of metalwork (1974, 211–22).

Bradley suggested that the metalwork distributions need not result from ritual activities alone, but could also owe something to the presence of rich and powerful riverside settlements (1978, 118–19). Hilltop enclosures gained more prominence too during this period, although their character would seem to be quite different from the later hillforts, with an emphasis on storage rather than defended settlement; swords and horse-riding may have provided the flamboyant element inherited from earlier times (Bradley, 1978, 119–22). Thus, the decline of Wessex was reflected in an expansion of settlement from the coastal plain, and in the Thames Valley a more ranked society effectively took over from the Wessex Culture (Bradley, 1980, 66). The river finds might represent a substitute funerary ritual or may have been discarded in a competitive display of wealth (Bradley, 1980, 66). A 'prestige trade' developed, based on riverside settlements, as well as a more developed bronze industry with provision for the recycling of 'scrap'. Both would need to have access to major rivers as lines of communication (Bradley, 1980, 67). In contrast to this system in the Thames Valley, Wessex had become a 'poor relation': effort was now turned towards agricultural re-organisation in order to create a surplus. The end of the exchange of bronze affected both social systems in their separate areas (Bradley, 1980, 68–9). In this context, bronze may have become too widespread, no longer a prestige artefact, at which point iron presented itself as a suitable substitute. Iron was much easier to produce than bronze and would soon become popular and widely available: again the system had to satisfy everyone, and again we have greater control over land (Bradley, 1980, 69–71). These points were reinforced by Barrett, who identified ceramic style zones, which might reflect territorial groupings in this period, and also "vertical patterns of obligation within an emerging hierarchy" (1980a, 92). He went on to indicate how hillforts emerged on the edges of these pottery style zones, integrating a number of social and geographic areas and handling the transfer of prestigious objects between zones; later, the growth of political control centralised power at these sites themselves and led to the developments of the Iron Age (Barrett, 1980a, 92–4). He concluded by noting that, whereas rank in the earlier Bronze Age was attained by access to 'symbolic' trappings, in the later Bronze Age rank was achieved by the availability and quantity of wealth or goods available for external exchange (1980a, 95).

Bradley has also supplemented these ideas with the additional context of conspicuous consumption of metalwork, in an attempt to integrate the patterns already seen in the separate categories of data (1984, 106–24). He was able to conclude that there was a relationship in some areas between quality of objects and access to agriculturally productive land. Beyond this, deposition should take place in periods of economic stability, while hillforts were possibly built in times of conflict (1984, 125). Again, there was the contrast between Wessex and the Thames Valley: the former an area of increasing isolation, the latter much more wide–ranging in its contacts and political relations (Bradley, 1984, 126). Bradley visualised a system with successive levels, in which Wessex and the Thames Valley may have interacted at a low level to make best use of agricultural products, while at a higher level economic success could be converted into power and prestige through feast giving, the destruction of wealth, and the formation of long–distance alliances. At the highest level, there would be international connections, covering large areas of Europe, but also more subject to outside changes (1984, 126–7). The size of this system produced its own downfall, as supplies of fine metal became harder to procure, and fluctuations in the amount of bronze in circulation proved impossible to control (Bradley, 1984, 126–7).

As has become clear, the discussion begins to involve a much wider region. We must now turn from the Bronze Age in southern Britain to its broader setting.

THE BRITISH BRONZE AGE IN A EUROPEAN SETTING

The whole chronology of the British Bronze Age, as derived from metalwork, is supported by cross–comparison with the European sequence. However, beyond this one–to–one correlation, how do we explain the links? We have tended to view the Bronze Age in an insular and regional way, overlooking the probable social links with other communities in mainland Europe.

For Childe the explanation of links could be referred to migrations and trade routes, linking all of Europe, especially the more primitive 'fringes', such as Britain, with developments in the Mediterranean (1930). Behind this, he recognised a closer relationship between adjacent communities in Europe and stressed the capabilities of the indigenous inhabitants (1930, 167). He recognised that they would have more in common with the primitive peoples of our time, than with the civilisations of the eastern Mediterranean (1930, 239). In part, this problem reflects the nature of our evidence (plenty of artefacts and not much else), and this still colours our syntheses of European prehistory (Coles and Harding, 1979, 537) and makes it difficult to see the wood for the trees. At a low level, it has been suggested that in western Europe rich Early Bronze Age graves were a feature of regionally centralised societies,while in central Europe hierarchies developed during the Early Bronze Age, with a change in grave goods to accommodate this (Champion *et al*, 1984, 211). As part of this organisation, "exchange of marriage partners would have been essential and the symbolic communication of status on a regional scale" (Champion *et al*, 1984, 213). Fortified settlements began to appear in many areas by the middle of the Bronze Age in central Europe and continued to function for some time; the evidence is less clear in western Europe (Champion et al, 1984, 214–5). In the later Bronze Age, this pattern was continued to some extent, but the emphasis changed: the Urnfield cremation rite was adopted in much of Europe along with sophisticated grave goods at the beginning of the period, and then, at the end of the Bronze Age, rich burials in chambers, sometimes with wheeled vehicles, appeared (Champion *et al*, 1984, 290–91). This was correlated with competition for agricultural land linked with aggression and the proliferation of defended sites; thus, the elite would manipulate surplus production to enhance the position of a leader, and status would be achieved between groups by armed conflict, gift exchange, and "lavish entertaining" (Champion *et al*, 1984, 291–2). This type of social organisation was expansionist but unstable and lasted into the Iron Age, when the much more general availability of iron undermined the control of the metal supply. This led to a less differentiated society in northern Europe, but in central Europe, new links with the Mediterranean world reinforced the competition for status, now marked by the acquisition of 'foreign' goods (Champion *et al*, 1984, 292–3). Exchange was an important part of status competition, and it was inferred that bronze was taken out of circulation to maintain its prestige by deposition in graves and hoards; however, "these patterns of exchange, circulation and deposition are as yet little understood" (Champion *et al*, 1984, 294). A similar point has been made by Bradley, who has also pointed to the more independent and regional nature of the British Early Iron Age, and a decrease in long–distance exchange at that time (1984, 131–3).

Barrett has lent more precision to the role of long–distance contact in Britain in his discussion of later Bronze Age pottery (1980b). He pointed out that the pottery forms of the southern and eastern coastal zones represent "one half of a system which borders both sides of the North Sea and Straits of Dover" (1980b, 315). The success of this system was matched by the failure of Wessex, but a re-alignment of exchange around the eighth century BC led to fresh settlement in Wessex and the upper Thames basin, and a renewed investment in long-distance exchange (Barrett, 1980b, 315-6). Barrett felt that material culture can be viewed "as a system of communication" (1980b, 314). This may be the best way to view our material and to move away from an artefactually orientated study.

Rowlands has stressed the importance of trade and exchange to the social system (1973). He postulated that Bronze Age Europe was connected "by a number of interlocking regional exchange networks, in which goods moved internally by such mechanisms as gift or redistribution and in the peripheral areas and between networks by barter and trade" (1973, 596). These 'exchange spheres' remained stable until the beginning of the Iron Age, when iron affected the balance, and there was increased influence from the city states of the Mediterranean (Rowlands, 1973, 596-7). More recently, Rowlands has 're-built' the structure of Bronze Age society in an attempt to discuss the exchange links within Europe; so, he has suggested that settlements in the later Bronze Age in Britain were organised with separate male and female units, reflecting the strong male focus of society (1980, 32). He went on to suggest, as we have already seen from other authors, that certain groups were able to manipulate local and long-distance exchange, and thus to accumulate metal surpluses and resources (1980, 33). This could be seen in the siting of downland sites, which might have been producing a surplus for exchange with coastal communities, who were better placed to take advantage of long-distance exchange (Rowlands, 1980, 34-5). These coastal sites then formed part of an Atlantic regional economy, which existed alongside, and reacted with, the Urnfield Culture complex of central Europe. Ultimately, each formed separate relations with the Mediterranean (Rowlands, 1980, 37-41). This Atlantic economy then went into a phase of expansion in the eighth to sixth centuries BC, as can be seen by the quantities of metal objects available at this time. In the same way, more of the products of central Europe were required in the Mediterranean (Rowlands, 1980, 41-5). However, the demand was not maintained, and the whole economy collapsed. Bronze objects lost their value, and iron came into its own in the more fragmented social system that ensued (Rowlands, 1980, 45-6). Rowlands summarised his discussion with a series of points for further research towards a "scientific prehistory" (1980, 46).

Thus, we have dealt with the position of southern Britain in the Bronze Age of Europe in a summary fashion, but it is possible to see how regional patterns may have developed out of a wider social setting within this period: the shift away from the 'artificial ritual' of the Wessex culture, organising exchange to its own ends, to the growth of the coastal regions, manipulating long-distance exchange. The latter were stimulated by European contacts, in turn stimulated by the city states of the Mediterranean, only to fail together. As Rowlands noted, we can only look at our available evidence, but it is possible to read more from it than other descriptive commentaries on the European Bronze Age would suggest.

SUMMARY AND CONCLUSION

The basic elements of Bronze Age settlement and material culture have been drawn together at regional, national, and European levels in an attempt to provide a framework against which to set the metalwork, principally the hoards. This has been done through discussion of other authors' opinions on these aspects of the Bronze Age. Most seem generally agreed on the overall arrangement of the evidence, although interpretations can differ markedly, but it is in the social setting of this material that most dissension lies. This is common to much of modern archaeology: questioning the tenets and unsupported presuppositions in all areas. In a period of patchy material record, too much emphasis and stress can be laid upon particular ideas and interpretations, but nevertheless, it should be clear from the foregoing that the 'social' interpretation is favoured here. Invaders, traders, and environment may have had some effect on Bronze Age societies, but they do not 'explain' them.

It would seem much more sensible to view the regional pictures as part of a larger system, which acted in concert with neighbouring exchange partners on a European scale. We have noted the rise and decline of Wessex, the rise in importance of the Thames Valley, and the specialist nature of settlements in the Somerset Levels and the Fens. Overall, these can be explained as networks of interactions between social groupings in Bronze Age Britain. The gain of power and prestige and the formation of long-distance exchange networks help to explain many of the problems presented by the data. When these networks had extended so far across Europe, there was always a latent instability in the system, and towards the end of the Bronze Age it collapsed, and we find a return to the more regional patterns of the Iron Age.

Metalwork has been placed within this overview, where necessary, and particularly in the later Bronze Age. An attempt has also been made to fill in other evidence for this period. The wide picture of the Bronze Age will be useful in our attempts to explain hoarding. Hoards arose during the course of a society's existence and as a result of some social experience: we must attempt to define these elements and to consider in what ways they can be studied.

CHAPTER 3

FRAMEWORKS OF EXPLANATION

INTRODUCTION

We have already seen in the previous chapters how hoards have been interpreted and the role which they play in our models of explanation for the Bronze Age. We have suggested various ways in which they might have functioned within the Bronze Age. It is the intention here to examine how they might be built into a more theoretical framework of explanation for the Bronze Age.

EXPLANATORY MODELS

The methodology of Kristiansen's work on Danish hoards has already been mentioned: the theoretical side, however, has always appeared to be somehow separate and not fully linked to the examples under discussion. We can look again at how the theory is derived, using information gained on a visit to Denmark (described in Chapter 4) and some more recent papers by Kristiansen.

The hardest part of Kristiansen's work to understand has been the link between the analysis of wear patterns and the economic model for Bronze Age Denmark (remarked in Chapter 1; Kristiansen, 1979, 169 ff; 1981, 250 ff). One of the pivotal factors here is the importance of agricultural wealth in gaining access to other wealth resources through exchange (Kristiansen, pers. comm.). He also combines estimates of population density, land–use patterns, and subsistence strategies, with population figures based on the number of graves. Of particular importance is the relationship in each area between population density and the productive potential of the land (Kristiansen, 1979, 169, 173, Fig. 12). This raises several difficulties: graves may not be representative of the total population, and we cannot assume that the same proportion of people were buried from period to period. Population levels and land quality were a major factor in Kristiansen's interpretation and were assessed by considering the productive potential of each parish, eliminating areas that could not be used as arable land (Kristiansen, 1979, 171; 1980, 6–7; 1981, 251). However, this does include 'moors', which may or may not have been present to the same extent in the Bronze Age. Nor can we be sure that recent assessments of productive potential bear much relation to the prehistoric situation; they may very well be influenced by later factors. Nonetheless, Kristiansen uses the material to postulate "different developmental trajectories" in separate regions of Scandinavia. As part of this process, the Bronze Age economies themselves were divided into two groups with two sub–groups each (Kristiansen, 1979, 174–5).

Kristiansen's main analysis attempted to explain the evolutionary and devolutionary developments in the Bronze Age in relation to a model of tribal structure. Throughout, the emphasis was on economic factors (Kristiansen, 1979, 182). The argument, however, rests on a large number of basic assumptions about the original data; it is hard to see the connection between his data analysis and his basic social model, which has simply been 'fitted' around the empirical observations. However, it is obvious that much of the argument is derived from Marxist analyses, and especially from the work of Friedman and Rowlands, a point confirmed in another article by Kristiansen himself (1984b, 95n.). We need to examine these studies to trace the links.

In a more recent paper, Kristiansen has shown how the degree and nature of wear on sword blades across time in Bronze Age Denmark can be linked to the social position of their users (1984a). Certain sword types were more ostentatious than others and although worn on the hilt, the blades were not heavily sharpened through use in fighting. Thus, they would have belonged to a distinct group in society; "man vermeint hier die Konturen zweier Gruppen in der bronzezeitlichen Gesellschaft zu erkennen: Krieger und Häuptling" (Kristiansen, 1984a, 198). This conclusion was backed up by reference to the grave groups and to underlying differences in the associated grave goods, although the difference was not so clear cut in 'Period III', as it had been in 'Period II' (Kristiansen, 1984a, 199–202). Kristiansen draws a picture of a society based on leading chiefly families who exercised control over politics and ritual. They combined these roles with military might and ranked above the warrior groups. This position also enabled them to manipulate the bronze supply, and consequently the access of lower ranks to this prestigious material (1984a, 203). This is the 'prestige good system' described in anthropological works and noted in a number of prehistoric situations (Kristiansen, 1984a, 203–4). Kristiansen concludes that further studies into Bronze Age social structure are needed, and in particular a consideration of the role of hoards and also of women's ornaments: "Durch einen Vergleich dieser beiden Variablen hoffe ich, das Verhältnis zwischen sozialen und ideologischen Veränderungen beleuchten zu können, welches eines der zentralen Probleme der Archäologie darstellt" (Kristiansen, 1984a, 204).

Kristiansen has also recently dealt more specifically with Marxist theory in archaeology, in a volume devoted to this theme (Spriggs, 1984). Having summarised prevalent trends of explanation in archaeology, Kristiansen suggests that we can move beyond "mechanical theory" in seeking to construct a framework, which maintains the evolutionary and systemic perspectives, and "which is able to account for the explanation of societies in their structural and cultural totality with regard to their genesis, reproduction and transformation"; such a theory is Marxist theory (1984b, 74). How is this to be applied? In the first instance, Kristiansen cites the need for more case studies, which would look at the interaction between social systems in their local, regional, and 'global' setting (1984b, 75). Secondly, we have to take into account how aspects of the record become obscured by the actions of the societies themselves, as well as by post-depositional factors (Kristiansen, 1984b, 76). He goes on to discuss the role of ideology in "pre-depositional and depositional processes" (1984b, 76). "Thus ideology is not considered to be a passive reflection of society, but, on the contrary, an active factor that can be used by competing individuals and social groups to establish and legitimize their dominance through an ideology bearing upon society as a whole and expressed in symbols, social norms, rules and rituals"; contrast and harmony on various levels may be involved (Kristiansen, 1984b, 77, Figs. 1 and 2). Examples are taken for the Neolithic and Bronze Age in Denmark (the evidence of wear and consumption of bronzes already discussed elsewhere in this thesis) and explained in terms of the Marxist framework; social, economic, and ritual change interact with each other, but are also linked to changed conditions of production with decreasing supplies of bronze, changes in wealth consumption from burial to hoarding, and increases in communal ritual and in the display of female wealth (ornament sets) (Kristiansen, 1984b, 95). The prestige-goods system with its political and social dynamics create the momentum, but their development is restricted by the ecological and technological conditions "of a small-scale economy" (Kristiansen, 1984b, 95). Eventually, the cycle of the prestige-goods system reached a point at the transition to the Iron Age "that would not allow the tribal cycle to continue or to be repeated" (Kristiansen, 1982, 273). Kristiansen concludes that we should consider "cultural form within a larger framework of production and reproduction in order to determine its material functions" (1984b, 95).

This makes clearer the position in Kristiansen's earlier papers and the apparent gap between data and theory (discussed above). Kristiansen postulated an evolutionary and a devolutionary tendency in the Danish Bronze Age: the first leading to the 'Asiatic' state, and the second possibly devolving into a 'pre-feudal mode of production'; both would have been governed by economic processes (1979, 182). As seen from Godelier's work, "economic relations may be embedded in kinship relations, political relations or even ideological relations" (Kristiansen, 1981, 239). The dominant relations of production are defined by the specific combination of these factors (Kristiansen, 1981, 239; 1982, 244). As already noted, Kristiansen conceives of the use of structural Marxism as a way to develop archaeological theory, while following the work of Friedman – latterly a Global Systems Approach (cf Spriggs, 1984, 5, 7).

The published version of Friedman's thesis is prefaced by a note explaining a change in his theoretical position, while the thesis itself remains unchanged (1979, 9–20). Friedman would argue that his use of 'structural Marxism' is different to that of Godelier, and that Godelier reduces the idea to meaninglessness, because his notions of religion are tautological (1979, 18–19). Using this model, he demonstrated the way in which internal properties generated developmental tendencies in social forms: "The emergence, in devolution, of proto-feudal property, and the evolution of 'asiatic' states on the basis of 'tribal' property will both be shown to be related to the functioning of a single social system over time" (1979, 31). Friedman would now tend to replace the concepts of transformation resulting from ecological degradation and hierarchisation leading to continuous warfare with a 'global system' model, one of whose characteristics is the relationship between centre and periphery (1979, 9–10). "Within such systems there are centers of accumulation, producing a whole range of manufactured goods, surrounded by peripheries or supply zones – less developed areas that exchange their raw materials and labor power for center-produced goods that are instrumental in defining the power of local elites. A third zone can be added to this representation, one containing 'primitive' societies, beyond the center/periphery structure and totally dependent upon local resources, resources which are themselves limited by the expansionist nature of the centers" (Friedman, 1979, 10–11). Thus, Friedman is able to criticise his own work and to suggest alternative methods of explanation; we have already seen a version of the centre (core)/periphery model in use in archaeological explanations of the southern British Bronze Age. Political location would shift from core to periphery "in a wider system of transformations in space and time", with a need for access to external exchange, arising out of the internal structuring of the society (Rowlands and Gledhill, 1977, 156).

Having now reviewed the setting for Kristiansen's analysis of the Danish Bronze Age and the impact of 'global systems' theory, we can review some related works in an attempt to deepen our understanding of these approaches.

Parker Pearson has rightly pointed to the problem of relating Marx's theory of capitalism to prehistoric societies (1984, 60). However, the important point is that artefacts are not just objects, but embody facets of their originating society: "all practice and the technology employed to implement that practice is mediated through ideology with each item taking its meaning from the whole set of material conditions, social practices and belief systems" (Parker Pearson, 1984, 61). Thus, in pre-capitalist societies economy is mediated through religion, whereas it becomes one of the "main components of capitalist ideology" (Parker Pearson, 1984, 61). A study of burial practices within a society indicates the ritual used to establish a social position for the living; the role of ancestors and deities can be far more important in a primitive society, than other aspects of material culture (Parker Pearson, 1984, 63–4). Archaeology can thus give us social insights in a way not possible for other areas of human study, such as anthropology, which lacks spatial time-depth; archaeological knowledge can be turned into "a source of generalisation concerning the role of history in society as well as the history of societies" (Rowlands, 1984, 113).

Kristiansen and Friedman used the concept of the Asiatic mode of production to explain one of the possible forms of transition from classless to class societies (discussed above), such as the transition from the Bronze Age to the Iron Age. In this mode of production there is a regular surplus, which then forms the basis for social differentiation with the emergence of a minority of individuals exploiting the community. They then develop into a higher community or State, which controls high-level developments, such as cities and foreign trade (Godelier, 1978, 221–4). The concept of the Asiatic mode of production has, however, been criticised for being ambiguous in its application and "riddled with theoretical problems", since many of its characteristics seem to be determined by technology rather than relations of production; the concept was originally evolved to contrast with capitalism in Europe, and not as a theoretical concept in its own right (Bottomore, 1983, 35–6). Thus, the explanatory potential of this concept would seem to be very limited and inappropriate to our discussion, while arguments as to the exact nature and definition of it rage on (summarised by Bailey, 1981).

Ekholm defines another method of explanation – the global system: nations are linked by an interdependent network of exchange, and the mode of production and social formation are only part of this much larger system (1981, 241–2). The local level 'exists' in its own right, with its local system of production and a local social structure, but it is also influenced by external factors. Exchange plays a central role in this process (Ekholm, 1981, 246–7). Evolution occurs unevenly through "centre/periphery relations", where the 'centre' moves from one region to another, leaving an underdeveloped periphery as a result; the centres and peripheries are also organised within a larger system, to which are added 'primitive societies' (Ekholm, 1981, 247–8, fig. 9.4).

Each sphere can evolve within itself, but will not necessarily develop to another level. At the same time, both the centre and its periphery may combine to form a single political unit, reflecting the larger system (Ekholm, 1981, 248–9). Just as societies within this system can evolve, they can also devolve and collapse (Ekholm, 1981, 249–50). As these local systems develop, so does competition, and this eventually results in warfare: "War, like production, is a ruling class project in which producers are forced to participate" (Ekholm, 1981, 257). Following warfare, we have "internal confrontation between classes", and eventual contraction due to destruction: the crisis and ensuing contraction are part of the shift of centres in global systems, and the total collapse and destruction of centres arises from competition within the social structure (Ekholm, 1981, 259). Finally, we can see that evolution is not always progressive, and "the next 'mode of production' may... belong to the same family of structures that preceded it" (Ekholm, 1981, 259). As Ekholm makes clear, the world-system approach seeks to integrate history and social science into an historical social science, which can then be united with politics: the eventual aim being to understand our present world in its total context (Kahn and Llobera, 1981a, 322–4). Wallerstein used an analysis of the political economy of sixteenth-century Europe to comprehend the world-system today: this economy was based around capitalist forms of production, but was divided into areas of core, semiperiphery, and periphery (1979, 37–8). The semiperipheral areas were in transition between core and periphery, and all three represented various stages of economic, political, and social development (Wallerstein, 1979, 38–9). The world-system perspective denies that there are units of analysis, such as state or nation: "social action takes place in an entity within which there is an ongoing division of labor..." (Wallerstein, 1979, 155). However, we need to consider further the explanatory potential of such models for our analysis.

Friedman summarised a series of points about such approaches (1982, 179–81):

1. The unit of analysis is neither society nor a particular institution, but the total process of reproduction. Smaller cycles are embedded in larger cycles of the structural totality: intersocietal cycles of exchange, intrasocietal exchange cycles, life cycles, and production cycles. These are socially determined and are not reducible to internal social processes.
2. Social reproduction is governed by social operators; the latter are structures that organise the dynamic properties and direction of social activity, and thus determine the nature of the reproductive process. The general conditions of agricultural production tend to alter the shapes of the cycles.
3. The social categories of a social system do not contain the totality of the system, but "the social space within which reproduction occurs can and must be divided into that part that is directly organized by social operators and that part that is beyond social control and intentionality".
4. This is in contrast to the 'evolutionary' process, which is characterised by crisis and sudden transformations: "A social reproductive system is constituted by a number of interlocking dynamic processes that are functionally necessary to one another and, at the same time, possess properties that diverge from one another".

Friedman concluded that regional systems of civilisations, with commercial centres, peripheral chiefdoms and tribes, and marginal bands, were stable organisations until the 'modern period', when world systems changed radically with the appearance of industrial capitalism and the emergence of a dominant wage-labour sector (1982, 182). Thus, it would seem that, if we can identify certain characteristics of such a system within the archaeological record, we can reconstruct the likely social processes and events under study, such as we have seen for Denmark.

This has been effectively done by Rowlands and others in a series of articles, although Rowlands has also made some cautionary remarks (1982). He points to recent trends in contemporary Marxism, where many arguments have foundered on the problem of applying a set of principles, originally formulated by Marx in relation to nineteenth-century capitalism, to inappropriate data; but Marxism can be used to generate new principles (1982, 161). "The material culture record also does not appear to exist as a unity that can be correlated with any discrete behavioral activity. It forms a category only because archaeologists classify it as such, as part of the taxonomic space within which they operate and as part of the definition of their own discipline" (Rowlands, 1982, 164). Rowlands goes on to indicate how we can view the primary role of politics within the economy, where the economy becomes "a complex relation of forces between different social agents, and the productive forces are themselves subject to a rationality imposed on them by these relations" (1982, 167). Thus, political relations can determine the level of exploitation of material resources, the development of production processes, labour divisions, circulation and exchange, and the reproduction of these patterns through symbolism and ideology within a given set of environmental conditions (Rowlands, 1982, 167). The political structure inspiring these developments is set apart from them, and status insignia, such as prestige items, legitimate access to this high status, while being under effective control: the 'value' of the items is defined by their political functions and the status of participants involved in their ceremonial exchange, and not by any qualities intrinsic to the items themselves (Rowlands, 1982, 168). Herein lies an inherent weakness: lower-ranking groups could collude with outside agents, or trade for prestige items on the boundaries of the community, and subsequently gain control over local and external sources of demand, destabilising the existing hierarchy, unless the 'state' has maintained "control over the functioning of material flows" (Rowlands, 1982, 169).

Two applications seem of note here: those of Friedman and Rowlands (1977) and Frankenstein and Rowlands (1978). Frankenstein and Rowlands were dealing specifically with Early Iron Age society in south-western Germany, but the implications extended forwards and backwards in time (1978, 73). They first formulated a model of a 'prestige-good' economy, where political advantage is gained through exercising control over access to resources only obtained through external trade, and which is articulated through core centres (external trading partners) and periphery (local level centres), with middlemen in the semiperiphery (1978, 75-81). There is some loss in analytical depth when they address the archaeological record, but a picture can be presented all the same (Frankenstein and Rowlands, 1978, 81). Thus, craft activities, such as metalworking, potting, and weaving, would be directly controlled at the local level to ensure redistribution and use for exchange, while more utilitarian objects would be produced at a domestic level; the settlement pattern and burial evidence could indicate numbers of dependants in the chiefly clan and their ranking in relation to primary 'chiefly' burials (Frankenstein and Rowlands, 1978, 82). The taking of foreign status items and exotic raw materials should be evidenced, with the most important items coming from a centralised place of manufacture in the settlement of a paramount chief (Frankenstein and Rowlands, 1978, 82). The position of the paramount depends on control of the external exchange of highest status goods, so that he is, in a sense, a dependant of an external system, and may take on the dress, custom, and burial rite of cultures with which he is in contact (Frankenstein and Rowlands, 1978, 83). The contradictions in the structures might manifest themselves in the evidence of hostilities and "dynastic change" at the centre; the establishment of exchange links at lower levels would show as a collapsed pattern of competing centres within a previously uniform domain (Frankenstein and Rowlands, 1978, 83-4). After a lengthy review of the detailed evidence, Frankenstein and Rowlands concluded that the development of political units in this area of south-western Germany in the Early Iron Age was dependent on contemporary Mediterranean civilisations and was of a form to provide advantages to external trading partners seeking raw materials and possibly slaves (1978, 109). Also, these units evolved on the periphery of the highly centralised states, providing conditions for further evolution and development of these states (Frankenstein and Rowlands, 1978, 109). "The differential development of such systems and their dependence on each other for their own local evolution determines the nature of the kind of interaction that occurs between them", and therefore we need to understand why the dominant systems at the centre compete and transform the less-developed societies on the periphery to enable their own continued evolution (Frankenstein and Rowlands, 1978, 109-10).

Friedman and Rowlands set out at length the 'ground rules' for the development of 'simple' to 'complex' societies (1977). This was an attempt to reconstruct the structures of reproduction of particular social forms: "These are the social structures that dominate the processes of production and circulation and which therefore constitute the socially determined form by which populations reproduce themselves as economic entities" (1977, 203). The local population can be represented by a model of successive levels, each of which is autonomous, but limited by a hierarchy of constraints, and the entire process of social reproduction is dominated and organised by the relations of production (Friedman and Rowlands, 1977, Fig. 1). The system breaks down and structural transformations occur because of these dominant relations of production and the functional incompatibilities of the larger totality. The model envisages a series of evolutionary 'stages' generated from previous stages (Friedman and Rowlands, 1977, 204).

Factors external to the local society influence the local situation, in which production for exchange is a constant factor (Friedman and Rowlands, 1977, 204). The expansion of a tribe into a state takes place alongside other tribes, connected by warfare and exchange to the evolving unit. These tribes may be transformed into a politically acephalous periphery of the emergent state, which then imports a large part of their labour force and their products. Long-distance trade between emergent chiefdoms and states may stimulate intensification of local production and political development of local centres at the expense of the immediate peripheries (Friedman and Rowlands, 1977, 205). The local unit is taken to be the tribal system with its basic production and exchange units arranged in local lineages, which are no more than four or five households linked by a set of rituals to a founding ancestor: this would be self-sufficient in material reproduction, but matrimonial alliances through exogamy satisfy its biological reproduction, and in this way the alliance structure may be a dominant relation of production (Friedman and Rowlands, 1977, 206). Lineage is important in this respect because ancestors form a link with the supernatural, and the higher spirits can be used as part of the economic activity, obtaining wealth for the group. A surplus could be converted into a community feast, gaining prestige for that local lineage: an older lineage would be nearer the supernatural and able to provide more of a feast (Friedman and Rowlands, 1977, 207). Women would then be given to other lower status groups in exchange for a bride-price, equal to the social value of the wife-giver, thus providing a 'matrilateral link' to the source of wealth. Thus, differences in prestige are continually converted into the relative ranking of lineages (Friedman and Rowlands, 1977, 207). This tribal system uses valuables as indicators of status rather than its source. It has three relations of production (Friedman and Rowlands, 1977, 208):

1. Control of the local group over its immediate production process and its capacity to dispose of output;
2. Matrimonial exchange, with 'superior' wife-givers, because of the value of the wife of the prestige group;
3. The relations between lineage and community as a whole, which arise because of the prestige generated by distributive feasts resulting from lineage surplus.

High-rank lineages tend to emerge from this system because of the increase in surplus generated by them through status, gained by feasting. Relative rank derives from increased bride-price for lineage daughters, and high rank is reinforced by the accumulation of dependent labour or 'slaves' (Friedman and Rowlands, 1977, 208–9).

In time a particular line becomes dominant in feast giving and affinal exchange and is identified as the direct descendant of the territorial deity. At this stage other lines are ranked in terms of genealogical distance from the deity and the social form now becomes a conical clan (Friedman and Rowlands, 1977, 211). The chief, and his lineage, is entitled to tribute and is thus able to control a sizeable portion of the total labour of the community, in return for overseeing the welfare of that community: this is a new vertical relation of production (Friedman and Rowlands, 1977, 211). The alliance and exchange relations are continually extended into a wider region, obtaining a range of valuables, access to which depends on position in the hierarchy. The whole range is only available to those at the top (Friedman and Rowlands, 1977, 211). Powerful aristocratic lineages are thus formed, accumulating increased control over the wealth in circulation, and also gaining direct control over the total labour of the community which can be used in the expanding external exchange network (Friedman and Rowlands, 1977, 213). The growth in demand for surplus means the import of captured slaves as labour from surrounding groups and leads to a regional pattern with expanding centres of power, surrounded by acephalous societies, which may once have had similar structures (Friedman and Rowlands, 1977, 213). In the fully formed conical structure, local exchange is undermined by rank, because wife-giving now serves as a form of tribute. The conversion of surplus into status by an act of 'generosity' is replaced by an expression of segmentary position: the 'verticalisation' process is accentuated because wealth appears as the result of the supernatural power of the chiefly ancestors and their descendants (Friedman and Rowlands, 1977, 217). This new class of noble lineages related to a single sacred royal line is identical to the state and resembles the 'Asiatic' mode of production. In this sense, the emphasis is on the "dominant *economic* function of the monopolisation of the supernatural" (Friedman and Rowlands, 1977, 218).

The growth of the potential agricultural surplus permits an increased division of labour, with artisans being brought into the centre to form a full-time class of specialists, and a demand for new and more productive techniques in the production of wealth objects and 'public works' (Friedman and Rowlands, 1977, 219). Specialist craft production produces valuables for the elite, and there is also a large increase in interregional exchange, bringing in exotic objects. Thus, a number of relatively small states are interconnected at the top by elite exchange, while expansion can be realised in the larger region (Friedman and Rowlands, 1977, 219). As the size of the local domain grows, so does the potential for fission: centrally controlled luxury items may have to be distributed to peripheral chiefs in order to maintain their loyalty. Succession within the royal lineage becomes a major area of conflict (Friedman and Rowlands, 1977, 220). The difficulty of determining the relative rank of sons from the many wives of the chief may induce changes in the kinship relations; the lower ranks probably control the actual distribution of prestige goods, allowing for personal accumulation; and the techno-environment of the centre may be strained by increasing population density (Friedman and Rowlands, 1977, 221). The monopolisation of valuables, necessary for the social reproduction of all local groups, is a new development of domination, arising out of the now autonomous economic sector of prestige good production (Friedman and Rowlands, 1977, 222).

With the expansion of the old domain to new territories and the creation of a new kind of political hierarchy and economy based on prestige good production, we have the beginning of the next period (Friedman and Rowlands, 1977, 224). "The former tribute relation becomes a somewhat more reciprocal relation between the central royalty and more peripheral aristocrats who in exchange for goods from the centre maintain a supply of local products to that centre"; there is more of a settlement hierarchy over a large area and expansion depends on a major structural change in the aristocracy (Friedman and Rowlands, 1977, 224–5). The royal 'sons' may be sent out to govern provinces, resulting in concentric dualism between centre and periphery. Now the development of the prestige good economy undermines the former control based on proximity to the deities: the state is functionally split into two halves, with one representing religious power and the other concerned with external politico-economic relations (Friedman and Rowlands, 1977, 226). The massive increase in production for exchange creates a high demand for labour, satisfied by the importation of slaves employed directly at the centre, and the valuable products of the centre are traded for slaves, raw materials, and other products of the local areas: this is the characteristic relationship between the Mediterranean states and their northern European neighbours in the bronze and iron ages (Friedman and Rowlands, 1977, 227; outlined above from Frankenstein and Rowlands, 1978).

The expansion of this prestige good system encourages the development of new centres capable of autonomous production, especially of local specialised products, and thus ultimately undermines central control by competition for labour and land between centres and their peripheries: these competing urban centres have the beginnings of a commercial city state economy (Friedman and Rowlands, 1977, 228–32). The prestige items now tend to be increasingly generalised and serve as money in the growing number of exchanges. This enables the aristocrats with the original power of accumulation to become a class of wealthy individuals (Friedman and Rowlands, 1977, 235). Hierarchy collapses, as position becomes related to wealth, and the conical clan structure is destroyed, because the clan lands are no longer inalienable: a class of landless labourers develops and merges with the former slaves to form a single class of expropriated producers. The relations of production are now separated from the state structure, resulting in a superstructural state and a bureaucracy controlling the economy (Friedman and Rowlands, 1977, 236).

This outline indicates a general model: it "predicts a multi-linear evolutionary trajectory in which variant pathways are generated by the constraints imposed by particular local conditions" (Friedman and Rowlands, 1977, 241). These tendencies are summarised in a series of diagrams (Friedman and Rowlands, 1977, 244–6, Fig. 6). This is an attempt to overcome the narrow definitions characterising societies as bands, tribes, chiefdoms, and states, by defining specific social forms of the reproduction of populations. This reproduction takes place over time as part of a developmental and transformational process: "the structures with which we are concerned are the structures of processes and not of institutions, [so] we must deal with systems of trajectories in which elements are internally transformed as they take on new roles in the larger system of material reproduction" (Friedman and Rowlands, 1977, 267). A fixed set of institutions is hard to define for a particular 'stage', since we are taking a cross–section of a complex of processes; we can define a new stage, when a period begins with the emergence of new dominant structures, frequently accompanied by a spatial shift often from 'centre' to 'periphery' (Friedman and Rowlands, 1977, 269). Friedman and Rowlands conclude that we must try to comprehend the larger system, which articulates the local societies, local and regional conditions of reproduction, and exchange (1977, 272).

THE BRONZE AGE CONTEXT

We now need to place this model more firmly in the Bronze Age context. This has been attempted by Rowlands (1980) and by Bradley (1984).

In comparing kinship structure with a 'Crow–Omaha' system, Rowlands seems to be suggesting a different approach to the alliance structure, based on the wife – giver / wife – taker relationship already outlined: in this case, kin alliances are formed with groups that have provided marriage partners, and new alliances have to be formed with groups outside this relationship (1980, 16–18). However, the net result would appear to be the same, with those groups having the most extensive alliance networks also accruing more wealth and surplus labour product to be converted into status, with control over rituals, worship of ancestors, and genealogies (Rowlands, 1980, 19–20). Another feature of this kind of system is the way in which new relations of dominance develop through access to outside trade networks. The emphasis is placed directly on the accumulation of wealth and its use in status rivalry (Rowlands, 1980, 20). The manipulation of relations of circulation and exchange support the relations of dominance and hierarchy: weapons and ornaments form one system of circulation, 'politico–ritual' in function and stimulating food production; the relationship is indirect, however (Rowlands, 1980, 46). The exchange/alliance networks are the cause of, and also result from, competition between social groups: alliances depend on maintaining the flow of goods in exchange, and in turn support local leaders in their competitions with each other through feasting and fighting, recitation of heroic deeds, and claims to ties with ancestors and spirits (Rowlands, 1980, 47). Ranking between groups would be unstable, with competition for succession to title, and thus the necessity of maintaining support from allies through the redistribution of prestige items, which "symbolically encode allocations and transferences of prestige and power" (Rowlands, 1980, 47). Centralisation occurs by monopolisation of the allocation of titles, which could also lead to fragmentation through the desertion of supporters. The networks of exchange expand over large areas, forming total social networks, often on the periphery of the more dominant commercial states of the Near East and the Mediterranean. This is counterbalanced by an emphasis on territorial rights and ancestral sites, with patrilineal and patrilocal residence passing rights, title, and prestige over several generations (Rowlands, 1980, 47–8). This can be confirmed in the archaeological record for the British Middle Bronze Age and Iron Age respectively, through observations of the social units at settlement sites, weapon and ornament distributions, and pottery evidence (Rowlands, 1980, 48; 32–7). Thus, we can argue that artefacts should not be studied in isolation, but as part of their social context, and that the social context was itself a facet of a regional economy. The scale of the latter would have fluctuated in relation to economic processes involving a large area of Europe (Rowlands, 1980, 48). Bradley concentrates more on the archaeological evidence in this picture (1984; already noted above, Chapter 2). Of direct interest to this enquiry are the topics discussed by Bradley in the middle of his book, ie from the later Neolithic onwards, when a prestige goods system can be discerned (1984, 46ff). This system is explained as circulating certain items in an exclusive way, which have to be excluded from general distribution, either by separation from other goods in 'spheres of exchange', or by control through destruction, as suggested by Meillassoux (Bradley, 1984, 47). In fact, Meillassoux suggests a combination of spheres of exchange and destruction of goods, when talking about the ancient kingdom of Dahomey: the circulation of goods necessary for life is separate from the circulation of prestige goods in the courts. the latter goods are produced by slaves, who are regularly put to death to restrict their productive capacity (1977, 168–71). Nevertheless, Bradley's argument is persuasive. He concludes that a prestige goods economy existed in the later

Neolithic, because of the association of certain items with special classes of sites, the small degree of overlap shown by entire assemblages, and the deliberate deposition of specific objects at this time (1984, 57). Thus, different elites were able to develop out of the earlier Neolithic, on the basis of agricultural wealth, control of lithic artefacts, and feasting. This period saw the growth of core areas across Britain and changes in their relative importance, first from Wessex to the Orkneys and then back again at the end of the Neolithic (Bradley, 1984, 65). However, the importance of Wessex in the earlier Bronze Age was shortlived, in the sense that decline again set in despite attempts by the elite to re-emphasise their status through monument building and complex burials (Bradley, 1984, 94–5). Bradley suggests that the elements of the prestige goods economy continue during the Bronze Age, but the potential for accumulation of wealth and thus prestige enabled competition from the periphery to usurp the power of the core areas (1984, 102–6). Here he is drawing together a panoply of interpretations to shed light on the problems of metalwork and their deposition. Thus, we can place the emphasis on the economic, where deposits are made to maintain the scarcity value of prestige objects, or on the symbolic, where objects belonging to an individual have to be destroyed after death. The same applies when bridewealth loses its function. The act of deposition may also be important, for the destruction of valuables enhances the status of the participants and, at the same time, restricts the supply of material available to other people, so that it is harder for competitors to mount a challenge (Bradley, 1984, 104–5). This last idea is derived from Gregory's observations on gift exchange and *potlatch* (1980). The point of Gregory's argument was somewhat different to that under discussion here, as he was setting such practices within a modern economic context, but he does point to the importance of the destruction of wealth in *potlatch*, noting that "it is the ranking achieved by the alienation that is important, not the mode of alienation" (Gregory, 1980, 647–9). Nonetheless, Bradley is able to show that two of these principles were probably in operation during the Bronze Age: in the Middle Bronze Age ornament hoards could represent 'bridewealth' deposits, purging the social debt incurred by the breaking of such a link; and in the Late Bronze Age, weapon deposits in rivers could be part of a flamboyant destruction of wealth, since the wealth and status items were effectively removed from circulation (1984, 106–24).

Bradley has suggested that bronze objects can be viewed as part of a two–level system, governed by social distance; objects could be prestigious gifts at the local level, but beyond that group they could become mere commodities, traded for their metal content (1985a, 694–6). He went on to illustrate this argument with some examples from Britain, showing hoards lying at the edge of possible distribution zones, and emphasising how hoards of one type of object can dominate the record in one area and occur in more mixed hoards outside that area (1985a, 698–701). Bradley's contention was that the character of the item exchanged (gift or commodity) was governed by the relationship between the parties to the transaction, although, as archaeologists, we only have the objects themselves to work from and their patterns of distribution. Bradley conceded that these could cause serious problems of interpretation (1985a, 702–3). These ideas were developed in more detail in Bradley's Munro lecture (1985b), where deposits of metalwork were analysed using concepts taken from social anthropology, in particular the work of Gregory (1982) on gifts and commodities. Gregory drew a distinction between clan– and class–based societies, which employ different forms of exchange and reproduction. In a clan–based society the clansman is seen as surrounded by concentric spheres of relations, with almost complete strangers at the periphery. Only in the latter case does exchange assume a commodity form (1982, 41–2). However, when gifts are exchanged, these are regarded as inalienable and the very act of giving creates a debt. In this way, the donor expresses his superiority over the receiver and puts him under an obligation to reciprocate (Gregory, 1982, 43–7). Gregory showed that objects used as gifts possess rank or 'exchange–order', rather than exchange–value: objects from different ranks cannot be taken to be equivalents, although a range of products within any single rank may be equal to each other (1982, 48–50). The system accumulates large gift–debts, and if an individual maximises his net outgoings, he acquires a large following of debtors. At the same time, the stock of gifts can be kept low by the regular destruction of some of them, limiting the gift–credit that can be created (Gregory, 1982, 51–61). Thus, Gregory showed that the consumption of objects was important in a gift exchange relationship, while the production of objects was more important in commodity exchange (1982, 71). The complexities of the systems involved and their social settings go beyond this, but Gregory's work does show how we can potentially use this kind of information to differentiate the types of deposits in the archaeological record. It is arguable, however, that the commodity exchange should be invisible in the hoard record, as the objects would have been passed on and used, probably by re–casting. This is a weakness in Bradley's interpretation. However, some unusual pieces in hoards may be the residue of such transactions. These points have been reinforced by Barrett (1985). He has pointed out that we should consider single finds as being as important as hoards, and that we should begin to study and understand hoards by an examination of production and circulation. The latter must be done by taking into account the alienation of goods in commodity exchange, and the inalienability of goods in gift exchange. The two can be of variable 'value' (1985, 95–100). The same may be true of commodity exchanges, in that long–distance exchange was probably made up of a series of transactions over short distances. On the other hand, with each transaction the objects would be passed on with a different 'value', so that the further they moved away from the source, the more exotic they became (Barrett, 1985, 102). Different objects are found in hoards and graves, because these deposits were concerned with signalling rank and status in different ways: "Hoards contain particular artefacts which represent a core of symbols which may be contrasted with the symbols found in graves" (Barrett, 1985, 104). Daggers in graves could signal individual status, while axes in hoards could represent 'gifts to the gods', thus achieving the alienation of the inalienable. Axes in graves could result from particularly important gift exchanges and confirm that graves and hoards were not mutually exclusive in the Early

Bronze Age (Barrett, 1985, 104–6). Barrett concluded that: "People do live their lives by formulae but they employ the cultural values available to them, sometimes in an imaginative way" (1985, 106), indicating that we must be flexible in our approaches to an understanding of the processes behind deposition.

We can begin to see a social role for artefacts, and we can argue that the prestige imbued in them became directed into long–distance alliances. In the end, these led to the collapse of the Bronze Age system, because it became more susceptible to outside fluctuations, such as the supply of raw materials, which were needed for the increased production of prestige goods (Bradley, 1984, 125–7). At this point, iron technology makes its appearance, and there are signs of fragmentation into regional groups and indications of conflict; the exchange networks broke down and local groups would have to be more self–sufficient (Bradley, 1984, 144). However, the seeds of the upward movement of the cycle were present at the same time, and large–scale exchange became necessary once more to maintain the political superstructure: this led to the resumption of cross–Channel contacts (Bradley, 1984, 144).

These contacts eventually led Britain to become a supplier of raw materials on the periphery of a large system with Rome at the core, and subsequently to be subjugated (Bradley, 1984, 156). Bradley recognises the cyclical nature of this model, as would be predicted by the more abstract version (discussed above), but is also at pains to point to the need to maintain a flexible and eclectic approach, free from dogmatic adherence to the principles of a single system; he also stresses the changing rate of these cyclical developments, such that it would seem that we were dealing with an ever more compressed spiral of events (1984, 165–7).

This discussion has served to place artefacts in a social context as an aid to understanding the archaeological record: the artefacts are part of broader patterns predicted from the model. We are in a stronger position to address ourselves to the problems of "the duality of the symbolic relations between past artefacts and past peoples, that is how the artefacts signified for the people who used them in the past and how the artefacts signify that process in turn for us, and how this process is mediated by power and the objectification of power" (Miller and Tilley, 1984, 5). Further, ideology and power are manifested in material products, which can be studied archaeologically, and are a component of human *praxis*, "by which is to be understood the actions of agents on and in the world, serving as an integral element in the production, reproduction and transformation of the social" (Miller and Tilley, 1984, 14). However, this may be an unnecessarily philosophical standpoint in the present context (although some would argue that the notion of praxis goes beyond philosophy itself (Bottomore, 1983, 389)). It may be sufficient to suggest that we can arrive at meaningful statements about the past by viewing objects as part of a whole cultural dynamic, in which the symbols and ideologies are a small part. This puts the stress back on the economic and the overall model.

SUMMARY

The proposed model and theoretical framework have now been laid out, and it is as well to summarise the main points here.

The explanatory potential of Kristiansen's model for Bronze Age Denmark was examined and criticised, but the basic elements of his Marxist theory were felt to be useful in constructing a model for the circulation and deposition of artefacts. Some of these theoretical elements were examined in more detail, in particular, aspects of the structural Marxism. It was felt that a global systems approach had much to offer in defining the elements of these systems and their total process of reproduction. These factors were then examined as part of a broader social model. This described the expansion of the tribal system through production, alliance, and exchange, and its transformation into a prestige goods economy. We went on to follow its development through an 'Asiatic' mode of production to the formation of the state. The relationships between centres and peripheries are important in determining the course of this development: often peripheral areas are able to re–align exchange to themselves from the centres, and thus become centres in their own right. Thus, we have a continually shifting pattern of development, in which some areas must appear to be experiencing devolution, whilst others are evolving just as rapidly. The use of this model can be seen in explaining the nature of the Bronze Age in Britain and Europe. The most relevant element is undoubtedly the prestige goods economy. This may have its roots in the Neolithic. We may be able to explain the apparent shifts in wealth and resources in the Bronze Age in these terms – the re–alignment of exchange from core to periphery – in a rapidly increasing sequence, which eventually led to the more complex social structure of the Iron Age, when Britain was part of a much larger network of alliance and exchange on the fringe of the Roman empire. Alliance and exchange provide the means for change.

CONCLUSION

How are we to identify the operation of a prestige goods economy? How can we relate theory to practice? Indications have already been given above, but now we can list some of the expected patterns for metalwork and hoards.

1. We have postulated the existence of core/periphery relationships during the Bronze Age of southern Britain. For example, Wessex may have formed a core area in the Early Bronze Age with the Thames Valley as its periphery. Later, the roles were possibly reversed with the rise of the Thames Valley as a core area in its own right. This relationship can be used to explain the divergence of archaeological and material evidence in these two areas, and hoards are one part of that evidence. The hoards are inextricably bound up in the social processes that define the core and periphery and lend support to the growth and strength of the core. Major

differences in the circulation and consumption of metalwork may be one indication that an area was changing its dominant position in the regional system. This should also be visible from distributional studies, and such shifts can be sought by mapping the hoards of the various phases of the Bronze Age. The picture will not be totally clearcut, however, as the core/periphery relationship is dependent on other factors which will not be reflected by the hoard record; indeed, some will not be archaeologically visible at all. However, the apparently discontinuous nature of hoarding highlights the distinction between the phases of the Bronze Age, and in this study can be used to illustrate the switches in emphasis between one region and another over time. It can also show the changing position of different areas within a single region.

2. We have suggested that hoards, and metalwork in general, were used by societies of the Bronze Age to emphasise their position in relation to others and also to indicate the status of individuals within a social grouping. Thus, deposition can be seen to be a facet of status expression, as in the *potlatch*, where vast quantities of valuables are 'wasted'. These acts of conspicuous consumption serve a social purpose and also play an 'economic' role to the extent that they limit the supply of valuables; they achieve the alienation of the inalienable, so that gifts to gods cannot be repaid. In this way, they reinforce the authority of an individual within the group. In these cases, hoards can say something about the status of their depositor: this could be done in crude terms by comparing hoard sizes, in which case the status of the depositor of the Isleham hoard could be seen to out-rank all-comers! However, the size of this hoard and of the other large hoards of the Late Bronze Age may be due partly to the increasing competitiveness of status-defining acts: larger deposits become necessary to achieve the same effect, because the raw material of the deposit has become more widely available. So, we must ask whether the increased size of the deposits in the Late Bronze Age was a manifestation of the efforts of individuals to gain ascendancy and to raise their status within the social group.

3. An adjunct of such status-defining acts is the need to maintain a supply of raw materials to support these activities. A feature of the Bronze Age social systems is the development of long-distance alliances, which can supply raw materials to a group; the re-alignment of exchange can favour an area at the expense of another and lead to the decline of the primary/core area. Britain seems to have belonged to a European network of alliances and exchange, and some of the links can be seen to cover very large distances indeed. The archaeological correlate of this activity could be the appearance of more 'foreign' objects in the standard Bronze Age metalwork repertoire, entering the prestige goods system through the exchange of objects or people. We can examine the contents of our Bronze Age hoards for such pieces, and we can look at the mechanisms by which such materials may have arrived. Bronze Age wrecks were mentioned and the 'peculiarity' of the pieces in their cargo of bronzes; it seems that 'foreign' pieces did appear within Britain, but were 'converted' to more locally acceptable forms, although often in imitation of the original pieces. This is the foundation for typology: the similarities between British bronzes and their European counterparts have led to the erection of vast schemes of relationships and the creation of a finer chronology than for other periods of prehistory. Thus, our hoards do not have a 'direct' component as a result of these long-distance exchanges, but will have 'imitations', as can be seen in the ornament sets of the Middle Bronze Age; these sets could be interpreted as the personal equipment of 'exchanged' women manufactured in a local style.

4. The prestige goods system with its long-distance alliance and exchange supported the core areas with supplies of raw material and prestige artefacts and enabled the core areas to grow at the expense of their peripheries, because of their control over the supply of such materials. However, in the long term, land-use in the core area might not be productive enough to support the population, so that it became dependent on the peripheries to supply it with agricultural surplus. Therein lies a weakness of the system, as the peripheries would be able to turn the agricultural surplus to their advantage, cutting off the supply to the core area and re-aligning long-distance exchange to the peripheries themselves. As we have already suggested, this process will be visible in the distribution of hoards. While such a process was taking place, the pressure within each local system will have been intense. Thus, the status insignia will perhaps have been kept in circulation, when otherwise they would have been deposited. This seems to have happened in Bronze Age Denmark, and the increased wear on objects should become detectable in comparison with material dating from earlier and later periods or with finds from other regions. So, if we codify wear patterns on objects within hoards and compare the scales of wear across time and region, we should be able to identify these phases of increased circulation time and locate the major periods of stress in the local system. Another clue may come from recognising phases of intermittent deposition. We have already noted how the deposition of hoards might have happened at the end of chronological phases. If it is correct, it might reflect the 'holding' of prestige material for longer periods. This would also be exhibited by the degree of wear on the component artefacts. Alternatively, other types of activity might have been used to define status during lacunae in the deposition of hoards. This is perhaps supported by the chronological distribution of river metalwork. Such a process may well be analogous to hoard deposition.

5. Hoards may thus be part of a social system based around exchange, prestige, and status-defining acts, and as such would not have been recoverable. Indeed, some of their contents could have been subject to breakage, as in the example of *potlatch*. Here, pieces are deliberately broken to remove their use value and to take those pieces out of circulation and exchange: a greater gift-debt is accrued and the supply for repayment is reduced. Here are two facets which could well be reflected in our Bronze Age hoards: breakage and non-recovery. It has often been noted that pieces were apparently deliberately broken, as in the case of swords snapped into several pieces, although the objects might still have been serviceable when this occurred. This observation can be examined by wear analysis. We have hoards in the archaeological record, because they were not

recovered in the past. We must ask whether they were ever intended for recovery. How many could have been easily located and retrieved? An analysis of contextual information is useful in this case. Some writers suggest that certain hoards do not resemble the other material at all and give the appearance of the dumping of old-fashioned, worn-out, incomplete pieces. If this is true, these might not result from a status-defining act by the depositor, unless the value of the raw material itself was the crucial element. These hoards may also result from attempts to restrict the supply of metal for re-smelting into new status items; indeed, both functions could have been served by the same deposit, as in the *potlatch* ceremony, which combines the expression of status through deposition and the removal of material from circulation in order to restrict supply. So, the collections of broken and worn pieces are not necessarily inconsistent with our model. Some material must have been re-melted to provide the supply of new objects, but this was most probably heavily supplemented by the supply of raw material in the form of 'foreign' objects obtained through the long-distance exchange networks. Only a re-examination of the hoard finds themselves can shed light on these questions.

6. The development of core/periphery relationships in the Bronze Age could have led to changes in the social structure itself. It seems feasible that with the passage of time social complexity increased and a growing number of individuals may have sought access to prestige goods and status insignia. Only a restricted number of pieces may have been available in the Early Bronze Age and the Wessex graves. The ornaments and weapons of the Middle Bronze Age were more widely available, and a still broader range of equipment is found in the Late Bronze Age. The content of the hoards can be analysed for changes across time and region that might indicate the growing complexity of society over this time. Also, the 'lower' ranks may have had some access to bronze supplies, as evidenced by the more functional tools deposited in the hoards, and the great quantities of socketed axes of the Late Bronze Age. If there are phases when the tool content of hoards are clearly in the ascendant, this may reflect the attempts of other ranks in society to gain access to the 'upper echelons'. We must ask whether the elite were emphasising their position at the same time by other forms of deposition, such as placing swords in rivers.

7. The mechanisms of production were separate from the consumers of those products. Perhaps the manufacture of prestige objects took place in peripheral areas or as a 'client service'. The core areas would require the prestige objects for their status insignia and consequently for status-defining acts of deposition. We must ask whether this might explain the apparent contradiction in the distribution of places of manufacture, well away from the centres of maximum deposition of those objects. The higher ranks in the core areas were able to maintain their ascendancy over the peripheries, who were responsible for the making of the objects. The distribution of hoards could again reflect this pattern of core and periphery, although the manufacturers in the peripheries may have been capable of deposits in their own right too. We shall consider whether this could be the nature of some of the so-called 'scrap' hoards, although these will require very careful definition, if we are to differentiate them from hoards simply of 'broken' pieces.

8. At the end of the Bronze Age, bronze was supplanted by a new raw material – iron – which was more widely available. The basis of the long-distance alliances and exchange was removed, and the whole social system collapsed at this point. Core areas, such as the Thames Valley, went into temporary decline, and peripheral areas, such as Wessex, fell back on their agricultural potential in order to re-build their position. The decline of this system and its prestige base is thought to have led to the 'debased' nature of deposits at the transition to the Iron Age, with poor quality token objects being deposited in hoards, as in the case of the Armorican axes with their low bronze content and high levels of lead. These would have been functionally useless. Was this a final attempt to save the system, using poor quality deposits? If so, did it fail in the face of the new material, when this was used for its novelty value, as perhaps in the hoard from Melksham? These transitional hoards are few however, and we must consider 'late' hoards in detail, if we are to address these issues.

As such, these suggestions must not be treated too dogmatically, but their explanatory value becomes obvious. It is senseless to view the tribes of the Bronze Age as subject to market factors more appropriate to modern capitalism, but by examining the ways in which capitalist systems have developed out of 'primitive' societies, we can begin to understand which factors are most relevant to this research. The artefacts, in our case the bronze objects in the hoards, played a real role in the social structure and could have been inextricably bound up in the types of process outlined above. We cannot hope to understand such things from the artefacts alone, but we can begin to put this material to work.

PART II

ANALYSIS

CHAPTER 4

THE METHOD

INTRODUCTION

Our literature survey, our discussion of the Bronze Age, and the explanatory model have all highlighted various areas for research and the reasons for undertaking a further study of hoard material. Various suggestions were put forward at the end of the last chapter, concerning the patterns in the hoard material to be expected according to the basic model. These patterns might be detected by analysis of the different facets of the hoards and their deposition. Thus, it was felt that distribution could indicate shifts from core to periphery within the social system. Context could be considered to see if there are any distinctions between hoards from different locations. The content of the hoards could be analysed to see if there are any compositional patterns, reflecting the contemporary social hierarchy; and the wear on the objects themselves could be analysed to detect any phases of increased circulation time, that might point to periods of stress within the social system. Related aspects, such as the weight of metal contained within hoards, can also be examined. These points will be developed here with a consideration of how best the material could be examined, followed by an outline of the actual methods used. This will form the basis of our consideration of the data listed in the catalogue and appendices.

Initially, it was proposed to catalogue hoards noting all the available information, to analyse their distributions, and then to seek significant correlations between their different attributes. An analysis of wear was seen as an adjunct to this work, as Kristiansen's research in this field had already provided such interesting results (discussed in Chapters 1 and 3; further detailed examination below). In the event, the analysis of wear patterns on hoard finds came to dominate the study. This new examination of the objects produced much fresh information: far more than the published sources would suggest. The justification for these apparently new methods of studying Bronze Age hoards already existed in the published articles: Evans obviously used a kind of scale of wear in his hoard descriptions (1881, 458–9); other authors noted that the contents of hoards had been carefully selected from the range of objects in use at the time. However, nobody had followed up these observations systematically. Kristiansen had demonstrated that striking patterns could be discerned from a solid analysis of the data. So what should we look for? What indicates wear?

WEAR

Obviously, our judgments can only be subjective, simple observations, unless we make an exact replica of the items and subject them to the treatment which could have produced the variations in shape and the surface changes that we observe. A number of writers have considered this topic. Rowlands drew together observations on the manufacture and working of palstaves. He noted that "the broad crescentic blade edge characteristic of many of the shield pattern palstaves is the cumulative result of a number of such stages in resharpening and was not a desired effect produced immediately after casting" (1976, 15). He went on: "Grinding marks can quite often be seen on the blade faces of spearheads which suggests that the surfaces of the casting were smoothed with a fine sand mixture and the blade edges were ground sharp" (1976, 15). Kristiansen demonstrated how garments could produce wear on ornaments and sword hilts, because of the movements of the wearer (1978 (published in English, 1985); 1983). Coombs observed sharpening and use marks on socketed axes from the Watford and Figheldean hoards (1979b, 199–203; 1979a, 256–60), but did not systematise this information, only remarking that "...post casting work certainly changes the shape of the axe" (1979a, 253). Farley made some similar remarks on the Aylesbury hoard, noting that, although the cutting edges of most of the axes were damaged, they were perfectly serviceable, and he was able to distinguish marks caused by recent handling from ancient damage (1979a, 140), a problem which Hodges warned against (1976, 206). Both Farley and Coombs referred to Curwen's paper on the hoard from Sompting, Sussex (1948). Curwen was able to show that two axes from the same mould had different degrees of expansion on their cutting edges due to sharpening (1948, 162–3). More hammering may have been necessary because of greater use. The swords from the Watford hoard gave occasion for a detailed study by Savage (1979). Savage was able to determine marks of manufacture, maintenance, repaired damage, tolerated damage, and final breakage (1979, 223). From this he was able to determine the 'life history' of each of the swords from this hoard and went into considerable detail on the occurrence, for example, of striking with another blade causing V–notches, which would then be ground down (1979, 226). All of these features could be taken together to illustrate the state of wear of the item at deposition and were applied to a number of other swords in a more wide–ranging study on the life–cycle of bronze swords (Savage, pers. comm.). However, the use of glass bristle brushes on corroded surfaces, when cleaning bronzes, may give rise to some random scratching of the surface, similar to the grinding marks discussed above.

Thus, the work of these authors suggested that some sort of intuitive classification of wear would be possible: various factors could be seen to be common to all objects, for example marks of abrasion, the hammering out of cutting edges, the tearing of rivet holes, and the simple cleaning up of objects after casting. Having selected the material and area of study, examination could proceed along these lines.

Preparatory work

It was necessary first of all to start a catalogue of the hoards to provide the data base. It was decided to examine hoard material from southern Britain for ease of access, travelling, and expense. Also, there is enough difference in concentrations of material in this well-worked area to suggest significant distribution patterns. To narrow the field slightly and to make the material more manageable, four particular regions were selected for study: East Anglia, the Thames Valley, Wessex, and the South West. These were crudely defined according to county boundaries, with East Anglia being made up of Cambridgeshire (including the former county of Huntingdonshire), Norfolk, and Suffolk, without Essex because of possible distortions from built-up areas around London and the influence of the Lower Thames. The Thames Valley consists of the Middle and Upper Thames and the respective hinterlands, the counties concerned being Berkshire, Buckinghamshire, Oxfordshire, and Gloucestershire. Wessex consists of Hampshire, including the Isle of Wight, Dorset, and Wiltshire, an area which coincides in broad terms with Piggott's original definition (1938, 53), as modified by Grinsell (1941, 73), but lacking Sussex and Surrey. Obviously, some of the sites listed under Berkshire in the Thames Valley section could also be in Wessex. Finally, the South West is conceived of as Avon, Somerset, and Devon, without Cornwall, giving a low-lying area surrounded by higher ground, and again including some sites from Gloucestershire. Indeed, all of these regions are designed to have some overlap at the edges and can partly be considered as a convenient way of dividing up the material for study. These regions were each mapped at a scale of 1:250,000.

Having defined our area of study, the subsequent approach was twofold: the inception of the catalogue and the canvassing of museums in the study areas. In order to make the catalogue as comprehensive and useful as possible, as much information as could be obtained from various sources would have to be recorded in a standard way. Published catalogues were examined and compared, those of Rowlands (1976) and Needham (1979) being among the best. This problem was also discussed with Stuart Needham at the British Museum, and it was decided to use the same headings as the National Bronze Index (NBI) housed there, thus ensuring a degree of compatability in the information recorded. The NBI was then used to provide preliminary entries of hoards in the study areas, alongside the published catalogues of other workers in the field and a literature search of the relevant local journals. Later, visits to museums provided information on individual hoards through their indexes, and revealed a number of examples not mentioned elsewhere. Additions were continually made to the catalogue, and descriptive entries of hoard contents have been added after examination of the actual objects. As much detail as possible is entered for the circumstances of discovery to enable a more complete picture of the find-spots to be built up, and to refine the grid references, which were otherwise worked out from the hoard names when they were not available from other sources. A note of the present and past collections in which the material has been placed enabled the writer to compile a list of museums to be visited in addition to those approached initially. The bibliography or sources for individual hoards are as complete as possible. The resulting catalogue would seem to be a fairly full list of all the hoards discovered and available, in publication or from first-hand observation, within the study regions (Appendix A). No attempt has been made to include finds reported or discovered since the study was carried out in 1980–81, although more recent references to the listed hoards have been included.

Meanwhile, the relevant county and local museums had been indexed from the publication "Museums and Art Galleries in Great Britain and Ireland – 1979" (ABC, 1979), and a standard letter was progressively sent to each requesting information, and giving advance warning of the intention to visit and examine any material concerned. The catalogue and other sources provided museums not listed in this way. The staff of all visited museums are acknowledged elsewhere. The reply of individual museums to this letter was varied or sometimes non-existent. Most museums managed a fairly prompt reply, stating what they had or a source where this information was available. Some museums had to be prompted a second time, stating what was known to be there. A few museums found it impossible to reply in any way at all. However, these were minor collections, with perhaps one or two objects each, and were not visited. Unfortunately, there is no other way of finding out about the collections of a museum. Nevertheless, it eventually proved possible to build up some sort of timetable of visits, although some repeated journeys could not be avoided.

Observations

The method of examination for the material had now been devised and was tested by inspection of a variety of material at Reading Museum, because this was conveniently close at hand. This led to refinement of the recording and the establishment of a set procedure, designed to produce consistent results. Objects were recorded with a number of crude numerical scales, using simple observation by eye, dimension and weight measurements with ruler and cheap, folding scales, and examination through a good x20 hand lens. This last allowed observations on the surface condition of individual objects, and the recording of the state of various attributes, such as casting seams and rivet holes. The entries were recorded, and the descriptions and comments subsequently transcribed to the catalogue (Appendix A), and the measurements to the list of results (Appendix B). The features recorded were as follows:

1. Number allocated to the object by the museum
2. Object number, according to the order examined
3. A simple description of the object
4. Whether the object was complete or not (Yes/No)
5. The length (or diameter – D) in millimetres
6. The present state of the object: patinated, cleaned, eroded, or diseased (P, C, E, D)
7. Weight of the object in grams
8. Ancient surface marks: 1) hammering, 2) fine, or 3) coarse

scratches
9. State of the loop or rivet–hole: 1) as cast, 2) cleaned out, 3) worn or torn
10. State of the casting seams: 1) as cast, 2) filed down, 3) hammered out, or 4) completely obliterated
11. The state of the edge: A) asymmetrical, 1) as cast, 2) hammered out, 3) resharpened, 4) notched, 5) broken, 6) milled, 7) bevelled
12. Any remarks on the state of the edge, the object, and so on.

Some of these headings need to be explained in more detail. Ancient surface marks can be detected with the aid of the hand lens: hammering (1) was associated with the working of the object in preparation for use or re–sharpening; fine scratch marks (2) were felt to indicate some kind of polishing or finishing of the object; deeper scrapes (3) could result from heavy usage or damage, the latter possibly since deposition. The loops and rivet holes were examined to see whether they were blocked, as would be expected with a fresh casting (1), whether they were simply cleared for use (2), or whether they were pulled or broken through use (3). The casting seams were sometimes visible around the objects, more prominently with their flashing from the moulds present (1), or worked down in some way such as grinding (2), or hammering (3), until at times they had been completely removed (4). The edge of an object, where it has one, should give the clearest indications of use and the degree of wear of that piece. Asymmetry (A) usually occurred with axes, probably due to the differential wear and sharpening of the blade in use. Casting seams would still be present on an as–cast edge (1). Some use was felt to be indicated by a hammering out of the edge (2); heavier use by further hammering for re–sharpening, typically producing on axes a widely curved blade with points (3). Damage to the edge could be seen in the form of notches (4), or breakage of the edge (5). Milling of a fine sharp edge could be detected with swords and spearheads (6); a coarser grinding of an edge could produce a bevel (7). These simple scales covered most cases encountered and could be supplemented by written descriptions when necessary. They are admittedly rather idiosyncratic and could lead to bias in observation, other factors being overlooked, but they were easy to apply and rapid to use on a large sample. In later analysis, it was found useful to reduce these observations to a generalised scale of wear, graded from A, for as cast, to E, for heavily worn, with NC for the unclassifiable element; this works because wear tends to affect the same groups of attributes in similar ways. Following this detailed examination of each object and its recording – on average, 60 objects were examined per day at a rate of roughly 6 minutes per object – the whole hoard would then be photographed. Due to the travelling, this process was refined to require the minimum of equipment: a camera with a standard lens (50 mm), a wide–angle lens (28mm), a flashgun, and centimetre scales. Black–and–white film was generally used – Ilford FP4 or Kodak Plus–X Pan – and the objects usually simply photographed in rows, laid out left to right, top to bottom, in the order in which they had been examined. The results are to be seen in the accompanying plates (1–117), which are adequate for record purposes. This saved considerable time on individual drawing, especially as many items already have published drawings.

Museum visiting was carried out periodically from April 1980 to October 1981 with continued work on the catalogue. A return visit was later made to Reading Museum to finish the recording of the hoards there, and remarkable consistency was found between the observations made at the outset and the new ones. This would suggest that the recording method is accurate, despite its limitations. Some visits were plagued by the inefficiency of the museums, many of whom failed to have looked out the material in readiness, resulting in some cases in the discovery that the objects were lost or in conservation. One trip was effectively wasted: at Dorchester Museum in Dorset, the majority of the objects were locked into cases, which apparently had no keys, or had been lost, unlabelled, in the metalwork store. Fortunately, this was not very often the case, and it was eventually possible to examine a sizeable proportion of the Bronze Age hoards from southern Britain.

TRIP TO DENMARK

Having established that it was possible and justifiable to record wear on objects from hoards in southern England, it was obviously of critical importance to compare these results with those of Kristiansen, which inspired this work. I therefore undertook a study trip to Copenhagen from 21 to 30 April 1981 to discuss his methods with Kristiansen and to examine his data at first hand. He was able to demonstrate how his study had been carried out, using material mainly in the National Museum, which I was then able to examine myself. Some of these Danish bronzes had also been used by Levy in her work (discussed in Chapter 1). The trip was successful in elucidating several points, enumerated here.

1. Various degrees of wear show very clearly on ornaments by the very nature of the objects themselves: they were designed to be worn. Sword hilts also exhibit this, due to the way in which they were worn on the person and rubbed by clothing. The nature of that clothing is apparent from the rich and well–preserved Danish burials. Sword blades also show different degrees of sharpening and re–sharpening with consequent changes in blade profiles: a point often ignored when deriving classifications from blade shape (Kristiansen, pers. comm.; 1978; 1984a, 189, Abb. 1; 1985).
2. Hoards of women's ornaments show various degrees of wear within individual groups. For example, the hoard from Simested, Rinds in Viborg Amt (Levy, 1982, 147 No. 273) has a large hanging vessel with decoration, which is not very worn but rather roughly applied, and it also has several holes in it, which have been repaired from behind. The neckring has quite smooth twists, which are not heavily worn, but the fibula has no pin and the decoration on it is very worn and smooth. So, if these were the possessions of one person, they must have been acquired gradually, or have come at the same time from previous owners. Alternatively, they were accumulated from several people and then deposited together. These variable factors could introduce some bias into Kristiansen's analysis which is based on the proportions

of examples exhibiting different degrees of wear. Also, he has actually selected material which exhibits wear best, and this gives rise to another bias, involving the representativeness of his sample.

3. There are other issues arising from a study of the objects themselves. For example, worn sword blades with new hilts are known, and there is much more material available for study from hoards, graves, and single finds. We should not restrict ourselves to the ornaments and swords, which could reflect quite specialised processes at work. For example, if we assume that axes are commonplace tools, do they exhibit long or short circulation times – in the same ways as the richer display items? Or were these also affected by differential access to the bronze sources, giving us a long circulation time for an axe, when the owner could not gather enough wealth for a new one? Again, it may be that axes are in fact rich possessions; the examples which have been discovered as single finds do not exhibit great degrees of wear, although they have plainly been used.

4. The zones, around which Kristiansen's analyses are based, are rather arbitrary, although, like my own regions in southern England, they do reflect some geographical reality. If Kristiansen were to do the analyses again, he would study the material within different geographical units (pers. comm.; 1980, 3, footnote 6). How this would affect the region by region, period by period analysis is a problem: for instance, if Zones 3 and 4 in Period III were combined, this would significantly increase the proportion of heavily worn examples in relation to unworn examples for the whole area (Kristiansen, 1979, Fig. 3).

5. A feature of Kristiansen's data gathering and subsequent analysis is the simplicity of the procedures that he used; for example, much work can be done from the published catalogues, which are of good quality, without recourse to the objects every time (Kristiansen, pers. comm.). The wear scale can then be derived from a simple inspection of the material, tracings of decoration, notes on profiles, and so on. Since this is a simple system, various computer analyses are possible for speedy data sorting and comparison (Kristiansen, pers. comm.).

6. Hoards have certain ascribed functions in Denmark, just as they do in Britain. Inspection of the Danish material with adequate contexts highlights the role of 'votive finds', which are really treated as a separate category of objects. These came from bogs and other 'wet places' and are considered to have some ritual function; this also includes single finds (Jensen, 1972; pers. comm.). This categorisation is readily accepted by Kristiansen, and he selects this material quite freely for his analyses (1979, 159), just as Levy assumed that ritual hoards are total assemblages for the purpose of her analysis and did not consider that particular items could have been selected for deposition (1977, 147). Both of these authors are considering different facets of a social model using a specific data base, so this should not surprise us, although the representativeness of the material must again be questioned, a point later stressed by Levy herself (1982, 4). We should not preempt analysis by accepting simplistic categorisations at the outset.

There can be no doubt that more questions could be posed and answered about this work and treatment of the material, despite this already lengthy outline of points raised. The trip helped me not only to understand the practical side of Kristiansen's work (and incidentally Levy's theories), not by contradicting it, but certainly by complementing it. It also allowed me to come to grips with some of the theoretical issues involved. Although my comments and criticisms may in some ways seem rather negative, Kristiansen's data analysis remains a source of inspiration, and one with considerable potential. The role of the theory in his work has already been considered (Chapter 3).

REPRESENTATIVENESS

How representative are our observations? This question is obviously important in considering our results. Would a more intensive search of the sources make a difference? In Suffolk, for example, Lawson has managed to list at least 48 hoards through intensive searching and local enquiry (pers. comm.): there are 42 in the catalogue (Appendix A), not all of them certain. However, uncertainty clouds most reported discoveries, and it is impossible to be more thorough. We cannot be sure of the rate of loss or non–discovery, two topics touched on in Chapter 1, although we shall attempt some rudimentary calculations. We can compare the number of hoards examined to those not examined, out of the possible total, and also the likely proportion of separate objects examined: Table 2.

Table 2: Numbers of hoards and objects examined

Region	Number of hoards		Number of objects		
	Examined	Total	Examined	Not examined in hoards seen	Total
TV	20	37	208	20	289
SW	27	41	341	136	543
W	57	80	573	70	842
EA	96	141	2152	6377*	8803
Total	200	299	3274	6603	10477

* 6245 of these pieces came from the Isleham hoard, which it was impossible to examine in more detail.

These figures can only be approximations, since some of these groups were not definitely hoards. There is often a discrepancy in the number of objects listed and those actually available for study, and not all accounts give precise figures for the contents of the hoards. In such cases, the totals have been estimated to fit in with the suggested amount at recovery ('dozens', 'a number', etc). Nevertheless, these figures are a suggestion of the material potentially available. We can provide percentages as a basis for more direct comparison: Tables 3 and 4. Again, these cannot be absolute because of the limitations of the original estimates.

Table 3: The hoards and objects as a percentage of the regional totals

Region	Percentage hoards		Percentage objects	
	Examined	Not examined	Examined	Not examined
TV	54%	46%	72%	28%
SW	66%	34%	63%	37%
W	71%	29%	68%	32%
EA	68%	32%	24% (82%)	76% (18%)

Table 4: The hoards and objects as a percentage of the overall total

	Percentage hoards		Percentage objects	
Region	Examined	Not examined	Examined	Not examined
TV	7%	6%	2% (5%)	1% (2%)
SW	9%	4%	3% (9%)	2% (5%)
W	19%	8%	5% (14%)	3% (7%)
EA	32%	15%	21% (48%)	63% (10%)
Total	67%	33%	31% (76%)	69% (24%)

The figures in brackets indicate the percentages of objects without the Isleham hoard, if we leave this out as an exceptional case; its exclusion does not greatly affect the percentage of hoards examined.

These figures indicate that a sizeable proportion of the available hoards have been examined (about two–thirds) and a fair proportion of the available objects (over two–thirds, if Isleham is not considered). On a regional basis, coverage of hoards and objects has usually been fairly good (over half), but even a quarter of the objects from East Anglia examined provides a reasonable basis for discussion given their frequency. As percentages of the total number of hoards in southern Britain, the other regions pale in comparison to East Anglia, but this reflects the huge amount of material deposited in this region. This is also demonstrated by the figures for individual objects, even if Isleham is disregarded. Given that about 60 objects could be recorded per day, the whole sample took 11 working weeks to examine; another 24 weeks would have been necessary to examine the remainder, including Isleham (3 weeks if not), but two–thirds of these objects would have been unavailable. Therefore, it does not seem unreasonable to base more complex calculations on this sample. Examination of more material is unlikely to change the results significantly. Of the estimated 6,500 objects from Isleham, 255 were examined, and these are used in the calculations as if they were the complete contents of a hoard. In any case, a large proportion of the metal from Isleham is plate scrap, which is unclassifiable in the terms of our analysis.

How far do the available and recorded samples reflect the past situation? As discussed in Chapter 1, both Kristiansen (1974) and Needham (1981) have considered this problem in some detail. Kristiansen plotted the frequency of hoards discovered according to years of registration for the whole of Denmark, as well as regionally, and also considered those finds resulting from various recent activities. He was able to conclude that the sample would not be significantly increased in the future (1974, 160). Indeed, the graph shows a decrease in discoveries in recent times (Kristiansen, 1974, 127, Fig. 1). Similar information about the British hoards has been abstracted from the catalogue: date of discovery was given in most cases or worked out from the first report or even the museum number. Despite the lack of precision, it gives some working figures. The way in which the object was discovered is often more scantily reported, but it has been possible to assign significant numbers to particular categories. The dates of discovery have been plotted as 9–year blocks from 1735, the first recorded hoard, to the present, with the bars representing the number discovered in each block (Figs. 1–3). The diagrams have also been subdivided according to the four regions. Uncertain hoards have been left out and the diagrams have been modified in the case of poorly recorded examples from the National Bronze Index, where discovery 'before 1950?' is more of a guess than an informed estimate. The diagrams show two interesting peaks: one just before the 1880s, and the other after the Second World War. The peak at 1881 marks the publication of Evans' book, which drew together many of the recent or contemporary accounts of hoards, and that after 1940 reflects the intensification of agriculture for the war effort and the increase of modern arable farming since that time (Groube and Bowden, 1982, 8). These graphs would suggest a slight fall in discoveries in recent years, being particularly intermittent in the South West, but at a fairly high level in East Anglia. Therefore, we can hardly be sure that all the hoards have now been found and our sample must be biassed by this fact. Figure 4 is an attempt to separate out some of the factors, which gave rise to these discoveries. It can be seen that factors such as excavation or accidental recovery yield a slow rate of discoveries, while discoveries due to agriculture and construction seem to be on the increase. The effects of quarrying on archaeological recovery seem to be non–existent in recent times, and peat cutting seems to have been a short–lived reason for discoveries, probably due to the replacement of manual cutting methods by machine stripping. A very recent innovation, of course, is metal detecting, which seems to be giving a sharp increase in the recovery rate. Drainage and mains trenches give a steady trickle of finds. The 'accidental' category includes finds from gardens and other diverse methods of recovery, such as watercress bed digging (W23) or explosives disposal (W70); it could be argued that most categories of discovery are accidental, but it is a convenient way of expressing the rest. The majority of finds recovered through agriculture are, of course, due to ploughing, and it is precisely the post–war increase in this activity which we can see reflected in this graph. Regionally, the most significant contribution to these figures comes from East Anglia, where vast areas of reclaimed fen are now subject to arable methods; the drastic increase of such agriculture in other regions such as Wessex, where the destruction of monuments is so critical (Groube and Bowden, 1982), does not seem to have greatly affected the rate of recovery.

This would seem again to reflect the prehistoric situation: in some areas, the hoards were not there in great numbers in the first place, whereas the situation in East Anglia is still in a state of flux. This is perhaps especially true of East Anglia, as the metal detecting line shows an increase due almost entirely to finds made here, although this may reflect the close association of archaeologists in this area with this particular fraternity (Lawson, 1979b, 173): in other areas, finds may be more readily disposed of without notification. However, the same emphasis on East Anglia is reflected in most of the other methods of recovery; only Wessex has a slight predominance in the case of finds from construction work or 'accidental' discoveries. Therefore, despite the variations described above, there seems to be a constant rate

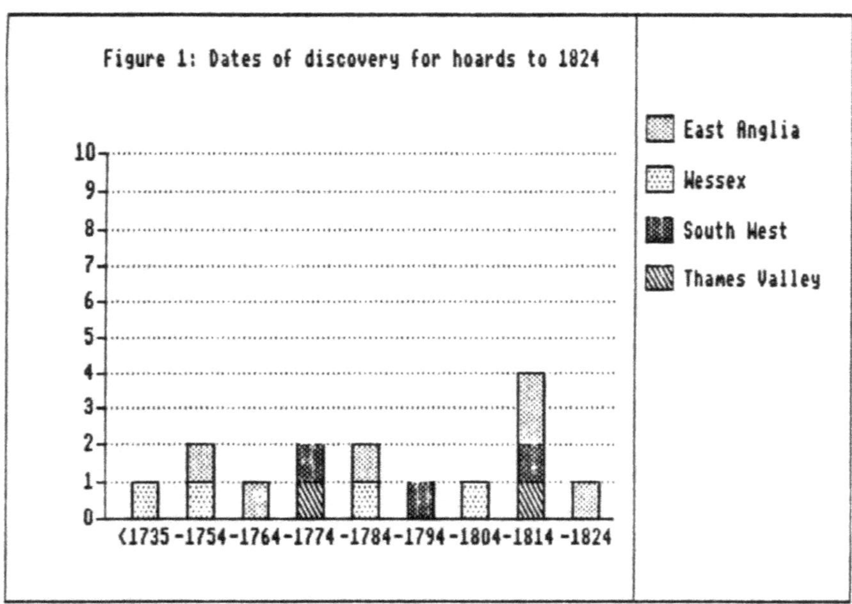

Figure 1: Dates of discovery for hoards to 1824

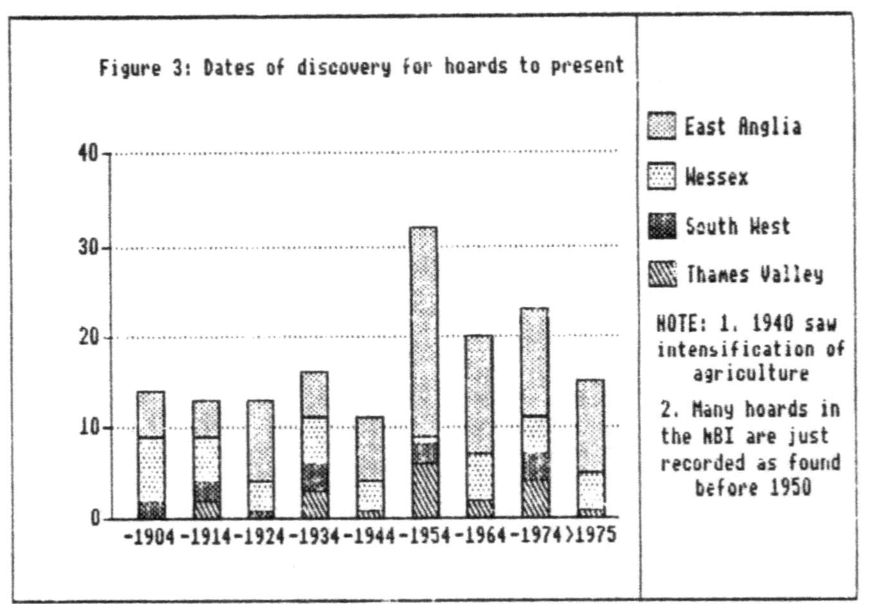

Figure 3: Dates of discovery for hoards to present

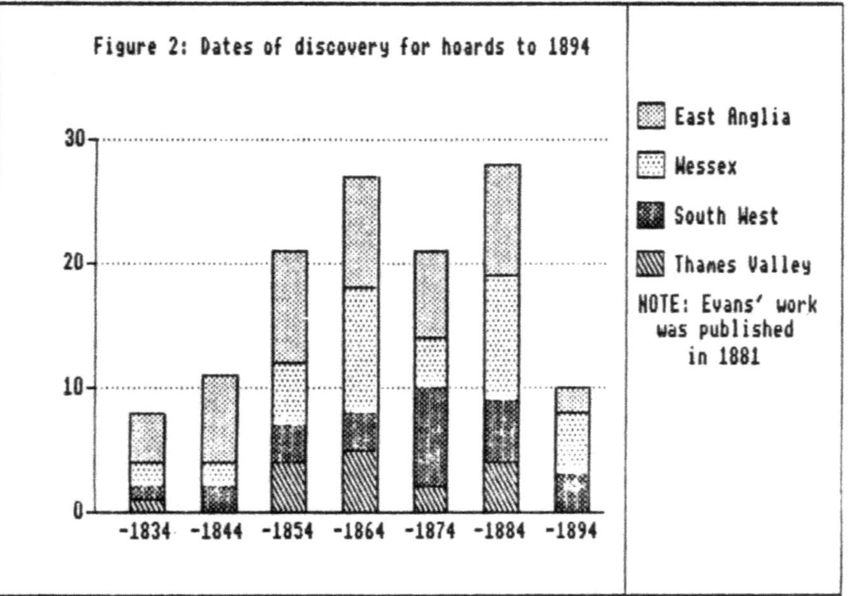

Figure 2: Dates of discovery for hoards to 1894

Figure 4: Dates of discovery for hoards according to factor

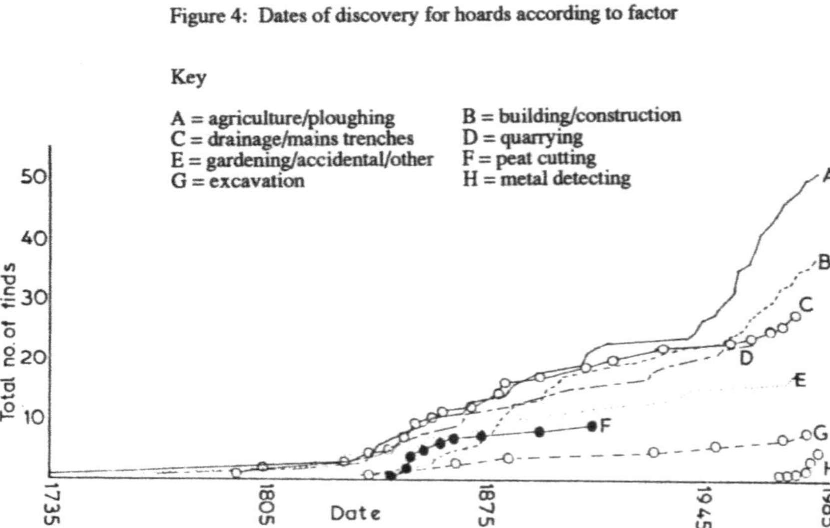

of recovery, which is far from dying out. This must influence the completeness of our distribution maps and the other results of our analysis.

Needham offered a more complicated approach to rates of recovery and associated factors (1981, 40ff). He was concerned to predict the likely ratio of bronze products to stone moulds. He showed that the actual number of objects recovered would be a small sample in proportion to the number of objects originally deposited (1981, 49, Fig. 13). We can calculate recovery rates for particular activities from our graph (Fig. 4); whether these will continue to obtain is another matter. Thus, the line for agriculture would seem to break into 3 segments, giving roughly:

1735–1838 1 find every 26 years
1838–1939 1 find every 5 years
1939–1980 1 find every 1.5 years

This suggests that the rate of discovery increases by a factor of about 5, implying the future recovery of 1 find every 3 or 4 months and assuming a continued increase in the uptake of land for agriculture. This is unlikely, now that mechanisation seems to have reached a peak, and the amount of land left unploughed is decreasing. The rate of discovery must slacken at some point; but when? Unfortunately, there are not enough figures on the depth of finds to suggest any correlation with an increase in deep ploughing, for example; the few figures would suggest a remarkably constant depth of discovery, with only a few exceptions found at greater depths. We can compare this with the rates of discovery from building and construction, activities which probably involve deeper excavation:

1835–1899 1 find every 10.5 years
1899–1950 1 find every 3 years
1950–1979 1 find every 2 years

Again, the figures for finds from drainage and mains trenches are important:

1794–1881 1 find every 5.5 years
1881–1931 1 find every 8.3 years
1931–1974 1 find every 7 years

Here, we see an increase in the recent rate of recovery in construction work, but finds from trenching seem to have become less frequent, although the situation may now be changing. Of course, these figures are rather crude representations, but they are worth comparing with recovery rates from two other agencies. The finds from excavation are divided into 2 parts:

1837–1928 1 find every 18 years
1928–1977 1 find every 16 years

Metal detecting is a recent development and provides only a small sample:

1968–1977 1 find every 4.5 years
1977–1980 1 find every year

Thus, the 'scientific' recovery of objects has always been very slow and this remains the case, while the deliberate search for antiquities recovers them more rapidly than recent agricultural activity.

Taken together, this would suggest that a considerable proportion of hoards still remain in the ground, but that the day when this rate will fall is also fast approaching. We also have no idea of what was recovered before 1735, particularly since remelting for metal has always been a problem and took place as recently as 1971 (Coombs, 1979a, 253). Our ancestors probably had less scruples about re–using antiquities, particularly when the law of Treasure Trove was designed to swell the coffers of the Treasury! Despite these caveats, we are left with our present sample to work on, and we can only hope that future finds will not significantly differ in character from this material. This particular aspect of the material should not seriously affect the observations on wear, outlined above, but it must still be taken into account.

EFFECTIVENESS OF THE METHOD

So far, we have outlined how the study of wear in hoards from southern England can be initiated and carried out, and methods have been compared with those applied to Danish material. We have also considered the representativeness of this material. Where discussions with other experts have helped to refine the observations, this has already been noted. The correction of my own work on re–visiting the collections at Reading has also been recorded. Other comments have been received after some preliminary presentations of the results of this research at lectures and conferences: for example, at the Fourth Theoretical Archaeology Group Conference (Durham, 13 to 15 December, 1981). Here, a consideration of hoards in the terms of rubbish deposition was presented and attracted comment on the applicability of the method. Questions centred around how we can detect wear at all, and how we can compare wear between objects of different functions. The presentation of other authors' observations on wear (above) demonstrates that we can detect this feature within hoards. However, the problem of comparing wear between a weapon and an ornament, for example, is harder to answer. At the root of this problem is the question of how the wear was caused in each case. Obviously, this would be through a particular use, but we must ask whether, for example, tools were more often used than weapons, and thus more susceptible to wear or to different forms of wear? Were ornaments worn all the time on the person or only occasionally? These are specifics which are probably impossible to answer, but we can observe the important fact that collections of objects with different amounts of wear on them were deposited together. Given the nature and content of most deposits, it is unlikely that this will be a problem of comparison, especially as we have no idea whether many hoards were really a collection of personal objects deposited at one time by one person from their own personal possessions. It may also be stressed that the approach aroused interest and supportive comment.

Another test of the method would be the comparison of some of my results against those derived from metallurgy and scientific analysis of a collection of objects. The only comprehensive report of this kind is that of Coghlan (1970) on the hoard from Yattendon, Berkshire (TV12). He made observations on a selection of the objects, where this was not precluded by the poor state of the metal, and found that in general they had been cold-worked to harden the cutting edges, except for the spearheads (1970). My observations on the same examples showed that some were worn and the majority were heavily worn. However, the hoard as a whole was very fragmentary, and we cannot place too much weight on observations in either case. Of the spearheads, Coghlan states that "the results suggest differences in fabrication technique and that the cutting-edges of the blades were not invariably heated and worked after casting" (1970, Notes on the groups). It is unlikely that this sort of scientific examination can be paralleled by surface observation and vice versa; therefore, a scientific check on the results presented here is difficult and perhaps not possible. Nevertheless, in this particular case it would seem justifiable to suggest that the majority of objects had been prepared for use and had subsequently been well worn. A much larger programme of sampling and sectioning is also needed, such as that presented by Northover (1982).

Northover has used metallurgy and metallography on an extensive series of samples from Bronze Age objects from all across Britain, on the basis of which he has begun to be able to make statements about bronze production and distribution across time (1982). He has been able to show that alloy differences within phases of the Bronze Age indicate changes in the sources of supply of raw materials or already processed metal (1982, 70). Interestingly, Northover has been able to extend analysis beyond the Early Bronze Age, which has been traditionally the subject of much of this kind of research, to the Late Bronze Age, when it has often been assumed that recycling of metal led to the mixing of alloys, thus confusing the derivation of sources for the metal. In fact, he has found that single sources of metal were in use in the Late Bronze Age, so that recycling of that metal did not involve much mixing with other alloys (1982, 50). This in turn has led to the identification of metal circulation zones, within which metal of a common source is used to make bronze products, although differentiation between everyday and prestige objects does occur, probably because its production was differently organised in each case; metal did not move in bulk across the boundaries of these zones, except in the case of the prestige items (Northover, 1982, 51). In the initial stages of copper and bronze working in Britain, metal seems to have been obtained fairly locally either from Ireland or from within Britain, but with the advance of the Bronze Age, Britain becomes part of a European metal supply zone (Northover, 1982, 51–9). During the later Bronze Age, Europe seems to supply most of the British metal, probably in the form of scrap, but there is also some use of local sources, with the 'foreign' metal perhaps reserved for the more prestigious items (Northover, 1982, 59–67). Northover indicated that the actual process of production could have more effect on the final use of an object, for example tool production in metal moulds allowed extensive cold re-working, which weapon production in clay moulds could not match (1982, 70). The importance of this work is clear, but still limited in its application, and it is hard to relate it to the nature of the analysis undertaken here. For this reason, metallurgy has not been used at all in the presentation of the hoard data analysed for wear patterns.

COMPUTER ANALYSIS

The nature of our records of wear and related factors lends itself to analysis by computer. This was also an attractive proposition because of the sheer volume of data recorded for all the individual objects in a number of hoards. Computer analysis could help to sort out large quantities of information – an impossible task by hand – and would give some depth to the results. Nevertheless, the computer analyses were themselves time-consuming exercises, and the results still had to be interpreted. Here, a description is given of the various procedures employed to assist in the analysis of this material: no doubt, the research could have been better designed to fit in with computer analysis, and the more extensive use of computers could gain further and deeper insights into the complex nature of hoards, but available computing capacity grew and changed during the course of this research. Cheap personal computers have since become commonplace. Future research should benefit from these possibilities: for example, a portable microcomputer would have made the task of recording observations and subsequent analysis much simpler and quicker.

Some tests were done using automatic clustering procedures on all the observations for complete axes, the best represented objects in the hoards, on mainframe computers: an ICL 1904S and Nord 500 of the University of Reading Computer Centre. These clustering procedures have been used before in archaeology, particularly by Hodson (1970, 299–320), although he eventually concluded that a K-means procedure was more satisfactory than other methods of clustering. Orton has summarised other work (1980, Chap. 2). However, we can subject our data to cluster analysis, using a library program available at Reading, called here ASF4, which offers a variety of flexible approaches. The program is particularly useful for sorting and classifying large numbers of related observations made on individual items.

Complete axes were analysed because they had the best representation of the variables of wear recorded. Columns were set aside for the condition of surface, loop, casting seams, and edge (as explained previously above). Some variables, which were not consistently recorded for many objects, were omitted, giving 17 columns of information in a form acceptable to the program. Each step of the several scales used in recording was made equal to one column, so that, for example, the edge was defined by A, 1, 2, 3, 4, 5, 6, 7, and each one of these was taken to be one column, with 1 or 0 indicating whether that feature was present or absent in the object. Certain characteristics are more applicable to certain types of axe, of course, and perhaps loopless palstaves should have had an 'unclassifiable' notation or another value for missing data (Sneath and Sokal, 1973, 115). However, 1 and 0 notation to indicate presence/absence was used for the sake of simplicity. Only a limited amount of computing time was available; indeed, since it was not possible to carry out the analysis of more than 100 objects on the ICL computer, the program had to be transferred and run on the Nord research machine, when calculation on more than 500 objects was possible.

The data was punched on computer cards with a unique identification number for each object, and the data files created for Wessex and East Anglia (with more than 100 objects each) were transferred from ICL to Nord for analysis. The program ASF4 allows a number of parameters to be specified and different forms of analysis to be carried out. The method chosen for simplicity and ease of use was Group Average, with a distance measure of unstandardised Euclidean distance. This distance measure is discussed by Sneath and Sokal (1973, 124) and measures the difference between objects (known as Observational Taxonomic Units or OTUs), defined by their variables (or characters), re–ordering the data by dissimilarity in a matrix. This matrix is then stored in the computer and subjected to further analysis, resulting in a final printout in the form of a dendrogram. The Group Average method used is equivalent to the unweighted pair–group method using arithmetic averages (UPGMA) of Sneath and Sokal and "computes the average similarity or dissimilarity of a candidate OTU to an extant cluster, weighting each OTU in that cluster equally, regardless of its structural subdivision" (1973, 230). Therefore, clusters are built up by measuring which are the least dissimilar of the OTUs, and which are the least dissimilar clusters, resulting eventually in a single stem joining the clusters, where all are related. The measure of dissimilarity provides a scale, against which the levels of clusters can be read off (cf Sneath and Sokal, 1973, 230–34). The resultant dendrograms are considered in Chapter 5.

Individual categories of objects were also examined in more detail, extending the analysis beyond that of complete axes as described above, and the amounts of wear between them were compared. This was done for three of our regions – Thames Valley, South West, and Wessex – using a commercial sorting program with the BBC microcomputer: *Collector's Catalogue* by Acornsoft. This program allows data to be entered in a format suitable to the user and then sorted by one or other of the recorded variables or fields, which are defined for each record: a form of electronic card index. All the objects from the hoards examined in these regions were entered into the computer, with details of type, date, wear, and completeness. Limitations of memory space with the BBC microcomputer prevented the use of this program for data from East Anglia. The data for each of these three regions was then sorted by type, date, and wear, so that a simple count could be made of wear by object and date. These were converted into percentages for ease of comparison, and the results are presented in Chapter 5.

The distribution of hoards was also plotted on the BBC microcomputer to enable rapid comparison for different phases and random plotting. This was done using a simple program (App. E: Program 3), which generates a grid of 20 x 20 squares on the screen and plots asterisks as co–ordinate points. The screen co–ordinate points were obtained by measuring the position of each hoard from an origin defined for each regional map and were then entered at the keyboard. A grid of 20 x 20 was used as affording the best approximation of the area covered by regional maps. This fitted with the possible range of the graphics screen of the computer of 1279x1023 points (Coll, 1982, 161 and 495). Therefore, each square on the screen represents a step of 50, or is equivalent to a grid square on the regional map. The screen results were then printed out or 'dumped', using a published screen dump program (Hill, 1984, 86–7), giving a series of figures (Chap. 5). A simple conversion of this plotting program (App. E, Program 4) enables us to plot a random set of co–ordinates for each region, using the microcomputer. The number of required co–ordinates is entered; this must be equivalent to the number of hoards for each region. The possible range of X and Y co–ordinates for each region is determined by inspection of the regional maps. The resulting screen picture is again dumped. The computer calculates random numbers in the range of 0 to the maximum of X and Y, and as such produces 'pseudo–random' numbers (Prigmore, 1981, 146–7), but these should be sufficiently 'random' for our purposes. Also, because it would be complicated, using limited equipment and a simple program, to define exactly the area within which points can occur, for instance the coastline and areas of sea, some of the points generated are impossible in terms of the local topography. However, the majority of points do fall on 'dry land' and provide us with a rough picture of what a random distribution of hoards might look like for each region. These regional results are discussed in Chapter 5.

SUMMARY

The underlying method for a renewed study of Bronze Age hoards in southern England has now been outlined and has been set against the background of earlier work on related material. The representativeness of the sample has also been considered, with special reference to the factors causing hoards to be discovered. It seems that the sample is still increasing, but cannot continue to do so for much longer; in the meanwhile, we probably have a fairly even cover of finds in our four regions on which to assess our distributions. Some space has been devoted to the justification of a 'novel' method of examination: it is felt that this kind of study can suggest wear patterns on British bronzes, and that this is a factor of some interest in the analysis of hoards. We have also compared our working methods with those used in Kristiansen's research on Danish Bronze Age material. The method of recording and analysing data from the objects in hoards has been described, including a review of computer–assisted procedures. The place of metallurgy and metallography in the study of hoards has been briefly outlined and discussed. With all this as background, we can now present a review of our results and their interpretation.

CHAPTER 5

ANALYSIS AND RESULTS

INTRODUCTION

The method for a re–examination of the hoards from southern Britain has been described: now the results of that study are presented, along with our analysis of the raw data. Various aspects are considered, from the chronological correlations of the hoards to their contextual and distributional patterning, and from the weight of the objects to the degree to which they are worn. A summary draws together these results and the archaeological setting for the hoards.

REGIONAL DIFFERENCES IN DEPOSITION

It was observed at the end of Chapter 3 that the relationship between core and periphery would predict a shift in the level of hoarding by period and between regions: we can test this observation by looking at the regional differences in chronological distribution of the hoards. This can be done quite simply on the basis of the number of hoards relating to each phase of the Bronze Age, compared with each other and across regions.The dating for each catalogued hoard was listed according to the four regions, as outlined previously (Chaps. 2 and 4), from which it was possible to calculate the relative proportion of deposits dating to each phase (App. C). Several phases include some examples not certainly attributable to them, but those examples for which it is impossible to determine any dating, are listed as undatable (N.D.). The results were converted into a graph (Fig. 5), using a published computer program (Sandford, 1985, 77–9), from the data in Table 5. A broader chronological division of hoards into MBA2, LBA3, other, and undated (N.D.) can be used to give a visual representation of regional differences (Map 5).

Table 5: Numbers of hoards by phases

	EBA2	MBA1	MBA2	LBA1	LBA2	LBA3	LBA4	EIA1	ND	TOTAL
TV	4	0	10	0	1	21	0	0	1	37
SW	3	0	28	1	0	4	0	0	4	40
W	3	1	38	0	4	15	11	0	7	79
EA	3	0	19	8	5	73	4	1	28	141

Crudely, the graph shows the preponderance of deposition of hoards of LBA3 date in the Thames Valley and East Anglia, whereas MBA2 hoards account for a large proportion of Wessex hoards and nearly three–quarters of all South West hoards. Some phases are not represented at all in some of the regions: for example, there is no MBA1, LBA1, or LBA4 representation in the Thames Valley, no MBA1, LBA2, or LBA4 in the South West, and no LBA1 in Wessex, while East Anglia has all periods but MBA1, although EIA1 here results from one transitional gold hoard.

Thus, phases of deposition seem to occur intermittently across our regions during the Bronze Age, possibly due to a switch to deposition in other forms, or a need to keep the metal in circulation. Alternatively, it could have been passed straight on for re–casting without a significant amount of deposition. This does seem to vary regionally. For example in MBA2, when regions such as Wessex and the South West are probably in the ascendant according to the core/periphery model. This contrasts with the concentration of deposits in the Thames Valley and East Anglia in LBA3. Some phases are poorly represented across all the four regions, and this must represent a phase of restriction in the metal supply in all areas, as well as the channelling of a scarce resource to other kinds of deposit, eg grave goods. The number of LBA4 hoards in Wessex can be taken as the attempt by this region to re–align exchange at the end of the Bronze Age, a process which was ultimately undermined by the appearance of iron.

Hoard weight

Of course, this regional pattern does not account for the size of deposits – it assumes equal importance for each hoard – nor does it take into account the actual quantities of metal involved in deposition: this can be calculated from rough weight measurements taken for the hoards examined in detail (listed in App. B). This cannot be a particularly accurate figure because of the incomplete nature of many of the hoards studied, through loss of objects or separation into different collections, not all of which are accessible. It also leaves out weights of gold in hoards (App. D). We can move from statements about individual hoard weight to an assessment of the regional importance of the weights of metal deposited.

Table 6: Hoard weight

	Total in grams	Number of hoards	Mean in grams
TV	42976	20	2149
SW	55247	26	2125
W	114353	56	2042
EA	373255	90	4147
Total	585831	192	3051

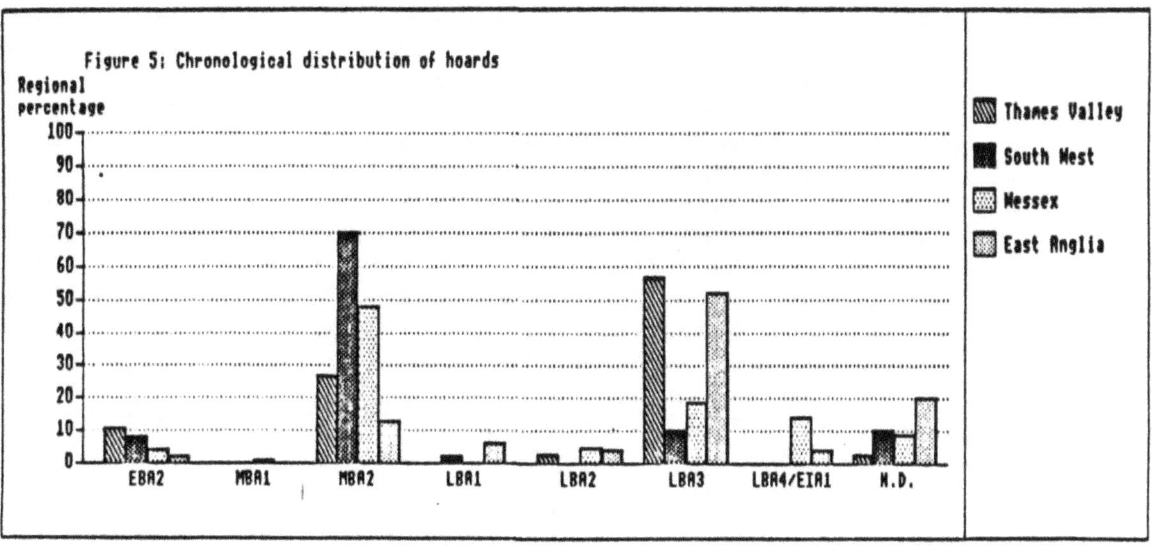

The mean (and standard deviation) are calculated using program 1 (App. E). Interestingly, this shows that the average weight for a hoard in the Thames Valley, the South West, and Wessex was around 2 kg, but twice as much in East Anglia. We can estimate the total weight of bronze from known deposits, if we multiply the remaining hoards, which were not examined, by the mean:

Table 7: Estimated hoard weight

	Non-examined hoards	x mean	Estimated total	Overall total
TV	17	2149	36533	79509
SW	14	2125	29750	84997
W	21	2042	42882	157235
EA	47	4147	194909	568164
Total				889905

Therefore, for the whole of the Bronze Age around 890kg of bronze were deposited, which does not seem to be a particularly vast quantity of metal. It amounts to less than 1 tonne deposited over 1,500 years. Of course, as we have already seen, its deposition varies across the various phases of the Bronze Age, and the weights should be divided up accordingly.

If we look more closely at these figures, we can see how some larger groups have biased the mean weight of these hoards (Table 8).

Table 8: Weights of hoards in grams and their average weights

	Total	Number	Mean	Median	Modal range
TV	42976	20	2149	1095	1- 500
SW	55247	26	2125	943	1- 500
W	114353	56	2042	902	501-1000
EA	373255	90	4147	992	501-1000
TV M2	17064	9	1896	1038	
L3	25912	11	2356	1128	
SW E2	5386	2	2693	2693	
M2	24838	20	1242	856	
L3	23905	3	7968	1520	
W E2	5868	3	1956	2272	
M2	58922	29	2032	869	
L2	10177	4	2544	1424	
L3	19313	13	1486	1106	
L4	14641	6	2440	509	
EA M2	13647	13	1050	732	
L1	4536	7	648	778	
L2	111800	5	22360	519	
L3	238434	61	3909	1350	
L4	2711	3	904	1142	

Thus, the median weight for hoards from all four regions is around 1 kg, while the most commonly occurring weights are in the range of 1–500g for the Thames Valley and South West, whereas Wessex and East Anglia have a range of 501–1000g as the most common. Divided up by period divisions, we can see that the median weight for hoards for each region lies around 0.5 kg to 2.5 kg. This would still suggest that average hoard weights were small: small enough to be transported and handled as personal possessions. The large hoards are the exception: the massive weight of metal in East Anglian hoards, like Isleham and Wilburton, of LBA2 date, which increase the mean weight to over 22 kg, when the median weight for this region is just 0.5 kg. The reasons for this kind of deposit must differ from those accounting for the smaller hoards.

Table 9: Mean weights for complete, examined hoards

		Mean weight in grams	Number of hoards	Standard deviation
TV	All hoards	2275.4	12	3056.3
	MBA2	953.7	4	419.4
	LBA3	2936.3	8	3551.6
SW	All hoards	2930.2	17	4944.9
	EBA2	2693.0	2	1727.0
	MBA2	1764.0	11	1439.9
	LBA1	1118.0	1	0
	LBA3	7968.3	3	9872.5
W	All hoards	1703.9	32	2319.9
	EBA2	1501.0	2	771.0
	MBA1	5432.0	1	0
	MBA2	1658.6	18	2572.1
	LBA2	959.0	3	919.1
	LBA3	1867.3	7	2122.8
	LBA4	289.0	1	0
EA	All hoards	4200.3	56	12564.8
	All but Is'hm	2622.0	55	4611.7
	MBA2	858.3	6	333.3
	LBA1	556.5	4	364.5
	LBA2	30605.0	3	42705.8
	LBA3	3280.8	41	5174.8
	LBA4	755.5	2	386.5

In Table 9 we have taken the total weight of bronze in those hoards, which we know, or can be fairly certain, are complete deposits. The total weight for hoards in East Anglia has been calculated with and without Isleham (EA27), since the weight and total number of objects seems at best an estimate. The total weights, number of objects, and other details are given in Appendix F; weights for gold, iron, and artefacts of other material included in hoards have been subtracted from the individual figures where necessary.

Comparing these figures with those obtained from all the hoards examined, we can see that the mean figures for all hoards in the Thames Valley and East Anglia are very similar, and those for the South West and Wessex are increased by 800g and decreased by 300g respectively: this would represent the weight of less than 5 objects in both cases. However, this does make more of a difference for individual periods in each region: the mean weight for a hoard in MBA2 in the Thames Valley is effectively halved, those for LBA2 and LBA4 in Wessex are greatly reduced, and LBA2 in East Anglia has been greatly increased (again mainly due to the exceptional size of Isleham). Therefore, the overall figures do not seem to have been greatly altered, but we may have a more accurate estimate of mean hoard weight for each of the periods.

We can also calculate the average weight of objects in these complete hoards, since we know how many pieces there are in each hoard:

Table 10: Mean object weight

	Mean hoard weight	Number of hoards	Number of objects	Mean object weight
TV	2275.4	12	156	175
SW	2930.2	19	322	173
W	1703.9	32	287	190
EA(+EA27)	4200.3	56	7594	31
EA(-EA27)	2622.1	55	1094	132

These figures show a close correspondence, disregarding the figure for East Anglia including Isleham, and would suggest that roughly the same kinds of objects were being used in similar proportions to make up the hoards in all the regions. Socketed axes and palstaves dominated and have probably contributed most to these figures. For example, we can take a typical hoard of socketed axes – EA52, Foulsham – and work out the mean weight of the complete examples: 107 axes give a mean weight of 230g, a figure not far removed from those considered above. The nature of a hoard, although exhibiting some regional differences, seems to have had a remarkable conformity across southern Britain.

Returning to the distribution of hoards across time and space, we can use these estimates of weight to calculate a new set of percentages (biased by our sample).

Table 11: Comparing percentages obtained from total numbers and total weights

	EBA2		MBA1		MBA2		LBA1		LBA2		LBA3		LBA4		ND
%	1	2	1	2	1	2	1	2	1	2	1	2	1	2	1
TV	11	0	0	0	27	40	0	0	3	0	57	60	0	0	3
SW	8	10	0	0	70	45	2	2	0	0	10	43	0	0	10
W	4	5	1	5	48	52	0	0	5	9	19	17	14	13	9
EA	2	1	0	0	13	4	6	1	4	30	52	64	3	1	20

Note: 1 = Percentage of total number of hoards, as per Table 5.
2 = Percentage of total weight of hoards, as per Table 9.

Therefore, if the actual weight of metal deposited was an important factor, MBA2 and LBA3 are roughly equal in terms of deposition in the South West, despite the preponderance of MBA2 hoards, whereas in Wessex both seem to be equally represented. The same applies to the Thames Valley, allowing for the bias of our sample, but in East Anglia the deposits of LBA2 and LBA3 seem to be more significant, and those of MBA2 lose some of their importance. Again, we are not comparing like with like, as we have fairly large percentages attributable to undatable hoards, although these can be equally split between the periods, altering the figures only by a few percent. This would suggest that a limited pool of metal existed in each region and that in each period in Wessex and the Thames Valley it was roughly equally divided. By contrast, MBA2 hoards in the South West were reduced in size because of the larger number of deposits, while a very few deposits in LBA2 East Anglia gained more of the metal. This would appear to be a chronological reason for deposition beyond the need of the individual to secure his own deposit.

Remarkably, we have detected a uniformity in the size of the average hoard and its apparent content (in terms of weight content per types of object) for the Bronze Age across the four regions. One phase, LBA2, seems to have seen the deposition of enormous quantities of material in a few hoards, with the majority of that material in one region, East Anglia. However, we can also see that, despite the importance of the South West in MBA2 in terms of numbers of deposits, the same quantities of material were buried in less hoards during LBA3. So, we can see internal differences within our regions, as well as differences between regions during the various phases of the Bronze Age. According to our model, Wessex should have an early importance in terms of deposition and less importance later in the period: this is confirmed both by the number of hoards and the weight of metal deposited. Equally, the Thames Valley later rises to importance in terms of numbers and weight of hoards deposited. The South West seems to have declined in importance in the later Bronze Age with fewer hoards, but the weight of metal equals that of the important MBA2 period of deposition; this could reflect its changing status, from a core area with its important ornament hoards of MBA2, to a peripheral region in LBA3. On the other hand, it had one special asset: the production of bronze objects used outside the region. The evidence for bronze manufacturing is scarce in southern Britain, but there is good evidence for it in the South West, closer to the likely sources of copper and tin. In East Anglia, a small amount of the metal goes into several early hoards, but the major phase of deposition is in the Late Bronze Age, with perhaps a few individuals making massive statements about position and status during LBA2 before a more general phase of deposition in LBA3, as the importance of the region grew relative to the others.

Hoard size and distribution

We can take these figures for size and weight of hoards a step further: the size and mean weight of hoards have been examined to ascertain whether or not hoards conform to a roughly 'standard' size. If we use these figures and the standard deviation, as calculated using Program 1 (App. E), we can find which of the complete hoards examined lie more than one standard deviation from the mean: For the regions, the basic figures are as follows (weights in grams; '–' = negative number):

Table 12: High and low hoard weights

		Weight under	Weight over
TV		-	5332
	MBA2	534	1373
	LBA3	-	6488
SW		-	7875
	EBA2	966	4420
	MBA2	324	3204
	LBA3	-	17841
W		-	4024
	EBA2	730	2272
	MBA2	-	4231
	LBA2	40	1878
	LBA3	-	3990
EA		-	16765
	-Isleham	-	7234
	MBA2	525	1192
	LBA1	192	921
	LBA2	-	73311
	LBA3	-	8455
	LBA4	369	1142

This results in the following hoards being singled out: TV9 (MBA2), TV14 (LBA3), TV35 (MBA2); SW32 (MBA2), SW34 (LBA3), SW37 (MBA2); W23 (LBA2), W27 (MBA2), W28 (MBA2), W65 (LBA3), W80 (LBA2); EA10 (LBA1), EA27 (LBA2), EA29 (LBA3), EA40 (MBA2), EA53 (LBA3), EA101 (LBA1), EA109 (MBA2), EA118 (MBA2), and EA129 (LBA3).

Naturally, this selection consists of the smallest and largest complete hoards in each region (in terms of their weight), and these will lie on the limits of the range of hoard weights for each period. These are small hoards of ornaments (TV9, EA109), or huge tool and scrap hoards (EA129), for example. Other hoards which are notable for their small size here contain some interesting and unusual combinations: SW32 has a tanged chisel and two sickles, W80 has a socketed spearhead and a tanged knife, EA10 consists of shield and spearhead, and EA118 with three miniature palstaves, like those from Stibbard (EA50). The large hoards range from a collection of palstaves (TV35, W27, W28), through combinations of axes, other pieces, and cake metal (TV14, SW34, SW37, W23 (mostly weapons), W65, EA27, EA29, EA40, EA53, EA129), to the two swords from Barrow (EA101), both of interesting early type (classified as 'wide–U' and 'Medway' types of grip–tang sword (Brown, 1982, 2–3, 33)). The geographical distribution of these hoards can now be inspected (hoard distribution in general is discussed below): in the Thames Valley, only TV35 lies outside areas of usual deposition; in the South West, SW32 lies on the edge of an area of deposition, and SW34, the large hoard of Stogursey, lies close to the coast; in Wessex, W27 and W28 lie right on the coast, while the other three lie inland, but within areas containing other deposits; in East Anglia, EA27 lies in the centre of a large number of deposits, while EA53 and EA129 are effectively coastal, and the others, small and large, lie close to, or in the area around, EA27.

Is there anything notable in this distribution of statistically selected hoards? Subjectively, it can be argued that access to the sea was of importance in relation to choice of deposition site in three of our areas. This would be useful where the hoards are too large and heavy to transport overland easily. The others would seem to conform to the patterns established by the remaining hoards. Equally, in the Thames Valley access to rivers seems to be of importance, except for TV35 which lies on the Downs, in an area with relatively little metal in any context. However, these hoards do little to alter the overall picture of hoard distribution in these regions, where the majority picture of deposition must be of interest. They are few in number compared to the overall total of hoards; nevertheless, they indicate that some individuality in deposition did exist.

HOARD CONTENT

Another factor which has usually been considered to be of importance in the interpretation of hoards is that of content: the objects that actually make up the hoards. Thus, LBA3 hoards with all their lumps of metal and small pieces of broken objects are usually called 'scrap' or 'founder's' hoards, and the Broadward Complex is typified by its weapon hoards (Coombs, 1975, 64). However, as always, sweeping generalisations tend to be just that, and not all hoards fit the bill. Rowlands attempted to overcome this difficulty by using a more systematic classification based around tool, weapon, and ornament combinations (1976, 100–102). He found that 120 Middle Bronze Age hoards could be divided between the seven possible combinations of these categories. Over half were composed of tools only, but both weapon hoards and composite hoards of all three types were rare (1976, 102). Rowlands also noted that these hoard combinations had a distributional significance (1976, 103).

Where possible, hoards from our four regions were listed according to their content of tools, weapons, ornaments, miscellaneous items, and metal. Tools were taken to be represented by: axes, palstaves, knives, chisels, gouges, and awls; weapons by: swords, spearheads, and halberds; ornaments by: bracelets, torcs, and pins; miscellaneous items include horse trappings, razors, ferrules, chapes, and casting jets; metal would consist of lumps from cakes of metal and pieces of melted metal, such as the 'plate' from Isleham (EA27). Overall, we can get an average percentage representation of each category for the regions as in Table 13.

This clearly shows that metal only occurs in LBA2 and LBA3 hoards for all regions (with a small percentage of undatable material in East Anglia). This reflects the usual view of Late Bronze Age deposition. Miscellaneous items also tend to be a Late Bronze Age feature, again in character with the nature of the assemblages.

Table 13: Showing the mean percentage composition of hoards for each phase

	No.hoards	Tools	Weapons	Ornaments	Misc	Metal
TV-EBA2	4	37	63	0	0	0
MBA1	0	0	0	0	0	0
MBA2	10	76	13	10	1	0
LBA1	0	0	0	0	0	0
LBA2	1	50	0	0	0	50
LBA3	21	56	25	2	12	5
LBA4	0	0	0	0	0	0
EIA1	0	0	0	0	0	0
ND	1	100	0	0	0	0
W-EBA2	3	35	65	0	0	0
MBA1	1	100	0	0	0	0
MBA2	37	57	3	40	0	0
LBA1	0	0	0	0	0	0
LBA2	4	13	70	0	17	0
LBA3	15	59	14	8	11	8
LBA4	10	85	12	2	2	0
EIA1	0	0	0	0	0	0
ND	4	77	11	0	12	0
SW-EBA2	3	94	6	0	0	0
MBA1	0	0	0	0	0	0
MBA2	28	71	10	19	1	0
LBA1	1	0	75	0	25	0
LBA2	0	0	0	0	0	0
LBA3	4	50	22	12	13	3
LBA4	0	0	0	0	0	0
EIA1	0	0	0	0	0	0
ND	2	50	50	0	0	0
EA-EBA2	3	98	0	2	0	0
MBA1	0	0	0	0	0	0
MBA2	19	45	13	42	0	0
LBA1	8	18	49	11	22	0
LBA2	5	5	77	1	16	2
LBA3	72	62	14	2	7	15
LBA4	4	87	13	0	0	0
EIA1	1	0	0	100	0	0
ND	21	71	22	0	2	5

Surprisingly, in MBA2 – the 'Ornament Horizon' – ornaments are a fairly minor element in the hoards, especially in the South West. Of course, the bias is created by the large percentage of tools in these deposits, and there is a more even split between tools and ornaments in MBA2 Wessex and East Anglia. Tools seem to be a major component or predominant element in many phases, although weapons take the lead in EBA2 in Wessex and the Thames Valley, in LBA1 in the South West (only one hoard), in LBA2 for Wessex, and in LBA1 and LBA2 for East Anglia.

If we take Rowlands' sevenfold classification (above), and use the same principle with our five possible classes of information, the range of possible combinations would seem to rise to 31! It does not seem particularly helpful to classify, say, a hoard of 20 tools and one ornament, as a tool and ornament combination. The contents of hoards may just as easily represent what was available for deposition, as what was selected for deposition; tools predominate in any scheme, because they were probably the most widely available of all items, although there does seem to be selection of weapons for deposition in LBA2. We can confirm this impression by plotting a frequency diagram showing the relative number of occurrences of each combination in each region during the two best represented periods: MBA2 and LBA3 (Fig. 6). The East Anglian frequency distribution is lent more weight by the number of examples, but we can see how tools are dominant in virtually all combinations of material. Even metal, supposedly a significant part of LBA3 hoards, most often makes up less than half of any hoard. The results are of course based only on the contents of hoards; the balance of deposition could be altered by other forms of deposit, such as single finds.

Therefore, tools are the most common element of hoards across time, save some regional and chronological variation, and we should look to variations within that element to deepen our understanding of hoard content. This preponderance of tools in hoards would seem to contradict the argument of our model, where we see the deposition of prestige objects as part of status–defining acts. Do the prestige objects always have to be weapons or flamboyant ornaments? Some of the socketed axes in LBA3 hoards are extremely fine and must surely rise above the purely functional ascription implicit in the term 'tool'. Other axes are no doubt fairly coarse implements, and all categories or types were subjected to use, as can be seen from an analysis of wear. Thus, tools were obviously considered acceptable for deposition in hoards and were suited to this kind of deposit, in contrast to the quantities of swords and spearheads from rivers, for example. The sheer quantities of metal involved in the deposition of axes must have had some meaning in our scheme, and obviously axes were readily available. The deposition of quantities of tools, prestigious and functional types, still displayed someone's ability to discard a valuable asset and still served to restrict the supply of tools and metal to any competitors for social position. Equally, some of the largest hoards are made up of many little pieces of objects, often broken, and this accords with the idea that deposition served to restrict the metal supply and that objects were broken to ensure that re–use was not possible. The objects may well have been accumulated as broken pieces, first intended for recasting, but could have been pressed into service as a significant deposit of metal. So, we can see that the ready availability of tools for deposition may still reflect the need to make a hoard for prestige purposes: some of the smaller hoards of tools could be interpreted as smaller scale deposits, gaining lower levels of prestige for the depositors.

WEAR

Wear is considered to be important in our analysis of hoards, because it can demonstrate the circulation time of pieces contained in hoards and indicate phases of stress in the core/periphery relationship, when the circulation of objects had to be maintained for longer, due to restrictions in the metal supply. The measurements and observations on the individual objects in the hoards were designed to examine this aspect.

We have seen how it is possible to detect degrees of wear on an object and to convert those observations into an average scale of wear (Chap. 4; scale from A to E indicating worn to heavily worn). Having obtained a large set of observations, we have to break it down in various ways for analysis: there are the fairly obvious divisions of region, date, and type of object, and we can also consider the completeness of those objects. In addition, these divisions can be combined in other ways and tested.

To gain some measure of the usefulness of these various combinations of observations, it was decided to calculate chi–squared from the data and obtain measures of significance in relation to three null hypotheses:

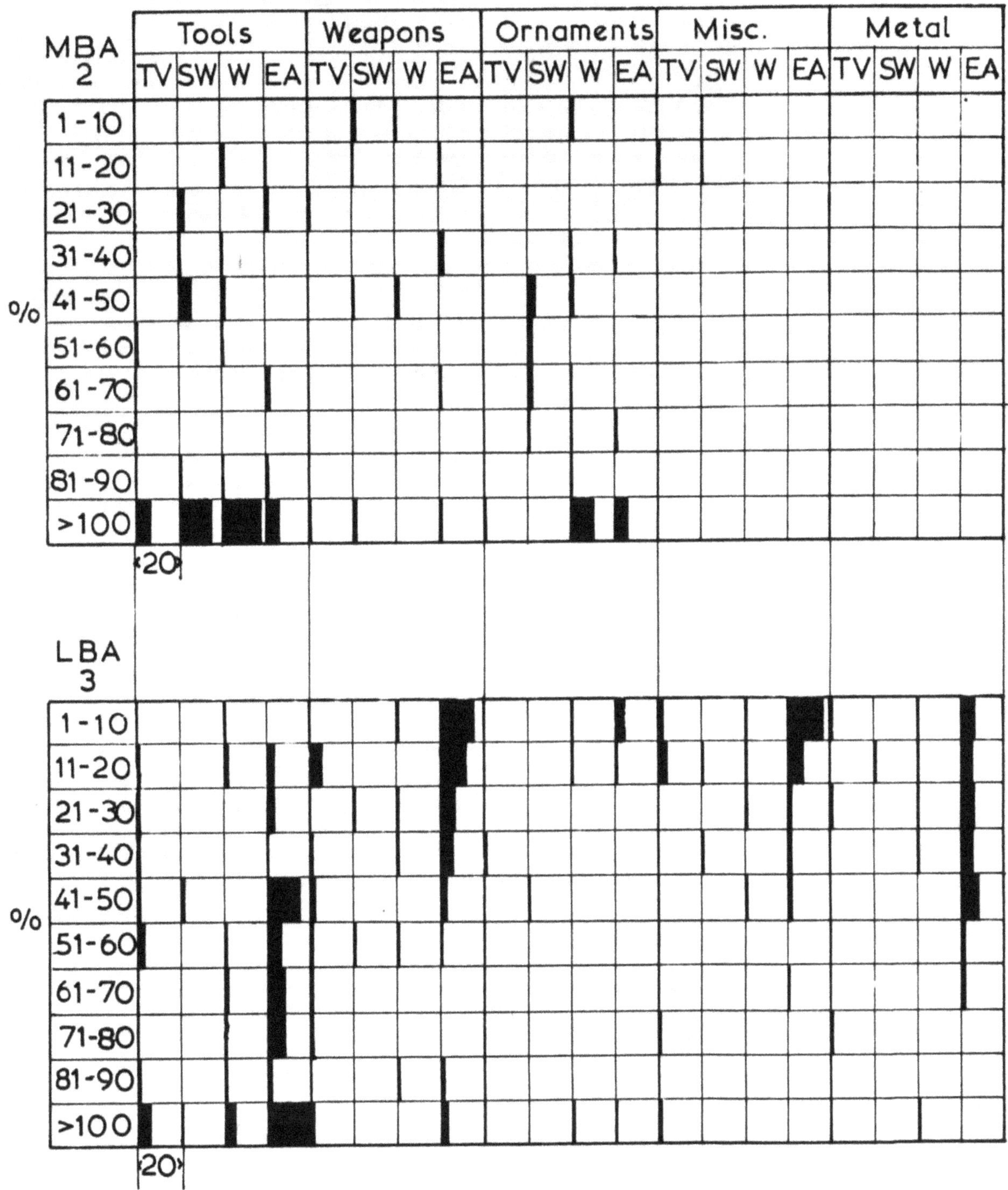

Figure 6: Showing the number of occurrences of a percentage composition in MBA2 and LBA3

1. That there is no significant relationship between object and completeness.
2. That there is no significant relationship between degree of wear and completeness.
3. That there is no significant relationship between degree of wear and object.

The data were divided up according to date and region to produce the contingency tables in Appendix G, from which chi–squared values and degrees of freedom (D.F.) are relatively simple to calculate, using Program 2 (App. E), except in the use of 2 x 2 tables with cells containing numbers less than 10, when Yates' correction is applied (cf. Bruning and Kintz, 1977, 230–7). The contingency coefficient is also calculated (C; this was only done for MBA2, LBA2, and LBA3). Using statistical tables, we can look up the level of significance for each of the values of chi–squared at those degrees of freedom and thereby gain a measure of confidence in our original null hypotheses. The table given by Kmietowicz and Yannoulis suggests the following levels of significance for our four regions and the three null hypotheses (1976, 20, Table 13):

Table 14: Levels of significance

	Thames Valley		South West		
	M2	L3	E2	M2	L3
1	0.5	0.001	0.25	0.001	0.001
2	0.5	0.001	0.75	0.005	0.025
3	0.005	0.001	0.75	0.001	0.001

	Wessex				
	E2	M2	L2	L3	L4
1	0.1	0.001	0.75	0.001	0.25
2	0.5	0.001	0.001	0.75	0.005
3	0.75	0.001	0.005	0.001	0.001

	East Anglia				
	M2	L1	L2	L3	L4
1	0.01	0.025	0.25	0.001	0.75
2	0.025	0.25	0.005	0.001	0.5
3	0.001	0.5	0.001	0.001	0.5

NOTE: 0.001 = 0.1%)
0.01 = 1.0%) Chances of accepting the
0.1 = 10.0%) null hypothesis
0.5 = 50.0%)

Thus, we can see a highly significant relationship between degree of wear and object (3) in MBA2 and LBA3 in all 4 regions, in LBA2 in Wessex and East Anglia, and in LBA4 in Wessex. EBA2 in the South West and Wessex and LBA1 and LBA4 in East Anglia show no such relationship. There is also a highly significant relationship between an object and its completeness (1) in LBA3 in all areas, and a significant to highly significant relationship between degree of wear and completeness of an object (2) in LBA3 in the Thames Valley, South West, and East Anglia, but not at all in Wessex. MBA2 shows a fairly significant relationship between object and completeness (1), and degree of wear and completeness (2) in all regions but the Thames Valley, where we can neither accept nor reject the null hypothesis.

These results confirm that there is some sort of relationship between these factors of wear, object, and completeness, and that it does differ by date and region, but what is that relationship and what might it represent? We can assess our confidence in these relationships with a contingency coefficient, indicating the degree of relationship between the variables (cf. Bruning and Kintz, 1977, 233 and 237; C in the results): this lies between 0 and 1 and has effectively the same meaning as the correlation coefficient. So, where there is no association C equals zero, and at the other extreme C should attain a value of 1. In fact, this varies with the number of categories studied, with maximum values known for square tables (eg 2 x 2; 5 x 5), but not for rectangular tables (eg 2 x 5, 3 x 6) (Yeomans, 1968, 292–3). Thus, for the Thames Valley and Wessex in LBA3 we have a measure of relationship between degree of wear and object (3) returning values of C of 0.7485 and 0.6721 respectively from 5 x 5 contingency tables; since the maximum value for C from a 5 x 5 table is 0.894 (Yeomans, 1968, 293), we can see that both of these values indicate a high degree of correlation between degree of wear and object in LBA3 for the Thames Valley and Wessex. In fact, this significant relationship can be seen in the other regions too, both in MBA2 and LBA3. In the South West and Wessex in LBA3 there is also a significant relationship between object and completeness (1).

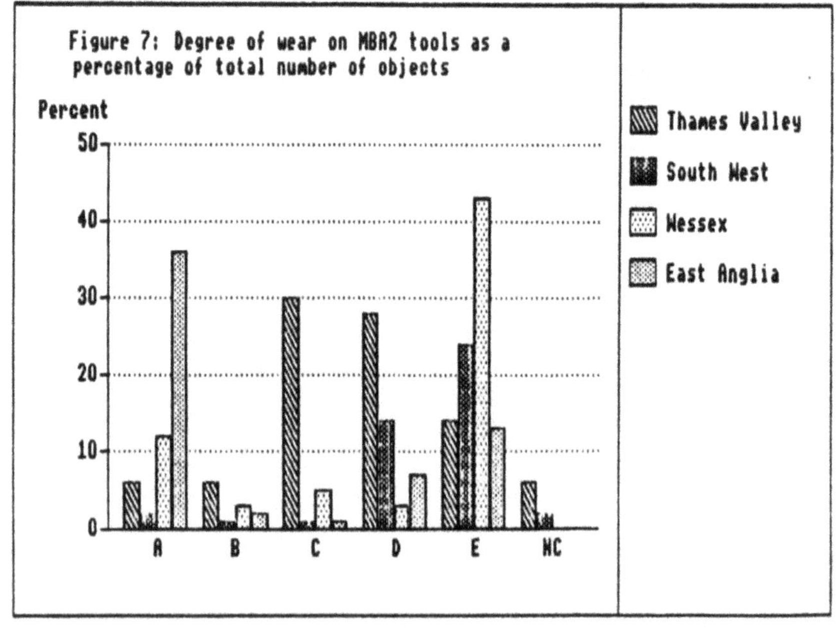

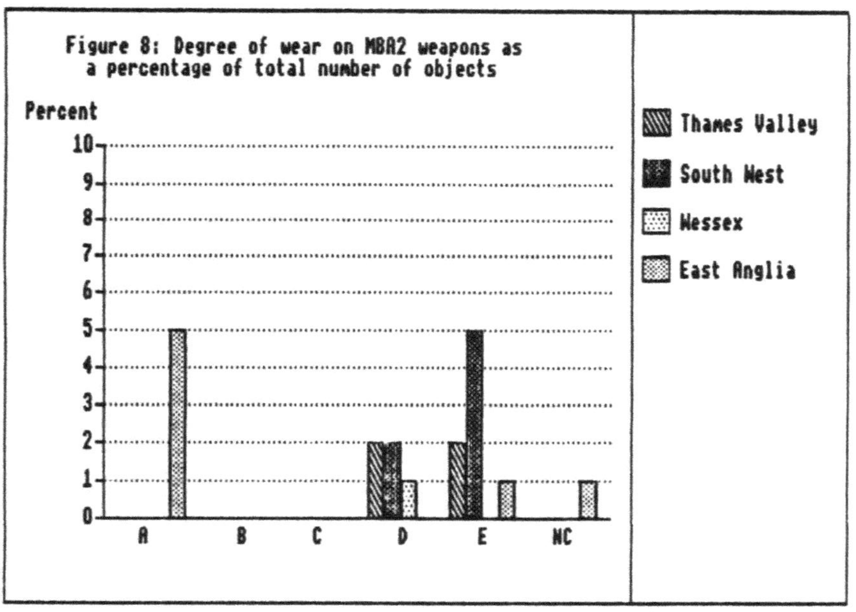

Figure 8: Degree of wear on MBA2 weapons as a percentage of total number of objects

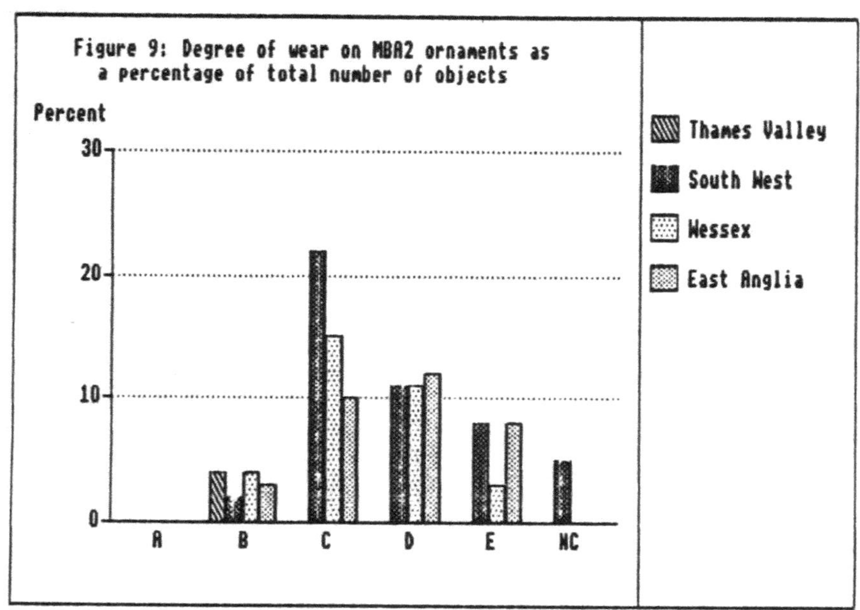

Figure 9: Degree of wear on MBA2 ornaments as a percentage of total number of objects

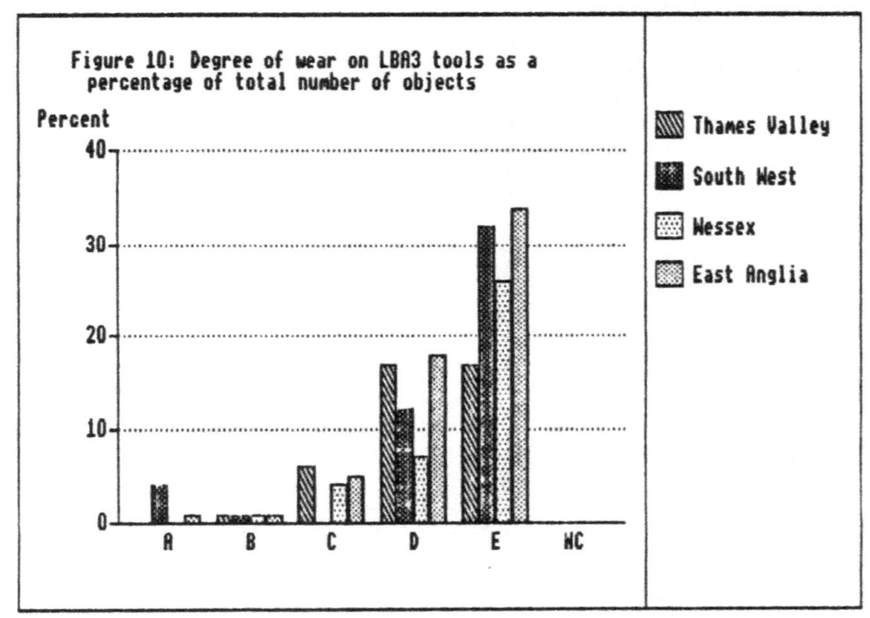

Figure 10: Degree of wear on LBA3 tools as a percentage of total number of objects

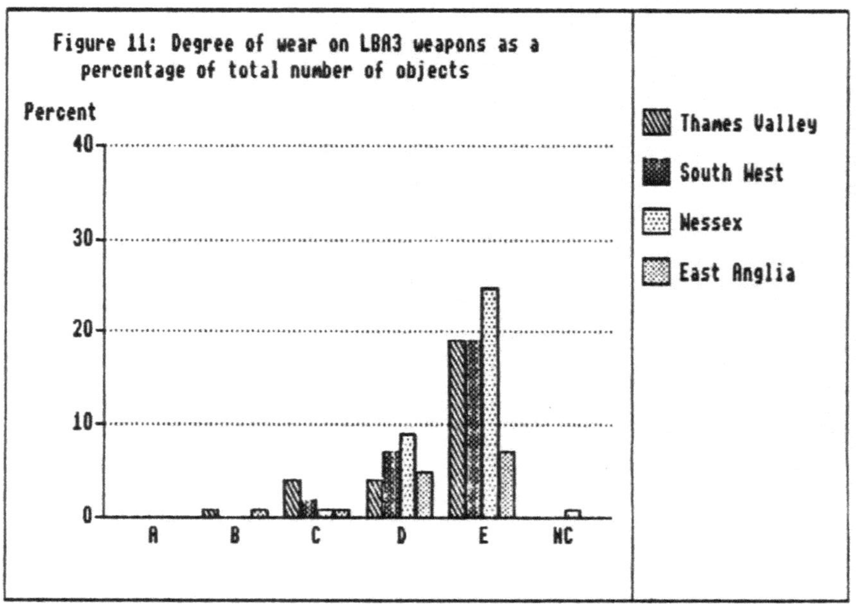

Figure 11: Degree of wear on LBA3 weapons as a percentage of total number of objects

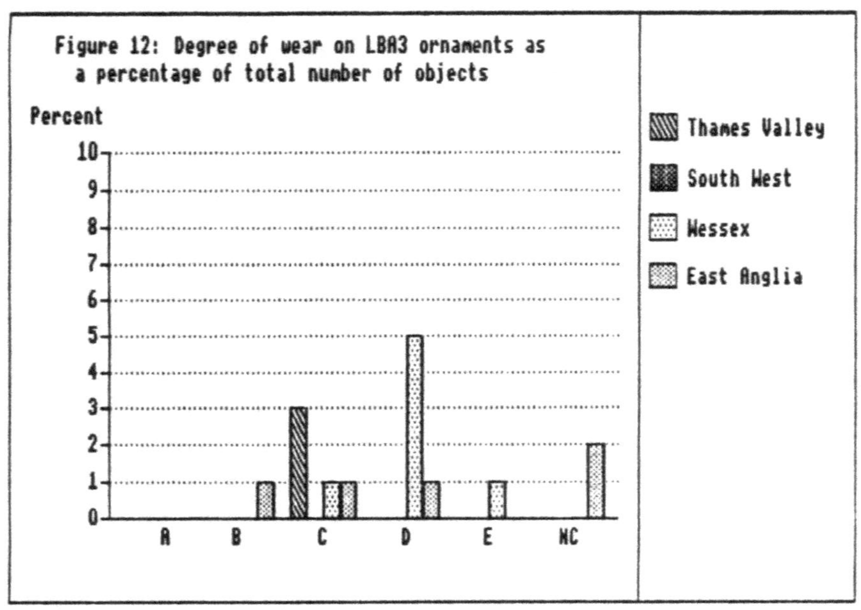

Figure 12: Degree of wear on LBA3 ornaments as a percentage of total number of objects

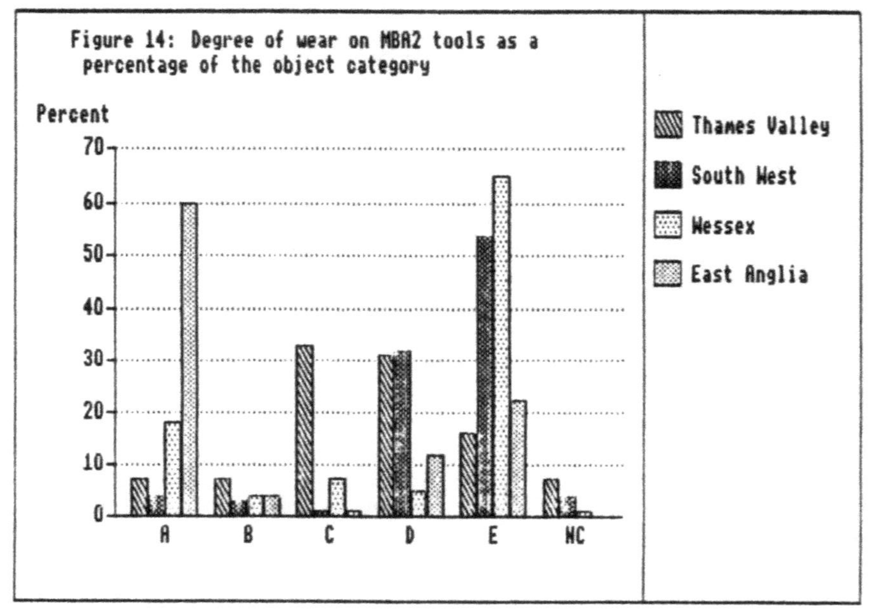

Figure 14: Degree of wear on MBA2 tools as a percentage of the object category

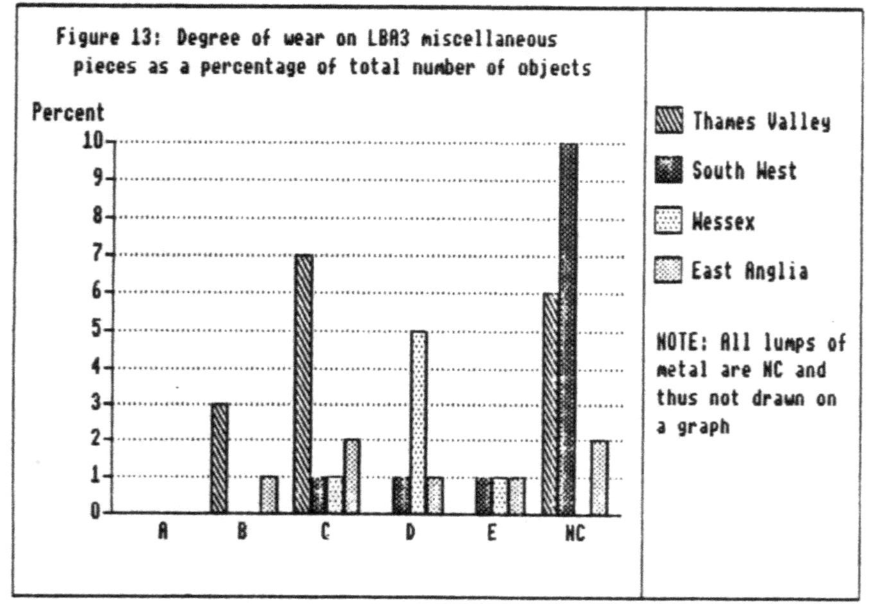

Figure 13: Degree of wear on LBA3 miscellaneous pieces as a percentage of total number of objects

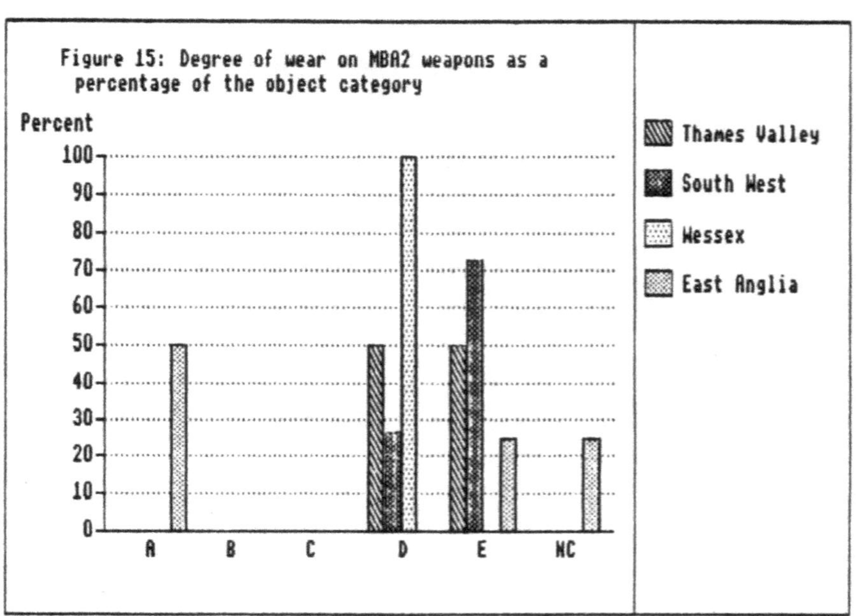

Figure 15: Degree of wear on MBA2 weapons as a percentage of the object category

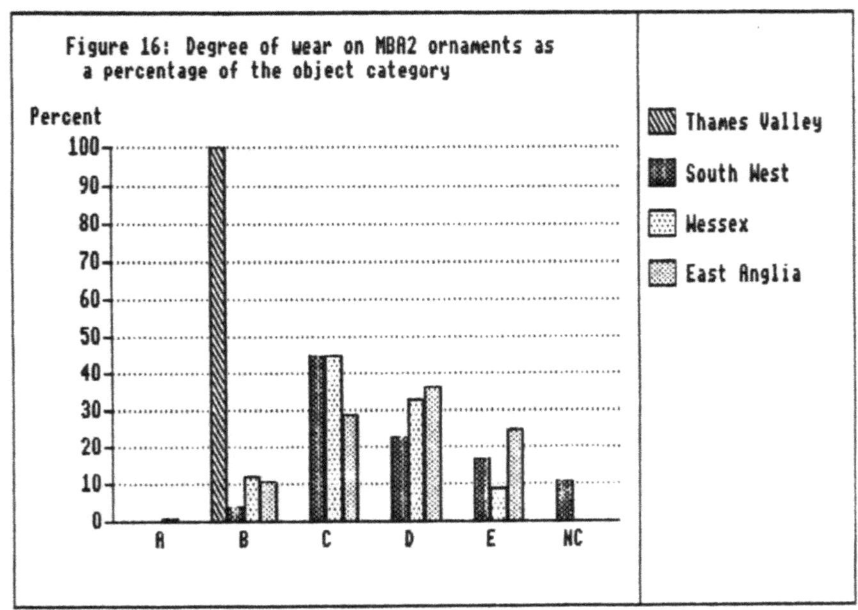

Figure 16: Degree of wear on MBA2 ornaments as a percentage of the object category

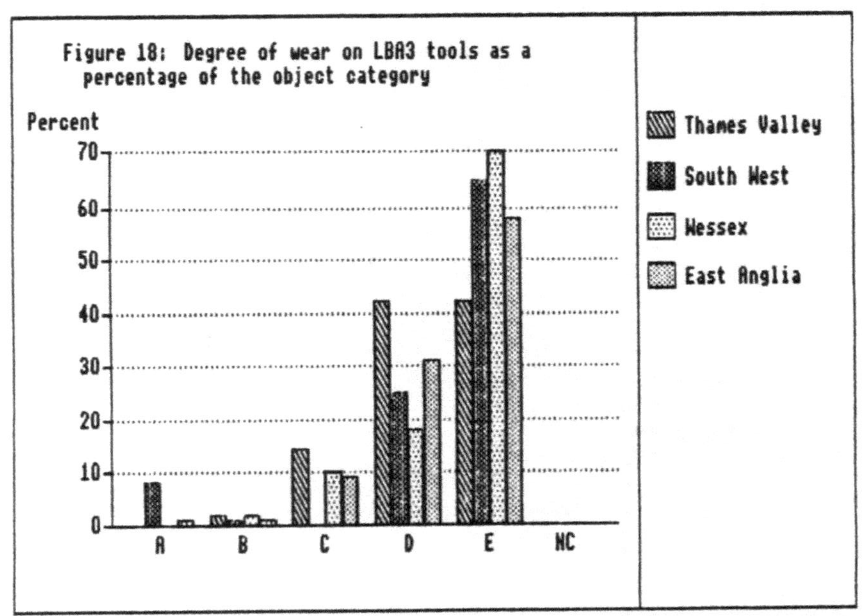

Figure 18: Degree of wear on LBA3 tools as a percentage of the object category

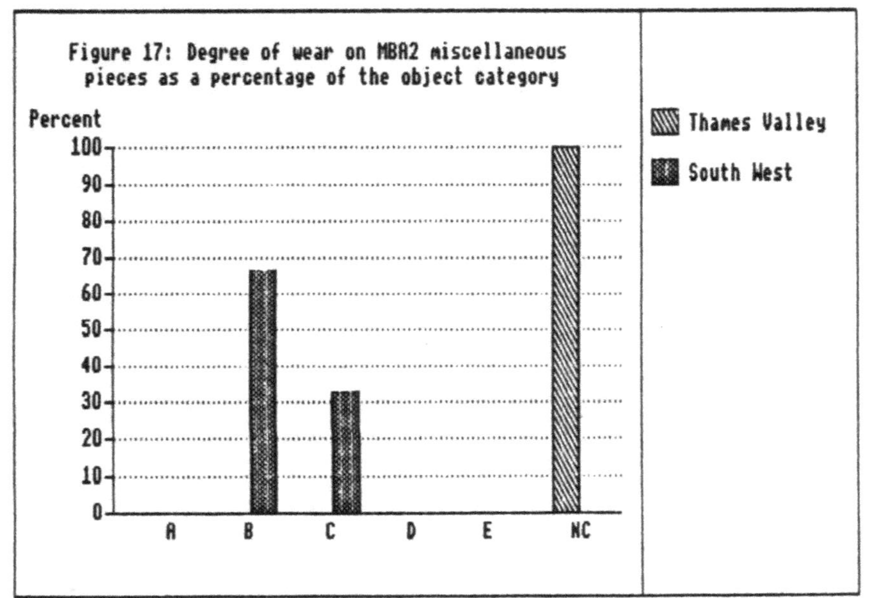

Figure 17: Degree of wear on MBA2 miscellaneous pieces as a percentage of the object category

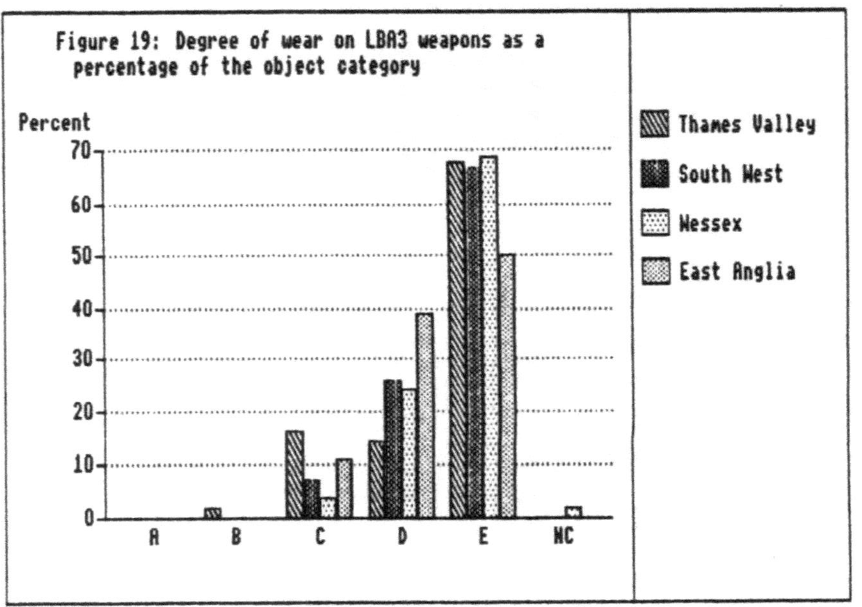

Figure 19: Degree of wear on LBA3 weapons as a percentage of the object category

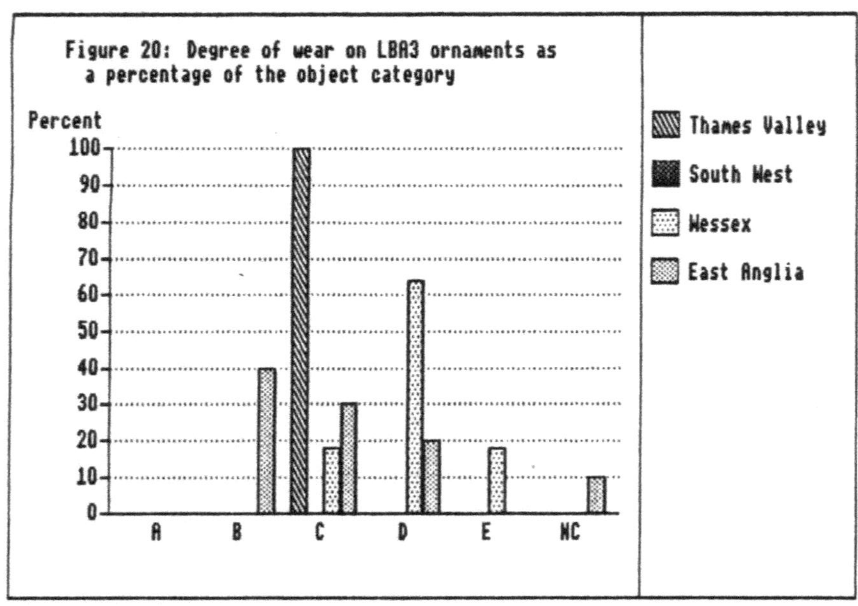

Figure 20: Degree of wear on LBA3 ornaments as a percentage of the object category

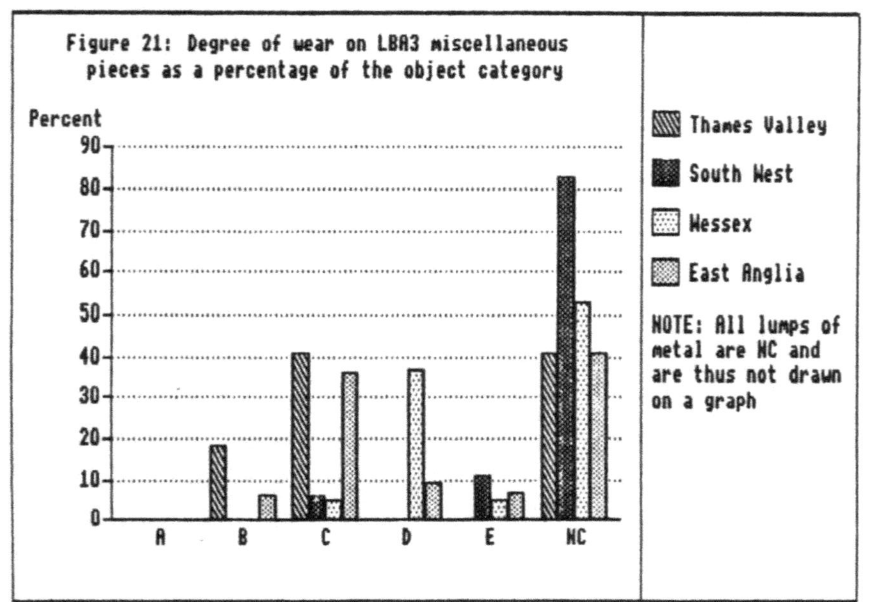

Figure 21: Degree of wear on LBA3 miscellaneous pieces as a percentage of the object category

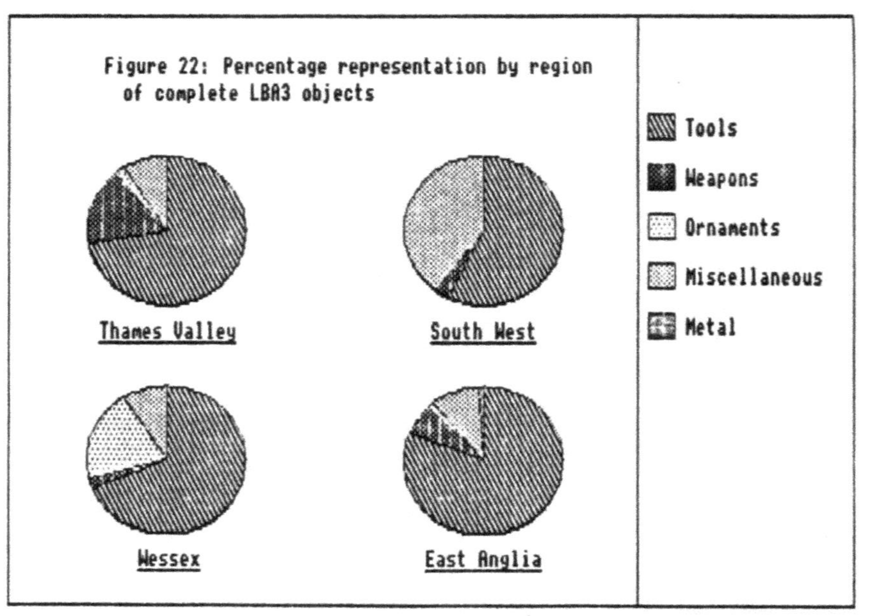

Figure 22: Percentage representation by region of complete LBA3 objects

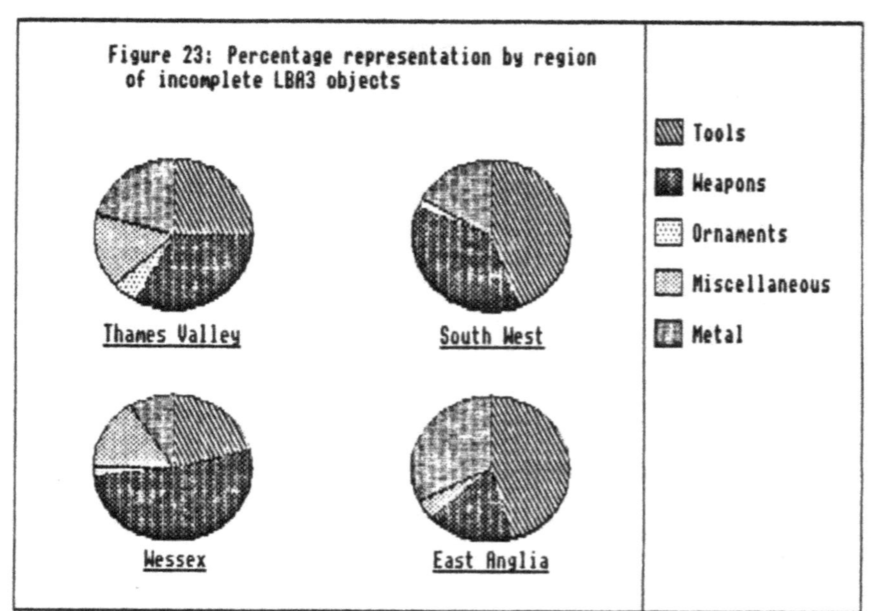

Figure 23: Percentage representation by region of incomplete LBA3 objects

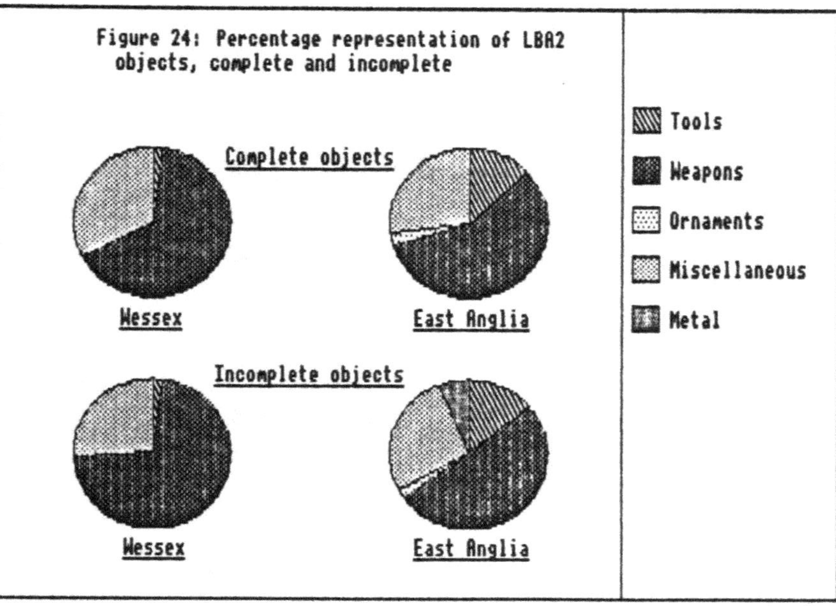

Figure 24: Percentage representation of LBA2 objects, complete and incomplete

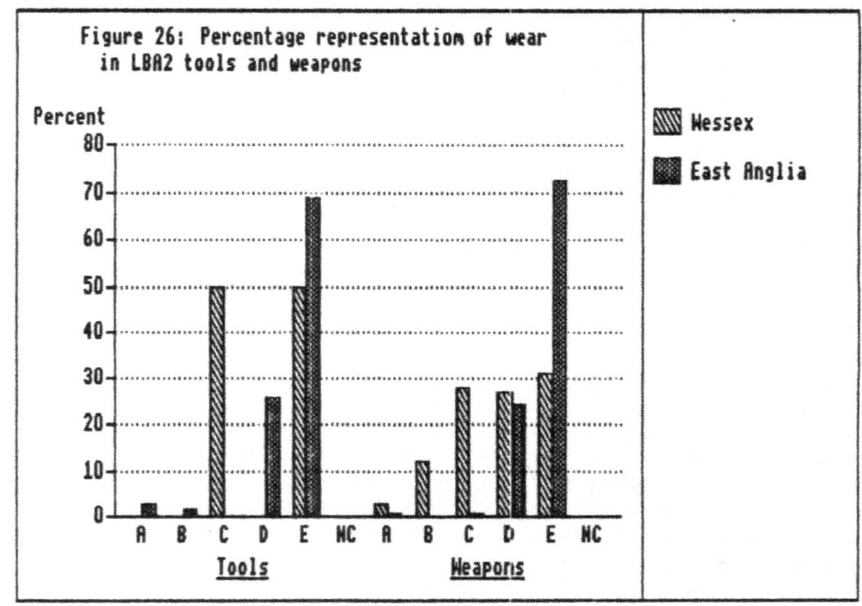

Figure 26: Percentage representation of wear in LBA2 tools and weapons

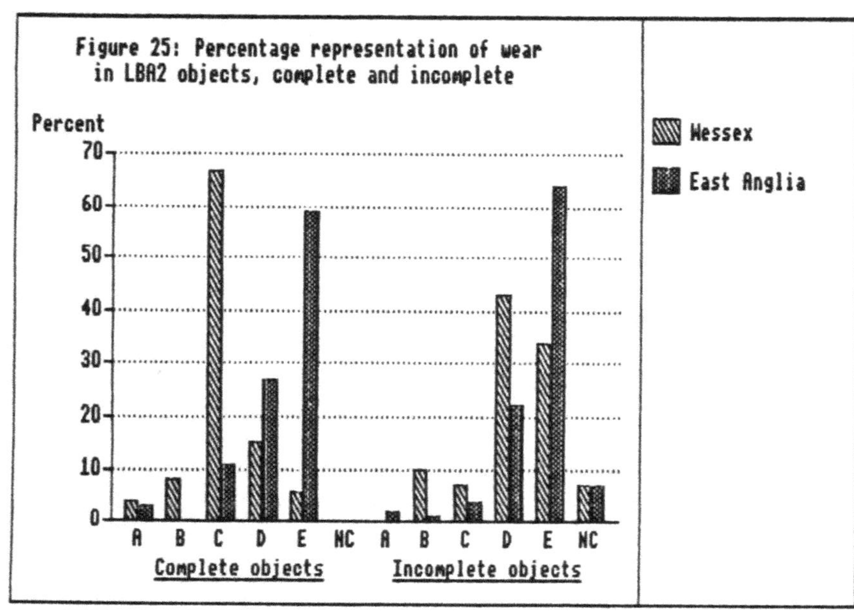

Figure 25: Percentage representation of wear in LBA2 objects, complete and incomplete

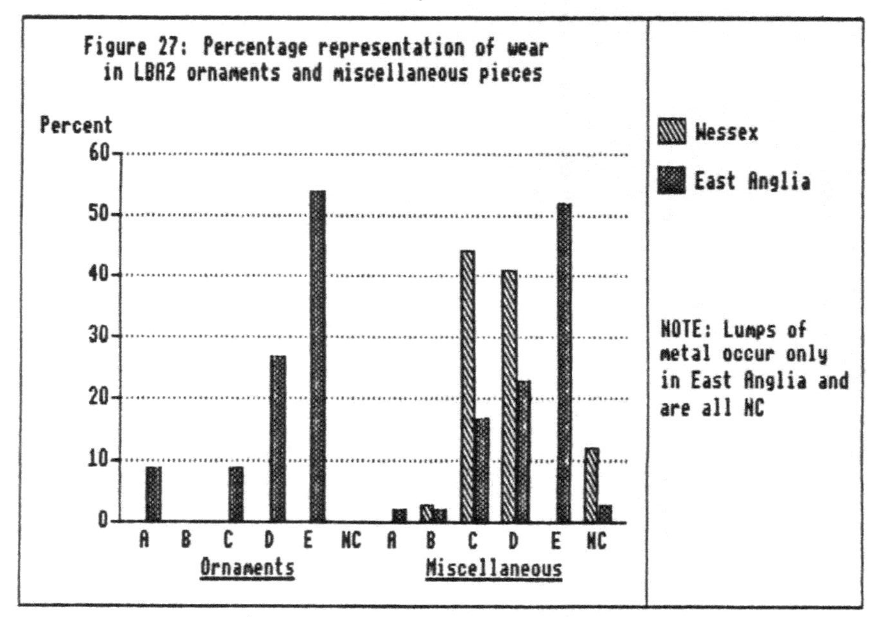

Figure 27: Percentage representation of wear in LBA2 ornaments and miscellaneous pieces

All the other regions too, both in MBA2 and LBA3. In the South West and Wessex in LBA3 there is also a significant relationship between object and completeness (1). All the other values of C given show very little or some slight relationship between the variables observed, with the relationship between degree of wear and completeness (2) hardly attaining any significance in all regions. This is a refinement of the previous observations of level of significance and provides support for the further analysis of patterning by date and region. There is a positive relationship, empirically observed and statistically tested, between object and degree of wear: obviously, we need to compare degrees of wear across time, region, and by object.

The graphs (Figs. 7–13) show degree of wear for each object category as a percentage of wear for all objects in each region for MBA2 and LBA3. We could also take each category of object as a separate entity and graph the percentage of these in each wear category for each region (Figs. 14–21).

The graphs for tools (Figs. 14 and 18) amplify the previous graphs, but those for other categories are clearer and show the distribution of wear patterns across different objects. In MBA2, ornaments seem to be subject to more moderate wear than tools or weapons – perhaps not surprisingly, since we would expect wear to be stronger and more destructive in the case of functional objects. This was not the case in East Anglia, where tools and weapons are generally less worn, or in the Thames Valley where the ornaments do not seem to be so worn (although here we are dealing with a very small sample) (Map 6). LBA3 also shows heavy wear for tools and weapons, and moderate wear for ornaments and miscellaneous pieces (Map 7). This would seem to suggest that most objects were subjected to fairly heavy usage before they became available for deposition. This would tend to support traditional interpretations, in which scrap hoards were collections of worn–out pieces, but it casts doubt on the reality of merchant's hoards which are supposed to consist of unworn pieces. In this case, it is interesting that the relationship in LBA3 between degree of wear and completeness of the object is not so clear cut, whereas the relation between the type of object and its completeness is quite striking. We can again calculate the relative proportions in these observations.

We can see that tools make up the major proportion of complete objects in hoards of LBA3 date, but, where objects are incomplete, weapons become as important as tools (Figs. 22–3; Map 8). Thus, weapons are more likely overall to be deposited broken than tools in LBA3. Interestingly, the figures show that about twice as many broken objects occur in hoards as complete ones. The figures for wear against completeness suggested that this factor was not so important, but we can modify these figures by leaving out the unclassifiable element in hoards (usually incomplete metal lumps) and re–calculating the scale of wear against the total for each category: complete and incomplete. The figures indeed suggest heaviest wear for incomplete objects, with complete objects suffering only moderate wear. This supports the idea that some objects would disintegrate through heavy use before their deposition, but more generally objects, whether whole or broken, were only worn to a moderate degree, when they entered the hoards of LBA3. This suggests that the objects had not circulated for long before their deposition.

So far, we have concentrated mainly on the results for MBA2 and LBA3, because these periods are particularly well and consistently represented in all four regions. For Wessex and East Anglia we can examine the results for LBA2: these would seem to suggest different relationships between our variables from those seen in the succeeding phase (LBA3). As we can see from the values of the contingency coefficient (C; App. G), there is no significant relationship between object and completeness in either area (1), some significance in the relationship between degree of wear and completeness for Wessex but not East Anglia (2), and a fairly significant relationship between degree of wear and type of object for both areas (3). We can again confirm this with charts of the percentage representation of each category in both regions (Figs. 24–7). Weapons predominate over other objects, whether complete or incomplete, as they are such a feature of LBA2 (1). In Wessex, a degree of wear seems to be correlated with completeness and heavier wear with incompleteness, but in East Anglia heavy wear seems to occur on complete and incomplete objects fairly equally (2). Tools seem to suffer more wear in East Anglia than Wessex, weapons more heavy wear in East Anglia, and there is heavier wear on miscellaneous objects in East Anglia too (3). Some aspects of this patterning seem to continue into LBA3, with heavy wear on tools and weapons, though the more even distribution of degrees of wear in LBA2 weapons have given way to higher levels of wear among LBA3 ones. For East Anglia there seems to be a reversal of the treatment of ornaments, heavy wear in LBA2 giving way to much less wear in LBA3. The wear on miscellaneous pieces seems to decrease from LBA2 to LBA3 in East Anglia, the position in Wessex being more uncertain because of the presence of unclassifiable pieces.

This gives the impression of series of objects – tools, weapons, and ornaments – which overlap in time between LBA2 and LBA3, either coming into use again as newly–modelled pieces, or falling into disuse as old pieces are replaced, presumably by new ones. The deposits represent records of these transitory moments in time and, as such, are far more likely to represent a selection of objects continuously available in various styles across time, than a single phase of deposition induced by some outside event. However, because our chronology is based upon contents and associations of hoards, we cannot easily pick out these changing relationships, nor derive suitable timespans for individual objects. Across greater timespans than those considered here, eg between MBA2 and LBA3 – c 600 years – change is magnified and complicated by a lack of depositional evidence in some areas in the intervening periods. This erratic pattern does favour the explanation of deposition induced by external influences. Surely too, the change in proportions of objects deposited indicates something about the nature of the deposits: a change from majority weapon to majority tool deposition cannot be easily explained.

The differences in degrees of wear between different types of object of LBA2 and LBA3 in different regions also indicates the nature of circulation time. Circulation time appears to have been longer in LBA2 for East Anglia than Wessex with heavier wear on tools, weapons, and ornaments; the circulation time seems to remain long for tools and weapons in LBA3, but the ornaments reach hoards sooner. Although East Anglia was in the ascendancy in the Late Bronze Age in our core/periphery model, this therefore had to be achieved on the basis of long circulation times for the objects in the hoards, indicating a restriction in the metal supply from the peripheries and through exchange. Meanwhile, communities in Wessex, a peripheral area in this period, were able to deposit less–worn items. Thus, there would be internal tensions within the system, as well as the influence of external relationships. However, we must return to the major topic of this section: wear.

Computer analysis

We have examined different aspects and correlates of wear across time and region by using a generalised scale of wear (A to E and N.C.) derived from the original in–depth observations. This intuitive classification has been used on all categories of material, but may be more obviously suited to tools and weapons than to ornaments and miscellaneous pieces, as discussed above (Chap. 4). It also 'evens out' the wider range of original variables recorded, although these pose considerable problems because of the variety of possible combinations. Some tests were done, using automatic clustering procedures (ASF4) on all the variables recorded for complete axes, the best represented of objects in the series, using mainframe computers, as described in Chapter 4.

Having submitted the data to analysis and got the computer to print out the relevant dendrograms, we need to consider what these diagrams tell us about the data. We have an illustration of the dissimilarity between objects, based on their range of characteristics (the state of loops, casting seams, and edges): the objects have been classified according to these variables of wear. Of course, the result of this might not be readily interpreted: an observation made by Orton, when commenting that clusters of Roman spearheads were not analytically useful in leading to fruitful developments (1980, 62). More analysis or other techniques could lead to refinements of the observations, but we shall deal here with the raw dendrograms from our four regions.

Initial inspection of the results from complete Thames Valley axes shows a broad separation into three clusters (1, 2, 3 on Fig. 28) on the basis of similar wear patterns: cluster 1 is composed mainly of LBA3 axes, cluster 2 of MBA2 axes

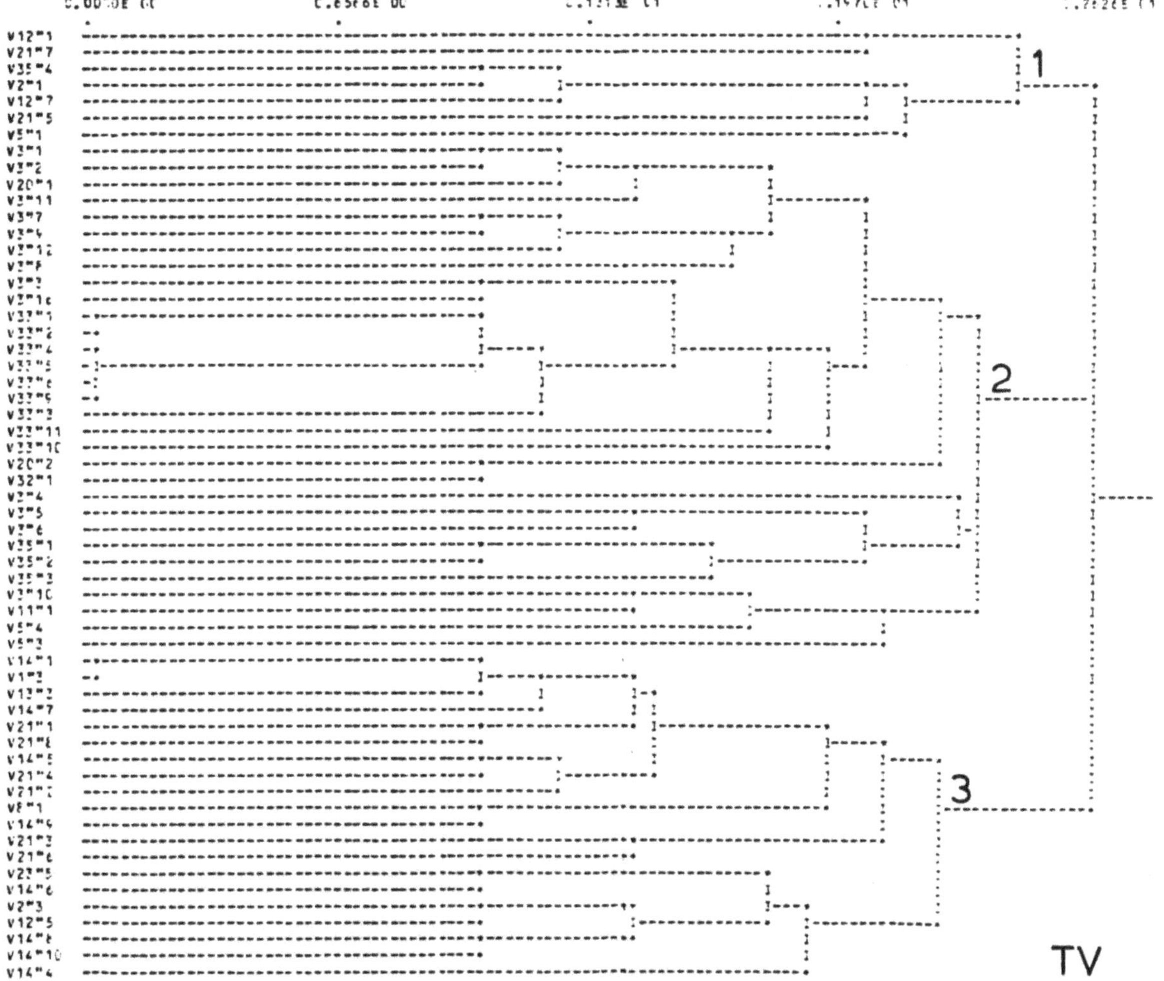

Figure 28: Computer dendrogram for wear on Thames Valley axes

(bar two examples), and cluster 3 entirely of LBA3 axes. This would suggest a chronological difference between aspects of wear; the generalised, intuitive scale for wear, when compared with these results, does not immediately suggest any real patterning, although various small clusters of objects with similar scales of wear can be detected, eg between TV33/4 and TV33/10, where all the pieces are 'worn' (C). The results for complete South Western axes show two main divisions, with the first subdivided into two (1a, 1b, and 2 on Fig. 29). The difference between clusters 1 and 2 is fairly clear: the small group of objects in 2 are unworn, or as cast, except for SW34/35, which is classified as well–worn on the basis of the edge, but other features on it suggest an as–cast state. The difference between 1a and 1b is not so clear–cut, but 1b contains all worn and heavily worn axes, and 1a has separated off a sub–group of EBA2 axes, with other internal groupings being formed within the clusters. Small differences in individual pieces then determine the position of the remainder in the clusters: distinctions which cannot be made in the A to E scale. Therefore, these two results would indicate that the intuitive A to E scale can be used in analysis of these complex objects, but the fineness of some of these distinctions results from the use of the original numerical scales by the computer program ASF4.

Larger numbers of objects were analysed for Wessex and East Anglia. The results for Wessex divide into two groupings, which each subdivide into two other groupings (Fig. 30). The main groupings differ in the clustering of worn and heavily worn axes in 1, and unworn material in 2. The subsidiary groupings refine on this slightly: 1a consists of heavily worn material in the main, with a group of EBA2 axes separated off into a cluster with two LBA3 axes and one MBA2 axe; 1b contains finds of different dates, tending to concentrate less worn examples at the right–hand edge of the cluster; 2a consists of MBA2 and LBA4 axes, mostly unworn; and 2b has one LBA3 axe among MBA2 worn examples. Again, this reinforces the individual nature of each object and the amount of wear, to which the object is subject before it is combined with other pieces in a hoard, but there is a tendency for certain categories to come together. The axes from East Anglia had to be divided into two groups to enable computer analysis to take place, because of the sheer quantity of examples; an unequal division was achieved on the criterion of context: those with good contextual information were analysed together, and those without any information on find circumstances formed the other group. Figure 31 shows the results of clustering all axes from hoards with secure contexts: notable are the size of cluster 1, compared to 2, and the multiple groupings of exactly similar axes, ie those joined together at the base line. Also, it is immediately obvious that the difference between clusters 1 and 2 is due to degree of wear: 2 being made up entirely of unworn examples. Cluster 1 can be subdivided into the masssive 1a, containing worn and heavily worn axes mainly of LBA3 date (the major component of East Anglian hoards), and the four examples of lb, which are of MBA2 date, three from the same hoard. Cluster 2 does not need to be subdivided any more finely, although it is again interesting to note the joining of unworn MBA2 examples along the base line, many from the same hoard: EA50, from Stibbard, one of Evans' merchant's hoards (1881, 460 No 8). The palstaves and spearheads from here are, however, of an exceptional nature and probably non–functional. The second analysis of East Anglian material, of those axes from hoards with poor contextual detail, gives the results in Figure 32. Here we have a division into three main groups. Cluster 1 divides into two, with 1a consisting of worn items mainly of LBA3 date, and lb of more heavily worn items, again mainly of LBA3 date. Cluster 2 is formed of two objects of MBA2 date which are not so worn, their individual character separating them from the rest. Cluster 3 groups mainly unworn items of MBA2 date in 3a, but also contains some of LBA3, and two anomalous pieces, EA75/3 and EA83/7, whose individual characteristics place them in cluster 3b.

These larger scale analyses indicate the same overall results: division and clustering based on wear of individual items, whatever their date, but with some grouping of similar dated objects, suggesting that some aspects of wear are a function of object morphology, the same morphology on which classification is based. To set against those hoards with examples that fall together in terms of wear, there are those whose objects are widely distributed for the same reasons. The results also bear out the effectiveness of our intuitive classification of wear, reinforcing the possibilities of analysis using a generalised scale of wear, rather than every single attribute. Of course, many more measurements and observations could be made on individual objects, resulting in still better definition, but also in a much larger database. So, are hoards merely 'random accumulations' of objects, or are they made up of carefully selected items? Or are they a mixture of both? These are the problems raised by wear analysis, but to answer these questions we must also look to other correlates and the role of objects other than axes.

We can examine other categories of objects in more detail and compare the amount of wear between them. This was done for three of our regions – Thames Valley, South West, and Wessex – using a commercial sorting program with the BBC microcomputer, as described in Chapter 4. The program can correlate various attributes of individual pieces, placing similar objects together and subdividing them by wear and so on. The quantities assigned to these sorted categories can then be converted to percentages. The results are illustrated by graphs (Figs. 33–43; Map 9).

With only two exceptions, tools, other than socketed axes and palstaves, seem to be generally well–worn at deposition in the three regions. The sample is small of course, but worn tools do seem to have been selected for deposition in all periods. Socketed axes and palstaves show more of a spread across the wear range and differ from region to region. Weapons on the whole seem well–worn at deposition in all regions, except for socketed spearheads in Wessex during LBA2, where there is a tendency to less wear before deposition. Again, this is based on a small number of hoards. Ornaments suffer less wear before deposition in all the regions, although they are tending to be more worn by LBA3 in Wessex, and torcs have more wear than bracelets – were they circulating longer than bracelets before their deposition?

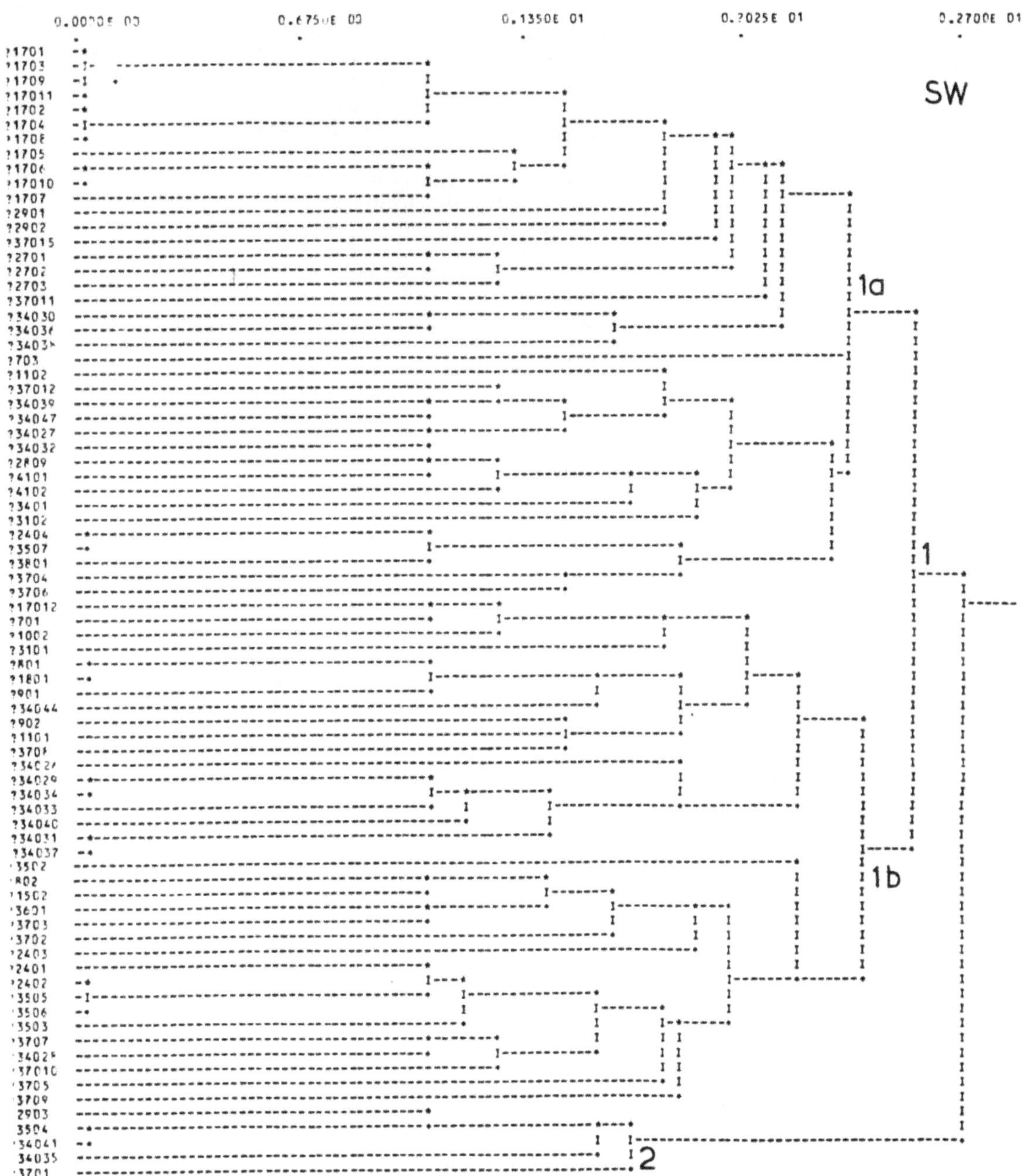

Figure 29: Computer dendrogram for wear on South Western axes

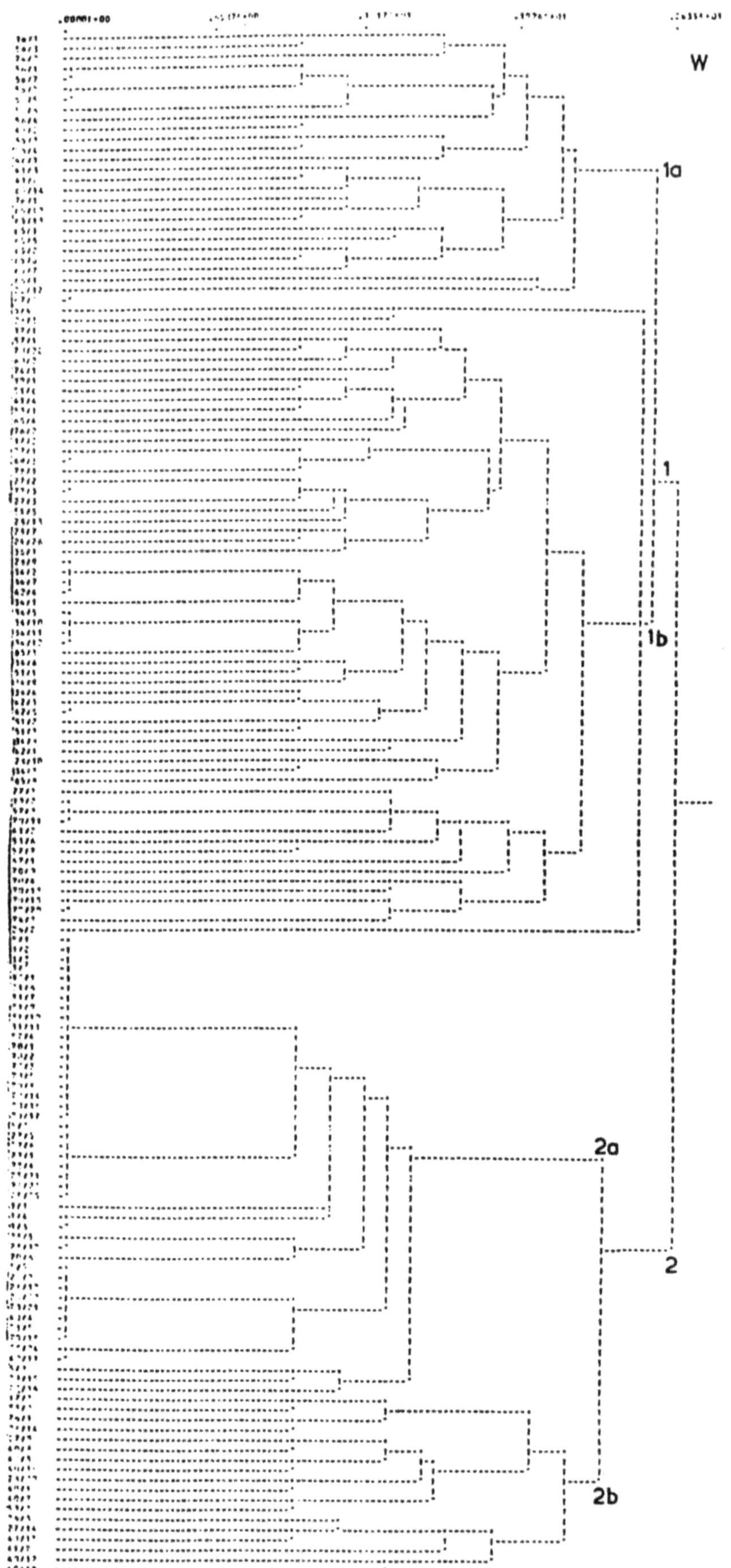

Figure 30: Computer dendrogram for wear on Wessex axes

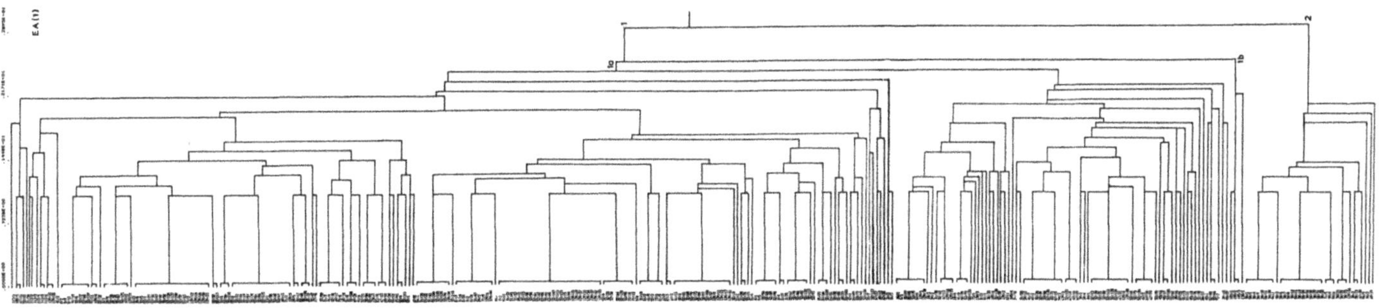

Figure 31: Computer dendrogram for wear on East Anglian axes from good contexts

Please view pages in original size at this link: https://doi.org/10.30861/9780860547488_original

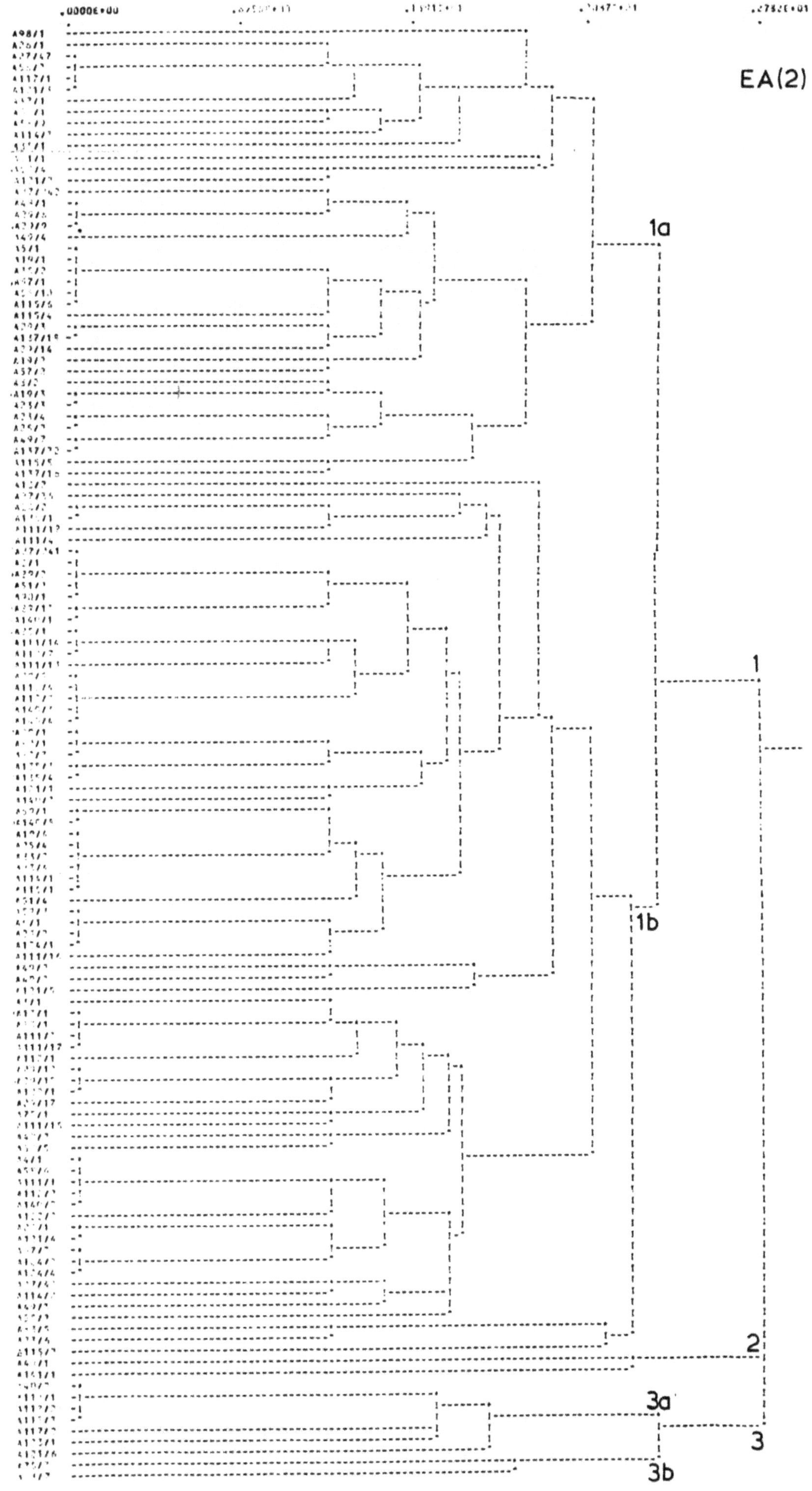

Figure 32: Computer dendrogram for wear on East Anglian axes from poor contexts

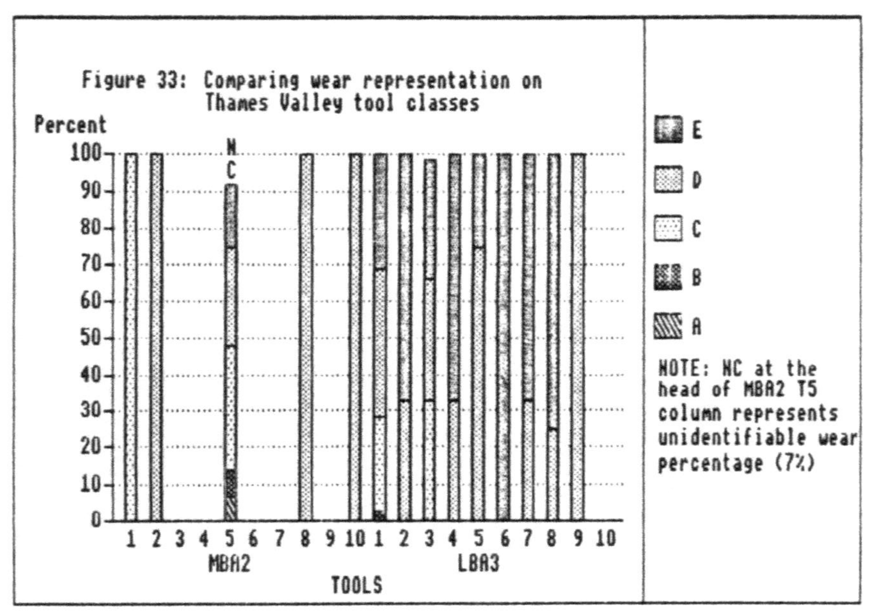

Figure 33: Comparing wear representation on Thames Valley tool classes

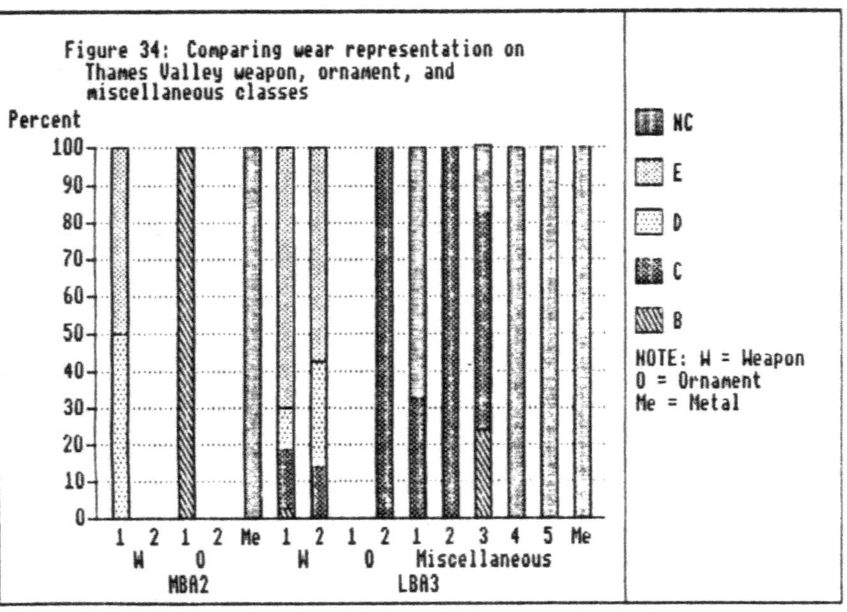

Figure 34: Comparing wear representation on Thames Valley weapon, ornament, and miscellaneous classes

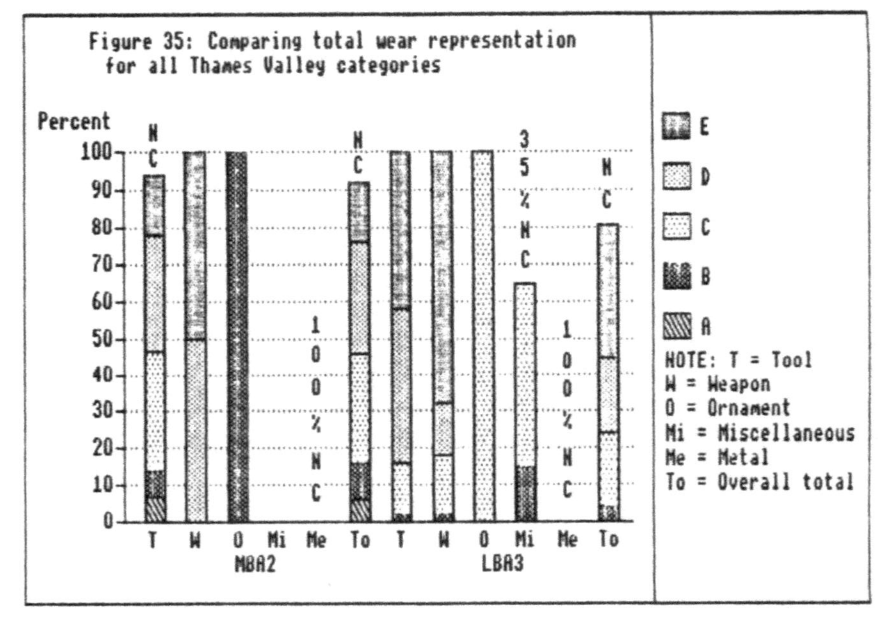

Figure 35: Comparing total wear representation for all Thames Valley categories

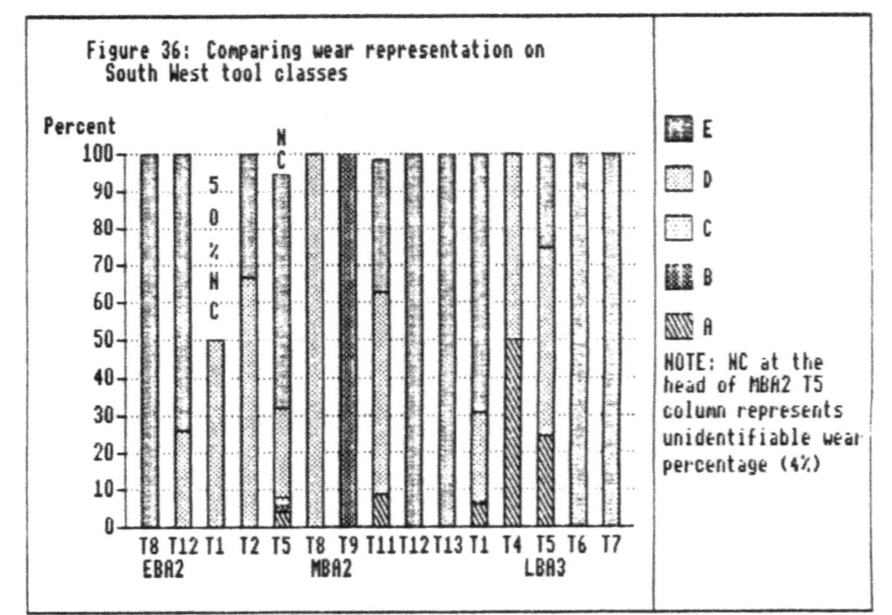

Figure 36: Comparing wear representation on South West tool classes

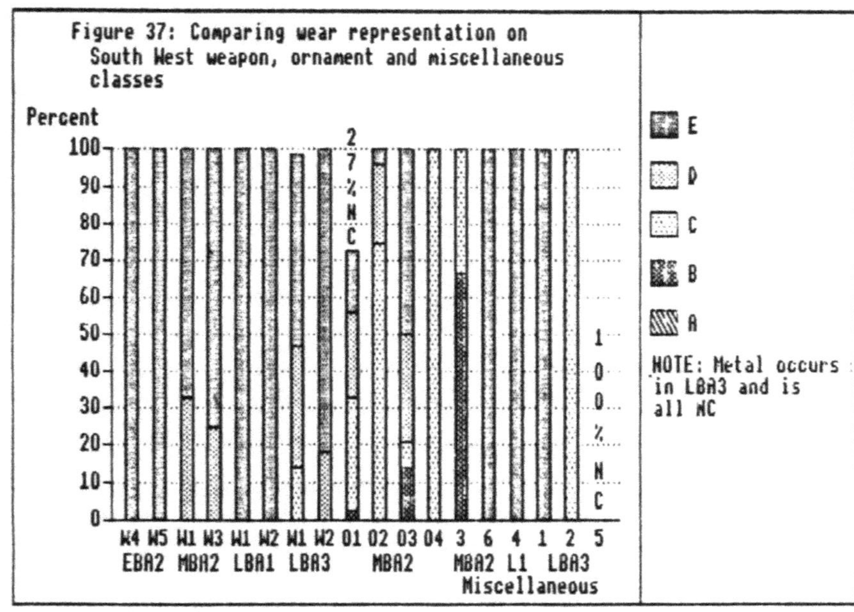

Figure 37: Comparing wear representation on South West weapon, ornament and miscellaneous classes

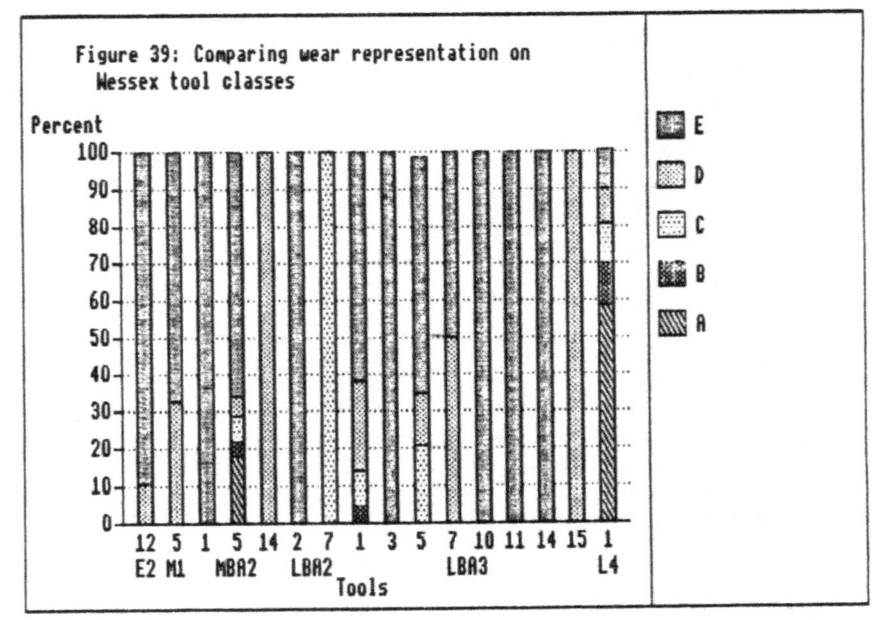

Figure 39: Comparing wear representation on Wessex tool classes

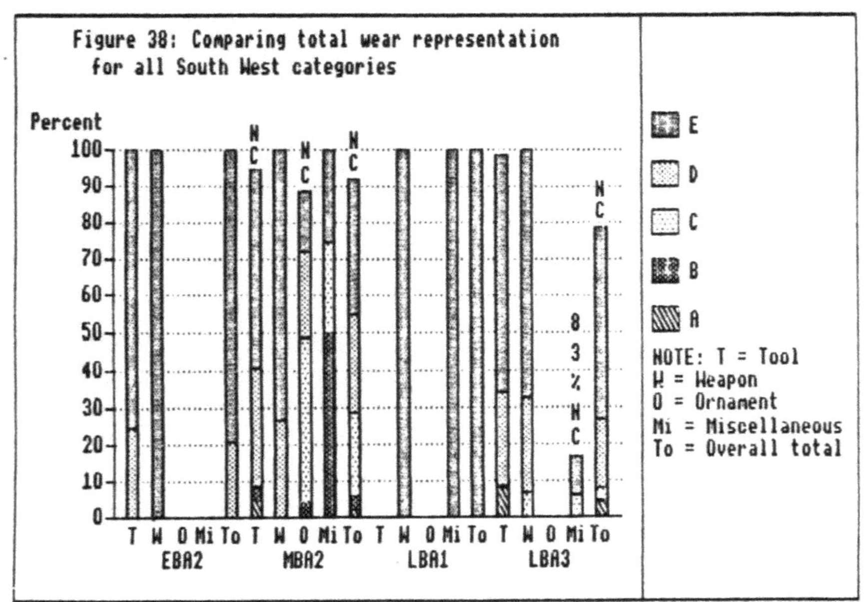

Figure 38: Comparing total wear representation for all South West categories

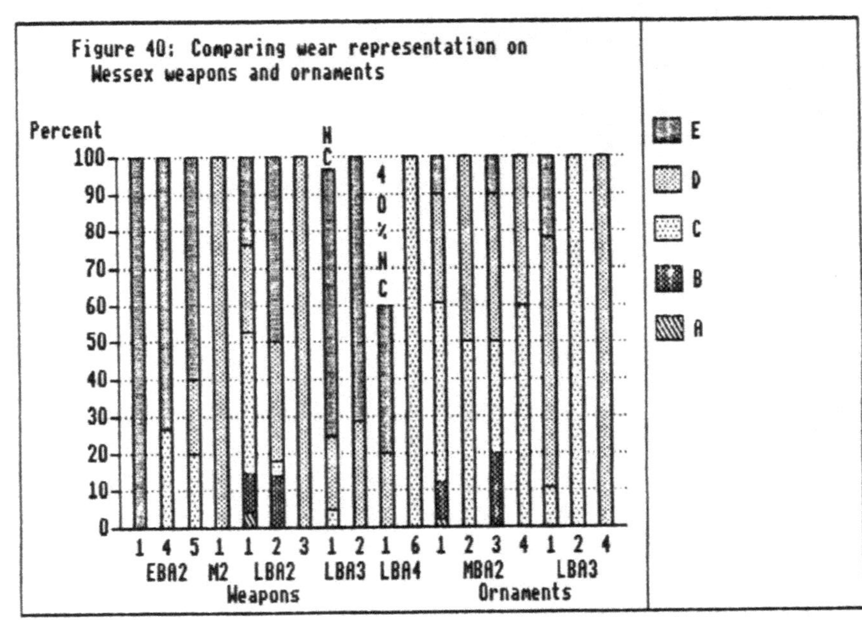

Figure 40: Comparing wear representation on Wessex weapons and ornaments

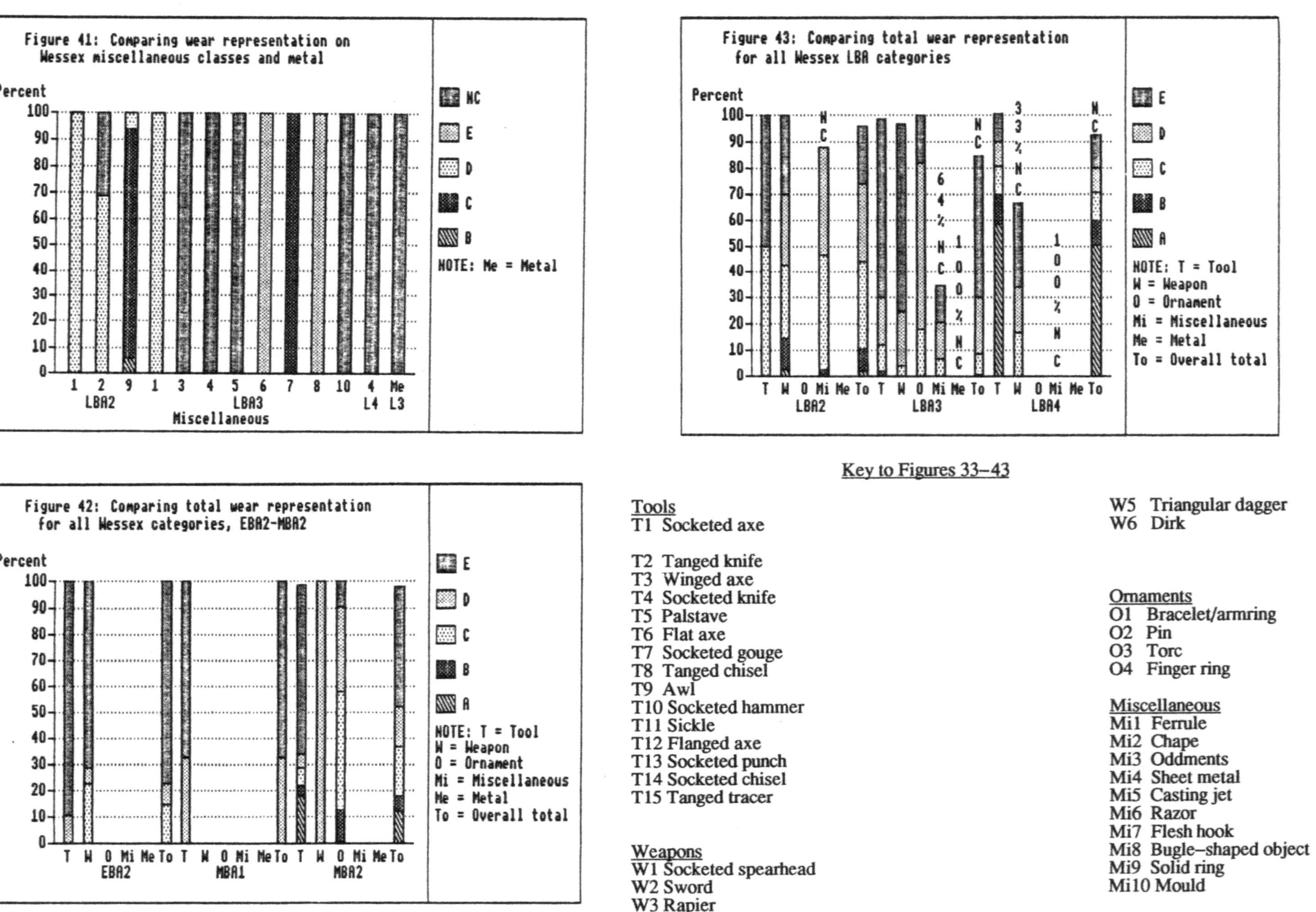

Key to Figures 33–43

Tools
T1 Socketed axe

T2 Tanged knife
T3 Winged axe
T4 Socketed knife
T5 Palstave
T6 Flat axe
T7 Socketed gouge
T8 Tanged chisel
T9 Awl
T10 Socketed hammer
T11 Sickle
T12 Flanged axe
T13 Socketed punch
T14 Socketed chisel
T15 Tanged tracer

Weapons
W1 Socketed spearhead
W2 Sword
W3 Rapier
W4 Tanged spearhead
W5 Triangular dagger
W6 Dirk

Ornaments
O1 Bracelet/armring
O2 Pin
O3 Torc
O4 Finger ring

Miscellaneous
Mi1 Ferrule
Mi2 Chape
Mi3 Oddments
Mi4 Sheet metal
Mi5 Casting jet
Mi6 Razor
Mi7 Flesh hook
Mi8 Bugle–shaped object
Mi9 Solid ring
Mi10 Mould

Me Metal

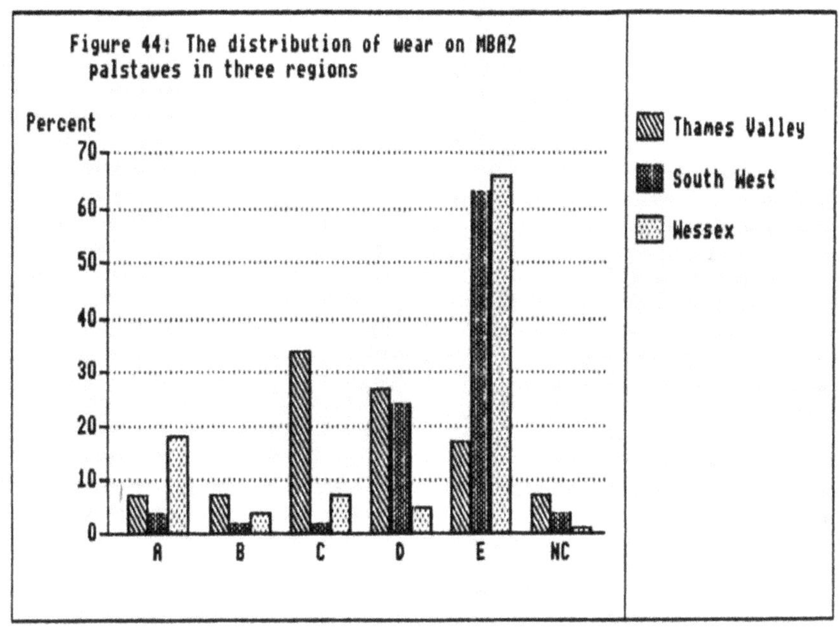

Figure 44: The distribution of wear on MBA2 palstaves in three regions

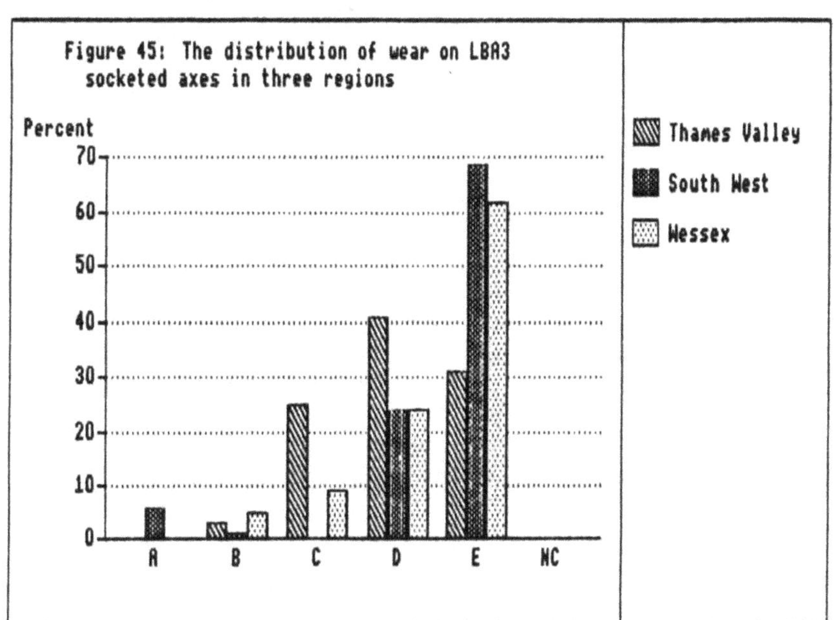

Figure 45: The distribution of wear on LBA3 socketed axes in three regions

Miscellaneous pieces are too infrequent to allow detailed observations, and a large number of them are unclassifiable; metal lumps are all unclassifiable and most are incomplete.

We can graph the differences between wear for palstaves and socketed axes for the regions in MBA2 and LBA3 (Figs. 44–5). There is greater emphasis on heavy wear of palstaves in Wessex and the South West, but there are also more unworn palstaves from Wessex. Moderate wear typifies palstaves from the Thames Valley. In LBA3, socketed axes are mainly subject to heavy wear before deposition, with the Thames Valley again exhibiting moderate wear. As these objects make up the larger proportion of tools in each region for these dates, it is no surprise that they reflect the general pattern of wear for tools. However, it does reinforce the point that these axes may be selected for deposition at various stages of their useful life, in contrast to the selection of other tools when they were worn. Perhaps axes were more freely available for deposition and represent less of a 'loss' than other tool types. The same principle would dictate that weapons were retained longer before deposition, and the deposition of a sword would represent a considerable loss in terms of investment and effort in manufacture. The weapons which characterise LBA2 in Wessex were deposited with less wear than in other periods and regions: did fashion dictate that these weapons be deposited at this stage, whereas later on it was possible for such objects to be used for a longer period before deposition? Or did the few hoards of this period attract the available objects, worn or not, because of problems affecting the metal supply? The conventional chronology may of course give a false impression of the components of each phase: some of the same objects may have been deposited later than the others and when they were more worn. Others may have been recycled immediately. Again, uncertainty clouds the picture.

Our analysis of wear has refined the picture of core/periphery relationships and has also highlighted variations in circulation time. Now we can see that not all objects of a particular phase circulated for equal lengths of time before their deposition. The wear on axes seems to indicate this best: when other pieces were quite heavily worn, axes with less wear could be deposited. Thus, certain classes of object do seem to have been more freely available and easily procured than others, despite any pressures on the metal supply that might have limited the deposition of other items. A phase based around weapons, such as LBA2, saw the deposition of less heavily worn items, possibly because prestige items were deposited in a more rapid cycle of consumption. Perhaps the number and size of hoards in LBA3 restricted the speed at which they could be deposited, because of the danger of reducing the metal supply too severely. This is perhaps reflected by the deposition of items with more wear. The supply of raw material from outside must have been quite limited in nearly all regions during LBA3. The one exception was the Thames Valley, where pieces with less wear were deposited, indicating the dominant position attained by this region within the overall system.

Individual patterns of wear on objects within hoards do not yield such a coherent picture: the patterns of wear seem to vary regionally and chronologically. Thus, hoards are hard to categorise on the basis of content and wear analysis alone: hoards are part of a larger system of metalwork production, distribution, and consumption, and wear is only one part of that system. Some bias is introduced by the incomplete state of many hoards. Also, it is uncertain whether or not particular deposits were sealed. Where we have reasonable contextual information, this should also be taken into account.

CONTEXT AND CIRCUMSTANCES OF DEPOSITION

As usual, the initial problem is the intractability of the information: many discoveries are poorly recorded or do not record any information about their exact contexts. 'From a field' does not tell us much about the actual location or context of the deposit. This is partly due to the inexpert ature of some of the finders (in other cases, the detail is surprisingly complete, even for finds made a century or more ago, and one wonders if this is perhaps a case of embroidering the detail). Often the quality of the record is partly due to the circumstances under which many hoards are found. Thus, a hoard may be ploughed to the surface and the pieces lie there until they are recognised and collected. Meanwhile, the plough has probably destroyed any traces of a hole or container. Other people remove things in their excitement, professionals included, and do not observe how the pieces may have been lying, or whether any other material was associated with them. We can only note the circumstances of many deposits as uncertain:

Table 15: The number of uncertain contexts for hoards from each phase and region

	Undated				EBA2			MBA2			
	TV	SW	W	EA	TV	W	EA	TV	SW	W	EA
Uncertain	1	3	5	50	2	1	3	5	16	20	15
Total hoards	1	4	6	51	4	3	3	10	28	38	20

	LBA1		LBA2			LBA3				LBA4	
	SW	EA	TV	W	EA	TV	SW	W	EA	W	EA
Uncertain	1	2	1	2	4	10	2	11	53	9	2
Total hoards	1	7	1	4	6	21	4	15	73	11	4

We can see from this that in some phases most, if not all, hoards come from uncertain contexts; in other periods, this is true of at least half the finds. However, in LBA1 in East Anglia only two of the seven hoards come from uncertain contexts, and this applies to only a third of the EBA2 hoards in Wessex. Some regions have complete contextual information for all the hoards in a particular phase: EBA2 hoards from the South West, for example, and MBA1 in Wessex (only one hoard found!).

We are left with a selection of information, which we can examine in various ways. We can work out the depths at which particular hoards were buried. The graphs (Figs. 46–9) show that the majority of hoards are buried at a fairly shallow depth, between 30 and 60 cm (1 and 2 ft). This would seem to be the rough depth penetrated when ploughing in recent times, and usually the depth of topsoil over subsoil. In other words, this would be the depth at which we would expect to see archaeological features cut into a 'natural' surface: that surface having first been eroded by more recent activities. First, this would seem to imply that many hoards are far from being 'closed' deposits, because some of their contents could previously have been ploughed up without record. Secondly, many hoards could easily be from undiscovered archaeological sites; other features or material might not have been apparent at the time of the discovery. Limited excavations around hoards or hoard find spots, however, have generally failed to find anything else of significance. For example, EA67, North Elmham I, was discovered after ploughing, but subsequent excavation found the very base of the pit which had contained the hoard, but no other features. Then, we do have hoards located in or around settlements or other known sites. These can be listed:

TV21	Bourton-on-the-Water	LBA3	Near ditches of 'Bronze Age settlements'
TV23	Nottingham Hill	LBA3	Hillfort, settlement context
TV34	Wallingford	LBA3	Possible settlement on bank of or island in Thames
SW23	Worth	LBA1	'In an ancient entrenchment'
SW28	Norton Fitzwarren	MBA2	Hillfort, scooped hole in bank outside
W16	Waddon Hill	EBA2	'At an earthwork'
W26	Bursledon Brick Pit	MBA2	Near a settlement site
W32	Danebury	LBA4	Hillfort, small pit under the rampart (possibly predates the site)
W37	Plaitford	MBA2	Near settlement site

However, the coincidence of 'hoards' with settlements is very slight, and beyond this we can cite the evidence mapped and discussed by Lawson for the area around Snettisham (1980c, 281, 284 Fig. 9), where he postulated a series of settlements on the basis of aerial photographs in an area with much deposition. We also have the examples collated by Coombs in his thesis (1971, 408–9), and the hoard from Petters Sports

Field from outside our study area (O'Connell, 1986).
Other associations for hoards would seem to be with possible burials, cremations, or barrows. Such finds are:

TV9	Charvil Farm	MBA2	Possibly with a skeleton
TV37	Hagbourne Hill	LBA3	Possible cemetery site
SW10	Lovehayne	MBA2	'Found in a barrow'
SW30	Priddy	ND	In a barrow
SW41	West Buckland	MBA2	With charcoal and burnt bone
W1	Eggardon Hill	LBA4	Possibly in a barrow
W60	Amesbury	LBA3	'On site of a ploughed out barrow'
W68	Durnford	MBA2	Found in a barrow
W74	Manton Copse	LBA3	'Found lying together with ashes'
W75	Salisbury	ND	'From tumuli'
EA20	'Granta Fen'	LBA1	'With human bones'
EA117	Eriswell I	LBA3	'Found in a Roman mound'
EA118	Eriswell II	MBA2	'From a tumulus now destroyed'

Again, the evidence is mainly circumstantial and possibly enhanced for the benefit of collectors, reporters, and the public. The objects supposedly from barrows appear to have been separate from any burials, except for W68, Durnford, where urns were also found, but not necessarily in association. The author has drawn attention to the association of hoards with burials in a paper on the hoard from West Buckland, SW41 (R Taylor, 1982). With TV9, Charvil Farm, there are two reports of the finding of the pair of armrings, one asserting that they were found with a skeleton, and the other denying this possibility. It would be hard to make much of this slight evidence (or easy to make too much of it!), and other contextual associations may have more significance.

Other information recorded about hoards and their discovery relates to the positioning of the objects, burial under stones, and burial in containers. The positioning of objects on discovery may be fanciful in certain cases, but there can be no doubting the veracity of other reports.

TV21	Bourton-on-the-Water	LBA3	'4 pairs in a circle', in a hole covered with flat stones
SW3	Westbury-on-Trym	EBA2	'Close together on a mat of twigs'
SW27	Milverton	EBA2	One on top of another
W27	HMS Sultan	MBA2	Palstaves set vertically in a small pit
W47	Brading Marsh	MBA2	Armrings set 'in a crescent' around socket of spearhead
W55	Arreton Down	EBA2	Axes laid on spearheads
W56	Totland	EBA2	'In a sort of little heap'
EA18	Grunty Fen	MBA2/ LBA1	Palstaves separated from torc by a turf
EA105	Bramfield	MBA2	In a circle, enclosing other examples

Other reports mention objects being found in a heap or confined within a small space or a specially dug hole. If we recall the deposit at Beeston Regis, EA41, where, although the objects were in a pot, they had possibly been tied together with string, we might suppose that some of these arrangements resulted from the deposition of a bundle of objects. The organic string or thong could have decayed and the pieces would have come to rest in an apparent arrangement, assuming a new importance on discovery. SW3, Westbury-on-Trym, was included here because of the careful arrangement of the pieces on a mat of twigs; equally, we may see the 'mat of twigs of tree or rush', as the remains of a coarsely woven container for the objects, perhaps a basket. Other containers that we know of are pots, boxes, a wooden tub, and possibly leather bags.

TV23	Nottingham Hill	LBA3	Possible traces of a box
SW24	Edington Burtle	MBA2	In a box
W29	Hinton	ND	'In a decayed earthen pot'
EA8	Green End Road	LBA3	Probably in a bag
EA21	Stuntney	LBA3	In a tub
EA27	Isleham	LBA2	In a pot-lined pit
EA41	Beeston Regis	LBA3	In a pot
EA53	Gorleston I	LBA3	Probably in a bag
EA93	Waterden	LBA3	Found 'in a round container'

Finally, attention has been drawn to a number of examples buried under stones or in similar places:

TV5	New Windsor	LBA3	'Under a stone'
TV17	Bradwell	LBA3	'Contained in a cist'
TV21	Bourton-on-the-Water	LBA3	Covered with flat stones
SW7	Bovey Tracey	MBA2	'Under a block of granite'
SW17	Plymstock	EBA2	Lying under a stone

These would seem to be variations on the need for a container for the objects, perhaps to seal the pit in which the pieces were buried. Alternatively, the stones could be the remains of barrows, or markers for the hoard site. Attention has been focussed on the exceptions because of this extra detail, as other hoards may originally have had such features that were not observed on discovery. Alternatively, they may have been buried in a more haphazard manner. Of course, when so many are ploughed up, we cannot hope to tell how carefully the pieces may have originally been deposited.

Another feature, relating to the discovery of hoards, is the frequent mention of wet conditions at the find spot. This has come to dominate many arguments about the interpretations of deposition. It is doubtful whether this factor is of particular significance when dealing with many of these hoards, particularly when 'wet conditions' are part of the natural surroundings of an area. This may be one of the reasons for a concentration of finds in an area of peat: simply that there has been much peat cutting in the area, bringing the finds to light. Again, the attraction may have been due to some other invisible factor, such as a nearby settlement, or even the need to hide objects in a more 'secure' place, as attested by Randsborg for historical times in Denmark (see Chap. 1 above). Against the number of hoards from wet areas can be set the number from dry land deposits. All this may amount to a red herring!

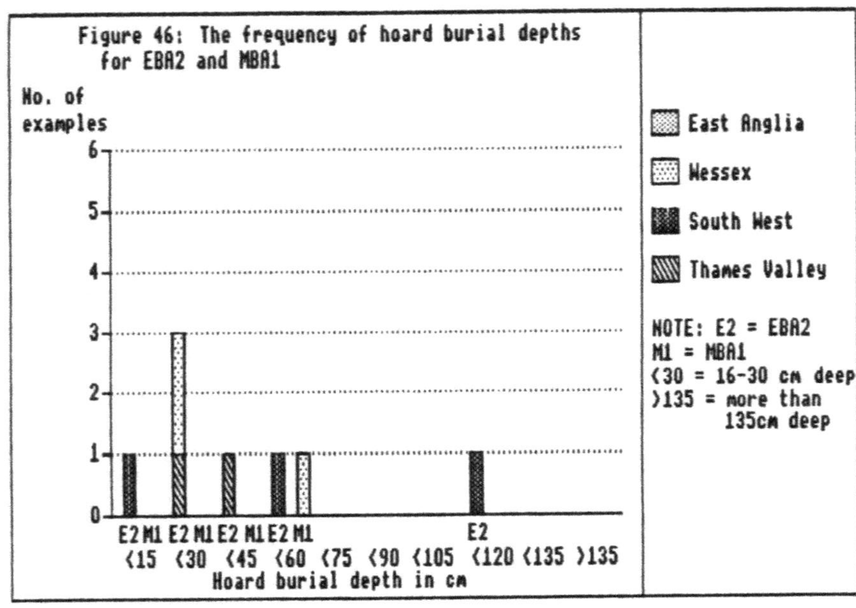

Figure 46: The frequency of hoard burial depths for EBA2 and MBA1

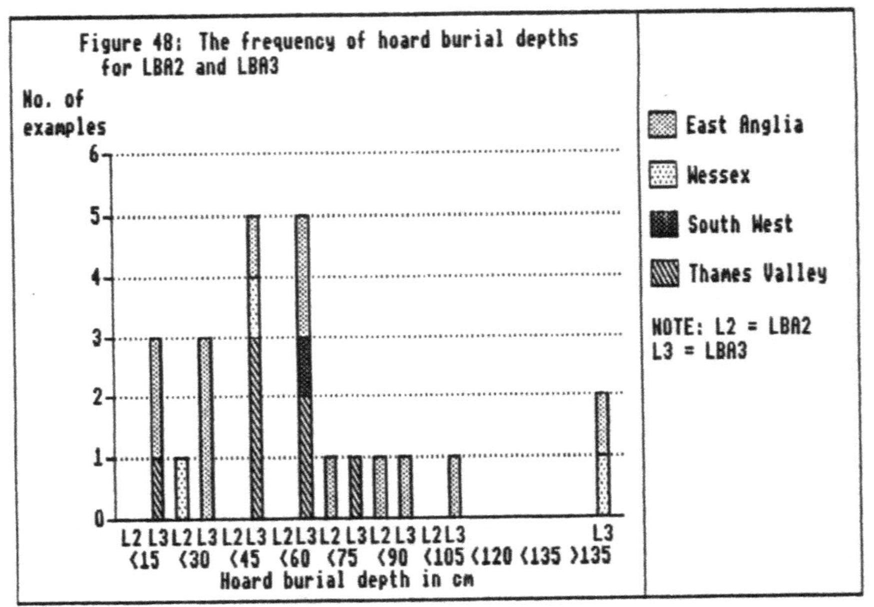

Figure 48: The frequency of hoard burial depths for LBA2 and LBA3

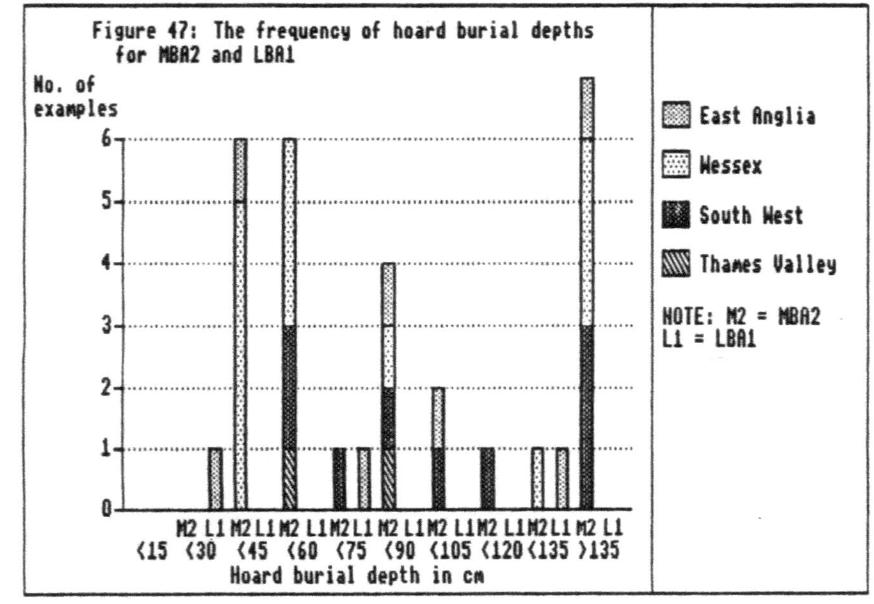

Figure 47: The frequency of hoard burial depths for MBA2 and LBA1

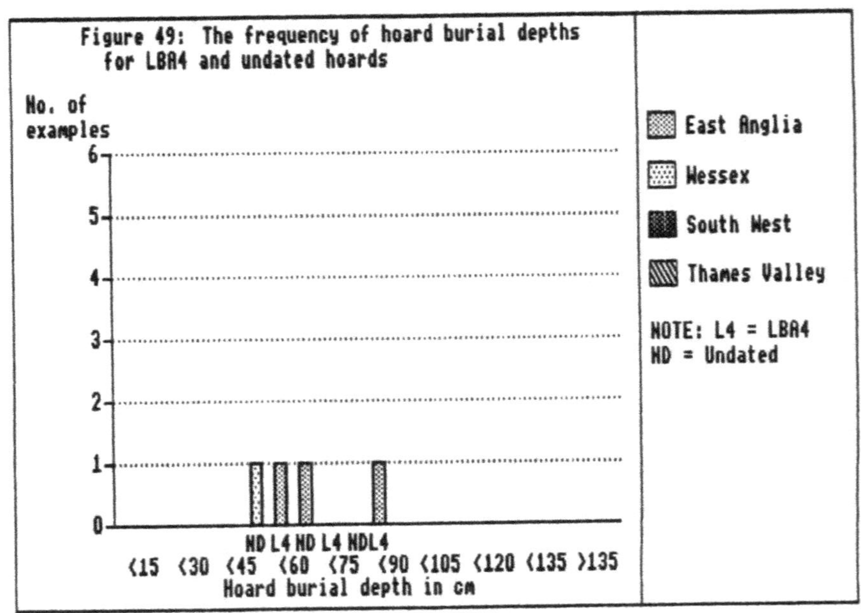

Figure 49: The frequency of hoard burial depths for LBA4 and undated hoards

TV10 Speen	LBA3	'Found in peat'
SW19 Bloody Pool	LBA3	'Found in a swampy hollow'
SW24 Edington Burtle	MBA2	8ft (240 cm) deep in peat
SW33 Spaxton	MBA2	In some marshy ground 6ft (180 cm) below surface
W23 Andover	LBA2	1ft (30 cm) down in peaty soil
W25 Blackmoor	LBA2	'Found under peat'
W41 Cobden Bridge	LBA3	13 or 14ft (390 or 420 cm) from surface below peaty soil
W49 Billingham House	MBA2	In a peat bed, 14ft (420 cm) from the surface
W54 Arreton	MBA2?	'From a piece of marshy land'
EA10 Chatteris	LBA1	Lying on clay under the peat
EA14 Coveney Fen	LBA1	'Considerable depth under peat, on the clay'
EA18 Grunty Fen	MBA2/ LBA1	Depth of 3ft (90 cm) in peat soil
EA21 Stuntney	LBA3	In a tub in peat fen
EA23 Whittlesey	LBA3	'Found in the turf'
EA24 Wilburton Fen	LBA2	On clay below peat surface
EA42 Boughton Fen	MBA2	Found digging peat
EA98 Wiggenhall	MBA2	'In the fens'
EA128 Lakenheath Fen	LBA2	'In fen'

In many of these cases, mention is made of the great depth of the discovery below the peat, or that they were found on the clay below the peat. It is possible that the build–up of peat took place after deposition and thus buried the hoard to a greater depth. In other cases, objects may well have been sunk in wet ground (literally, dropping to the bottom of the deposit), or have been buried near the surface of soft ground, sinking only later. Pryor's observations on fen deposition have been recorded in the literature survey (Chap. 1). Any associated organic material, which might indicate settlement alongside the hoards, would be easily missed in such contexts.

On the whole, we seem to have very little to go on in relation to contextual information about hoards: to talk about the circumstances of deposition of a hoard, when we know very little of the contemporary landscape, is perhaps to stretch the information too far. We can only make observations and hope that they make some sense overall; the reasons for deposition (may) transcend any of these factors. In conclusion, the majority of the evidence would seem to favour the simple burial of objects near the surface, possibly in some container or bundled up, and sometimes close to a known feature, such as a settlement, hillfort, or barrow. In certain cases, hoards may have been laid out on the ground and covered only later. The possibilities for post–depositional biases are enormous and hard to take into account: we can only assume that the few accounts of *in situ* hoards are representative of the wider pattern. Overall distributions of hoards within the regions and by date need to be examined for further information.

DISTRIBUTION

As already noted above (Chap. 4), the hoards were mapped according to their regional attribution, using National Grid References which were as accurate as possible. This gives us four basic maps (Maps 1–4), showing all hoards in each region whatever their date: two hoards, TV24 and TV26, are not on the Thames Valley map, because they fall well outside its boundaries; they are both EBA2 in date: TV24 is from the northern side of the Severn, and TV26 is from near Stroud north of the Cotswolds. Otherwise, all points have been plotted as listed in the Catalogue (App. A). Therefore, they include some collections which may not have been hoards and others which are doubtful or poorly attributed. Nevertheless, concentrations make themselves apparent in the distributions, or the distributions seem to conform to certain geographical factors. The distributions were also crudely plotted on the BBC microcomputer for rapid comparison and random plotting, as described in Chapter 4. The various regions can now be considered in more detail.

Thames Valley

What observations can we make about the distribution of hoards in the Thames Valley? Looking at the overall distribution (Map 1), we find that many hoards lie close to the river and fall into several small clusters of findspots, eg TV1–3, 5–7, and TV14–16, 18, 20. This pattern is reflected chronologically as well: the river seems to be most important in MBA2 and LBA3. Interestingly, the two EBA2 hoards within the area, TV4 and TV25, are peripheral to the areas with later deposits. The computer printouts show this broad patterning for all hoards (Fig. 50), MBA2 hoards (Fig. 51), and LBA3 hoards (Fig. 52). A random plot of 35 points within the range of the Thames Valley coordinates (Fig. 53) actually shows some small concentrations, but many of the points lie away from the river.

We can test this random distribution against the overall distribution of Thames Valley hoards using the chi–squared test, with the null hypothesis that there is no relationship between the patterning of hoards and a random distribution:

All hoards

		Present	Absent	
Random plot	Present	7	21	28
	Absent	13	69	82
		20	90	110

chi-squared = 1.1738 DF = 1
Significant at 0.5 level (50% chance of accepting null hypothesis)

Analysis is by the presence or absence of hoards in any grid square: no attempt has been made to take into account the presence of more than one hoard in a particular square, for this would otherwise lend more weight to an association. The level of significance suggests that the actual distribution of hoards could be random or non random. If we repeat the analysis between MBA2 and LBA3 hoards, we see the following:

MBA2

		Present	Absent	
LBA3	Present	4	11	15
	Absent	4	91	95
		8	102	110

Chi-squared = 9.687 DF = 1
Significant at 0.005 level

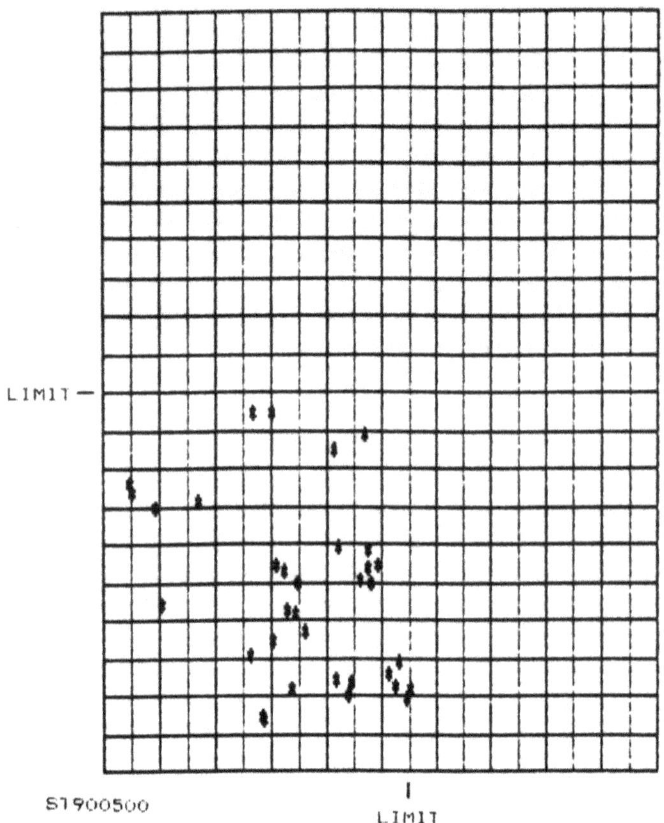

Figure 50: Computer plot of the distribution of all hoards in the Thames Valley

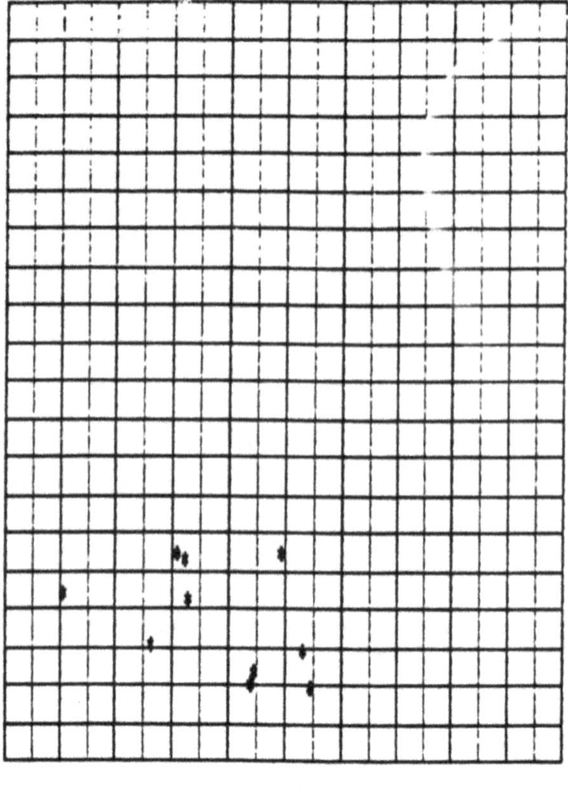

Figure 51: Computer plot of the distribution of MBA2 hoards in the Thames Valley

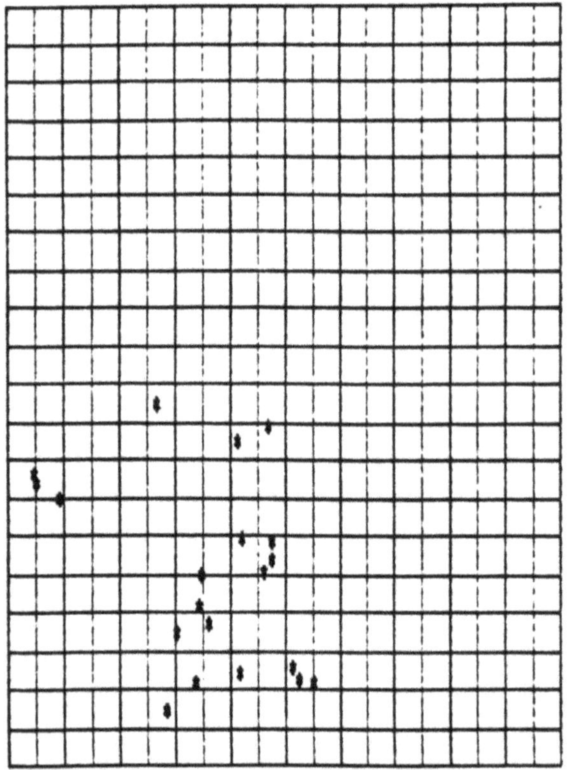

Figure 52: Computer plot of the distribution of LBA3 hoards in the Thames Valley

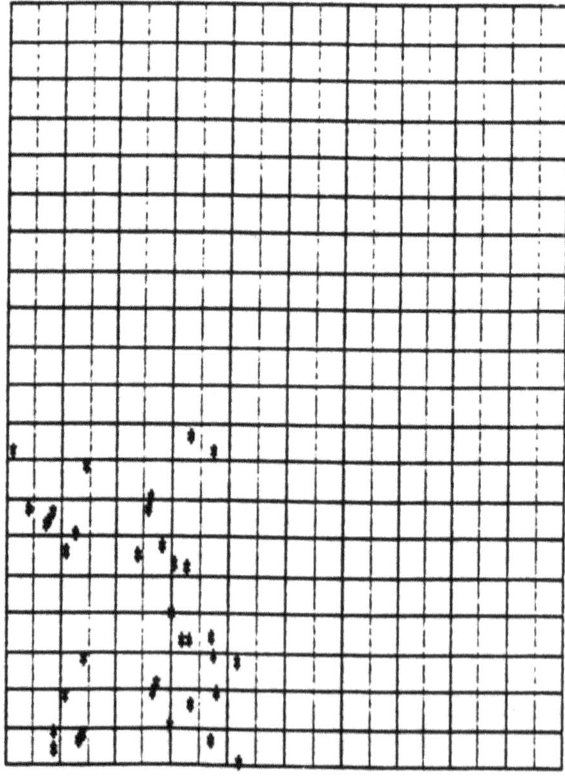

Figure 53: Computer plot of random distribution of hoards in the Thames Valley

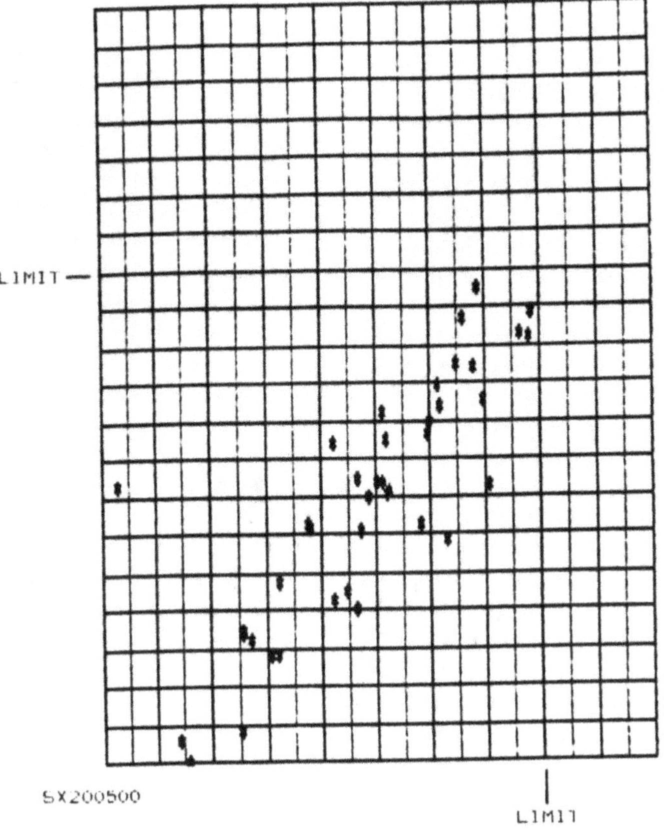

Figure 54: Computer plot of the distribution of all hoards in the South West

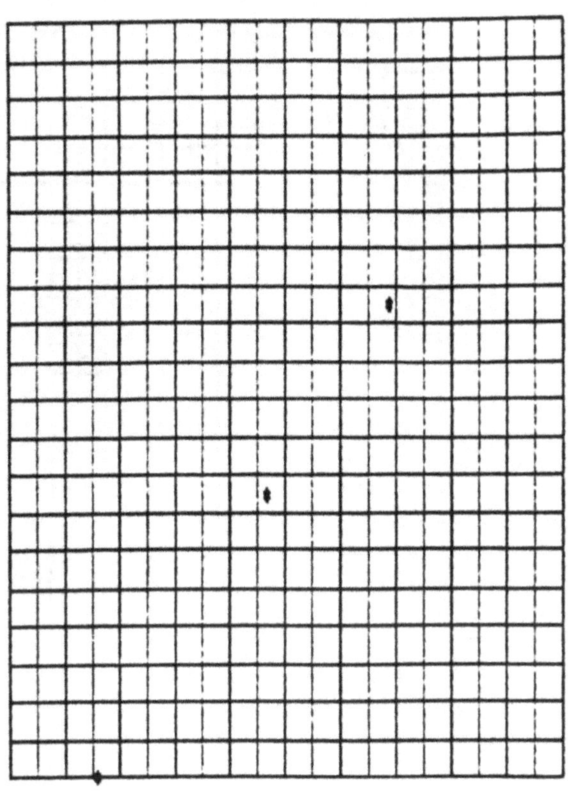

Figure 55: Computer plot of the distribution of EBA2 hoards in the South West

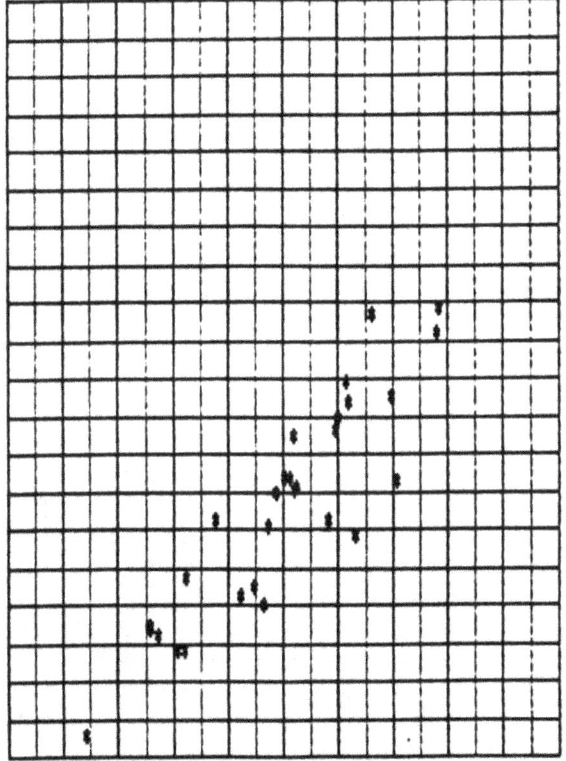

Figure 56: Computer plot of the distribution of MBA2 hoards in the South West

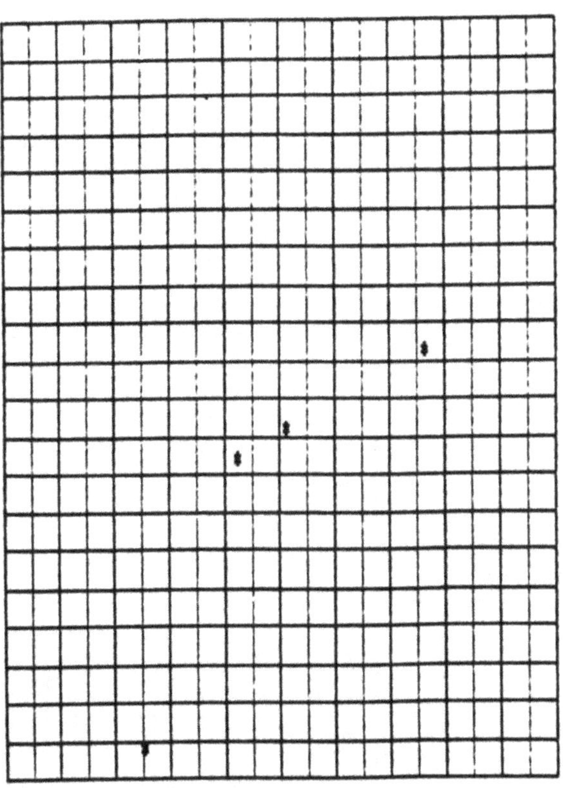

Figure 57: Computer plot of the distribution of LBA3 hoards in the South West

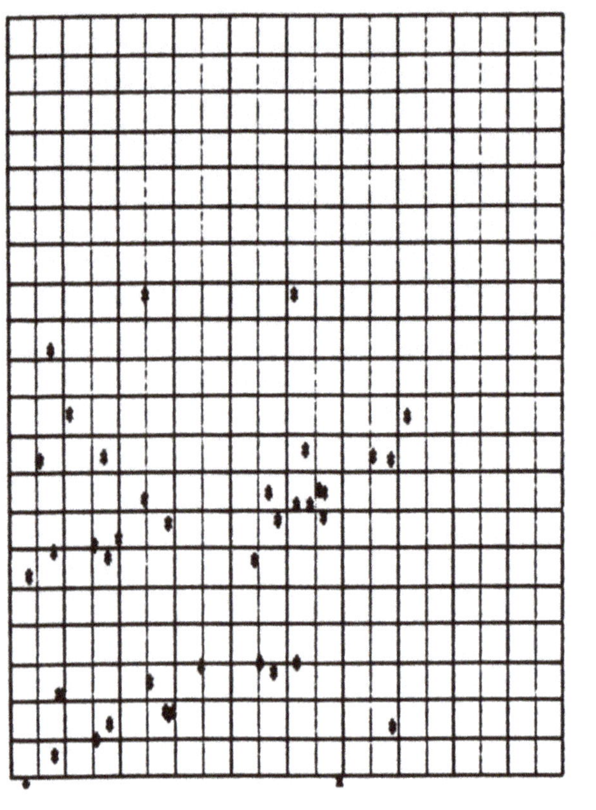

Figure 58: Computer plot of random distribution of hoards in the South West

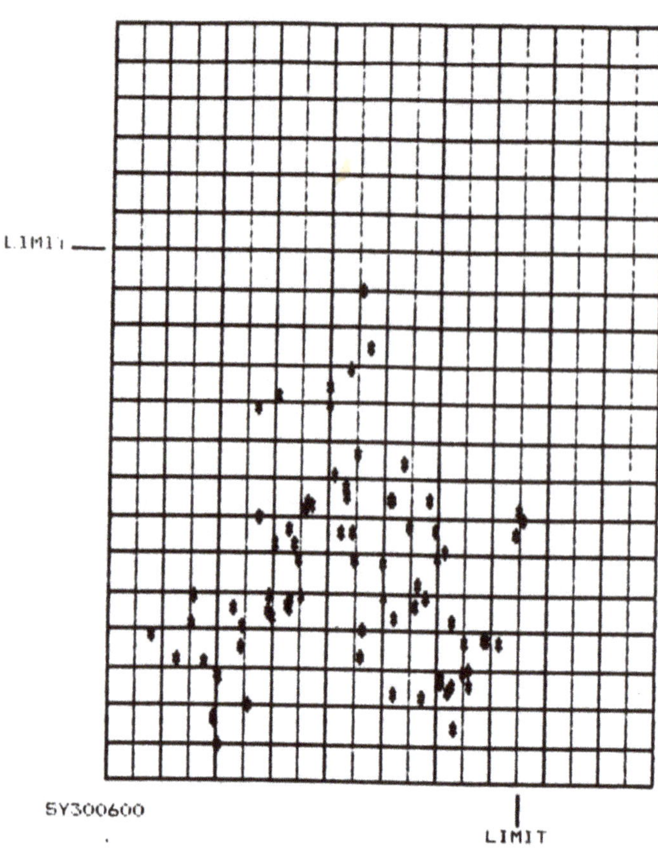

Figure 59: Computer plot of the distribution of all hoards in Wessex

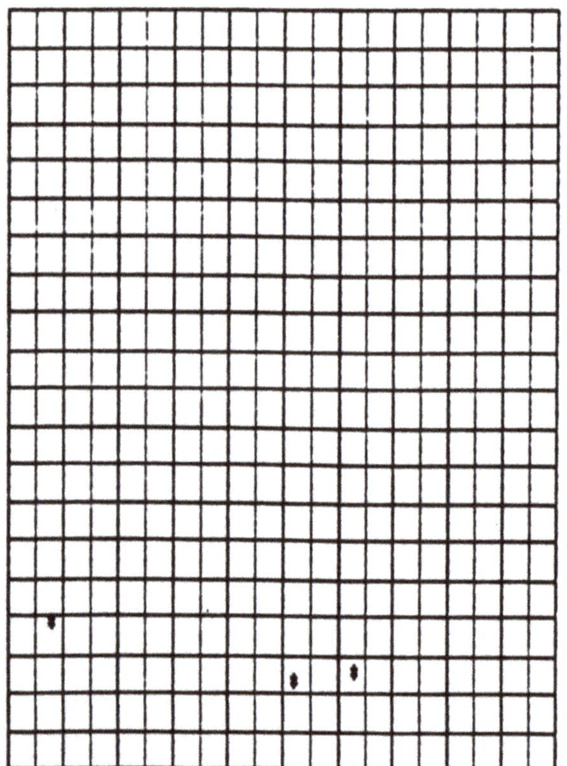

Figure 60: Computer plot of the distribution of EBA2 hoards in Wessex

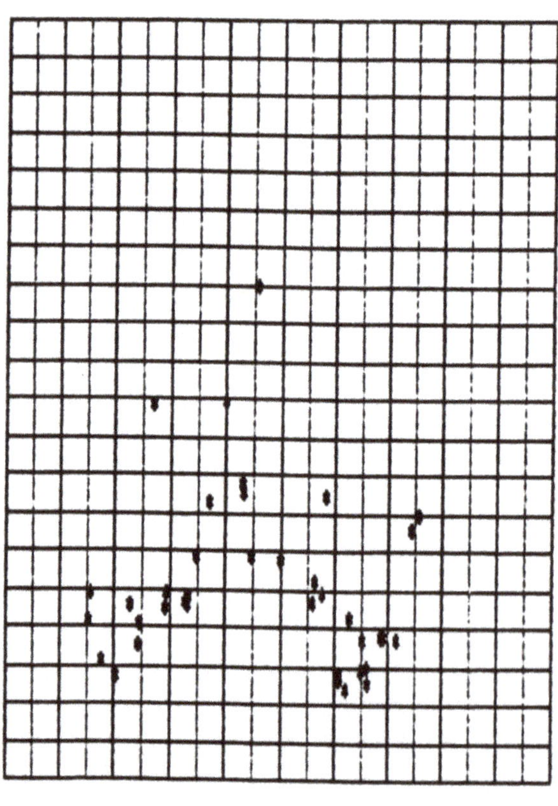

Figure 61: Computer plot of the distribution of MBA2 hoards in Wessex

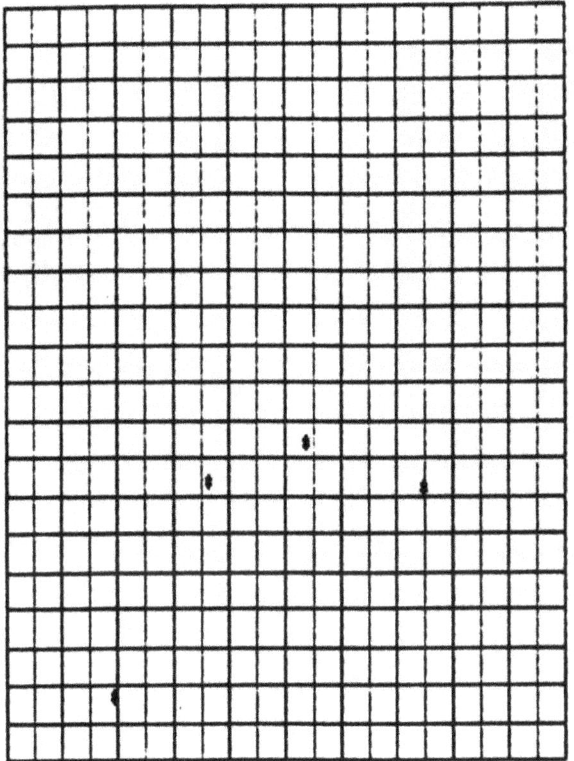

Figure 62: Computer plot of the distribution of LBA2 hoards in Wessex

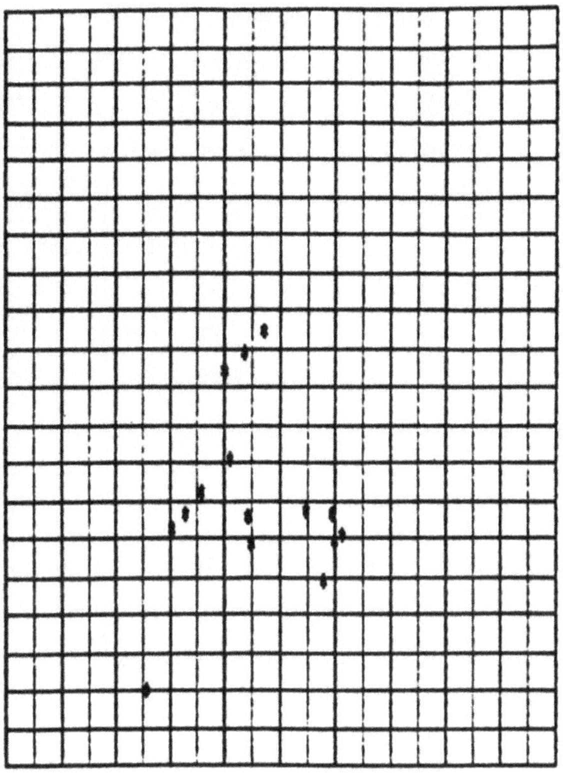

Figure 63: Computer plot of the distribution of LBA3 hoards in Wessex

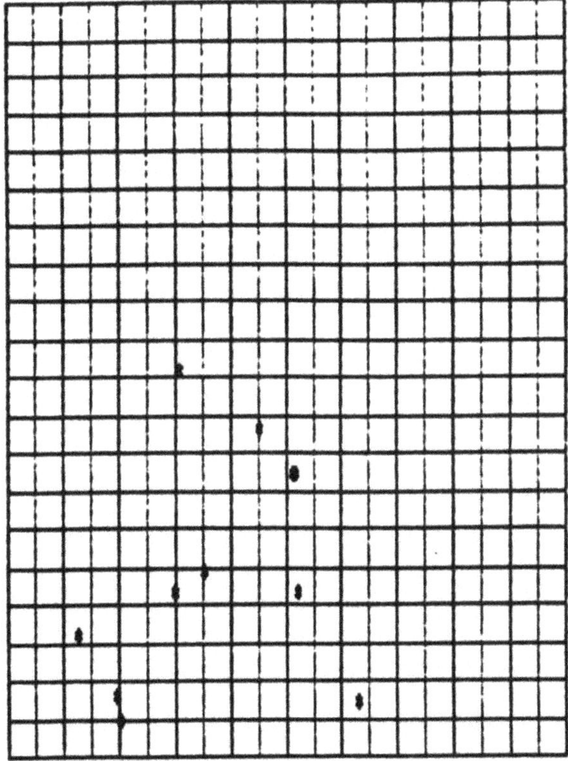

Figure 64: Computer plot of the distribution of LBA4 hoards in Wessex

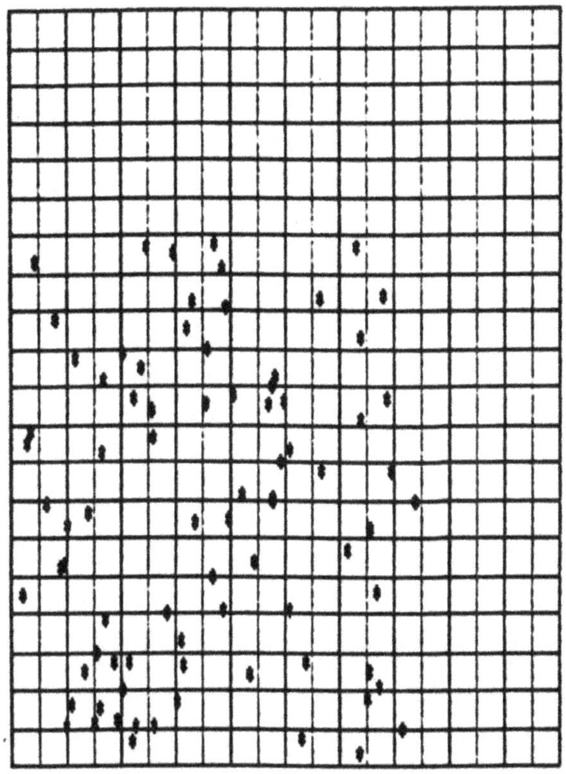

Figure 65: Computer plot of random distribution of hoards in Wessex

Therefore, there is a much more significant association here between the distribution of hoards in the Thames Valley in MBA2 and LBA3. This might suggest a selection of similar sites for deposition in both these periods. It suggests a greater continuity, than we might expect of material dating from two quite separate periods. This might suggest deposition at or near settlement sites, which were certainly present in the same areas in both the Middle and Late Bronze Ages, their positions being governed by the local topography and access to resources.

South West

Again, deposition seems to have taken place on lower ground with access to rivers; there are several such areas with a concentration of hoards, eg SW28, 35–7, and 41. Nearly 50% of SW hoards come from the low–lying area of the Somerset Levels (Map 2). The hoards in fact seem to lie along a north–east/south–west line, with SW12 as an outlier: an impression emphasised by the computer plots (Fig. 54). The three hoards of EBA2 are well–spaced (SW3, 17, 27), but lie along this same line (Fig. 55). The pattern is clearest in MBA2, with its preponderance of hoards, clustering at Taunton and on the fringe of Dartmoor (Fig. 56). The representation for LBA3 is sparse (Fig. 57), and the main phase of hoarding would seem to be restricted to MBA2. A random plot of 41 points within the range of the coordinates for the South West (Fig. 58) shows a fairly dispersed pattern in contrast to the 'linear' distribution of the actual deposits. We can repeat the chi–squared test for the South West distribution, as follows:

All

		Present	Absent	
Random plot	Present	7	27	34
	Absent	19	155	174
		26	182	208

Chi-squared = 2.431 DF = 1
Significant at 0.25 level

This shows once more that there is not much correlation between the actual distribution of hoards and a random plot, although there is some coincidence between the patterns. The same test between MBA2 and LBA3 gives the following:

MBA2

		Present	Absent	
LBA3	Present	1	18	19
	Absent	3	186	189
		4	204	208

Chi-squared = 1.2368 DF = 1
Significant at 0.5 level

There is even less correlation between these two distributions, but we must take account of the small number of observations for LBA3 and the large number of 'blank' squares, which will have a distorting effect on the calculation. Nevertheless, we cannot place much weight on a few dispersed hoards of LBA3 in relation to the pattern of deposition in MBA2.

Wessex

The distribution of hoards in the Wessex region shows several interesting features: a tendency for deposition to take place near to the coast, especially on the Isle of Wight, and proximity to rivers in lower lying areas (Map 3). Thus, we have a broad sweep of low–lying, well–irrigated land in the centre of the map with a spread of hoards. Then, nearer the coast, the hoards seem to be drawn to the sea. The north–east part of the Isle of Wight was also favoured as an area for deposition (Fig. 59).

The three EBA2 hoards (W16, W55, and W56) lie in the south of the region: W55 and W56 come from the Isle of Wight, but W16 comes from higher ground near to the coast and closer to rivers (Fig. 60). The MBA2 distribution seems to mirror the overall distribution of hoards in the area, and hoards are well represented at this time (Fig. 61). With the exception of one hoard the distribution seems to have moved further to the north in LBA2 (Fig. 62), an impression borne out by the spread in LBA3 (Fig. 63), possibly representing a move to higher ground. In LBA4 the distribution seems to move south towards the coast again (Fig. 64), which could correspond with the identification of some of these hoards as imports.

The random plot (Fig. 65) shows a wide scatter of points across the area, bearing little resemblance to the overall distribution, as borne out by the calculation of chi–squared:

All

		Present	Absent	
Random plot	Present	16	51	67
	Absent	32	111	143
		48	162	210

Chi-squared = 0.05845 DF = 1
Significant at 0.9 level

Thus, we can accept the null hypothesis that there is no relationship between a random distribution of points and the overall distribution of hoards in Wessex, which are therefore located in a particular way. The correlation between the distribution of MBA2 and LBA3 hoards can be given:

MBA2

		Present	Absent	
LBA3	Present	3	8	11
	Absent	22	177	199
		25	185	210

Chi-squared = 2.6141 D.F. = 1
Significant at 0.25 level

While this is not particularly significant, it does suggest some degree of association between these two distributions.

Access to the sea and rivers, in general, seems to have played a significant part in the distribution of hoards in Wessex: this should not surprise us, as this would have been a logical place for landing ships moving along the coast or across the Channel.

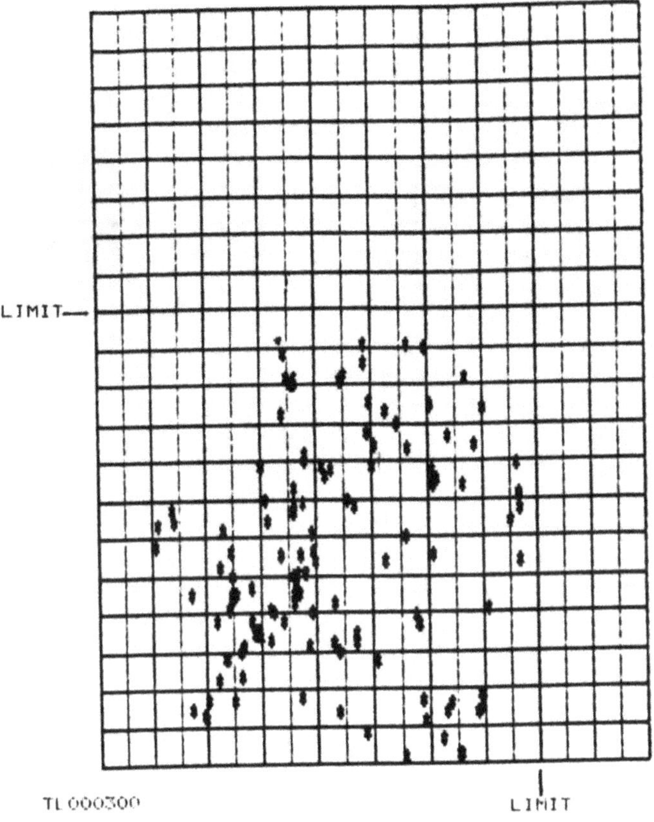

Figure 66: Computer plot of the distribution of all hoards in East Anglia

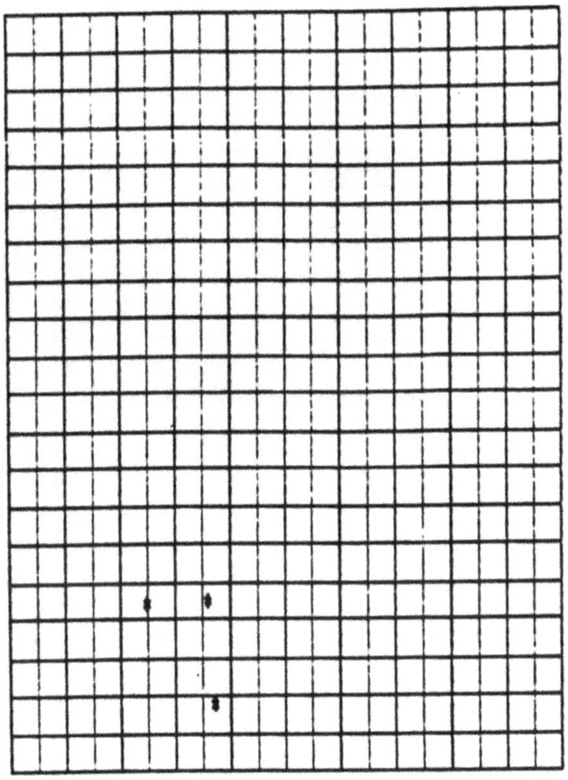

Figure 67: Computer plot of the distribution of EBA2 hoards in East Anglia

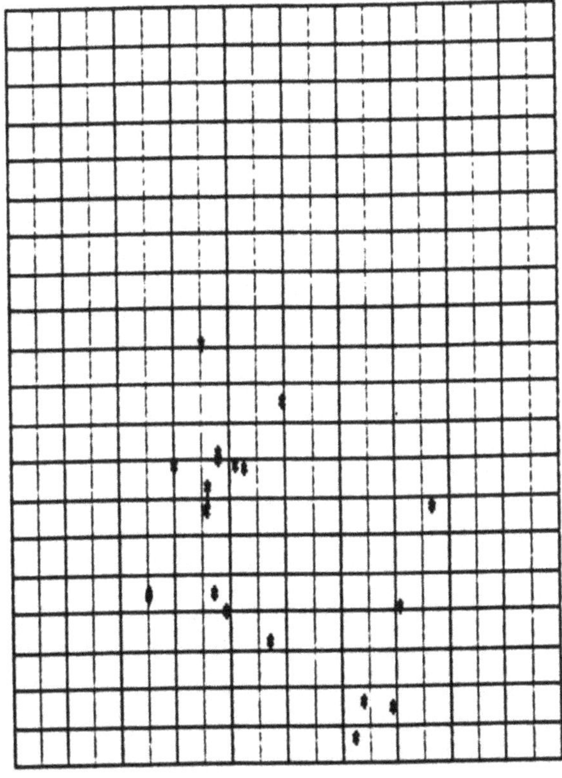

Figure 68: Computer plot of the distribution of MBA2 hoards in East Anglia

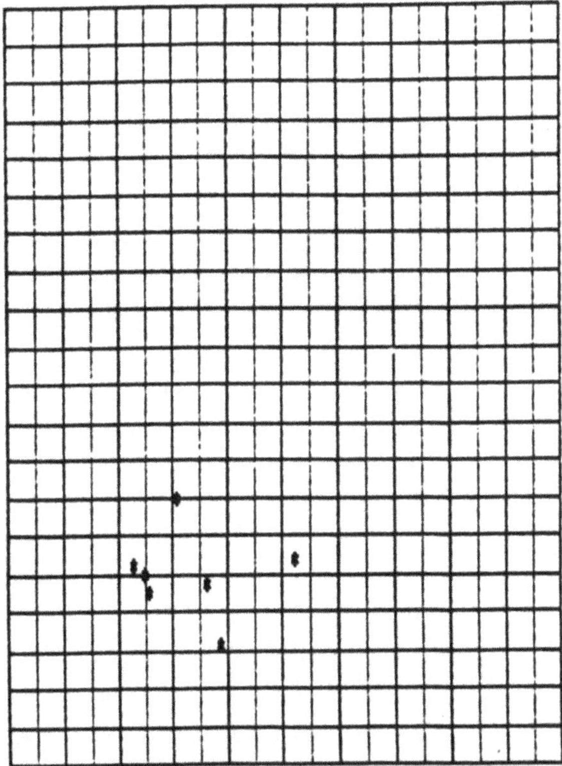

Figure 69: Computer plot of the distribution of LBA1 hoards in East Anglia

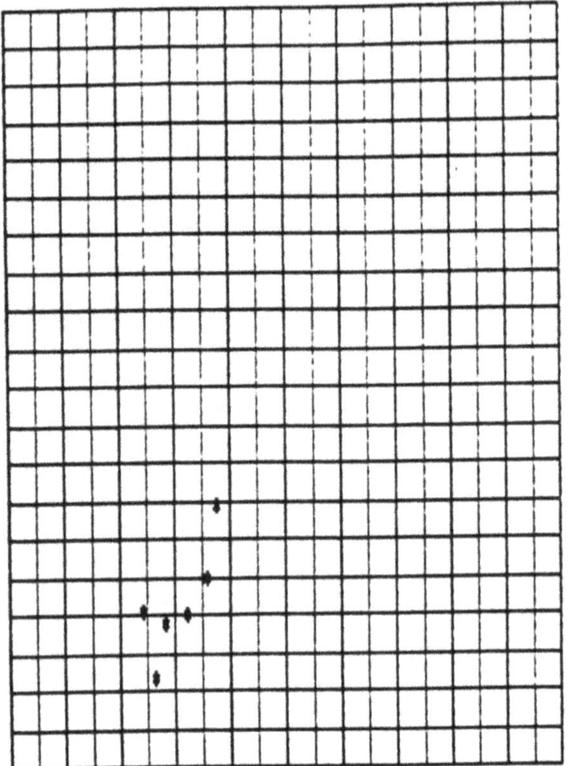

Figure 70: Computer plot of the distribution of LBA2 hoards in East Anglia

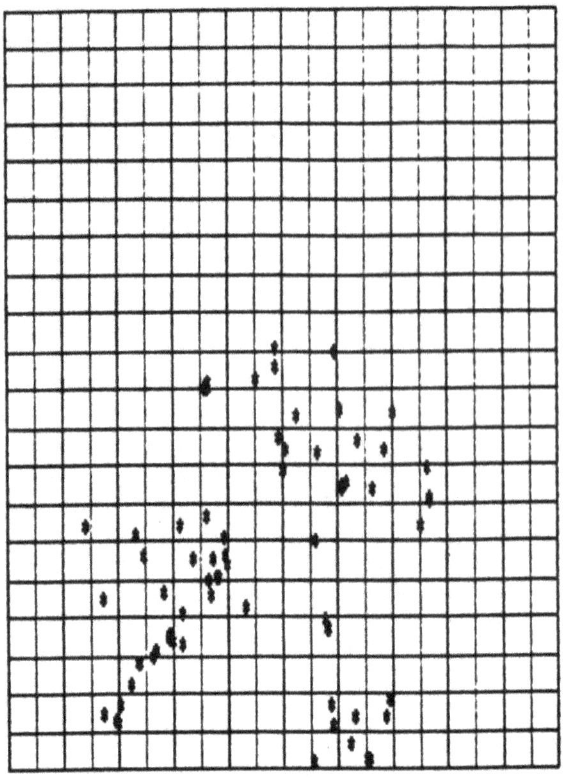

Figure 71: Computer plot of the distribution of LBA3 hoards in East Anglia

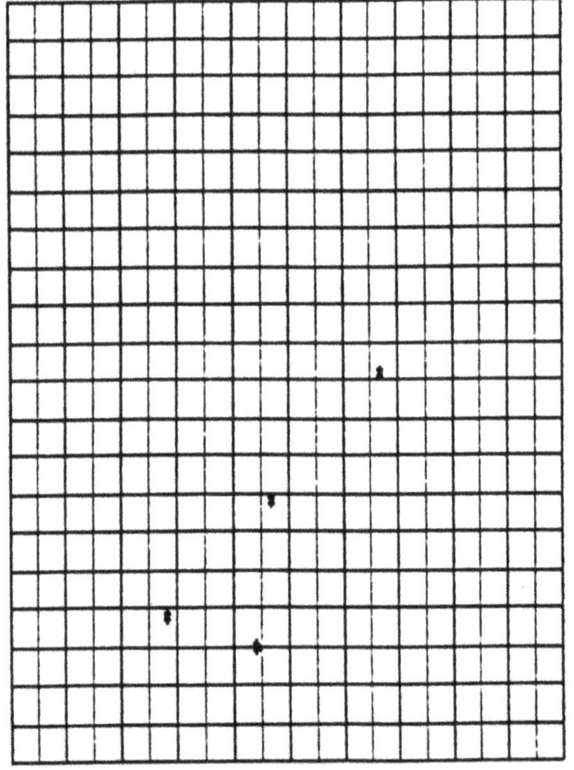

Figure 72: Computer plot of the distribution of LBA4 hoards in East Anglia

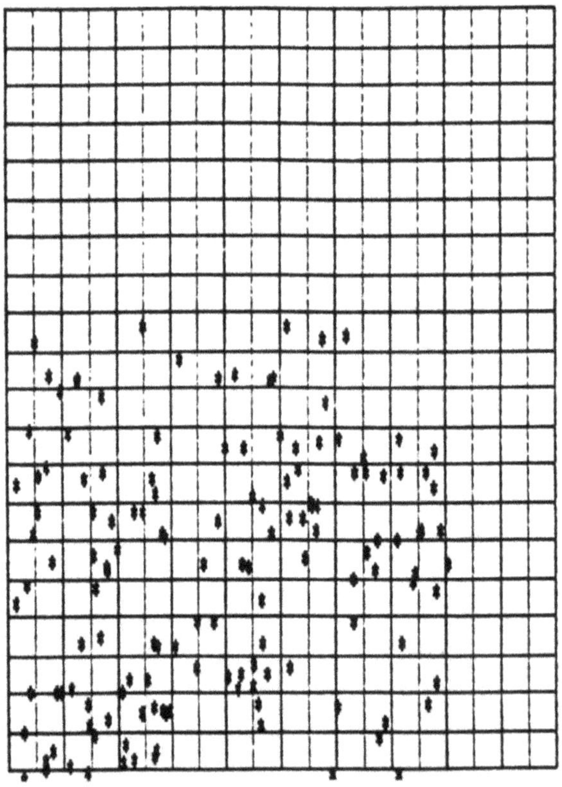

Figure 73: Computer plot of random distribution of hoards in East Anglia

East Anglia

Much of this region consists of fen, and here we find the greatest concentration of finds: a mass of hoards in the centre of the map (Map 4). Other groups were located on the coast or on the fringes of slightly higher ground. The hoards seem to 'map' the coastal outline on the computer plot (Fig. 66). The three EBA2 hoards lie in the centre of the region (EA15, EA113, and EA134), close to or in the fen (Fig. 67). The MBA2 hoards are central, and towards the coast as well, with most lying in the fen (Fig. 68). During LBA1 (Fig. 69) and LBA2 (Fig. 70), hoarding seems to have occurred mainly in the fens, but in LBA3 a sudden increase in numbers of hoards also extends the distribution to the north and east and reveals several concentrations of hoards (Fig. 71). The few LBA4 examples are fairly widely dispersed across the region (Fig. 72). A random plot of 141 co-ordinates within the range for all East Anglian hoards produces a scatter of points, as in the diagram (Fig. 73).

The chi–squared test for this against the plot of all hoards in East Anglia gives us:

		All		
		Present	Absent	
Random plot	Present	39	57	96
	Absent	32	64	96
		71	121	192

Chi-squared = 1.0951   DF = 1
Significant at 0.5 level

This leaves us uncertain whether we should accept the null hypothesis that there is no relationship between a random distribution and the 'real' distribution of hoards in East Anglia. Subjectively, the pattern does not appear to be random for the reasons already given. The calculation of chi–squared between hoards of MBA2 and LBA3 shows these figures:

		MBA2		
		Present	Absent	
LBA3	Present	7	35	42
	Absent	8	142	150
		15	177	192

Chi-squared = 5.8518   DF=1
Significant at 0.025 level

So, we have a significant association between the distribution of hoards in these two phases, suggesting again that similar areas were favoured for deposition at these times. The intervening periods, although not well represented, show the continuity of deposition in the fen area.

Conclusion

The distributional evidence would seem to be consistent with our model of the core/periphery relationships: either a distribution remains the same across time, as it does in the South West and the Thames Valley, or there are locational shifts, as in Wessex and East Anglia. This may have as much to do with topographical factors as with social determinants. Thus, hoards in the South West and the Thames Valley are 'fixed' in the areas best suited for settlement and human activity, while the range of possibilities is increased in Wessex and East Anglia. Some of the shifts within Wessex would seem clearly to reflect attempts to organise exchange through Wessex in preference to other regions, and the hoards found near to the coast may have been deposited to demonstrate the wealth of individuals in that area. The failure of these attempts within Wessex, and its decline to peripheral status, led to a shift in deposition northwards, while in the last phase of the Bronze Age, LBA4, Wessex again attempted to re–align exchange in its favour, and again this is reflected in a coastal distribution of deposits. The fen area of East Anglia seems to have attracted most hoards of all phases, but with phases in which their distribution shifted 'outwards' to the coast. Perhaps this change reflects attempts within the alliance network to bring metal into the region when it was in short supply. Generally, however, the distribution of hoards would seem to suggest the continuous use of the same areas for deposition. Most likely, these were the areas of densest settlement and activity in the Bronze Age.

SUMMARY

Various aspects of the Bronze Age hoards have been examined in detail in this chapter, and it is useful to summarise the main points here.

1. Chronology: there are nine periods based on metalwork typology which make up the span of the Bronze Age; hoards, however, can only be loosely dated within such a framework. For our four regions there is a preponderance of depositions of hoards of MBA2 and LBA3 date: the majority of Wessex and South West hoards were deposited in MBA2, and the majority of Thames Valley and East Anglia hoards belong to LBA3. This may reflect the shifts in core/periphery relations.
2. Hoard weights: less than 1 tonne of metal was deposited during the Bronze Age. The mean hoard weight for the Thames Valley, South West, and Wessex was about 2 kg, and for East Anglia 4 kg. The median weight for hoards in all regions was about 1 kg, and it is thus conceivable that the content of many hoards could have been carried by individuals before deposition. A limited pool of metal was equally split in each period for deposits in Wessex and the Thames Valley, but the size of MBA2 hoards in the South West was reduced due to the number of deposits, while a few LBA2 deposits in East Anglia gained more of the metal. It would also seem that roughly the same kinds of objects were used in similar proportions to make up hoards in all regions.
3. Hoard content: lumps of metal only occur in LBA2 and LBA3 hoards. Miscellaneous pieces are a feature of LBA hoards. Ornaments are only a small part of MBA2 hoards in the South West, and tools are the major component of hoards in all regions or predominate in many phases, although weapons take the lead in Wessex and Thames Valley during EBA2. This also happens in LBA2 in Wessex, and in LBA1 and LBA2 in East Anglia. Tools seem to predominate in all phases because they were probably more widely available.

The deposition of tools could have involved large quantities of metal in a status–defining act, although deliberate selection of weapons for hoards may have taken place in LBA2.

4. Wear: the detection of wear on hoarded items has proved to be of great interest. There is a highly significant relationship between degree of wear and type of object in MBA2 and LBA3 for all four regions, and also for LBA2 in Wessex and East Anglia, and for LBA4 in Wessex. There is a highly significant relationship between an object and its completeness in LBA3 in all regions, and a significant relationship between degree of wear and completeness in LBA3 in the Thames Valley, South West, and East Anglia, but not at all in Wessex. During MBA2, there is a fairly significant relationship for all the regions except the Thames Valley between the type of object and its completeness and between degree of wear and completeness.

5. The degree of wear and types of objects are positively related: ornaments are subject to more moderate wear in MBA2, but tools and weapons are generally less worn in East Anglia than elsewhere. In LBA3, tools and weapons show heavy wear, and ornaments and miscellaneous pieces show moderate wear. Weapons are more likely than tools to be deposited broken in LBA3. Some objects are broken through heavy use before deposition in LBA3, but generally objects are only worn to a moderate degree. These observations may reflect differences in the circulation time of objects deposited in hoards. This could be due to stresses between the core and the periphery. There would be phases of restricted metal supply and thus increased wear before deposition. This would happen in a core area, eg East Anglia in LBA3, where ascendancy was maintained by deposition of bronze after longer periods of circulation.

6. It would seem that a series of objects were available in LBA2 and LBA3 and were selected for deposition at different stages of their use–life. Hoards did not suddenly appear as a result of a single phase of deposition. However, the apparently erratic deposition of hoards in different periods of the Bronze Age could be a result of external influences intermittently affecting the depositors: most probably in the form of fluctuations in the amounts of metal obtained through alliance and exchange.

7. Computer analysis of wear figures indicates that some aspects of wear are a function of object morphology, ie certain types of object are regularly worn in a particular way. Tools, other than socketed axes and palstaves, were deposited worn at all times; axes and palstaves show more of a spread across the range of wear. Weapons were well–worn at deposition in all regions, except for socketed spearheads in LBA2 in Wessex. Ornaments suffer generally less wear before their deposition, but tend to show more wear by LBA3 in Wessex. On the whole, axes seem to have been selected at any stage of wear for deposition, including a small proportion of 'as cast' pieces, but this might mean that they represented less of a loss to the depositor than other types of artefact. Weapons seem to have been retained for longer before deposition, except in LBA2 in Wessex, where they were less worn. This shows that differences in wear patterns occur according to the types of objects in the hoards, regardless of the overall state of wear for that phase of hoarding. These patterns of wear nevertheless do seem to be regional and chronological, and form part of the wider process of production, distribution, and consumption.

8. Context of deposition: most hoards seem to have been buried very shallowly and at a depth at which archaeological features generally occur. Some of their contents may already have been removed deliberately or by cultivaton. Some hoards could come from settlement sites or could be 'substitute' burials. The objects were sometimes tied up as a bundle or placed in containers. The majority of the evidence, however, favours the simple burial of objects, near to the surface, with no 'other reasons' for their siting.

9. Distribution: for the Thames Valley it was suggested that the rivers formed an important focus for deposition, perhaps reflecting the presence of settlement sites in use from MBA2 to LBA3. In the South West, the Somerset Levels and the area around Taunton were favoured for deposition of all phases, again perhaps due to the nature of local settlement. In Wessex, deposition tended to be coastal or near to rivers and could reflect a need for access to water transport, whilst shifting within the region during the Bronze Age. Lastly, in East Anglia, the Fens attracted most deposits, perhaps reflecting continuous settlement in this area, but again deposition later moved outwards towards the coast.

CONCLUSION

This chapter has shown that it is possible to analyse hoards in a rigorous way and to derive more information from the individual objects than is at first apparent. Various patterns have been examined, tested, and interpreted. It is also abundantly clear that hoards represent a biased sample; some deposits offer limited information, and only a few are adequately documented. Therefore, it is not possible to offer a full survey of deposition across the whole of the Bronze Age, but we can suggest that the general patterning in our four regions accords with the model presented earlier. It now remains to justify this assertion and to place our hoards within the wider framework of Bronze Age studies.

PART III

SOCIAL ARCHAEOLOGY

CHAPTER 6

SUMMARY

INTRODUCTION

The point of this chapter is not to repeat everything that has already been said, but to draw together the threads of the argument in relation to the hoards of southern Britain. The enquiry was begun with a lengthy survey of other authors' observations on the subject of hoards in Britain and Europe, followed by an outline of the Bronze Age background. A theoretical framework and model of explanation have been offered. The methodology for my own research was then related, and the results described. Now, we shall see how these parts articulate and in the final chapter conclude this survey.

PREVIOUS RESEARCH ON BRONZE AGE HOARDS

The enquiry was basically divided into two parts: the interpretations of hoards offered in Britain as distinct from those in Europe. In Britain, we have tended to view hoards in economic terms of the crudest kind, various facets of the hoards themselves and the manner of their deposition being taken as indicative of their purpose. The basic divisions were seen in terms of merchant's, founder's, and personal hoards, the last of which could be 'sepulchral' in nature. We can summarise these traditional interpretations in the form of a diagram (Fig. 74). The interpretation of some hoards as 'votive' was adopted reluctantly in Britain, after the European example, to help explain the character of those deposits which did not fit easily into the other groups. Other supplementary groups of hoards were discerned: the domestic hoards of the householder, and tool–kit hoards of specialised craftsmen. Gradually, these 'basic' interpretations developed into social explanations for deposition, with particular classes of people, for instance warriors, responsible for depositing particular classes of hoards, such as finds of weapons. The reasons for deposition, when not implicit in the original hoard categorisation, were usually seen to result from troubled times, invasion, or ritual practice. Various authors have criticised these explanations or attempted new categorisations, but the old definitions tend to reappear thinly disguised.

If we look at hoards and deposition in a different way, for instance as part of the agricultural cycle, it is possible to suggest that hoards represent production residues or stocks of material produced at certain times of the year. This model, proposed by Rowlands, has a different theoretical emphasis to the other models, which are based on technological and traditional economic interpretations. For different reasons, other authors emphasised links between hoards and settlements, although these are seldom apparent in the material record. The current trend is to question the place of hoards within the frameworks of Bronze Age society, frameworks which are partly based on the metalwork, but corroborated with other archaeological material. We can now question the blind acceptance of such interpretations and try to develop new ways of looking at the evidence. It becomes apparent that there is still much information to be gained from the objects in hoards, and that there are other ways of explaining deposition.

The course of European research was to a certain extent equivalent to that in Britain, but more often it ran in parallel: votive deposits were seen as one of the simplest modes of explanation. The votive nature of hoards was a theme developed by many European scholars and still prevalent today, although this is not to deny that 'economic' explanations for hoards were and are widely used. As in Britain, the more recent trend has been to attempt to relate hoards to, or place them within, a social framework, often built up using the burial evidence. This has been most developed through the work of Kristiansen, although he has not confined his attention to metalwork from hoards, using the hoards of the later Bronze Age to supplement the metalwork from burials in the earlier Bronze Age. The importance of Kristiansen's work lay in his development of an analytical method based on the wear apparent on bronze objects. Particular forms of social organisation were postulated to account for these data and were built into a general model.

Underlying some of the interpretations of hoards and metalwork were the ethnographic parallels and anthropological models used by some authors. Initially, these were simple comparisons, such as the organisation of metalworking by African smiths; but many authors have been quick to point to the fallacy of direct comparison between unrelated environmental settings and different cultures, especially as ethnography has to contend with 'post–Colonialism' in so many cases. More recently, various authors have attempted to see the culture, ideology, and symbolism behind the production of particular artefacts, and thus build a notion of the kind of ideas which may have been utilised in the manufacture of objects. As the sophistication of the model increases, so do the difficulties of applying it to the archaeological record. It would seem more fruitful to consider the responses of a culture to particular situations and the ways in which it might be reflected in the material record. So, we can look at the symbolism of the object, but we can also consider its context, association, and method of deposition. The answer would seem to lie in social anthropology and not ethnography; we can use social theory, rather than direct

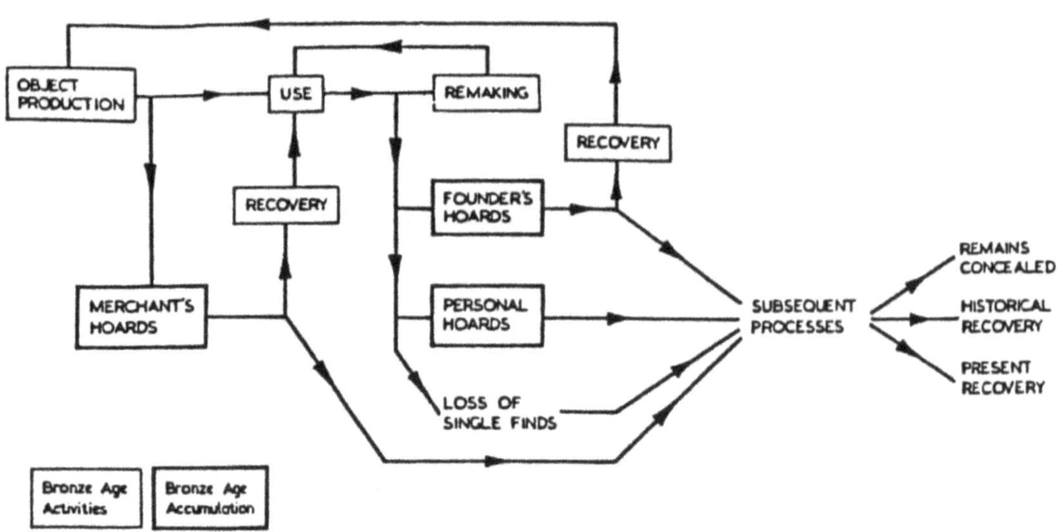

Figure 74: Traditional interpretation of hoard formation and deposition processes

parallels. These points are taken up in more detail in considering theoretical frameworks of explanation.

The outline survey of previous research into Bronze Age hoards and metalwork in Britain and Europe showed that the question of hoarding was still open to discussion and could prove a fruitful area for research. This set the scene for the whole enquiry.

THE BRONZE AGE

It was felt necessary to place the metalwork within the presently understood frameworks for studying the Bronze Age as a whole. We considered all the major categories of evidence on a regional, national, and European scale.

The evidence used in building chronologies was briefly reviewed and an outline scheme, based on metalwork technology and typology, adopted: this is over–precise in relation to pottery and settlement, but until a wider range of radiocarbon dates is available, it is the most convenient. This gives us a framework on which to 'peg' our hoards, although the problems of typology and association posed by hoard finds should not be overlooked. The dating can be conveniently, and more coarsely, visualised in terms of Early, Middle, and Late, or earlier and later, Bronze Age.

The archaeological evidence for these periods in the Thames Valley, Wessex, the South West, and East Anglia were reviewed, these being the chosen areas for further research. To a certain extent, these outlines were based on 'received information', and thus subject to authors' opinions and interpretations, but some attempt was made to contrast the approaches. Recent essays concerned with social analysis were considered the most rewarding. They suggested that the supremacy of Wessex in the Early Bronze Age faltered as the Thames Valley took over its dominant position in the Late Bronze Age. Already the evidence suggested a core/periphery relationship. The evidence from the South West and East Anglia, while to a certain extent paralleling developments in Wessex and the Thames Valley, shows how an adaptive response to the environment was also a necessary adjunct to life in these areas. A survey of current knowledge of Bronze Age environment bore out the general impression of a drier, warmer Early Bronze Age, followed by a wetter Late Bronze Age and Early Iron Age, but it is important to recognise that many of the environmentalists' dated horizons are actually derived from associated archaeological material and thus are not fully independent of changing fashions among prehistorians.

The archaeological setting of the Bronze Age within southern Britain was next considered, building on the evidence of these four different regions. This revealed a basic division between earlier and later Bronze Age society. This reflects a fundamental change from a society in which rank might have been achieved through access to prestige goods to one in which it was attained through access to, and control of, wealth and resources. External exchange provided the catalyst for this reaction, bringing in more foreign, prestige goods in exchange for local products: areas with access to external routes were able to exploit them to their own advantage.

Much of this took place against the background of the European Bronze Age. This is not to say that 'foreigners' or 'invaders' came into Britain with all the good ideas. Rather, exchange relationships stimulated the local situation. However, this was not a static phenomenon. A Britain with its own prestige goods economy in the Late Neolithic and earlier Bronze Age became a participant in larger European events, only to become more isolated as the system collapsed in the Early Iron Age. The underlying evidence for this pattern of social interaction came from the burials, settlements, and artefacts of the Bronze Age. When considered in conjunction, these suggested far–reaching developments in contemporary culture and society. It is against this background that we can visualise the hoard data.

FRAMEWORKS OF EXPLANATION

The tendency in the first two chapters, already outlined, was to give more interpretative emphasis to the evidence of the Bronze Age in general, and of metalwork in particular. Less attention was paid to the underlying theory.

To redress the balance, the theoretical position adopted by Kristiansen was examined, with reference to the interpretative works used by him in his analyses. Broadly, his position was seen to be allied to structural Marxism, as expounded by Friedman (but later criticised by him). Kristiansen postulated that a series of cycles with evolutionary and devolutionary tendencies transformed the social system across time; we do not need to see that as the replacement of one form of social organisation by another, but as part of a progressive tendency, influenced by local conditions. Friedman would now place the emphasis on the importance of the relationship between 'core' and 'periphery', notions already used to explain trends in the British Bronze Age.

The theory of Marxism, related as it is to capitalism and the forces that give rise to capitalism, might seem unrelated to the study of primitive economies, but it is precisely in such areas that Marxism has a powerful explanatory potential. In these terms, cores and peripheries exist alongside each other, but also contain the roots of change and contradiction, as shifts in power transform peripheral areas into new centres of power, and core areas themselves lose their status through the breakdown of the social system. These networks of core areas and their peripheries are conceived of as being very extensive. The connecting links can be glimpsed in a series of cycles governing exchange within and outside society – cycles of life and cycles of production. These are constantly changing in relation to each other and to the larger whole. The system tends to be governed by social 'operators', but these operators are also subject to the constraints of their environmental setting. All this might seem rather remote from actual archaeological practice, but a model of general applicability can be derived from the 'rules'.

Initially, we can visualise a tribal system at the local level developing a complex social structure with various levels of dominance through external exchange. The result of the control of trade and prestige is to change the social structure with time, until chiefly lineages can direct production and distribution to their own ends. However, this also has the result of 'cutting off' the highest ranking individuals from the rest of society, because now no–one can match their position in bride–giving. At this stage, we may be able to identify a dominant centre, with its peripheries controlled by local chiefs who supply that centre with goods in return for portable wealth: a characteristic of a prestige goods system. In the expansion of this system lies the potential for autonomous production in other areas, and the rise of new centres, which come into conflict with established ones. Herein are the roots of the commercial city state with a bureaucracy controlling production, social position defined by access to wealth, a class of landless producers, and the use of prestige goods as money tokens. Thus, we have been considering a system which possesses general evolutionary tendencies, but which is also subject to continuous transformation.

This is directly relevant to the Bronze Age situation. The all–important part of this model is the prestige goods system, with alliances based on access to wealth and exchange, and the redistribution of prestige items. In this system, Britain in the later Bronze Age lies on the periphery of the European core areas. Bradley saw this prestige goods system as operating from the later Neolithic onwards, changing the emphasis of exchange by exercising control through the destruction and consumption of wealth. This interpretation was couched in terms of the relationship between core and periphery. Thus, while Wessex declined as a core area in favour of the Thames Valley, at the same time the latter area was acting as a periphery to the greater core areas of Europe. The Early Bronze Age emphasis on status insignia became supplanted by a different system in the Late Bronze Age, which placed more emphasis on direct access to wealth. These two systems recall the early and late stages in the life of a prestige goods economy, as described by Friedman. The importance of the concepts discussed by Bradley lies in the articulation of the archaeological record to the overall model: an attempt to explain the apparent destruction of wealth objects and the consumption of items that legitimate rank. In other words, we can imbue the artefacts with a social role as reflections of the larger social system without identifying the specific ideological attributes governing their production.

From these theoretical and practical observations, it is possible to generate a further series of observations, which could be used in our analysis of the hoards and their contents. We could seek to place the objects within an economic framework, but not one where their position and use is defined in terms of crude value, but where they are part of a total social system, articulating relations through alliance and exchange.

THE METHOD

Preliminary work indicated that the study of wear patterns in Bronze Age hoards was likely to be a fruitful line of enquiry, and it was this study that was carried out in museums in southern Britain. Other authors had observed traces of wear on British socketed axes, palstaves, and swords, but there had been little attempt to systematise or synthesise this information.

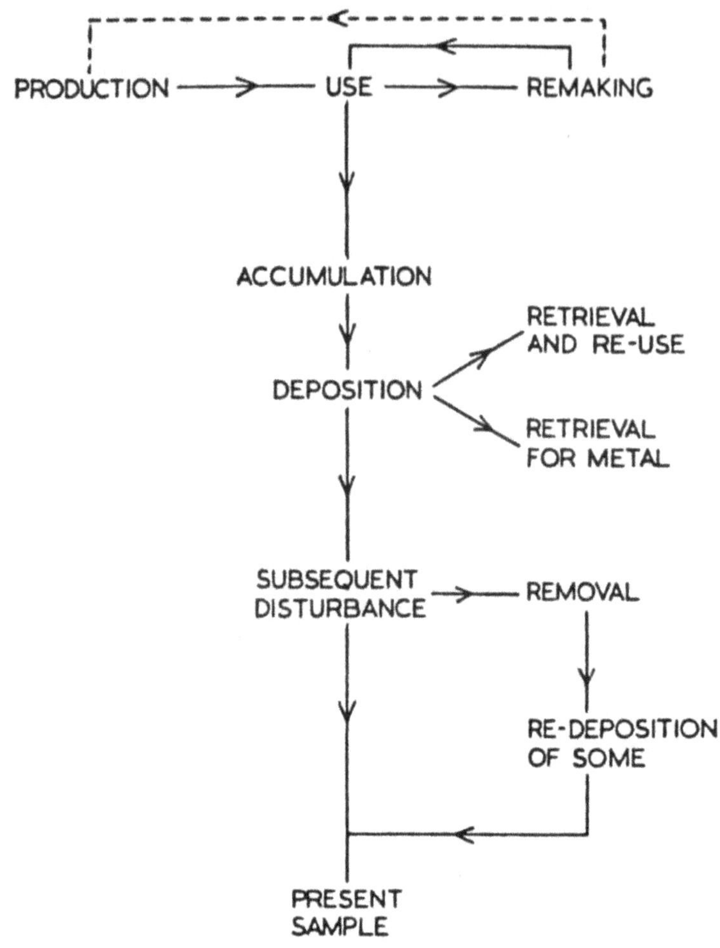

Figure 75: Factors affecting the hoard sample as seen in the archaeological record

Southern Britain was divided into four convenient regions for study: the Thames Valley, Wessex, the South West, and East Anglia. The hoards from these areas were catalogued as fully as possible from all available sources. The museums were visited in all the areas, and the information from the objects recorded, using a set procedure. It was not possible, nor desirable, to examine every piece of bronze from all hoards located in the four regions, but a large amount of data was gathered. Two–thirds of available hoards were examined, and about one–third of the available objects (this figure is smaller because it was not possible to examine the whole of the Isleham hoard). The representativeness of the sample was questioned in various ways. It was found that in all areas, except East Anglia, the rate of discovery of hoards had remained fairly steady in recent years, and was thus fairly likely to be a good sample of the available material, even if some hoards remain to be discovered. The figures suggested that recovery was likely to fall in the near future, even in East Anglia, where agriculture and metal detecting have contributed so significantly in recent years. We can think of our present sample as having been filtered by various activities (Fig. 75), particularly where we have no clear idea of how many pieces were recovered in prehistory or even historical time.

A trip to Denmark was undertaken to evaluate at first hand the working methods of Kristiansen. The simplicity of his methods had much to commend them, but it was also apparent that he was dealing with an 'ideal' sample, in other words the range of wear, and ways in which it is exhibited, were quite clear on the Danish pieces used for his analysis; also, he only dealt with swords and ornaments, probably the most prestigious artefacts, while there are large numbers of more functional objects, such as socketed axes that occur in similar contexts. Nevertheless, the overall result of my own investigations of the Danish material was encouragement that the principles of wear analysis could be used effectively. This was also the conclusion drawn from a comparison of my results with those of a scientifically investigated hoard, that from Yattendon (TV12), although obviously no direct comparison exists between my methods and those of metallurgy and metallography. Replication and experimentation in use of actual objects would seem to be a desirable course of further study: first, we must be sure that our replicas can match the originals in technology.

The method of examination of bronzes from hoards was devised to record the degrees of wear to which the pieces had been subjected before their deposition. This seemed to be a fruitful line of enquiry in elucidating the reasons behind deposition. The method is workable for a reasonable sample and sheds new light on the questions already posed of the material by other authors. Analysis using computers was useful in processing the large amount of data recorded. More traditional information, such as content and context, was also carefully recorded, as these were still felt to be significant to an understanding of the hoards.

ANALYSIS AND RESULTS

The data gathered were subjected to analysis in various ways. Statistical tests were used as appropriate, and various observations made. It is clear that any systematic reworking of this material will generate new insights, if we look beyond the limitations of technology and typology. Any future studies would do well to use a smaller sample and to investigate it in greater depth, as the results processed here showed that such a large database could hinder interpretation.

Hoards were dated according to the standard chronologies, in other words the latest examples in the hoard were taken to be indicative of its overall date: this would be the date of final accumulation, but not necessarily the date of deposition, although it would seem likely that deposition followed shortly after accumulation, as is generally accepted. For the four regions studied, there was a clear preponderance of hoards of MBA2 and LBA3 date, with the majority of hoards in Wessex and the South West deposited in MBA2, those in the Thames Valley and East Anglia deposited in LBA3 (Map 5). Hoards of other periods occurred in different proportions in the regions, and some periods are hardly represented or not at all. Thus, we could suggest that hoarding is a discontinuous phenomenon, or that the chronological phasing is meaningless in application to hoards. It seems most likely that objects of several technological stages, and thus dates, were available together at the same time, in a continuous sequence, and were selected at one point for deposition.

Using the rough weight measurements taken for individual objects examined, we can make a series of observations. The mean and median hoard weights indicate an average hoard of a size easily transported by one person, and probably in many cases the 'property' of that person. However, the size of deposits seems to have been limited by the size of the overall pool of metal available in each region, and thus it was equally split for each period in the Thames Valley and Wessex, but in the South West the number of MBA2 hoards deposited reduced their size, while in East Anglia the few hoards of LBA2 contain much more of the metal. So, although we might suggest one person or group making each deposit for most of the Bronze Age, there do appear to be chronological horizons, when deposition is increased.

The basic contents of hoards were enumerated according to whether they are judged to be a tool, weapon, ornament, miscellaneous piece (such as horse trappings), or metal. This shows that metal only occurs in LBA2 and LBA3 hoards, although it often only makes up less than half of any hoard; and miscellaneous pieces are generally a feature of Late Bronze Age hoards. In MBA2, ornaments are actually a small proportion of the objects deposited in hoards, especially in the South West, since the larger number have tools as the major component, although tools and ornaments were more equally split for Wessex and East Anglia. Tools seem to be a major component of hoards of all phases, although weapons predominate in Wessex and the Thames Valley during EBA2, the South West in LBA1, during LBA2 in Wessex, and in LBA1 and LBA2 in East Anglia. Generally, hoards would seem to be made up of the objects that were available for deposition in that phase, with tools predominating because they were most widely available in most phases. This suggests that deposition itself was important, and not the objects deposited in the hoard, but obviously hoards are not a complete cross-section of available material, and there was most likely to have been selection of particular items, though for what intrinsic reasons or purpose is not so clear.

Analysis was next concentrated on the recorded evidence for wear, using a generalised scale of wear for the objects in hoards ranging from A (as cast) to E (heavily worn) with NC for the unclassifiable element (usually lumps of raw metal). These observations were grouped according to region, date, and type of object, and then analysed using the chi-squared test to determine the significance of any relationships. Those considered were the relationship between different types of object and their completeness, types of object and their degree of wear, and between completeness and the degree of wear. The results can be most conveniently summarised as a table:

Table 16: Levels of significance between three relationships

Region/ date	Object/ Completeness	Degree of wear/ Completeness	Degree of wear/ Object
TV MBA2	Equal	Equal	High
TV LBA3	Very high	Very high	Very high
SW EBA2	Low	Not	Not
SW MBA2	Very high	High	Very high
SW LBA3	Very high	High	Very high
W EBA2	Low	Equal	Not
W MBA2	Very high	Very high	Very high
W LBA2	Not	Very high	High
W LBA3	Very high	Not	Very high
W LBA4	Low	High	Very high
EA MBA2	High	High	Very high
EA LBA1	High	Low	Equal
EA LBA2	Low	High	Very high
EA LBA3	Very high	Very high	Very high
EA LBA4	Not	Equal	Equal

Further testing of these relationships for all areas during MBA2 and LBA3 demonstrated that the correlation between degree of wear of an object and its completeness was low, while the correlation both between an object and its completeness and its degree of wear was usually high. Attention focused on hoards of MBA2 and LBA3 date, because these are the best represented periods, and comparison of trends or significance become difficult when dealing with a very small sample, as would be the case with most of the other periods. We can see that ornaments in MBA2 are subject to more moderate wear, while tools and weapons are more heavily worn, except in East Anglia, where wear on these objects seems to be less in this period (Map 6). During LBA3 the trend was for heavy wear on tools and weapons, with moderate wear on ornaments and miscellaneous pieces (Map 7). Breakage applied more to weapons than tools in LBA3, and, while some objects may have broken through heavy usage in this period, deposition was more usually of complete, worn objects (Map 8).

Computer analysis was used initially to test for groupings of wear observations for all types of axe, as recorded from the objects directly. These numerical scales brought out fine distinctions in the level of wear between objects, although they were shown to be broadly analogous to the generalised scale of wear derived from them. This also made clear that some wear was a function of the object's morphology, itself the basis of Bronze Age typology. In other cases, objects of the same date had the same kind of wear. This could mean that some typological analysis can provide inaccurate or misleading results, particularly where it relies on blade shape or width as an index of date. Some hoards were 'reconstituted' by the computer; their constituent axes came together again, due to similarities of wear, but again there were hoards whose contents spread themselves widely across the wear groupings. A simple computer sort procedure was also used with the generalised scale of wear to sift all objects from hoards in the Thames Valley, the South West, and Wessex (Map 9). This showed that, whereas axes were spread across the range of wear, other tools were deposited worn in all periods. Weapons were always well–worn, except for socketed spearheads in Wessex during LBA2. Ornaments were generally less worn, but in Wessex they tended to be more worn by LBA3; torcs were more worn than bracelets. It was further suggested that axes were more freely deposited, because they represented less of a 'loss', while weapons were more of an investment and thus were deposited when they were worn out, although this was not true of Wessex in LBA2. In that case, it must have been possible to deposit less–worn weapons, perhaps because 'fashion' dictated that weapons be hoarded at this point, or because there was less pressure on the metal supply, enabling replacements to be obtained easily. The regional and chronological patterning of wear is some indication of a wider network of interaction and change.

Analysis of the contextual information relating to hoard deposition did not necessarily show any meaningful overall patterns. Hoards were apparently buried at shallow depths, although no account can be taken of topsoil erosion, where and if this occurred; this may have influenced hoard content. There were associations of hoards with settlements and also burials; objects were sometimes 'bundled up' and sometimes placed in containers. In contrast to all the 'dry' land deposits, hoards from 'wet' places do not seem overly significant in southern Britain, and may simply represent hoards deposited in that particular landscape rather than any other. The net results would suggest that the positioning of hoards in the landscape was a factor of minor importance. 'Votive' hoards, if they exist, should not be explained by their context, but by their content.

Distribution mapping of hoards, and also some experiments with random plotting on the microcomputer, showed certain concentrations within the four regions. In the Thames Valley, the river was an important focus for deposition in MBA2 and LBA3; the slight evidence for earlier hoards of EBA2 fell well away from these areas. MBA2 saw the bulk of deposition in the South West, which occurred, as in other periods, in the low–lying regions, especially in the area of the Somerset Levels. In Wessex, the hoards concentrated on the river floodplains or towards the coast, but tended to move inland by LBA3 and back to the coast again in LBA4. The fen areas in East Anglia were favoured for all periods of deposition, but the coasts were also attractive. These distribution patterns either remain constant in the regions or move markedly. This must reflect both the siting of settlement areas and the need for access to communication routes. There need not have been any direct relationship between hoarding and settlement areas, but in many cases the domestic evidence is very poor. However, the 'hoarders' do not seem to have gone out of their way to deposit hoards in 'remote' areas. Alternatively, we could consider remote areas, for example Dartmoor, as being underexplored for hoards, and we may be making too much of a highly biased picture. After all, hoards have been discovered in places where man has conducted his more recent activities, and precisely through these agencies; many more could remain buried in relatively undisturbed areas. Set against this, archaeology and agriculture have had a great deal of coverage in Wessex and the Thames Valley, and discrete distributions are suggested by the evidence for these regions.

The results of our re–analysis of hoards from southern Britain showed some important patterning in regional and chronological terms. They do seem to reflect the people and societies that must have been responsible for their deposition. In the concluding chapter, we must return to the regional and chronological models on which our interpretations of Bronze Age society rest.

CHAPTER 7

CONCLUDING REMARKS

How, then, to conclude this survey of Bronze Age hoards in southern Britain? We could follow Evans' line (1881, 488) and suggest that the information contained herein will prove useful to others and let matters rest, but we have also discussed a model of social organisation for the Bronze Age, and we must consider how far it is consistent with our evidence. That evidence has been presented, discussed, and summarised; now we can attempt an interpretation.

The observations made about individual pieces can be related to the overall state of the objects, and, on this basis, we can postulate what part they played in a wider social and archaeological context. This is best presented in diagrammatic form (Fig. 76). However, it should be clear that any estimate of the likely process giving rise to these observations can only be at best an informed guess. For instance, we know what some objects look like after casting and before finishing from moulds or scrap pieces, but we have no clear associations of deposits of unfinished products with actual smithing evidence; we have very few hoards of 'as cast' objects. Further, what do we mean by 'consumption', 'loss', and 'discard'?

These are to a certain extent well–worn archaeological topics, and it is not proposed to go over the arguments again, but this is a clear example of the limitations of inference from the archaeological record. Hoards consist of objects associated with each other and very rarely with anything else: in other words, they are frequently without a well–defined archaeological context. Why? Because they are the archaeological residue of past actions, which left little or no other trace. In that case, how can we interpret hoards? By examination of the patterning and relationships between objects in hoards, and between hoards, across time and space. This is information that they can provide, but we can only place this within an overall framework developed from other archaeological evidence in conjunction with the metalwork. Of course, we run the risk of a circular argument, because a model has already been designed in the light of some of this evidence; it is to be hoped, however, that the evidence can reinforce or reject a position, which has sufficient supplementary evidence. Beyond that, we can only hope to provide information for further research.

EARLY BRONZE AGE

Hoards do not appear suddenly in the Early Bronze Age: polished stone and flint axe hoards are tolerably well known for the later Neolithic. In discussing our model in Chapter 3, we have already seen that a prestige goods economy may have been in operation during this period, and that these axe hoards were perhaps a facet of this. Deposition of prestige objects to enhance status: this was a recurrent theme of the Bronze Age.

Thus, by the Early Bronze Age prestige goods were part of an economy linking southern Britain with more distant areas. Stone axes had been obtained from 'exotic' locations within the British Isles; copper, bronze, and gold offered even more chance of obtaining a variety of prestige items. This is clearly reflected in the Wessex graves, although such a restricted group can assume too great an importance in our thinking. The hoards, however, occur in more peripheral areas and are made up of objects dated to EBA2, for instance those from the Isle of Wight. In our four regions such patterns can be picked out: in the Thames Valley, the EBA2 hoards lie well outside the areas favoured for later deposition and really on the fringes of the region; in the South West, deposition coincides more with later deposition, but each of the deposits is well spaced; in Wessex, the hoards are from the Isle of Wight or close to the coast, a pattern which is repeated in later periods, but one which contrasts with the burial evidence; and in East Anglia, the hoards lie close to or in the fen, as they do in later periods, but fewer barrows are found near to the fen edge, although this area was more favoured for settlement. Of course, barrows and hoards are only part of the archaeological record from the Early Bronze Age, and it is possible that the barrow distribution is also 'peripheral' to settlement areas. Hoards occur infrequently at this time too, perhaps due to the restricted supply of metal at this early stage, and thus the need to maintain more objects in circulation: a point confirmed by the heavy wear observed on the pieces. Another facet of the hoard pattern can be derived from the content of these EBA2 hoards: in the South West and East Anglia they are largely made up of tools, but in Wessex and the Thames Valley they are roughly two–thirds weapons to one–third tools. It is inevitable that tools contribute more weight of metal to hoards, but weapons may have held more prestige, although we cannot ignore the 'fancy' nature of many Early Bronze Age axes – the main 'tool' of the period – nor disregard the importance of axes in the later Neolithic. In other words, prestige could be gained at this time from the deposition of axes in the areas, where they still carried importance; weapons were more frequent in the Wessex area due to their use in barrow burials and may thus have assumed a greater importance than the axes for deposition. Overall, all the EBA2 objects deposited in hoards which were examined were heavily worn, suggesting a fair amount of use before deposition. There was no particularly significant association between degree of wear and type of object, degree of wear and completeness, or object and completeness, mainly because most pieces were whole and, regardless of type, all were heavily worn.

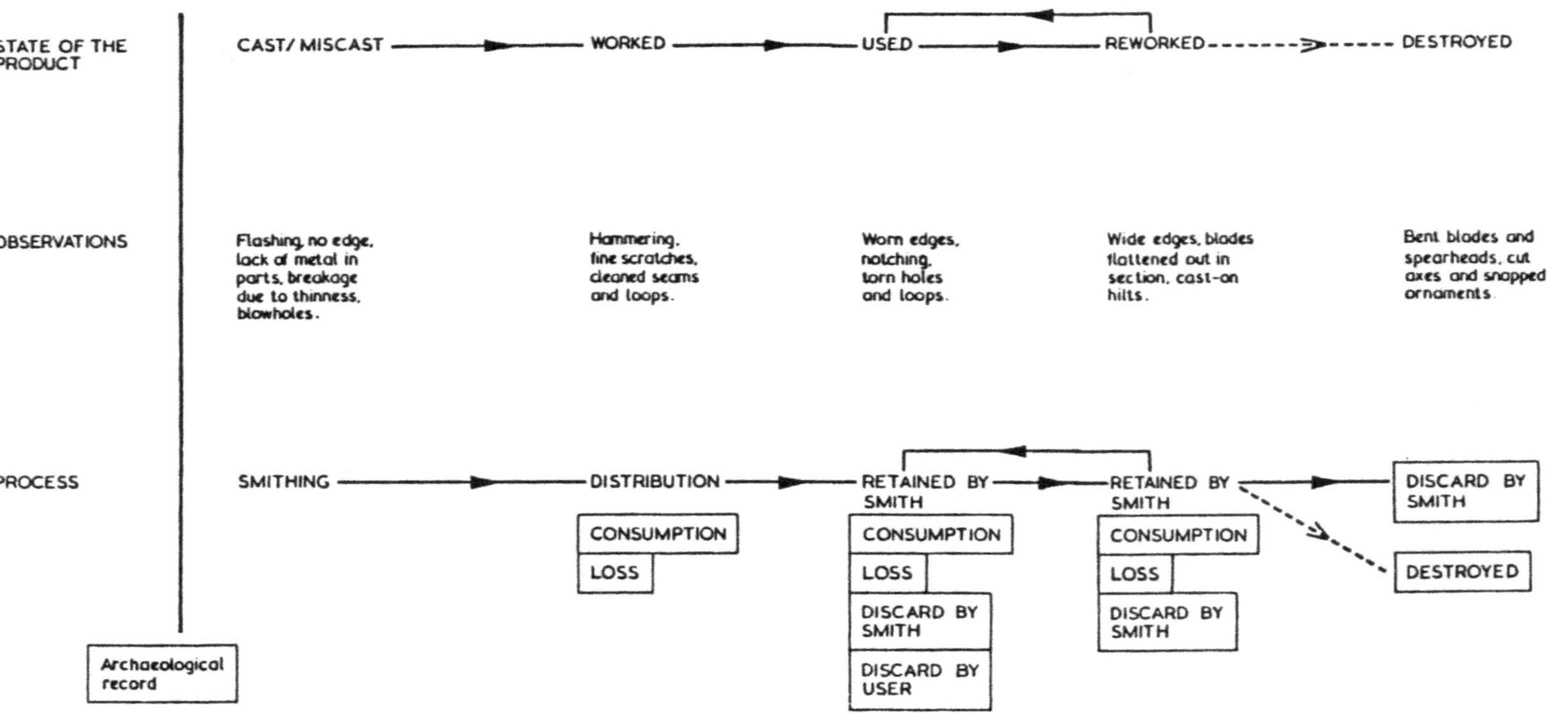

Figure 76: Dendrogrammatic illustration of the relationship between wear observations and possible entry into the archaeological record

Thus, deposition of hoards supplemented the display of valuables at funerals, and both were perhaps directed towards enhancement of prestige in these regions. The process is most visible in the archaeological record in the Wessex burials; objects circulated for a while at a high social level, but eventually they were gathered into a few widely spaced hoards. Ultimately, then, the items which had been circulated for a time as prestige goods were removed from circulation into hoards. The transfer of prestige associated with the movement of objects was focused by the accumulation of these objects and then fossilised by their deposition: a lineage had accrued more prestige items to itself, and then 'fixed' that prestige by an act of deposition, which also prevented any competitors from gaining access to the same objects. While individuals were also making similar prestige statements with barrow burial in the Wessex core area, the peripheries were beginning to control more of the metal supply through their access to the exchange networks, enabling them to make powerful statements through hoards, and eventually to weaken the Wessex power base entirely. Thus, the following period saw a shift into these 'peripheral' areas.

MIDDLE BRONZE AGE

The chronology imposes the discontinuity: the system cycles were continuous, but hoarding itself was not. We only have one hoard of MBA1 date, from Wessex (W34), consisting entirely of palstaves of an early typological date and all well-worn: deposition of this hoard in MBA2, but without any representative pieces of that phase, cannot be ruled out, but one hoard does not need special explanation. During MBA2 there was a massive phase of deposition.

In the Thames Valley, deposition now focused in the river valley, an area that continued to be used in this way during the Late Bronze Age. It was also the favoured location for settlement. In the South West, this was also a major period for hoards, which clustered in the low-lying areas again favoured for settlement. The positioning in relation to rivers and the coast, seen for EBA2 in Wessex, is repeated for this phase, reflecting access to communication routes for exchange. In East Anglia, there was a concentration on the fen area and also the coast, probably reflecting inland settlement and again stressing access to communication routes. In the Thames Valley and the South West, tools make up about three-quarters of the hoard contents with small numbers of weapons and ornaments; in Wessex and East Anglia, the tool content is reduced to around half in favour of ornaments with a few weapons. The results of wear analysis showed significant relationships between object and completeness, the degree of wear and completeness, and the degree of wear and object for all areas but the Thames Valley, where the correlation between degree of wear and object was the only significant one. Breakage of objects before deposition, often due to heavy wear, was becoming more frequent at this stage, although the wear on ornaments was generally not so heavy as that on tools or weapons. However, East Anglia showed generally less wear for tools and weapons, and ornaments in the Thames Valley suffered less wear, implying that objects were deposited sooner in these regions than in Wessex and the South West. If we take the more detailed comparisons between objects in three of our regions, we can see that Wessex and the South West suffered heavy wear for palstaves, while moderate wear typified palstaves from the Thames Valley. Again, the implication seems to be one of circulation and access to metal supplies. So, although the South West was in the ascendant in this period, deposition involved pieces that were kept in circulation longer, suggesting an internal tension in maintaining this position. Local metal production could have served in the main for exchange: a position which would be easily destabilised by the realignment of exchange, for example, through the Thames Valley. Wessex, meanwhile, was already in decline and the Thames Valley had access to sufficient quantities of material to enable deposition of moderately worn items to take place.

The ornaments often give the impression of being individual sets or pairs of pieces, most likely derived from an individual, or they sometimes occur as a single 'token' amongst a collection of palstaves, for example. This would suggest an importance for ornaments as prestige objects and probably status insignia: some ornament hoards could also be 'substitute' burials without their erstwhile owners. Palstaves seem to occur fairly universally in hoards and must be the 'standard' object of the period: prestige was probably not conferred by possession of single items, but by access to large numbers of these objects; large palstave hoards again 'freeze' the prestige for a lineage or individual, while restricting access to the objects and the metal contained in them.

The inspiration for the range of ornaments during this period was 'foreign', ie from within Europe, even if the objects themselves were manufactured within Britain. This probably conferred more prestige on those who had access to them: if they are taken to be female objects, then they might take on added significance in the wife - giver / wife - taker relationship. Some sets of ornaments do have a range of pieces from small, very worn items up to larger, less-worn pieces, which could have been gathered at different stages in the lifetime of the individual, and deposited together at death. Alternatively, they could have been a series of objects 'handed down' and deposited when a lineage was extinguished. The importance of the European link probably lay in the raw material provided by exchange and used to produce local items: societies with direct access to this exchange, in the coastal areas and river valleys, were in a commanding position to monitor the acquisition and selective distribution of these objects and the prestige associated with them. No doubt there would be attempts to control the flow of raw materials to prevent other groups and lineages establishing exchange links of their own, but those societies with access to supplies of other raw materials for exchange would manage to divert it to their advantage. This status rivalry may also be reflected in the increased number of deposits during this phase.

The South West in MBA2 had a number of important

ornament hoards and is traditionally seen as the main area of development for the objects of this phase of the Bronze Age: the Ornament Horizon. Evidence for production is not as extensive as for the Late Bronze Age, but the rapier moulds form Hennock (SW14) indicate that casting was taking place locally in MBA2. The presence of the raw materials for metal production in the South West must have provided a stimulus for this core area with innovative production, perhaps copying European prototypes for the ornament forms. Metal production continued into the Late Bronze Age, but the product would now seem to have been intended more for exchange with other areas, as the hoard record declines in this area, and it is suggested that the area becomes peripheral.

Thus we may be seeing several responses to the needs of the prestige goods system in the hoards of MBA2: there were individual hoards substituting for burials, which would concentrate prestige on the descendants of that individual; there were female sets possibly buried at the extinction of a lineage, removing the status which could not be conferred to anyone else; and there were a series of sizeable deposits, attempting to establish rank in different localities as access to external exchange became more widespread. The peripheries were once again drawing away from the power base established at the cores. Regionally, there were different emphases on the type and content of the hoards, but, during this period, deposition increased across southern Britain, due to the availability of a plentiful metal supply, before it again became more restricted. The South West contrasts with other areas because it contains so many hoards, but we must remember that less of the overall metal supply was available in this area. Another cycle completed its course.

LATE BRONZE AGE

Hoards now become larger, more frequent, and more complex and are drawn from a larger array of objects and metal pieces. The four chronological phases are also better represented in the hoard record. The production of metalwork was now on a 'mass production' scale with the evolution of complex core castings, and the possibility of repeated casting of the same object from rapidly produced moulds.

Hoards of LBA1 and LBA2 date are rather unevenly represented across the four regions: in the Thames Valley there is one hoard of LBA2 date, in the South West one of LBA1 date, in Wessex four of LBA2 date, and East Anglia has eight in LBA1 and five in LBA2. It is at this stage that we see the growing importance of East Anglia. The distribution of hoards is also important. We can observe that in Wessex the hoards seem to have moved away from the coast, which was earlier favoured for deposition, perhaps onto higher ground inland, possibly matching an expansion in the settled area. In East Anglia, the concentration in both phases is in the fens, which continued as a favoured area for at least seasonal settlement.

During these phases, miscellaneous pieces and lumps of metal begin to contribute to the content of hoards: thus the LBA1 hoard from the South West is three–quarters weapons and one–quarter small pieces; the LBA2 hoard from the Thames Valley is half tools and half metal; the LBA2 hoards from Wessex are mostly of weapons with some tools and miscellaneous pieces; and in East Anglia the proportion of weapons rose from 50% in LBA1 hoards to 75% in LBA2, with a corresponding decrease in the proportion of tools and ornaments. This preponderance of weapons in hoards at this time has been remarked before, but it is clearly of interest: weapons would seem to be prestige objects and, in the case of swords, must have represented a considerable investment in terms of the time and labour necessary for their production. Are we seeing the separation in society beween those primarily responsible for deposition and those responsible for production? In other words, tools had once been available for use in hoards, but now the high–ranking lineages had to resort to deposition of their own prestige objects, in the form of their weapons. The wear observations showed a high degree of correlation between degree of wear and completeness, and degree of wear and object in LBA2 Wessex, while the high level of significance accorded to the relationship between object and completeness in East Anglia in LBA1 was replaced by a similar relationship to that of Wessex in LBA2. The objects making up the LBA2 hoards were worn in Wessex, but tended to show even heavier wear in East Anglia whether complete or incomplete, while the Wessex hoards had heavier wear for the incomplete pieces. In East Anglia during LBA2, then, the emphasis seems to have been on depositing items which had otherwise been kept in circulation for a long time, while deposition occurred in Wessex before objects were greatly worn. So, although there was a consensus about the deposition of weapons at this time, it was delayed in East Anglia, or the objects were subject to more use than those in Wessex. Alongside the weapons, the selection of miscellaneous pieces for deposition included objects associated with weaponry, such as chapes and ferrules with their implications for horse–riding, and other 'aristocratic' trappings, which became more common during LBA3.

LBA3 saw another phase of massive deposition in most regions: over half of all the hoards in the Thames Valley and East Anglia were deposited in this phase, but only one–fifth and one–tenth in Wessex and the South West respectively, these two areas having had a higher proportion of deposits in MBA2. So, this was a phase when deposition was the norm, but Wessex and the South West must have declined in importance relative to the Thames Valley and East Anglia. This is entirely consistent with our core/periphery model. The areas for deposition were now well established: the river valley of the Thames, the low–lying areas of the South West, the inland areas of Wessex, and the fens of East Anglia, but in this last case the distribution extended towards the coast with a sudden increase in numbers. Tools once again became the major component of these hoards, being half or more of the total content in each region; weapons declined to a quarter or less; there was a small representation of ornaments and miscellaneous pieces, and a fairly small figure for pieces of metal, although they would have contributed more weight to individual hoards. The correlations between object and completeness, degree of wear and completeness, and the object and its degree of wear are very significant in all cases in all regions, except for Wessex, where the relationship between degree of wear and completeness is not at all significant. Tools and weapons were heavily worn before their deposition, and tools tended to be more often complete than weapons, while ornaments and miscellaneous pieces were more moderately worn, although the latter are largely unclassifiable. So, while tools once again become the major component of hoards, they are deposited in the main well-worn: prestige had switched back from the deposition of status objects to the deposition of objects *per se*, probably with more emphasis on the quantities of metal involved as part of the status-defining act. Interruptions to the metal supply from Europe could have led to greater reliance on British sources of metal. There does seem to be good evidence for extensive production in the South West at this time, and much of that product seems to have been passed to other areas through exchange. There was relatively little deposition in the South West in this period, and a peripheral status has been suggested, but with some importance as a metalwork producer. The sudden switch from the weapon vlposits of LBA2 to the 'scrap' hoards of LBA3 would also support this suggestion: a restriction in the supply had made the raw material as important as the objects manufactured with it. The deposition of lumps of metal could also embody this attitude.

The strength of the Thames Valley and East Anglia in this phase of deposition suggests that the core areas were now firmly sited in these two regions, while Wessex and the South West were more peripheral in this phase; there may even have been competition between the Thames Valley and East Anglia in terms of prestige. Although the Thames Valley did not match the numbers and size of East Anglian hoards, this was a significant phase of river deposition for the Thames Valley and 'wet' deposits change steadily towards the middle and lower Thames during the Late Bronze Age. We have tangible evidence for the handling of foreign exchange through sites such as Runnymede Bridge in the Thames Valley: this would lend much prestige to the controlling groups. The 'martial' element of the East Anglian hoards now included cauldron pieces and flesh hooks, suggesting that here too the concentration of prestige in certain lineages was being reinforced by feast-giving.

The Thames Valley exhibited moderate wear on socketed axes in LBA3 in our analysis of individual objects. The more generalised categories of objects showed how wear increased on tools and weapons from LBA2 to LBA3 in Wessex and East Anglia, while ornaments tended to less wear. Thus, we suppose that tools and weapons circulated longer in LBA3, although ornaments were deposited sooner, reflecting our suggestion of a restriction in the metal supply for this period. Ascendancy was maintained at a price: deposition had to take place, but it also meant the destruction of a valuable resource, obtained with difficulty.

The number of hoards falls again in LBA4, with only Wessex and East Anglia represented in this phase. The East Anglian hoards are only a small percentage of the number deposited overall, but in Wessex the figure is almost as high as that for LBA3, suggesting that Wessex was beginning to re-assert its former position as a core area. There is only one EIA1 hoard, from East Anglia (EA108), but it is composed of two gold bracelets and may represent an individual deposit, such as we saw for ornament hoards in MBA2. The LBA4 hoards in East Anglia seem dispersed across the region, but in Wessex the distribution appears to have moved south again towards the coast. This is consistent with the suggestion that many of these pieces were imported in this phase. In both regions, the hoard content is overwhelmingly tools (principally the well-known large socketed axes), but in Wessex there are some weapons, a few ornaments, and other miscellaneous items. The only significant correlations were in Wessex between degree of wear and completeness, and degree of wear and object, because the axes tended to be deposited whole and as cast, with some wear on a few examples; the weapons tended to be more heavily worn and were probably residual pieces from earlier phases. The small sample of tools from East Anglia had more of a spread across the range of wear, but in the main were less worn, while the ornaments tended to show heavier wear. The importance of hoard deposits would thus seem to have fallen off after LBA3, while Wessex may have been attempting to regain its former position as a core area by a re-alignment of exchange - also suggested by the slight evidence for shipwrecks in this phase, as discussed in a paper on an Armorican axe from the sea off Chesil Beach (Taylor, R., 1980). The imported material was quickly reaching hoards before usage or recasting into other pieces. After this, hoarding comes to an end for several hundred years, as the Atlantic network itself declined and could offer little further through exchange for Wessex or indeed any other region.

Thus, the hoards of the Late Bronze Age seem to reflect the build-up of prestige and status at an accelerating rate. Bronze Age society had become more complex, but these developments put considerable pressure on the social system, resulting in increased control of exchange and more assertive status-defining acts. Early in the period, the weaponry in the hoards indicates the use of high-prestige objects in direct deposition: prestige was accumulated into the hands of a small elite, and an attempt was made to fix that position through the deposition of weaponry. Perhaps these acts were not definitive enough and had to be underlined and later reinforced by deposits in rivers (less easily recovered), while more functional items and greater weights of metal went into the later hoards. The accent in LBA3 must have been on the prestige gained through control of the metal supply, hoards reinforcing that prestige, and thereby restricting the supply. The aristocratic lineages had now built up powerful social positions and were able to control and command tribute, production, and exchange; feast-giving also emphasised their position. Production was carried out mainly in the peripheral areas, such as the South West. This situation declined with the advent of iron, a product which was more widely available, until the core areas were able to reassert their authority, again by recourse to external exchange in the Late Iron Age. By then, southern Britain was part of the Roman periphery, and soon it was subsumed entirely.

CORE AND PERIPHERY

The linked concepts of core and periphery were derived from a model having its roots in structural Marxism and the Global Systems Approach: the principle of core areas, containing the seat of a strong lineage, with peripheries, supplying the core with goods and raw material, was seen to have some explanatory potential for the Bronze Age of southern Britain. In particular, the concept of a prestige goods system has helped in the interpretation of hoards, for this model stresses that their development is part of a continuous process, which includes constant shifts of power between the core area and its periphery. The success of the system is based in agricultural production, but potential for expansion lies in the exchange and alliance networks: prestige goods are necessary to support these and also result from them.

The archaeological evidence has suggested that relationships of this type can be recognised between the later Neolithic and the Late Iron Age of southern Britain; the Bronze Age hoards have reinforced this picture and added considerable detail at specific points in this process. The discontinuous nature of hoarding is partly a function of our own chronological framework, but it is also due partly to the cyclical nature of this kind of system. In the Early Bronze Age, the picture was on a regional scale with a Wessex core area and a Thames Valley periphery. In the Middle Bronze Age, each region seemed to have a series of hoards, perhaps suggesting smaller core/periphery relationships within each region (although Wessex was beginning to come under the influence of the Thames Valley), while the regions were clearly on the periphery of a larger European system. The patterns of internal competition seen in the Middle Bronze Age were over by the Late Bronze Age, when we see signs of a more regional core/periphery relationship, with the former peripheries in the Thames Valley and East Anglia forming the new core areas. These cores were themselves still on the periphery of a large European exchange network, but that began to break down towards the end of the period and, despite some attempts to re-establish links from the periphery in Wessex, Britain entered a period of isolation.

As usual, one has to enter a plea for more archaeological information to supplement the model: a picture has been built up, but it is inevitably a jigsaw with some of the wrong pieces and other pieces missing.

HOARDS

These were the subject of this enquiry: they have been recorded, analysed, and discussed. A vast amount of information is contained within these deposits, and yet in many ways they are as enigmatic as they have always been.

The traditional models were felt to be inappropriate with their rigid ascriptions of type and function: these have been replaced by a new model, where hoards could fulfil a variety of functions, but their principal purpose was that of developing prestige. The wear for individual objects has been recorded and variations observed on a majority scale: we have to consider why most hoards conform to certain wear patterns and show such consistent patterns of content, context, and distribution, but we are bound to overlook the exceptions. The overall principle has been discerned for the majority: there will always be some anomalies.

To consider hoards in isolation proves itself to be misguided, because we have to have the other categories of information, if we are to study the society that made these deposits. They are just one type of intentional deposit and other types certainly existed, not all of them involving metalwork. The archaeological record for the Bronze Age is discontinuous for this reason; we have discerned the components, but we have yet to recognise fully the larger system that lay behind it.

BIBLIOGRAPHY

ABC 1979 *Museums and Art Galleries in Great Britain and Ireland – 1979*, ABC Historic Publications, Dunstable

Akerman, J.Y. 1843–9 In *Proc. Soc. Antiq. London*, 1, first series, 234–5

Akerman, J.Y. 1859–61 In *Proc. Soc. Antiq. London*, 1, 233–4

Alexander, J., Ozanne, P.C. and Ozanne, A. 1960 "Report on the investigation of a round barrow on Arreton Down, Isle of Wight", *Proc. Prehist. Soc.*, 26, 263–302

Annable, F.K. and Simpson, D.D.A. 1964 *Guide Catalogue of the Neolithic and Bronze Age Collections in Devizes Museum*, Wiltshire Archaeol. Natur. Hist. Soc., Devizes

Anon 1851 "Catalogue of antiquities, exhibited in the museum formed during the Annual Meeting of the Archaeological Institute, held at Norwich, in 1847", *Proc. Archaeol. Inst. – Norwich volume*, xxiii–lvi

Anon 1853 In "Quarterly meetings", *Proc. Bury W. Suffolk Archaeol. Inst.*, 1, 154

Anon 1854 "A list of articles exhibited in the temporary museum at the Town Hall, Devizes, October 12th 1853", *Wiltshire Archaeol. Mag.*, 1, 57–67

Anon 1855 "A list of articles exhibited in the temporary museum at the Council Chamber, Salisbury, September 13th 1854", *Wiltshire Archaeol. Mag.*, 2, 26–39

Anon 1856 "Catalogue of antiquities exhibited in the museum formed during the annual meeting of the Archaeological Institute, held at Chichester, in July, 1853", *Sussex Archaeol. Collect.*, 8, 281–344

Anon 1862 "Presents and purchases, 1861–62", *Cambridge Antiq. Soc. Rep.*, 2, 9–11

Anon 1875 "The twenty-first annual meeting of the Wiltshire Archaeological and Natural History Society, held at Devizes, Tuesday, Wednesday and Thursday, September 8th, 9th and 10th, 1874", *Wiltshire Archaeol. Mag.*, 15, 117–39

Anon 1886 "Description of plates illustrating Hamdon Hill relics", *Proc. Somerset Archaeol. Natur. Hist. Soc.*, 32, 81–3

Anon 1894–6 "The sale of the collection of antiquities belonging to the Rev. E. Duke, of Lake House", *Wiltshire Archaeol. Mag.*, 28, 260–2

Anon 1901 "A find of Bronze implements near Bristol", *Archaeol. J.*, 58, 93

Anon 1928 "Bronze hoard from Suffolk", *Antiq. J.*, 8, 236–7

Anon 1943–7 "Recent accessions to the Museum of Archaeology and Ethnology", *Proc. Cambridge Antiq. Soc.*, 41, 78–9

Anon 1947–52 "Recent accessions to the Museum", *Rec. Buckinghamshire*, 15, 148

Anon 1962 "Archaeological notes from Reading Museum", *Berkshire Archaeol. J.*, 60, 114–20

Anon 1963–4 "Archaeological notes from Reading Museum", *Berkshire Archaeol. J.*, 61, 96–109

ApSimon, A.M. 1969–71 "1919–1969: Fifty years of archaeological research. The Spelaeological Society's contribution to archaeology", *Proc. Univ. Bristol Spelaeol. Soc.*, 12, 31–56

Babington, C.C. 1853 *Ancient Cambridgeshire: Or an Attempt to Trace Roman and other Ancient Roads that Passed through the County of Cambridge; with a Record of the Places where Roman Coins and other Remains have been found*, Publications Cambridge Antiq. Soc., Octavo series, 3

Babington, C.C. 1883 *Ancient Cambridgeshire: Or an Attempt to Trace Roman and other Ancient Roads that Passed through the County of Cambridge; with a Record of the Places where Roman Coins and other Remains have been found*, Publications Cambridge Antiq. Soc., 2nd edition, Octavo series, 20

Bailey, A.M. 1981 "The renewed discussions on the concept of the Asiatic mode of production", in J. Kahn and J. Llobera (eds), 1981, 89–107

Balkwill, C.J. 1978 "Archaeology in Suffolk, 1977", *Proc. Suffolk Inst. Archaeol. Hist.*, 34/2, 147–50

BAMNCM 1966 *Bronze Age metalwork in Norwich Castle Museum*, City of Norwich Museums

BAMNCM 1977 *Bronze Age metalwork in Norwich Castle Museum*, 2nd revised edition, Norfolk Museums Service, Norwich

Barnard, Miss 1918–22 In "Summary of proceedings", *Proc. Prehist. Soc. East Anglia*, 3/2, 315–22

Barrett, J.C. 1980a "The evolution of later Bronze Age settlement", in J. Barrett and R. Bradley (eds.), 1980, 77–100

Barrett, J.C. 1980b "The Pottery of the later Bronze Age in lowland England", *Proc. Prehist. Soc.* 46, 297–319

Barrett, J.C. 1985 "Hoards and related metalwork", in D.V. Clarke, T.G. Cowie and A. Foxon, *Symbols of Power at the Time of Stonehenge*, HMSO, Edinburgh, 95–106

Barrett, J.C. and Bradley, R.J. (eds) 1980 *The British Later Bronze Age: Settlement and Society in the British Later Bronze Age*, BAR 83, Oxford

Barrett, J.C. and Bradley, R.J. 1980a "The later Bronze Age in the Thames Valley", in J. Barrett and R. Bradley (eds), 1980, 247–69

Barrett, J.C. and Bradley, R.J. 1980b "Later Bronze Age settlement in south Wessex and Cranbourne Chase", in J. Barrett and R. Bradley (eds), 1980, 181–208

Basford, H.V. 1980 *The Vectis Report – A Survey of Isle of Wight Archaeology*, Isle of Wight County Council

Bateman, T. 1855 *A Descriptive Catalogue of the Antiquities and Miscellaneous Objects Preserved in the Museum of Thomas Bateman, at Lomberdale House, Derbyshire*, printed for the author, Bakewell

Baudou, E. 1960 *Die Regionale und Chronologische Einteilung der Jüngeren Bronzezeit im Nordischen Kreis*, Studies in North-European Archaeology , *1*, Stockholm

Beesley, T. 1853–5 "On Roman remains in the neighbourhood of Banbury; and on the late remarkable discovery of coins at Evenley", *Trans. Archaeol. Soc. North Oxfordshire*, 15–24

Binford, L.R. 1972 "Archaeology as anthropology", in M.P. Leone (ed.), *Contemporary Archaeology: A Guide to Theory and Contributions*, Southern Illinois University Press, Carbondale and Edwardsville, 93–101

Binford, L.R. 1982 "Meaning, inference and the material record", in C. Renfrew and S. Shennan (eds.), *Ranking, Resource and Exchange – Aspects of the Archaeology of Early European Society*, Cambridge University Press, 160–163

Boswell–Stone, W.G. 1893 *Prehistoric and Roman Remains in West Dorset, and the Neighbourhood of Bridport*, Bridport

Bottomore, T. (ed) 1983 *A Dictionary of Marxist Thought, Blackwell*, Oxford (paperback edition 1985)

Boyd Dawkins, Prof. 1885–7 In Proc. Soc. Antiq. London, 11, 42–51

Bradley, R. 1978 *The Prehistoric Settlement of Britain*, Routledge and Kegan Paul, London

Bradley, R. 1980 "Subsistence, exchange and technology – a social framework for the Bronze Age in southern England c. 1400–700 bc", in J. Barrett and R. Bradley (eds), 1980, 57–75

Bradley, R. 1982 "The destruction of wealth in later prehistory", *Man*, 17/1, 108–22

Bradley, R. 1984 *The Social Foundations of Prehistoric Britain: Themes and Variations in the Archaeology of Power*, Longmans, London

Bradley, R. 1985a "Exchange and social distance – the structure of bronze artefact distributions", *Man*, 20, 692–704

Bradley, R. 1985b "The archaeology of deliberate deposits", in R. Bradley, *Consumption, Change and the Archaeological Record*, University of Edingburgh Occ. Paper 13, 21–40.

Bradley, R., Lobb, S., Richards, J., and Robinson, M. 1980 "Two Late Bronze Age settlements on the Kennet gravels: Excavations at Aldermaston Wharf and Knights Farm, Burghfield, Berkshire", *Proc. Prehist. Soc.*, 46, 217–95

Briard, J. 1965 *Les Dépôts Bretons et L'Age du Bronze Atlantique*, Travaux du Laboratoire d'Anthropologie préhistorique de la Faculté des Sciences de Rennes, Rennes

Briard, J. 1971 "Epées de Bretagne et d'ailleurs jetées dans les rivières à l'âge du Bronze", *Annales de Bretagne et des Pays de l'Ouest*, 78, 47–58

Briscoe, G. and Furness, A 1955 "A hoard of Bronze Age weapons from Eriswell, near Mildenhall", *Antiq. J.*, 35, 218–9

Britton, D. 1960 "The Islesham hoard, Cambridgeshire", *Antiquity*, 34, 279–82

Britton, D. 1963 "Traditions of metalworking in the later Neolithic and Early Bronze Age of Britain: Part 1", *Proc. Prehist. Soc.*, 29, 258–325

Bruce, J. C. 1880 *A Descriptive Catalogue of Antiquities, Chiefly British, at Alnwick Castle*, Newcastle–upon–Tyne, printed for private distribution

Bruning, J.L. and Kintz, B.L. 1977 *Computational Handbook of Statistics*, Scott, Foreman and Co., Illinois, 2nd edition

von Brunn, W.A. 1968 *Mitteldeutsche Hortfunde der jüngeren Bronzezeit*, Römisch–Germanische Forschungen, Band 29, Walter de Gruyter & Co., Berlin

Bunny, E.B. 1860 In "Proceedings of the Association", *J. Brit. Archaeol. Ass.*, 16, 322–3

Burgess, B. 1858 "Earth–works at Hampden and Little Kimble", *Rec. Buckinghamshire*, 1, 138–42

Burgess, C.B. 1968a "The later Bronze Age in the British Isles and North–Western France", *Archaeol. J.*, 125, 1–45

Burgess, C.B. 1968b *Bronze Age Metalwork in Northern England c. 1000 to 70 BC*, Oriel Press, Newcastle–upon–Tyne

Burgess, C.B. 1968c "Bronze Age dirks and rapiers as illustrated by examples from Durham and Northumberland", *Trans. Architect. Archaeol. Soc. Durham Northumberland*, 1, 3–26

Burgess, C.B. 1974 "The bronze age", in C. Renfrew (ed), *British Prehistory – A New Outline, Duckworth, London*, 165–222

Burgess, C.B. 1979 "A find from Boyton, Suffolk, and the end of the Bronze Age in Britain and Ireland", in C. Burgess and D. Coombs (eds), 1979, 269–83

Burgess, C. 1980a *The Age of Stonehenge*, Dent, London

Burgess, C. 1980b "The Bronze Age in Wales", in J.A. Taylor (ed), *Culture and Environment in Prehistoric Wales – Selected Essays*, BAR 76, Oxford, 243–86

Burgess, C. 1982 Review of "Cross–Channel Relations in the Later Bronze Age – with Particular Reference to the Metalwork", *Proc. Prehist.* Soc., 48, 546–8

Burgess, C. and Coombs, D. (eds) 1979 *Bronze Age Hoards – Some Finds Old and New*, BAR 67, Oxford. Also preface (i–vii)

Burgess, C. and Cowen, J.D. 1972 "The Ebnal hoard and Early Bronze Age metalworking traditions", in F. Lynch and C. Burgess (eds), *Prehistoric Man in Wales and the West – Essays in Honour of Lily F. Chitty*, Adams & Dart, Bath, 167–81

Burgess, C., Coombs, D. and Davies, D.G. 1972 "The Broadward Complex and barbed spearheads", in F. Lynch and C. Burgess (eds), *Prehistoric Man in Wales and the West – Essays in honour of Lily F. Chitty*, Adams & Dart, Bath, 211–83

Burnard, R. 1906 "Early Man", *VCH Devon*, I, 341–72

Bush, T.S. 1901 Note added to "Notes on a socketed bronze celt" by Harper Gaythorpe, *Proc. Bath Natur. Hist. Antiq. Fld. Club*, 9, 299–300

Butler, J.J. 1963 "Bronze Age connections across the North Sea. A study in prehistoric trade and industrial relations between the British Isles, the Netherlands, N. Germany and Scandinavia, c. 1700–700 BC", *Palaeohistoria*, 9

Butler, J.J. 1981 Review of "The Age of Stonehenge", *Proc. Prehist. Soc*, 47, 350–3

Case, H. 1953 "The Mere, Roundway and Winterslow beaker culture knives", *Wiltshire Archaeol. Mag.*, 55, 135–8

Champion, T., Gamble, C., Shennan, S. and Whittle, A. 1984 *Prehistoric Europe*, Academic Press, London

Chantre, E. 1875–6 *Age du Bronze: Recherches sur l'Origine de la Métallurgie en France, Deuxième Partie – Gisements de l'Age du Bronze,* Etudes Paléoethnologiques dans le Bassin du Rhone, Paris

Childe, V.G. 1930 *The Bronze Age*, Cambridge University Press

Childe, V.G. 1956 *Prehistoric Communities of the British Isles*, Chambers Ltd., London & Edinburgh, reprint of 1940 edition

Chowne, P. 1980 "Bronze Age settlement in north Lincolnshire", in J. Barrett and R. Bradley (eds), 1980, 295–305

Clark, J.G. 1938 "Early Man", *VCH Cambs.*, I, 247–303

Clark, J.G.D. and Godwin, H. 1940 "A Late Bronze Age find near Stuntney, Isle of Ely", *Antiq. J.*, 20, 52–71

Clarke, E.D. 1821 "An account of some antiquities found at Fulbourn in Cambridgeshire", *Archaeologia*, 19, 56–61

Clarke, R.R. 1939 "A bronze cauldron and other antiquities from north–east Suffolk", *Proc. Suffolk Inst. Archaeol. Natur. Hist.*, 23, 219–23

Clarke, R.R. 1947–52 "Notes on recent archaeological discoveries in Norfolk (1943–8)", *Norfolk Archaeol.*, 30, 156–9

Clarke, R.R. 1955–7 "Archaeological discoveries in Norfolk, 1949–54", *Norfolk Archaeol.*, 31, 395–416

Clinch, G. 1901 "Early Man", *VCH Norfolk*, I, 253–78

Clinch, G. 1905 "Early Man", *VCH Bucks*, I, 177–93

Clinch, G. 1911 "The Bronze Age" and "Topographical list of Bronze Age and Early Iron Age antiquities found in Suffolk", *VCH Suffolk*, I, 263–70 and 275–7

Clough, T.H.McK. 1969 "Recent discoveries of Late Bronze Age metalwork in Norfolk", *Norfolk Archaeol.*, 34/4, 348–51

Clough, T.H.McK. 1971 "A hoard of Late Bronze Age metalwork from Aylsham, Norfolk", *Norfolk Archaeol.*, 35/2, 159–69

Clough, T.H.McK. and Green, C. 1978 "The first Late Bronze Age founder's hoard from Gorleston, Great Yarmouth, Norfolk", *Norfolk Archaeol.*, 37/1, 1–18

Clough, T.H.McK. and Wade–Martins, P. 1970 "A Late Bronze Age hoard from Foxburrow Farm, North Elmham, Norfolk, 1970", *Norfolk Archaeol.*, 35/1, 6–18

Cocks, A. Heneage 1904–9 "On a hoard of bronze implements from New Bradwell", *Rec. Buckinghamshire*, 9, 431–40

Coghlan, H.H. 1970 *A Report upon the Hoard of Bronze Age Tools and Weapons from Yattendon, near Newbury, Berkshire*, The Borough of Newbury Museum, Newbury

Coles, J.M. 1959–60 "Scottish Late Bronze Age metalwork: Typology, distributions and chronology", *Proc. Soc. Antiq. Scot.*, 93, 16–134

Coles, J.M. 1962 "European Bronze Age shields", *Proc. Prehist. Soc.*, 28, 156–90

Coles, J. 1963 "The Hilton (Dorset) gold ornaments", *Antiquity*, 37, 132–4

Coles, J.M. 1968–9 "Scottish Early Bronze Age Metalwork", *Proc. Soc. Antiq. Scot.*, 101, 1–110

Coles, J.M. 1971 "Bronze Age spearheads with gold decoration", *Antiq. J.*, 51, 94–5

Coles, J.M. 1978a "The Somerset Levels: a concave landscape", in H.C. Bowen and P.J. Fowler (eds), *Early Land Allotment in the British Isles: A Survey of Recent Work*, BAR 48, Oxford, 147–8

Coles, J.M. 1978b "Man and landscape in the Somerset Levels", in S. Limbrey and J.G. Evans (eds), *The Effect of Man on the Landscape: the Lowland Zone*, CBA Res Rep 21, London, 86–9

Coles, J.M. and Harding, A.F. 1979 *The Bronze Age in Europe: An Introduction to the Prehistory of Europe c.2000–700 BC*, Methuen and Co. Ltd., London

Coles, J. and Hibbert, A. 1975 "The Somerset Levels", in P.J. Fowler (ed), *Recent Work in Rural Archaeology*, Adams and Dart, Bath, 12–26

Coles, J.M. and Orme, B.J. 1980 *Prehistory of the Somerset Levels*, Somerset Levels Project, Cambridge and Exeter

Coll, J. 1982 *The BBC Microcomputer User Guide*, British Broadcasting Corporation, London

Collins, A.E.P. 1948–9 "Bronzes and Pottery from Wallingford", *Berkshire Archaeol. J.*, 51, 65–6

Colquhoun, I.A. 1979 "The Late Bronze Age hoard from Blackmoor, Hampshire", in C. Burgess and D. Coombs (eds), 1979, 99–115

Cook, N 1972–3 "Bronze Age spearheads from Horrington Hill, near Wells", *Somerset Archaeol. Natur. Hist.*, 117, 119–20

Coombs, D.G. 1971 *Late Bronze Age Metalwork in the South of England. Typology, Associations, Distribution, Chronology and Industrial Traditions*, Ph.D. thesis, University of Cambridge

Coombs, D. 1974 "Ein spätbronzezeitlicher Depotfund von Snettisham (Norfolk)", *Archäologisches Korrespondenzblatt*, 4, 31–5

Coombs, D. 1975 "Bronze Age weapon hoards in Britain", *Archaeol. Atlant.*, 1/1, 49–81

Coombs, D. 1979a "The Figheldean Down hoard, Wiltshire", in C. Burgess and D. Coombs (eds), 1979, 253–68

Coombs, D. 1979b "A Late Bronze Age hoard from Cassiobridge Farm, Watford, Hertfordshire", in C. Burgess and D. Coombs (eds), 1979, 197–220

Crawford, O.G.S. 1913 "Prehistoric trade between England and France", *L'Anthropologie*, 24, 641–9

Crawford, O.G.S. and Wheeler, R.E.M. 1921 "The Llynfawr and other hoards of the Bronze Age", *Archaeologia*, 71, 133–40

Croker, J.G. 1952 In "Proceedings at the meetings of the Archaeological Institute", *Archaeol. J.*, 9, 185–6

Cunliffe, B. 1984 *Danebury: An Iron Age Hillfort in Hampshire*, CBA Res Rep 52, London

Cunliffe, B. and O'Connor, B. 1979 "The Late Bronze Age hoard from Danebury, Hants.", in C. Burgess and D. Coombs (eds), 1979, 235–44

Cunnington, M.E. and Goddard, E.H. 1934 *Catalogue of Antiquities in the Museum of the Wiltshire Archaeological and Natural History Society at Devizes, Part II*, Devizes, 2nd edition

Cunnington, W. and Goddard, E.H. 1896 *Catalogue of Antiquities in the Museum of the Wiltshire*

Archaeological and Natural History Society at Devizes. Part I, The Stourhead Collection, Devizes

Curwen, E.C. 1948 "A bronze cauldron from Sompting, Sussex", *Antiq. J.*, 28, 157–63

Dale, W. 1897–99 In *Proc. Soc. Antiq. London*, 17, 129–31

Dale, W. 1898 "Bronze implements from the neighbourhood of Southampton", *Pap. Proc. Hants. Fld. Club Archaeol. Soc.*, 4/1, 75–8

Dale, W. 1905–7 In *Proc. Soc. Antiq. London*, 21, 462–3

Dale, W. 1913–14 In *Proc. Soc. Antiq. London*, 26, 32–4

Darwin W.E. 1894–7 "A hoard of bronze implements found at Bitterne", *Pap. Proc. Hants. Fld. Club*, 3, 53–66

Davey, P.J. 1971 "The distribution of later Bronze Age metalwork from Lincolnshire", *Proc. Prehist. Soc.* 37/1, *96–111*

Dawkins, Boyd 1885–7 In *Proc. Soc. Antiq.* London, 11, 42–51

Dechelette, J. 1924 *Manuel d'Archéologie Préhistorique, Celtique et Gallo–Romaine, Vol. II: Archéologie Celtique ou Protohistorique, Première Partie – Age du Bronze*, Picard, Paris, 2nd edition

Dennett, J. 1845 "Notes on discoveries which have been made in the barrows, etc. in the Isle of Wight, in the year 1816, and at several subsequent periods", *Trans. Brit. Archaeol. Ass., Winchester volume*, 148–60

Dent, E. 1877 *Annals of Winchcombe and Sudeley*, John Murray, London

Dillon, Viscount 1910 *Illustrated Guide to the Armouries, Tower of London*, HMSO, London

Dobson, D.P. 1931 *The Archaeology of Somerset*, Methuen, London

Doran, J.E and Hodson, F.R. 1975 *Mathematics and Computers in Archaeology*, Edinburgh University Press

Drew, C.D. 1934 "Bronze Age hoard from Haselbury Bryan", *Proc. Dorset Natur. Hist. Archaeol. Soc.*, 56, 131–2

Drew, C.D. 1935 "A Late Bronze Age hoard from Lulworth, Dorset", *Antiq. J.*, 15, 449–51

Dunning, G.C. 1931 "A Late Bronze Age Urnfield at Barnes, Isle of Wight, and notes on the Late Bronze Age in the Isle of Wight", *Proc. Isle Wight Natur. Hist. Archaeol. Soc.*, 2/2, 108–17

Dunning, G.C. 1932 "Bronze Age settlements and a Saxon hut near Bourton–on–the–Water, Gloucestershire", *Antiq. J.*, 12, 279–93

Dunning, G.C. 1936 "Hoard of palstaves found at Werrar, near Northwood", *Proc. Isle Wight Natur. Hist. Archaeol. Soc.*, 2/7, 616

Dunning, G.C. 1959 "The distribution of socketed axes of Breton type", *Ulster J. Archaeol.*, 22, 53–5

Dupré, G. and Rey, P.P. 1978 "Reflections on the relevance of a theory of the history of exchange", in D. Seddon (ed.), *Relations of Production: Marxist Approaches to Economic Anthropology*, Frank Cass, London, 171–208

zu Ehrbach–Schönberg, M–C. 1985 "Bemerkungen zu urnenfelderzeitlichen Deponierungen in Oberösterreich", *Archäologisches Korrespondenzblatt*, 15, 163–78

Ehrenberg, M.R. 1977 *Bronze Age Spearheads from Berkshire, Buckinghamshire, and Oxfordshire*, BAR 34, Oxford

Ekholm, K. 1981 "On the structure and dynamics of global systems", in J. Kahn and J. Llobera (eds), 1981, 241–61

Ellacombe, H.T. 1849 In "Antiquities and works of art exhibited", *Archaeol. J.*, 6, 81

Eogan, G. 1964 "The later Bronze Age in Ireland in the light of recent research", *Proc. Prehist. Soc.*, 30, 268–351

Eogan, G. 1967 "The associated finds of gold bar torcs", *J. Roy. Soc. Antiq. Ir.*, 97, 129–75

Eogan, G. 1983 *The Hoards of the Irish Later Bronze Age*, University College, Dublin

Evans, A.J. 1907–9 In *Proc. Soc. Antiq. London*, 22, 121–8

Evans, J. 1870–3 In *Proc. Soc. Antiq. London*, 5, 392–412

Evans, J. 1876–8 In *Proc. Soc. Antiq. London*, 7, 480–5

Evans, J. 1881 *The Ancient Bronze Implements, Weapons and Ornaments of Great Britain and Ireland*, Longmans, Green and Co., London

Evans, J. 1884 "On a hoard of bronze objects found in Wilburton Fen, near Ely", *Archaeologia*, 48, 106–14

Evans, J. 1885–7 In *Proc. Soc. Antiq. London*, 11, 8–12

Evans, J.G. 1975 *The Environment of Early Man in the British Isles*, Elek, London

Falconer, J.P.E. 1905 "Ancient interments at Newton St. Loe, near Bath", *Proc. Bath Natur. Hist. Antiq. Fld. Club*, 10, 312–14

Farley, M. 1979a "A Carp's Tongue hoard from Aylesbury, Buckinghamshire", in C. Burgess and D. Coombs (eds), 1979, 137–44

Farkey, M. 1979b "A small Late Bronze Age hoard from Ellesborough, Buckinghamshire", in C. Burgess and D. Coombs (eds), 1979, 145–8

Farrar, R.A.H. 1952 "Archaeological fieldwork in Dorset in 1952", *Proc. Dorset Natur. Hist. Archaeol. Soc.*, 74, 85–110

Farrar, R.A.H. 1964 "Recent discoveries and accessions", *Proc. Dorset Natur. Hist. Archaeol. Soc.*, 86, 115

Ffoks, W. 1850 In "Proceedings at the meetings of the Archaeological Institute", *Archaeol. J.*, 7, 64–5

Fisher, C.H. 1899–1901 "Two bronze spear–heads from Rodborough, near Stroud", *Proc. Cotteswold Natur. Fld. Club*, 13, 85–7

Fleming, A. 1973 "Models for the development of the Wessex culture", in C. Renfrew (ed), *The Explanation of Culture Change: Models in Prehistory*, Duckworth, London, 571–85

Fleming, A. 1978 "The prehistoric landscape of Dartmoor Part 1: South Dartmoor", *Proc. Prehist. Soc.*, 44, 97–123

Fleming, A. 1983 "The prehistoric landscape of Dartmoor Part 2: North and East Dartmoor", *Proc. Prehist. Soc.*, 49, 195–241

Flower, J.W. 1870–73 In *Proc. Soc. Antiq. London*, 5, 425

Fox, A. 1950 "Two Greek silver coins fron Holne, South Devon", *Antiq. J.*, 30, 152–5

Fox, A. 1955 "Twenty–second report on the archaeology and early history of Devon", *Trans. Devon Ass.*, 87, 319–26

Fox, A. 1956 "Twenty-third report on the archaeology and early history of Devon", *Trans. Devon Ass.*, 88, 212–21

Fox, C. 1923 *The Archaeology of the Cambridge Region – A Topographical Study of the Bronze, Early Iron, Roman and Anglo-Saxon Ages, with an Introductory Note on the Neolithic Age*, Cambridge University Press

Fox, C.F. 1928 "A Bronze Age refuse pit at Swanwick, Hants.", *Antiq. J.*, 8, 331–6

Fox, C. 1939 "The socketed bronze sickles of the British Isles with special reference to an unpublished specimen from Norwich", *Proc. Prehist. Soc.*, 5, 222–48

Fox, C. 1941 "The non-socketed bronze sickles of Britain", *Archaeol. Cambrensis*, 96, 136–62

Fox, C. and Burkitt, M.C. 1926 "Early Man", *VCH Hunts.*, I, 193–218

Foxon, A.D. 1982 "Artefacts in society", *Scot. Archaeol. Review*, 1/2, 114–20

Frankenstein, S. and Rowlands, M.J. 1978 "The internal structure and regional context of Early Iron Age society in south-western Germany", *Bull. Univ. London Inst. Archaeol.*, 15, 73–112

Franks, A.W. 1852 In "Proceedings at meetings of the Archaeological Institute", *Archaeol. J.*, 9, 303

Franks, A.W. 1853 "On the additions to the collection of national antiquities in the British Museum", *Archaeol. J.*, 10, 1–13

Franks, A.W. 1855 "Notes on bronze weapons found on Arreton Down, Isle of Wight", *Archaeologia*, 36, 326–31

Friedman, J. 1979 *System, Structure and Contradiction in the Evolution of 'Asiatic' Social Formations*, Social Studies in Oceania and South East Asia 2, The National Museum of Denmark, Copenhagen

Friedman, J. 1982 "Catastrophe and continuity in social evolution", in C. Renfrew, M. Rowlands and B. Segraves (eds), 1982, 175–96

Friedman, J. and Rowlands, M.J. 1977 "Notes towards an epigenetic model of the evolution of 'civilisation'", in J. Friedman and M.J. Rowlands (eds), *The Evolution of Social Systems*, Duckworth, London, 201–76

Gardiner, J.P. 1980 "Land and social status – a case study from eastern England", in J. Barrett and R. Bradley (eds), 1980, 101–14

Gerloff, S. 1975 *The Early Bronze Age Daggers in Great Britain . . . and a Reconsideration of the Wessex Culture*, PBF VI/2, Munich

Gillies, W. 1981 "The craftsman in Early Celtic literature", *Scot. Archaeol. Forum*, 11, 70–85

Gingell, C. 1979 "The bronze and iron hoard from Melksham and another Wiltshire find", in C. Burgess and D. Coombs (eds), 1979, 245–51

Goddard, E.H. 1911–12 "Notes on implements of the Bronze Age found in Wiltshire, with a list of all known examples found in the county", and "Bronze objects not included in the list in WAM 37, 117", *Wiltshire Archaeol. Mag.*, 37, 92–158 and 455

Goddard, E.H. 1913–14 "A list of prehistoric, Roman, and Pagan Saxon antiquities in the county of Wilts. arranged under parishes", *Wiltshire Archaeol. Mag.*, 38, 153–378

Goddard, E.H. 1915–17 "Bronze implements of the bronze age found in Wiltshire, not previously recorded. Supplementary list (Feb. 1917)", *Wiltshire Archaeol. Mag.*, 39, 477–84

Goddard, E.H. 1917–19 "Bronze implements found in Wiltshire not previously recorded", *Wiltshire Archaeol. Mag.*, 40, 359–60

Goddars, E.H. 1922–4 "Unrecorded bronze implements in the Blackmore Museum, Salisbury", *Wiltshire Archaeol. Mag.*, 42, 601–2

Godelier, M. 1978 "The concept of the 'Asiatic Mode of Production' and Marxist models of social evolution", in D. Seddon (ed), *Relations of Production: Marxist Approaches to Economic Anthropology*, Frank Cass, London, 209–57

Goodwin, C.W. 1848 "On two British shields, recently found in the Isle of Ely, and now in the collection of the Cambridge Antiquarian Society", *Miscellaneous Communications, Publications Cambridge Antiq. Soc., Quarto Series*, 2/2, 7–13 + 4 pl.

Gough, R. 1806 *Britannia: Or, A Chorographical Description of the Flourishing Kingdoms of England, Scotland, and Ireland, and the Islands Adjacent; from the Earliest Antiquity. By William Camden. Translated from the Edition Published by the Author in MDCVII. Enlarged by the Latest Discoveries*, printed for John Stockdale, London, 2nd edition

Gowing, C.N. 1961–5 "Two socketed axes from Princes Risborough", *Rec. Buckinghamshire*, 17, 128

Gray, H. St. George 1902 "The 'Walter Collection' in Taunton Castle Museum", *Proc. Somerset Archaeol. Natur. Hist Soc.*, 48, 24–78

Gray, H. St. George 1909 "The gold torc found at Yeovil, 1909", *Proc. Somerset Archaeol. Natur. Hist. Soc.*, 55, 66–84

Gray, H. St. George 1931 "Bronze implements found in the parish of Old Cleeve, Somerset", *Proc. Somerset Archaeol. Natur. Hist. Soc.*, 77, 136–7

Gray, H. St. George 1932 "Additions to the Museum", *Proc. Somerset Archaeol. Natur. Hist. Scc.*, 78, lxxvi

Green, C. 1935 "Some broze implements from Gloucestershire", *Antiq. J.*, 15, 196–8

Greenwell, W. and Parker Brewis, W. 1909 "The origin, evolution, and classification of the bronze spear-head in Great Britain and Ireland", *Archaeologia*, 61, 439–72

Gregory, C.A. 1980 "Gifts to men and gifts to god: Gift exchange and capital accumulation in contemporary Papua", *Man*, 15/4, 626–52

Gregory, C.A. 1982 *Gifts and Commodities*, Academic Press, London

Grinsell, L.V. 1941 "The Bronze Age round barrows of Wessex", *Proc. Prehist. Soc.*, 7, 73–113

Grinsell, L.V. 1957 "Archaeological Gazetteer", *VCH Wilts.*, I/1, 21–279

Grinsell, L.V. 1968 *Guide catalogue to the South Western British Prehistoric Collections*, City Museum, Bristol

Groube, L.M. and Bowden, M.C.B. 1982 *The Archaeology of Rural Dorset: Past, Present and Future*, Dorset Natur. Hist. Archaeol. Soc. Monogr. 4, Dorchester

Gurney, H. 1829 In "Appendix", *Archaeologia*, 22, 424

Hall, M. and Gingell, C. 1974 "Nottingham Hill, Gloucestershire, 1972", *Antiquity*, 8, 306–9

Halls, H.H. 1908–14 In "Summary of proceedings", *Proc. Prehist. Soc. East Anglia*, 1/1, 111

Harding, D.W. 1972 *The Iron Age in the Upper Thames Basin*, Clarendon, Oxford

Harford, C.J. 1803 "An account of some antiquities discovered on the Quantock Hills, in Somersetshire, in the year 1794", *Archaeologia*, 14, 94–8

Hart, C. 1967 *Archaeology in Dean*, Bellows, Gloucester

Hawkes, C.F.C. 1938–40 "The excavations at Quarley Hill, 1938", *Pap. Proc. Hants. Fld. Club Archaeol. Soc.*, 14, 136–94

Hawkes, C.F.C. 1941 In J.F.S. Stone – "The Deverel-Rimbury settlement on Thorny Down, Winterbourne Gunner, South Wilts.", *Proc. Prehist. Soc.*, 7, 114–33

Hawkes, C.F.C. 1942 "A bronze pin, torcs and pottery from a Late Bronze Age site at Plaitford, Hants.", *Proc. Prehist. Soc.*, 8, 44–7

Hawkes, C.F.C. and Clarke, R.R. 1963 "Gahlstorf and Caister-on-Sea: Two finds of Late Bronze Age Irish gold", in I. Ll. Foster and L. Alcock (eds), *Culture and Environment – Essays in Honour of Sir Cyril Fox*, Routledge and Kegan Paul, London, 193–250

Hill, G. 1984 "Dumping secrets", *Acorn User*, 29, 86–7, 105–8

Hillier, G. n.d. *The History and Antiquities of the Isle of Wight*, printed for the subscribers only, and not published, London

Hoare, R.C. 1827 "Account of antiquities found at Hamden Hill, with fragments of British chariots", *Archaeologia*, 21, 39–42

Hodder, I. 1982 *Symbols in Action: Ethnoarchaeological Studies of Material Culture*, Cambridge University Press

Hodges, H.W.M. 1957 "Studies in the Late Bronze Age in Ireland: 3. The hoards of bronze implements", *Ulster J. Archaeol.*, 20, 51–63

Hodges, H.W.M. 1960 "The Bronze Age moulds of the British Isles, Part 2: England and Wales – Moulds of stone and bronze", *Sibrium*, 5, 153–62

Hodges, H.W.M. 1976 *Artifacts: An Introduction to Early Materials and Technology*, John Baker, London, 2nd edition

Hodson, F.R. 1970 "Cluster analysis and archaeology: some new developments and applications", *World Archaeol.*, 1/3, 299–320

Hood, A.A. 1870–73 In *Proc. Soc. Antiq. London*, 5, 427

Hooley, E.E. 1936–7 "Bronze implements stolen from Winchester", *Mus. J.*, 36, 495–6

Howard, H. 1983 *The Bronze Casting Industry in Later Prehistoric Southern England: A Study Based on Refractory Debris*, Ph.D. thesis, University of Southampton

Hudd, A.E. 1899–1901 In *Proc. Soc. Antiq. London*, 18, 237–40

Hudd, A.E. 1900–1903 "Four bronze implements from Coombe Dingle, Gloucestershire", *Proc. Clifton Antiq. Club*, 5, 118–21

von Hügel, Baron 1906–8 "Some notes on the gold armilla found in Grunty Fen, together with Mr. Isaac Deck's original account of its discovery in 1844", *Proc. Cambridge Antiq. Soc.*, 12, 96–105

Hughes, M. and Champion, T. 1982 "A Middle Bronze Age ornament hoard from South Wonston, Hampshire", *Proc. Prehist. Soc.*, 48, 487–9

Hundt, H-J. 1955 "Versuch zur Deutung der Depotfunde der nordischen jüngeren Bronzezeit, unter besonderer Berücksichtigung Mecklenburgs", *Jahrbuch des Römisch – Germanischen Zentralmuseums Mainz*, 2, 95–140

Hutchins, J. 1861–70 *The History and Antiquities of the County of Dorset: Compiled from the Best and Most Ancient Historians, Inquisitiones post Mortem, and Other Valuable Records and MSS in the Public Offices and Libraries, and in Private Hands. With a Copy of Domesday Book and the Inquisitio Gheldi for the County: Interspersed with Some Remarkable Particulars of Natural History; and Adorned with a Correct Map of the County, and Views of Antiquities, Seats of the Nobility and Gentry, Etc.*, Westminster, London, 3rd edition

Inventaria Archaeologica (IA) 1955a Great Britain 1st SET: GB 1–8, *"Grave-groups and hoards of the British Bronze Age"*, International Congress of Prehistoric and Protohistoric Sciences

Inventaria Archaeologica 1955b 2nd SET: GB 9–13, *"Bronze Age hoards in the British Museum"*, International Congress of Prehistoric and Protohistoric Sciences

Inventaria Archaeologica 1956 3rd SET: GB 14–18, *"Grave-groups and hoards of the British Bronze Age (2)"*, International Congress of Prehistoric and Protohistoric Sciences

Inventaria Archaeologica 1958 6th SET: GB 35–41, *"Late Bronze Age hoards in the British Museum"*, International Congress of Prehistoric and Protohistoric Sciences

Inventaria Archaeologica 1959 7th SET: GB 42–47, *"Middle Bronze Age hoards from Southern England"*, International Congress of Prehistoric and Protohistoric Sciences

Inventaria Archaeologica 1960 8th SET: GB 48–54, *"Bronze Age grave-group and hoards in the British Museum"*, International Congress of Prehistoric and Protohistoric Sciences

Irving, J. 1859–61 In *Proc. Soc. Antiq. London*, 1, 369

Isaacson, Mr. 1853 In "Quarterly Meetings", *Proc. Bury W. Suffolk Archaeol. Inst.*, 1, 24–8

Jankhun, H. 1958 "Moorfunde", in W. Krämer (ed), *Neue Ausgrabungen in Deutschland*, Mann, Berlin, 243–57

Jensen, J. 1972 "Ein neues Hallstattschwert aus Dänemark: Beitrag zur Problematik der jungbronzezeitlichen Votivfunde", *Acta Archaeologica*, 43, 115–64

Johnson, G. 1845 In "Proceedings of the committee", *Archaeol. J.*, 2, 80–1

Johnson, G. 1846 In "Proceedings of the committee", *J. Brit. Archaeol. Ass.*, 1, 51

Johnson, N. 1980 "Later Bronze Age settlement in the South-West", in J. Barrett and R. Bradley (eds), 1980, 141–80

Jones, J.D. 1964 *Carisbrooke Castle Museum: A Guide to the Collections, Trustees of the Carisbrooke Castle Museum*, Newport, new edition, reprinted 1969

Jones, S.J. 1931 "Note on an anvil and a palstave found at Flax Bourton, Somerset", *Proc. Univ. Bristol Spelaeol. Soc.*, 4/1, 43–4

Kahn, J.S and Llobera, J.R. 1981 *The Anthropology of Pre-Capitalist Societies*, Macmillan, London and Basingstoke

Kahn, J.S and Llobera, J.R. 1981a "Towards a new Marxism or a new anthropology?", in J. Kahn and J. Llobera (eds), 1981, 263–329

Kemble, J.M. 1863 *Horae Ferales: Or Studies in the Archaeology of the Northern Nations*, Lovell Reeve and Co., London

Kendrick, T.D. and Hawkes, C.F.C. 1932 *Archaeology in England and Wales: 1914–1931*, Methuen, London

Kennett, D.H. 1969 "The New Bradwell Late Bronze Age hoard", *J. Northampton Mus.*, 6, 3–7

Kennett, D.H. 1975 "The Wymington hoard and other hoards and finds of the Late Bronze Age from the South Midlands", *Bedfordshire Archaeol. J.*, 10, 5–18

Kersten, K. 1936 *Zür älteren nordischen Bronzezeit*, Forschungen zur Vor- und Frühgeschichte aus dem Museum vorgeschichtlicher Altertümer in Kiel, 3, Wachholtz, Neumünster

King, E. 1812 "A description of antiquities discovered on Hagbourn Hill", *Archaeologia*, 16, 348–9

King, J. 1846 In "Proceedings of the central committee", *J. Brit. Archaeol. Ass.*, 1, 309–10

Kirwan, R, 1867–8 "Memoir of the examination of three barrows at Broad Down, Farway, near Honiton", *Trans. Devon Ass.*, 2, 619–49

Kirwan, R. 1870 "Notes on the prehistoric archaeology of East Devon, Part III", *Trans. Devon Ass.*, 4, 295–304

Kmietowicz, Z.W. and Yannoulis, Y. 1976 *Mathematical, Statistical and Financial Tables for the Social Sciences*, Longman, London

Kolling, A. 1968 *Späte Bronzezeit an Saar und Mosel*, Saarbrücker Beiträge zur Altertumskunde, Rudolf Habelt, Bonn

Kristiansen, K. 1974 "En kildekritisk analyse af depotfund fra Danmarks yngre bronzealder (periode IV–V): Et bidrag til den arkaeologiske kildekritik (A source-critical analysis of hoards from Late Danish Bronze Age (periods IV–V): A contribution to archaeological source-criticism)", *Aarbger for Nordisk Oldkyndighed og Historie*, 119-160 (English summary)

Kristiansen, K. 1978 "Periodeovergange i bronzealderen: Et indlaeg om den kronologiske forsknings metodiske grundlag og videnskabelige funktion (Period transitions in the nordic Bronze Age: An essay concerning the methodological foundations and the scientific function of chronological studies)", *Hikuin*, 4, 77–88; English summary, 157–8

Kristiansen, K. 1979 "The consumption of wealth in Bronze Age Denmark. A study in the dynamic of economic processes in tribal societies", in K. Kristiansen and C. Paludan-Müller (eds), *Studies in Scandinavian Prehistory and Early History, 1*, National Museum of Denmark, 158–90

Kristiansen, K. 1980 "Besiedlung, Wirtschaftsstrategie und Bodennutzung in der Bronzezeit Dänemarks", *Praehistorische Zeitschrift*, 55/1, 1–37

Kristiansen, K. 1981 "Economic models for Bronze Age Scandinavia - towards an integrated approach", in A. Sheridan and G. Bailey (eds), 1981, 239–303

Kristiansen, K. 1982 "The formation of tribal systems in later European prehistory: Northern Europe, 4000–500 BC", in C. Renfrew, M. Rowlands and B. Segraves (eds), 1982, 241–80

Kristiansen, K. 1983 "Kampen om Bronzen", *Skalk*, 5, 18–25

Kristiansen, K. 1984a "Krieger und Häuptlinge in der Bronzezeit Dänemarks: Ein Beitrag zur Geschichte des bronzezeitlichen Schwertes", *Jahrbuch des Römisch-Germanischen Zentralmuseums Mainz*, 31, 187–208

Kristiansen, K. 1984b "Ideology and material culture: an archaeological perspective", in M. Spriggs (ed), 1984, 72–100

Kristiansen, K. 1985 "The place of chronological studies in archaeology: a view from the Old World", *Oxford J. Archaeol.*, 4/3, 251–66

Kubach, W. 1977 *Die Nadeln in Hessen und Rheinhessen*, PBF XIII/3, Munich

Kubach, W. 1978-9 "Deponierungen in Mooren der südhessischen Oberrheinebene", *Jahresbericht des Instituts für Vorgeschichte der Universität Frankfurt A.M.*, 189–310

Kubach, W. 1985 "Einzel und Mehrstückdeponierungen und ihre Fundplätze", *Archäologisches Korrespondenzblatt*, 15, 179–85

Langmaid, N.G. 1970 "Excavations at Norton Fitzwarren, 1970", *Somerset Archaeol. Natur. Hist.*, 114, 105–6

Langmaid, N.G. 1971 "Norton Fitzwarren", *Curr. Archaeol.*, 28, 116–20

Larsson, T.B. 1984 "Multi-level exchange and cultural interaction in Late Scandinavian Bronze Age", in K. Kristiansen (ed), *Settlement and Economy in Later Scandinavian Prehistory*, BAR S211, Oxford, 63–83

Larsson, T.B. 1986 *The Bronze Age Metalwork in Southern Sweden: Aspects of Social and Spatial Organization 1800–500 BC*, Archaeology and Environment 6, Department of Archaeology, University of Umeå

Lawson, A.J. 1979a "A late Middle Bronze Age hoard from Hunstanton, Norfolk", in C. Burgess and D. Coombs (eds), 1979, 43–92

Lawson, A.J. 1979b "A Late Bronze Age hoard from West Caister, Norfolk", in C. Burgess and D. Coombs (eds), 1979, 173–9

Lawson, A.J. 1980a "A late bronze age hoard from Beeston Regis, Norfolk", *Antiquity*, 54, 217–9

Lawson, A.J. 1980b "The Horning hoard", *Norfolk Archaeol.*, 37/3, 333–8

Lawson, A.J. 1980c "The evidence for later Bronze Age settlement and burial in Norfolk", in J. Barrett and R. Bradley (eds), 1980, 271–94

Lawson, A.J. 1981 "III: The barrows of Norfolk", in A. Lawson, E. Martin and D. Priddy, 1981, 32–63

Lawson, A.J. and Ashley, S.J. 1980 "The Hilgay hoard", Norfolk *Archaeol.*, 37/3, 328–33

Lawson, A.J., Martin, E.A. and Priddy, D. 1981 *The Barrows of East Anglia*, E. Anglian Archaeol. Rep. No. 12

Lee, S (ed) 1927 *The Dictionary of National Biography: Supplement January 1901–December 1911*, Vol. 1, Oxford University Press, London, reprint

Leeds, E.T. 1915–16 "Two Bronze Age hoards from Oxford", *Proc. Soc. Antiq. London*, 28, 147–52

Leeds, E.T. 1928 "The Evans Collection", *Antiquity*, 2, 351–3

Leeds, E.T. 1939 "Bronze Age", *VCH Oxon.*, I, 241–51 and index 262–66

Lethbridge, T.C. and O'Reilly, M.M. 1930–1 "Archaeological notes", *Proc. Cambridge Antiq. Soc.*, 32, 59–66

Levy, J.E. 1977 *Social and Religious Change in Bronze Age Denmark. A Dissertation Presented to the Graduate School of Arts and Sciences of Washington University in Partial Fulfillment of the Requirements for the Degree of Doctor of Philosophy*, Saint Louis, Missouri

Levy, J.E. 1979 "Evidence of social stratification in Bronze Age Denmark", *J. Fld. Archaeol.*, 6/1, 49–56

Levy, J.E. 1982a *Social and Religious Organisation in Bronze Age Denmark – An Analysis of Ritual Hoard Finds*, BAR S124, Oxford

Levy, J.E. 1982b "The Bronze Age hoards of Denmark", *Archaeology*, 35/1, 37–45

Lewton-Brain, C.H. 1954 *The Sandringham Estate and its Archaeology*, privately printed pamphlet

Lockhart, C. 1869 *A General History of the Isle of Wight*, supplement to: B.B. Woodward, T.C. Wilks and C. Lockhart, *A General History of Hampshire, or the County of Southampton, including the Isle of Wight*, Vol. III, Virtue & Co., London

Longworth, I. 1959 "Notes on excavations in the British Isles, 1958", *Proc. Prehist. Soc.*, 25, 270–82

Longworth, I.H. 1970–2 "Two gold bracelets from Nowton, Bury St Edmunds", *Proc. Suffolk Inst. Archaeol.*, 32, 271–2

Lort, Rev. 1779 "Observations on celts", *Archaeologia*, 5, 106–18

Lowsley, L. 1872–5 "Note on some ancient bronze implements found at Yattendon Park in 1878", *Trans. Newbury Dist. Fld. Club*, 11, 255

McNeil, R. 1973 "A report on the Bronze Age hoard from Wick Park, Stogursey, Somerset", *Somerset Archaeol. Natur. Hist.*, 117, 47–64

Manby, T.G. 1980 "Bronze Age settlement in eastern Yorkshire", in J. Barrett and R. Bradley (eds), 1980, 307–70

Mandera, H–E. 1972 "Zur Deutung der spätumenfelderzeitlichen Hortfunde in Hessen", *Fundberichte aus Hessen*, 12, 97–103

Mandera, H–E. 1985 "Einige Bemerkungen zur Deutung bronzezeitlicher Horte", *Archäologisches Korrespondenzblatt*, 15, 187–93

Maringer, J. 1973 "Das Wasser in Kult und Glauben der vorgeschichtlichen Menschen", *Anthropos*, 68, 705–76

Martin, E.A. 1981 "IV: The barrows of Suffolk", in A. Lawson, E. Martin and D. Priddy, 1981, 64–88

Maynard, G. n.d. "Section V – The bronze and iron ages", in G. Morris (ed), *An Outline Survey of Saffron Walden and its Region*, Saffron Walden Survey Society

Megaw, B.R.S. and Hardy, E.M. 1938 "British decorated axes and their diffusion during the earlier part of the Bronze Age", *Proc. Prehist. Soc.*, 4/2, 272–307

Meillassoux, C. 1977 *Terrains et Théories*, Editions Anthropos, Paris

Mercer, R. 1975 "Settlement, farming and environment in South West England to c.1000 BC", in P.J. Fowler (ed), *Recent Work in Rural Archaeology*, Adams and Dart, Bath, 27–43

Miller, D and Tilley, C. 1984 "Ideology, power and prehistory: an introduction", in D. Miller and C. Tilley (eds), *Ideology, Power and Prehistory*, Cambridge University Press, 1–15

Minnitt, S. 1974 "Early Bronze Age hoard from Milverton, Somerset", *Somerset Archaeol. Natur. Hist.*, 118, 51–3

Mohen, J–P. 1977 *L'Age du Bronze dans la Région de Paris. Catalogue Synthétique des Collections Conservées au Musée des Antiquitiés Nationales*, Editions des Musées Nationaux, Paris

Moore, C.N. 1969 "Five unpublished bronze implements from Wiltshire", *Wiltshire Archaeol. Mag.*, 64, 114–16

Moore, C.N. and Lewis, E.R. 1969 "A hoard of Breton socketed axes from Nether Wallop", *Proc. Hampshire Fld. Club Archaeol. Soc.*, 26, 19–20

Moore, C.N. and Rowlands, M.J. 1972 *Bronze Age Metalwork in Salisbury Museum*, Salisbury and South Wiltshire Museum Occasional Publication, Salisbury

de Mortillet, G. 1894 "Cachettes de l'âge du bronze en France", *Bulletins de la Société d'Anthropologie de Paris*, 5 (4th series), 298–340

Moule, H.J. 1900 "Notes on bronze", *Proc. Dorset Natur. Hist. Antiq. Fld. Club*, 21, 40–104

Moule, H. 1904 In "Exhibits, Winter session, 1903–1904", *Proc. Dorset. Natur. Hist. Antiq. Fld. Club*, 25, xxiii–iv

Muckelroy, K. 1981 "Middle Bronze Age trade between Britain and Europe: a maritime perspective", *Proc. Prehist. Soc.*, 47, 275–97

Müller, S. 1884–9 "Trouvailles danoises *d'ex-voto*, des ages de pierre et de bronze", *Mémoires de la Société Royale des Antiquaires du Nord*, 225–50

Müller-Karpe, H. 1958 "Neues zur Urnenfelderkultur Bayerns", *Bayerische Vorgeschichtsblätter*, 23, 4–34

NBI *National Bronze Index*, complete archive housed at the British Museum, Dept. of Prehistoric and Romano-British Antiquities

Needham, S. 1979 "A pair of Early Bronze Age spearheads from Lightwater, Surrey", in C. Burgess and D. Coombs (eds), 1979, 1–40

Needham, S. 1980 "An assemblage of Late Bronze Age metalworking debris from Dainton, Devon", *Proc. Prehist. Soc.*, 46, 177–215

Needham, S. 1981 *The Bulford–Helsbury Manufacturing Tradition – The Production of Stogursey Socketed Axes during the Later Bronze Age in Southern Britain*, British Museum Occas. Pap. No.13, London

Needham, S. and Burgess, C. 1980 "The later Bronze Age in the Lower Thames Valley: the metalwork evidence", in J. Barrett and R. Bradley (eds), 1980, 437–69

Needham, S. and Longley, D. 1980 "Runnymede Bridge, Egham: A Late Bronze Age riverside settlement", in J. Barrett and R. Bradley (eds), 1980, 397–436

Needham, S. and Saville, A. 1981 "Two Early Bronze Age flat bronze axeheads from Oddington", *Trans. Bristol Gloucestershire Archaeol. Soc.*, 99, 15–19

Needham, S.P., Lawson, A.J. and Green, H.S. 1985 "A1–6 Early Bronze Age hoards" in *British Bronze Age Metalwork, Associated Finds Series*, British Museum Publications, London

Neville, R. 1854 In "Antiquities and works of art exhibited", *Archaeol. J.*, 11, 294

Norris, H. 1846 In "Proceedings of the Committee", *Archaeol. J.*, 1, 165

Norris, H. 1853 In "Antiquities and works of art exhibited", *Archaeol. J.*, 10, 246–54

Northover, J.P. 1982 "The exploration of the long–distance movement of bronze, in Bronze and Early Iron Age Europe", *Bull. Inst. Archaeol. Univ. London*, 19, 45–72

O'Connell, M. 1986 *Petters Sports Field, Egham: Excavation of a Late Bronze Age/Early Iron Age Site*, Surrey Archaeol. Soc. Res. Vol. No. 10, Guildford.

O'Connor, B. 1980 *Cross–Channel Relations in the Later Bronze Age: Relations between Britain, North–Eastern France and the Low Countries during the Later Bronze Age and the Early Iron Age, with Particular Reference to the Metalwork*, BAR S91, Oxford

Okeley, J. 1979 "An anthropological contribution to the history and archaeology of an ethnic group", in B.C. Burnham and J. Kingsbury (eds), *Space, Hierarchy and Society: Interdisciplinary Studies in Social Area Analysis*, BAR S59, Oxford

Oliver, V.L. 1936 "Bronze Age rapiers and swords from Dorset", *Proc. Dorset Natur. Hist. Archaeol. Soc.*, 58, 26–9

O'Neil, B.H.St.J. 1941 "Hoard of axes from Bourton–on–the–Water, Gloucestershire", *Antiq. J.*, 21, 150–1

Organ, R.M. 1953–6 "Further notes on an anvil and a palstave found at Flax Bourton, Somerset", *Proc. Univ. Bristol Spelaeol. Soc.*, 7, 184–6

Orton, C. 1980 *Mathematics in Archaeology*, Collins, London

O'Shea, J. 1981 "Coping with scarcity: Exchange and social storage", in A. Sheridan and G. Bailey (eds), 1981, 167–83

Owles, E.J. and Smedley, N. 1966 "Archaeology in Suffolk, 1966", *Proc. Suffolk Inst. Archaeol.*, 30/3, 275–83

Owles, E.J. and Smedley, N. 1968 "Archaeology in Suffolk, 1968", *Proc. Suffolk Inst. Archaeol.*, 31/2, 188–201

Palmer, S. 1860 In "Proceedings of the association", *J. Brit. Archaeol. Ass.*, 16, 322–8

Palmer, S. 1870–3 In *Proc. Soc. Antiq. London*, 5, 429

Parker Pearson, M. 1984 "Social change, ideology and the archaeological record", in M. Spriggs (ed), 1984, 59–71

Passmore, A.D. 1905–6 "Notes on recent discoveries", *Wiltshire Archaeol. Mag.*, 34, 308–12

Passmore, A.D. 1930–32 "A hoard of bronze implements from Donhead St. Mary, and a stone mould from Bulford, in Farnham Museum, Dorset", *Wiltshire Archaeol. Mag.*, 45, 373–6

Passmore, A.D. 1949–50 "Bronzes from the Duke Collection once at Lake House", *Wiltshire Archaeol. Mag.*, 53, 257–8

Pauli, L. 1985 "Einige Anmerkungen zum Problem der Hortfunde", *Archäologisches Korrespondenzblatt*, 15, 195–206

Peake, H. 1931 *The Archaeology of Berkshire*, Methuen, London

Pearce, S.M. 1974 "A palstave hoard from South Petherton, Somerset", *Somerset Archaeol. Natur. Hist.*, 118, 54–5

Pearce, S.M. 1976 "The Middle and Late Bronze Age metalwork of the South–West, and its relationship to settlement", *Proc. Devon Archaeol. Soc.*, 34, 17–40

Pearce, S.M. 1983 *The Bronze Age Metalwork of South Western Britain*, BAR 120, Oxford

Pearce–Serocold, Col. 1933 "Bronze hoard from Burnham", *Antiq. J.*, 13, 55 + Pl.

Pearson, G.W. and Stuiver, M. 1986 "High–precision calibration of the radiocarbon time scale, 500–2500 BC", *Radiocarbon*, 28/2B, 839–62

Pettigrew, J.T. 1865 In "Proceedings of the Association", *J. Brit. Archaeol. Ass.*, 21, 232

Phelps, W. 1839 *The History and Antiquities of Somersetshire; Being a General and Parochial Survey of that Interesting County. Containing an Historical Introduction with a Brief View of Ecclesiastical History; and an Account of the Druidical, Belgic–British, Roman, Saxon, Danish and Norman Antiquities, Now Extant*, printed for the author, London

Phillips, W. 1864 In "Antiquities and works of art exhibited", *Archaeol. J.*, 21, 90

Piggott, C.M. 1946 "The Late Bronze Age razors of the British Isles", *Proc. Prehist. Soc.*, 12, 121–41

Piggott, C.M. 1949 "A Late Bronze Age hoard from Blackrock in Sussex and its significance", *Proc. Prehist. Soc.*, 15, 107–21

Piggott, S. 1938 "The Early Bronze Age in Wessex", *Proc. Prehist. Soc.*, 4, 52–106

Piggott, S. 1947 "The Arreton Down Bronze Age hoard", *Antiq. J.*, 27, 177–8

Piggott, S. and C.M. 1944 "Excavation of barrows on Crichel and Launceston Downs, Dorset", *Archaeologia*, 90, 47–80

Prigg, H. 1880 "On a hoard of bronze antiquities from Reach, Cambridgeshire", *J. Brit. Archaeol. Ass.*, 36, 56–62

Prigg, H. 1885 "On the recent discovery of a bronze sword, at Chippenham, Cambridgeshire, with notices of similar discoveries in the western district of Suffolk", *Proc. Suffolk Inst. Archaeol. Natur. Hist*, 6/2, 184–94

Prigmore, C. 1981 *30 Hour BASIC*, National Extension College, Cambridge

Pring, J.H. 1880a *The Briton and the Roman on the Site of Taunton*, Taunton

Pring, J.H. 1880b "On some evidence of the occupation of the ancient site of Taunton by the Britons", *Archaeol. J.*, 37, 94–8

Proudfoot, E.V.W. 1963 "Report on the excavation of a bell barrow in the parish of Edmonsham, Dorset, England, 1959", *Proc. Prehist. Soc.*, 29, 395–425

Pryor, F. 1976 "Fen–edge land management in the Bronze Age: An interim report on excavations at Fengate, Peterborough 1971–75", in C. Burgess and R. Miket (eds), *Settlement and Economy in the Third and Second Millennia BC*, BAR 33, Oxford, 29–49

Pryor, F. 1980 "Will it all come out in the Wash? Reflections at the end of eight years' digging", in J.Barrett and R. Bradley (eds), 1980, 483–500

Pryor, F. 1982 *Fengate*, Shire Archaeology, Princes Risborough

Pryor, F. 1984 *Excavation at Fengate, Peterborough, England: The Fourth Report*, Northamptonshire Archaeol. Soc. Monogr. 2/Royal Ontario Museum Archaeol. Monogr. 7

Pryor, F., French, C. and Taylor, M. 1986 "Flag Fen, Fengate, Peterborough I: Discovery, reconnaissance and initial excavation (1982–85)", *Proc. Prehist. Soc.*, 52, 1–24

Randsborg, K. 1974 "Social stratification in Early Bronze Age Denmark: A study in the regulation of cultural systems", *Praehistorische Zeitschrift*, 49, 38–61

Randsborg, K. 1980 *The Viking Age in Denmark*, Duckworth, London

Rathje, W.L. 1978 "Melanesian and Australian exchange systems: A view from Mesoamerica", *Mankind*, 11/3, 165–74

Renfrew, C., Rowlands, M.J. and Segraves, B.A. (eds) 1982 *Theory and Explanation in Archaeology: The Southampton Conference*, Academic Press, London

Richmond, I.A. 1950 "Stukeley's lamp, the badge of the Society of Antiquaries", *Antiq. J.*, 30, 22–7

Ridgeway, W. 1919 "An Irish decorated, socketed bronze axe", *Man*, 19, 161–4

Rittershoffer, K–F. 1983 "Der Hortfund von Bühl und seine Beziehungen", *Bericht der Römisch – Germanischen Kommission*, 64, 139–415

Roberts, R. 1882 "A description of some ancient gold ornaments found in Dorsetshire", *Proc. Dorset Natur. Hist. Antiq. Fld. Club*, 4, 158–9

Robertson, A.S. 1974 "Romano–British coin hoards: Their numismatic, archaeological and historical significance", in J. Casey and R. Reece (eds), *Coins and the Archaeologist*, BAR 4, Oxford, 12–36

Rolls, J.E. 1861 In "Proceedings at meetings of the Archaeological Institute", *Archaeol. J.*, 18, 161

Roskill, V. 1938 "The bronze implements of the Newbury region", *Trans. Newbury Dist. Fld. Club*, 8, 10–41

Rostovtseff, M. 1923 "Commodus–Hercules in Britain", *J. Roman Stud.*, 13, 91–109

Rowlands, M.J. 1971 "The archaeological interpretation of prehistoric metalworking", *World Archaeol.*, 3/2, 210–24

Rowlands, M.J. 1973 "Modes of exchange and the incentives for trade, with reference to later European prehistory", in C. Renfrew (ed), *The Explanation of Culture Change: Models in Prehistory*, Duckworth, London, 589–600

Rowlands, M.J. 1976 *The Organisation of Middle Bronze Age Metalworking – The Production and Distribution of Metalwork in the Middle Bronze Age in Southern England*, BAR 31, Oxford

Rowlands, M.J. 1980 "Kinship, alliance and exchange in the European Bronze Age", in J. Barrett and R. Bradley (eds), 1980, 15–55

Rowlands, M.J. 1982 "Processual archaeology as historical social science", in C. Renfrew, M. Rowlands and B. Segraves (eds), 1982, 155–74

Rowlands, M.J. 1984 "Objectivity and subjectivity in archaeology", in M. Spriggs (ed), 1984, 108–113

Rowlands, M.J. and Gledhill, J. 1977 "The relation between archaeology and anthropology", in M. Spriggs (ed), *Archaeology and Anthropology: Areas of Mutual Interest*, BAR S19, Oxford, 143–58

Rutland, R.A. and Coghlan, H.H. 1971–2 "Bronze Age flat axes from Berkshire", *Berkshire Archaeol. J.*, 66, 45–59

Rutland, R.A. and Greenaway, J.A. 1970 "Archaeological notes from Reading Museum", *Berkshire Archaeol. J.*, 65, 53–60

Sandford, P. 1985 "Charting success", *Acorn User*, 31, 77–9, 99–102

Sanford, W.A. 1880 In "Antiquities and works of art exhibited", *Archaeol. J.*, 37, 107

Sasse, B. 1977 "Versuch einer statistischen Systematik der jungbronzezeitlichen Hortfunde im Mittelelbe–Saale–Gebiet", *Jahrenschrift für Mitteldeutsche Vorgeschichte*, 61, 53–84

Savage, R.D.A. 1979 "Technical notes on the Watford sword fragments", a contribution to D. Coombs, 1979b, 221–8

Savory, H.N. 1958 "The Late Bronze Age in Wales: some new discoveries and new interpretations", *Archaeol. Cambrensis*, 107, 3–63

Scarth, H.M. 1859 "Some account of the investigation of barrows on the line of the Roman road between Old Sarum and the port at the mouth of the River Axe, supposed to be the 'Ad Axium' of Ravennas", *Archaeol. J.*, 16, 146–57

Schauer, P. 1974 "Der urnenfelderzeitliche Depotfund von Dolina, Gde. und Kr. Nova Gradiska, Kroatien", *Jahrbuch des Römisch–Germanischen Zentralmuseums Mainz*, 2, 93–124

Selborne, Lord 1875 "Appendix on the Roman–British antiquities of Selborne", in F. Buckland (ed),

Natural History and Antiquities of Selborne by Gilbert White, Macmillan and Co., London, 559–74

Selborne, Lord 1877 "Appendix on the Romano-British antiquities of Selborne", in T. Bell (ed), *The Natural History and Antiquities of Selborne in the County of Southampton, by the late Gilbert White*, John van Voorst, London, 378–93

Sheppard, T. 1922 "Hoard of bronze axes from Windsor", *The Naturalist*, July 1, 217–22

Sheridan, A. and Bailey, G. (eds) 1981 *Economic Archaeology: Towards an Integration of Ecological and Social Approaches*, BAR S96, Oxford

Sherwin, G.A. 1936a "Arreton Down bronze hoard", *Proc. Isle Wight Natur. Hist. Archaeol. Soc.*, 2/7, 612–3

Sherwin, G.A. 1936b *The Isle of Wight in the Bronze Age, Vols. I and II*, unpublished MS in the library of the Society of Antiquaries, MS 767

Sherwin, G.A. 1942 "A second bronze hoard of Arreton Down type found in the Isle of Wight", *Antiq. J.*, 22, 198–201

Shortt, H. de S. 1949–50a "A hoard of bangles from Ebbesbourne Wake, Wilts.", *Wiltshire Archaeol. Mag.*, 53, 104–12

Shortt, H. de S. 1949–50b "A bronze founder's hoard near Ansty Hollow", *Wiltshire Archaeol. Mag.*, 53, 134

Shortt, H. 1961–2 "Accessions", in *Salisbury Mus. Annu. Rep.*, 95, 18–22

Shrubsole, O.A. 1906 "Early man: Bronze Age", *VCH Berks.*, I, 173–96

Silvester, R.J. 1980 "The prehistoric open settlement at Dainton, south Devon", *Proc. Devon Archaeol. Soc.*, 38, 17–48

Skinner, E. 1885–6 "British bronze weapons found near Norwich", *The East Anglian; or, Notes and Queries on Subjects Connected with the Counties of Suffolk, Cambridge, Essex and Norfolk*, I, 57–8

Slapp, T.P. 1846 "Celts, etc. found at Carleton Rode, Norfolk", *Archaeologia*, 31, 494

Smedley, N. and West, S.E. 1955–7 "Archaeology in Suffolk, 1954–1955", *Proc. Suffolk Inst. Archaeol.*, 27, 41–6

Smith, C.R. 1849–53 In *Proc. Soc. Antiq. London*, 2 (1st series), 83

Smith, C.R. 1851 In "Proceedings of the association", *J. Brit. Archaeol. Ass.*, 6, 88

Smith, C.R. and Thorp 1882 "A hoard of bronze bracelets at Brading, I.W.", J. *Brit. Archaeol. Ass.*, 38, 423–4

Smith, M.A. 1959 "Some Somerset hoards and their place in the Bronze Age of southern Britain", *Proc. Prehist. Soc.*, 25, 144–87

Smith, R. 1903–5 In *Proc. Soc. Antiq. London*, 20, 179–95

Smith, R. 1907–9 In *Proc. Soc. Antiq. London*, 22, 337–43

Smith, R. 1914–15 In *Proc. Soc. Antiq. London*, 27, 69–74

Smith, R.A. 1920 *A Guide to the Antiquities of the Bronze Age in the Department of British and Mediaeval Antiquities, British Museum*, Oxford, 2nd edition

Smith-Masters, J.E. 1929 *Yattendon and its Church, with Records of the Manor and the Village from the 10th Century to the Present Day*, Cornwall Press, London

Sneath, P.H.A. and Sokal, R.R. 1973 *Numerical Taxonomy: The Principles and Practice of Numerical Classification*, W.H. Freeman and Co., San Francisco

Spriggs, M. (ed) 1984 *Marxist Perspectives in Archaeology*, Cambridge University Press. Also introduction: "Another way of telling: Marxist perspectives in archaeology", 1–9

Stahlhofen, H. 1977 "Ein Bronzedepotfund von Wallwitz, Kr. Burg", *Ausgrabungen und Funde*, 22, 211–13

Stein, F. 1976 *Bronzezeitliche Hortfunde in Süddeutschland: Beiträge zur Interpretation einer Quellengattung*, Saarbrücker Beiträge zur Altertumskunde, 23, Bonn

Stevens, F. 1932–4 "Bronze implements", in "Notes", *Wiltshire Archaeol. Mag.*, 46, 520–6

Stjernquist, B. 1962–3 "Präliminarien zu einer Untersuchung von Opferfunden: Begriffsbestimmung und Theoriebildung", *Meddelanden Från Lunds Universitets Historiska Museum*, 5–64

Stjernquist, B. 1964 "New light on spring-cults in Scandinavian prehistory", *Archaeology*, 17, 180–4

Stodart, E. 1836 "Torques found at Boyton, in Suffolk", in *Appendix, Archaeologia*, 26, 459–85

Stradling, W. 1854 "A young turf-bearer's find in the turbaries", *Proc. Somerset Archaeol. Natur. Hist. Soc.*, 5, 91–4

Stuiver, M. and Pearson, G.W. 1986 "High-precision calibration of the radiocarbon time scale, AD 1950–500 BC", *Radiocarbon*, 28/2B, 805–38

Stukeley, W. 1776 *Itinerarium Curiosum: Or, An Account of the Antiquities and Remarkable Curiosities in Nature or Art, Observed in Travels through Great Britain*, Centuria I, 2nd edition, and II, Baker and Leigh, London

Suckling, A. 1848 *The History and Antiquities of the County of Suffolk: with Genealogical and Architectural Notices of its Several Towns and Villages*, Vol. II, printed for the author, London

Sumner, Heywood 1927 "Bronze hoard in the New Forest", *Antiq. J.*, 7, 192–3

Taylor, A. 1981 "Appendix II: The barrows of Cambridgeshire", in A. Lawson, E. Martin and D. Priddy, 1981, 108–120

Taylor, J.J. 1980 *Bronze Age Goldwork of the British Isles*, Cambridge University Press

Taylor, R.J. 1980 "An Armorican socketed axe from the sea off Chesil Beach, Dorset", *Archaeol. Atlant.*, 3, 133–7

Taylor, R.J. 1982 "The hoard from West Buckland, Somerset", *Antiq. J.*, 62, 13–17

Thomas, R., Robinson, M., Barrett, J. and Wilson, B. 1986 "A Late Bronze Age riverside settlement at Wallingford, Oxfordshire", *Archaeol. J.*, 143, 174–200

Tinsley, H.M. 1981 "The Bronze Age" (with C. Grigson), in I.G. Simmons and M.J. Tooley (eds), *The Environment in British Prehistory*, Duckworth, London, 210–49

Torbrügge, W. 1960 "Die bayerischen Ims-Funde", *Bayerische Vorgeschichtsblätter*, 25, 16–69

Torbrügge, W. 1970–71 "Vor- und frühgeschichtliche Flussfunde - Zur Ordnung und Bestimmung einer Denkmälergruppe", *Bericht der Römisch-Germanischen Kommission*, 51–2, 1–146

Torbrügge, W. 1985 "Über Horte und Hortdeutung", *Archäologisches Korrespondenzblatt*, 15, 17–23

Trinder, H.W. 1907–10 "The Meon Valley", *Pap. Proc. Hampshire Fld. Club Archaeol. Soc.*, 6, 65–89

Tucker, C. 1855 In "Proceedings at meetings of the Archaeological Institute", *Archaeol. J.*, 12, 84–5

Tucker, C. 1867 "Notice of antiquities of bronze found in Devonshire", *Archaeol. J.*, 24, 110–22

Turner, J. 1981 "The Iron Age", in I.G. Simmons and M.J. Tooley (eds), *The Environment in British Prehistory*, Duckworth, London, 250–81

Tylecote, R.F. 1979 "The effect of soil conditions on the long-term corrosion of buried tin-bronzes and copper", *J. Archaeol. Sci.*, 6/4, 345–68

Varndell, G.L. 1979 "The Andover hoard – a Late Bronze Age hoard of Wilburton tradition from Hampshire", in C. Burgess and D. Coombs (eds), 1979, 93–7

Veasey, D. 1849–53 In *Proc. Soc. Antiq. London*, 2, 103–4

Verron, G. 1973 "Méthodes statistiques et étude des cachettes complexes de l'Age du Bronze", in *L'Homme, Hier et Aujourdhui, Recueil d'Etudes en Hommage à André Leroi-Gourhan*, Editions Cujas, Paris, 609–24

Wallerstein, I. 1979 *The Capitalist World-Economy*, Cambridge University Press, London and Editions de la Maison des Sciences de l'Homme

Ware, S. 1843–9 In *Proc. Soc. Antiq. London*, 1, 83

Ware, S. 1846 "Battle-axe-heads, found near Clare in Suffolk", *Archaeologia*, 31, 496–7

Warne, C. 1866 *The Celtic Tumuli of Dorset: An Account of Personal and Other Researches in the Sepulchral Mounds of the Durotriges*, John Russell Smith, London

Warne, C. 1872 *Ancient Dorset. The Celtic, Roman, Saxon, and Danish Antiquities of the County, including the Early Coinage*, privately printed, Bournemouth

Way, A. 1860 *A Catalogue of the Museum Formed at Gloucester during the Meeting of the Archaeological Institute of Great Britain and Ireland*, Gloucester

Way, A. 1869 "Antiquities of bronze found in Devonshire", *Archaeol. J.*, 26, 339–51

Welbourn, D.A. 1981 "The role of blacksmiths in a tribal society", *Archaeol. Rev. Cambridge*, 1/1, 30–40

Wells, P. 1981 *The Emergence of an Iron Age Economy: The Mecklenburg Grave Groups from Hallstatt and Sticna*, Peabody Museum, Harvard

Westropp, H.M. 1879–81 In *Proc. Soc. Antiq. London*, 8, 312–3

Whitehead, J.L. 1911 *The Undercliff of the Isle of Wight, Past and Present*, Knight's Library, Ventnor

Whitmarsh, J. 1884 In "Ninth report of the committee on scientific memoranda: V. Archaeological", *Rep. Trans. Devonshire Ass.*, 16, 75–6

Wilde, W.R. 1857 *A Descriptive Catalogue of the Antiquities of Stone, Earthen, and Vegetable Materials, in the Museum of the Royal Irish Academy*, Royal Irish Academy, Dublin

Wilde, W.R. 1861 *A Descriptive Catalogue of the Antiquities of Animal Materials and Bronze in the Museum of the Royal Irish Academy*, Hodges, Smith and Co., Dublin

Wilkins, E.P. and Brion, J. 1859 *A Concise Exposition of the Geology, Antiquities, and Topography, of the Isle of Wight. The Favourite Localities of the Tourist, No. 1*, E. Stanford, London

Worsaae, J.J.A. 1866–71 "Sur quelques trouvailles de l'age de bronze faites dans des tourbières", *Mémoires de la Société Royale des Antiquaries du Nord*, 61–75

Wright, T. 1863 "On some antiquities recently found at Cirencester, the Roman Corinium", *J. Brit. Archaeol. Ass.*, 19, 100–5

Yates, J. 1849 "Use of bronze celts in military operations", *Archaeol. J.*, 6, 363–92

Yeomans, K.A. 1968 *Statistics for the Social Scientist: 2. Applied Statistics*, Penguin Education Studies in Applied Statistics, Harmondsworth

Zimmermann, W.H. 1970 "Urgeschichtliche Opferfunde aus Flüssen, Mooren, Quellen und Brunnen Südwestdeutschlands", *Neue Ausgrabungen und Forschungen in Niedersachsen*, 6, 53–92

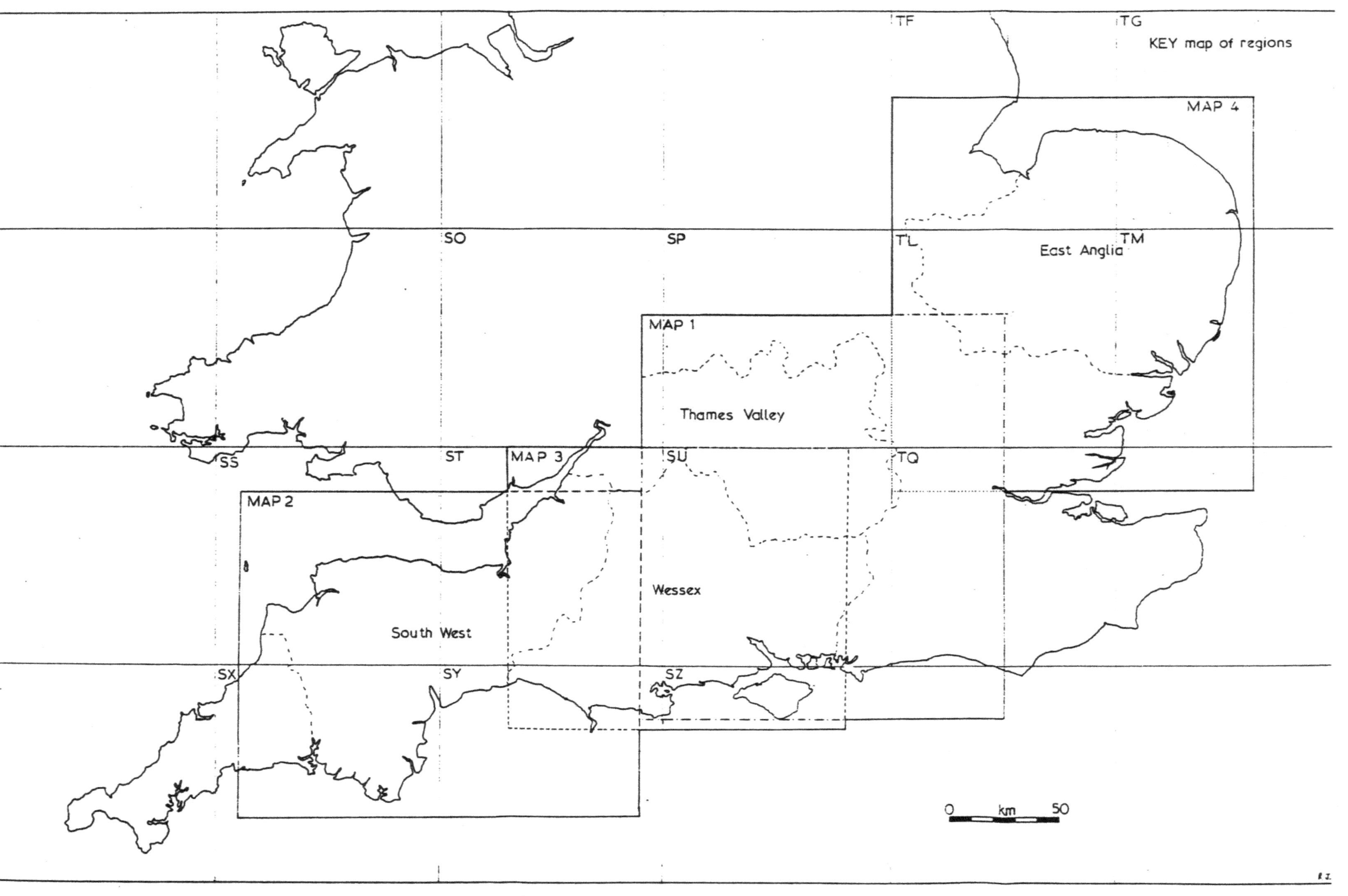
KEY map of regions
TF
TG
MAP 4
East Anglia
SO
SP
TL
TM
MAP 1
Thames Valley
SS
ST
MAP 3
SU
TQ
MAP 2
Wessex
South West
SX
SY
SZ
0 km 50

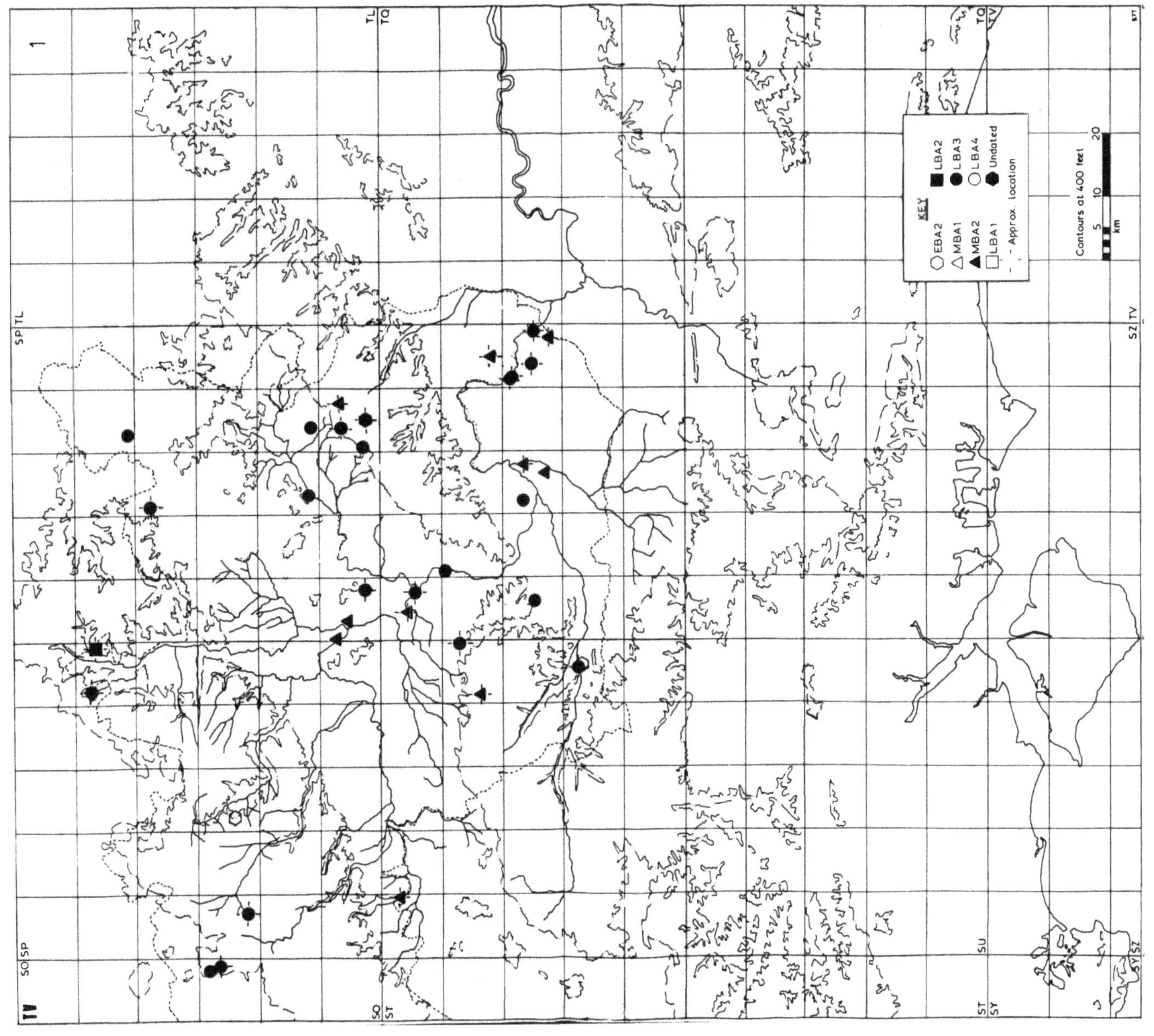

Please view pages in original size at this link: https://doi.org/10.30861/9780860547488_original

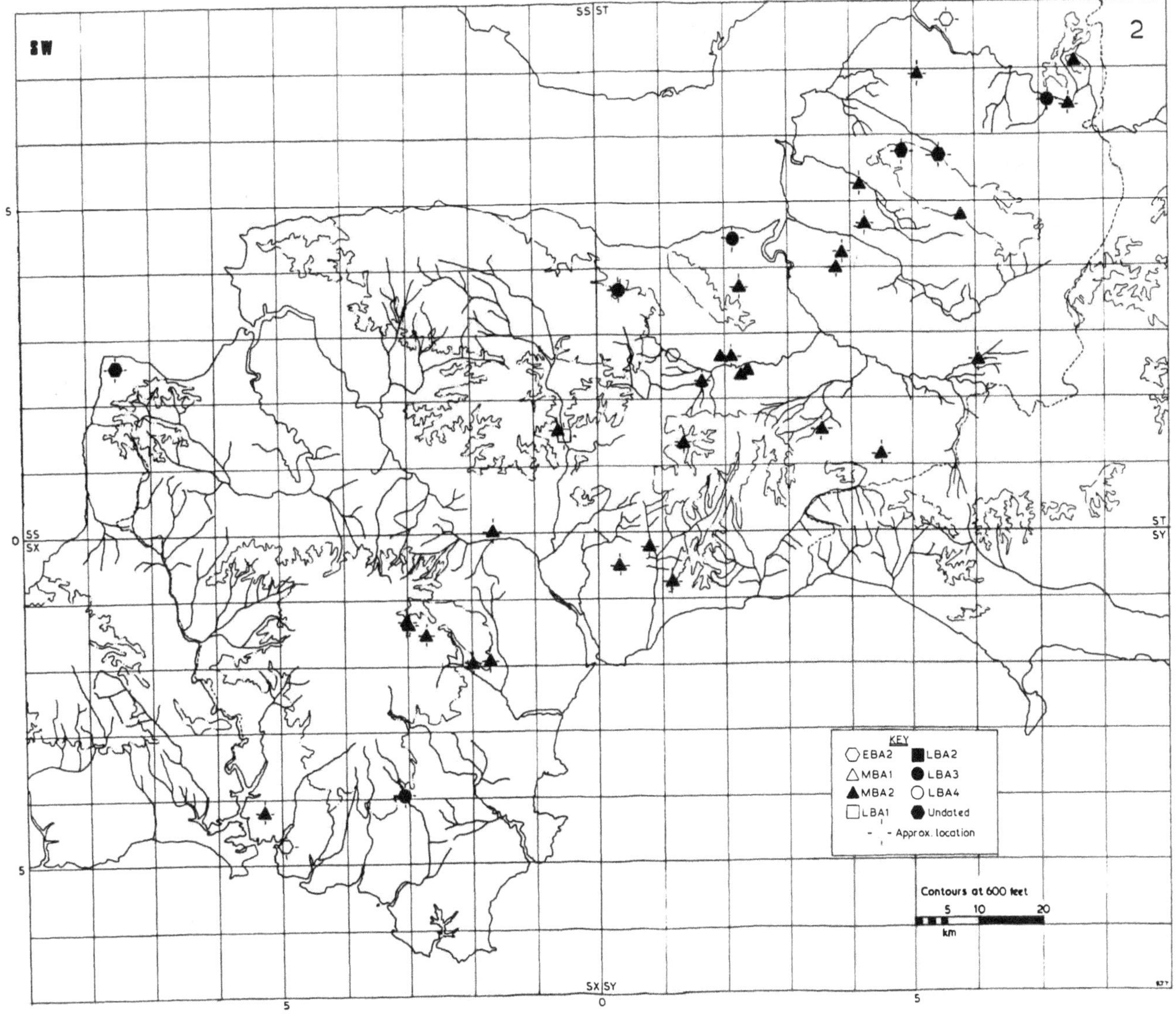

Please view pages in original size at this link: https://doi.org/10.30861/9780860547488_original

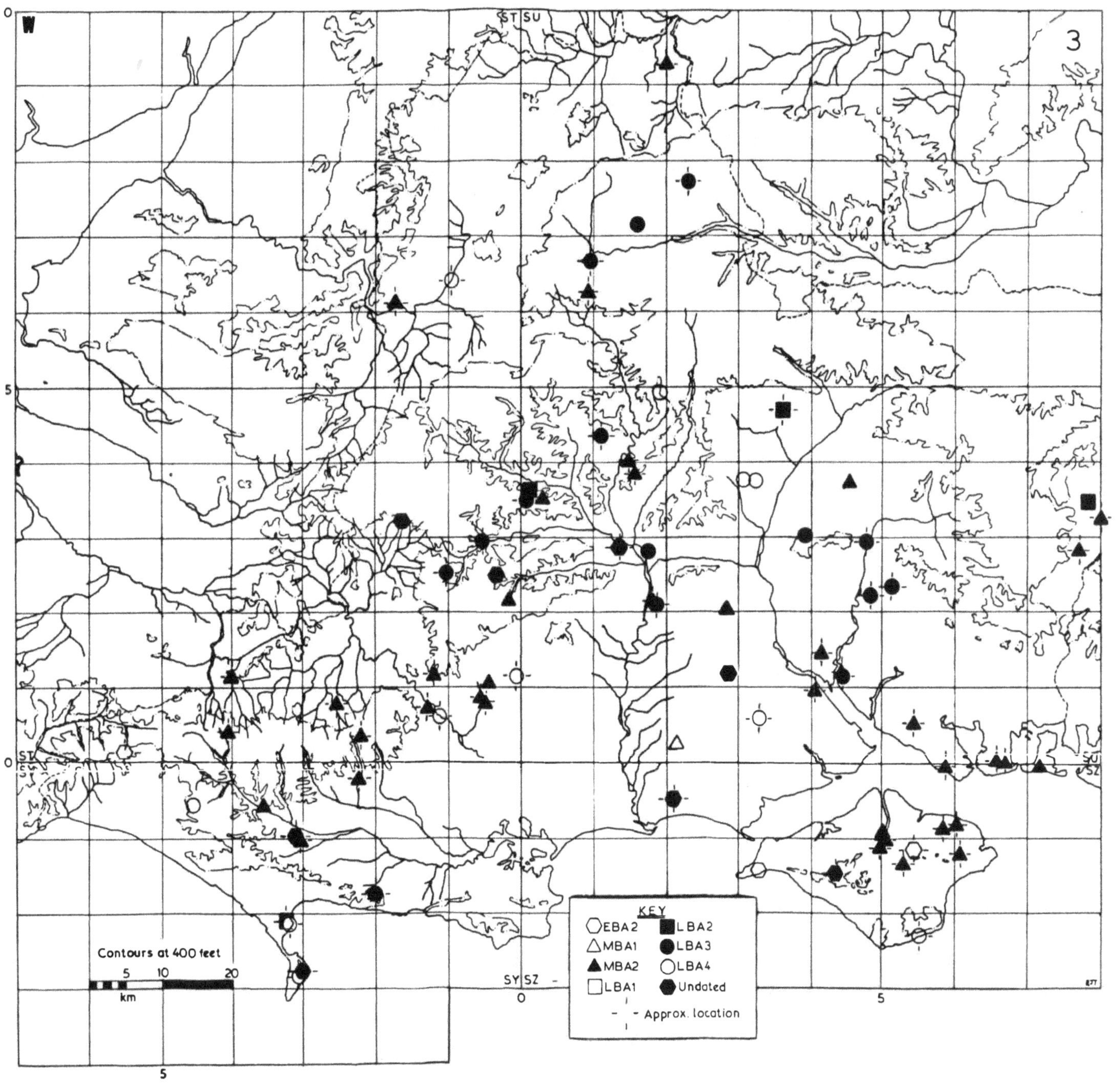

Please view pages in original size at this link: https://doi.org/10.30861/9780860547488_original

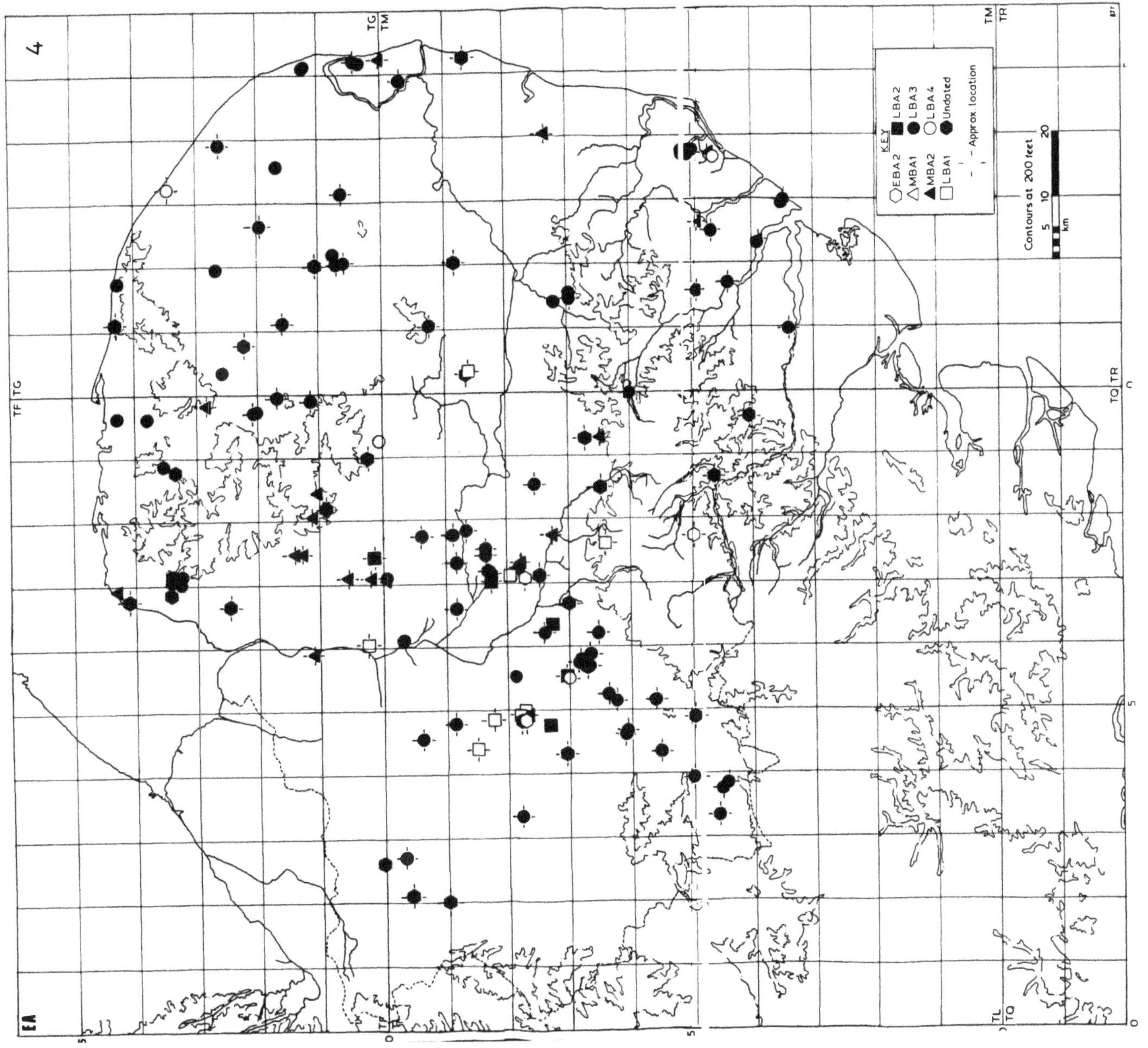
4
KEY
EBA2
MBA1
MBA2
LBA1
LBA2
LBA3
LBA4
Undated
- Approx. location
Contours at 200 feet
km
EA

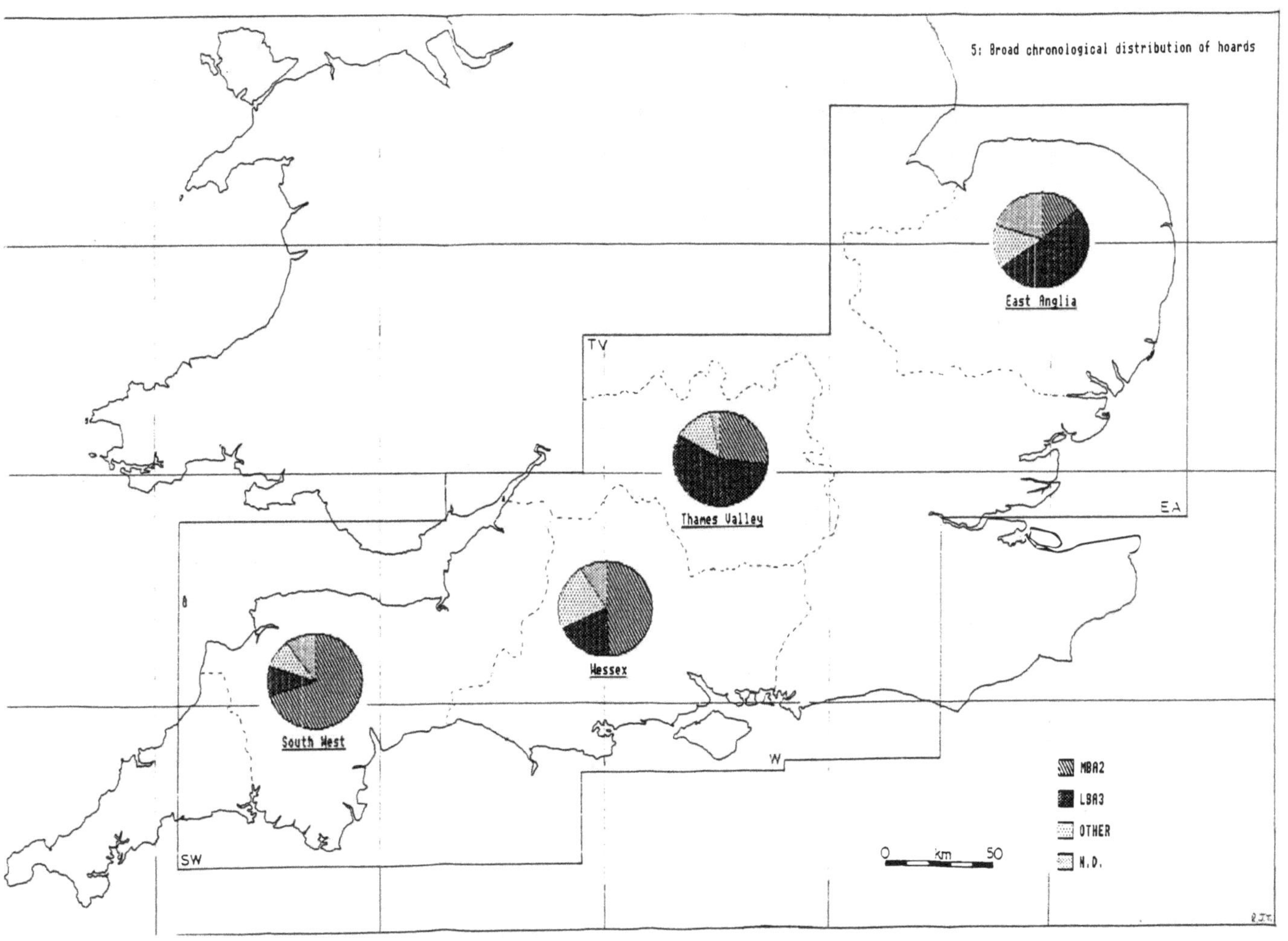

Please view pages in original size at this link: https://doi.org/10.30861/9780860547488_original

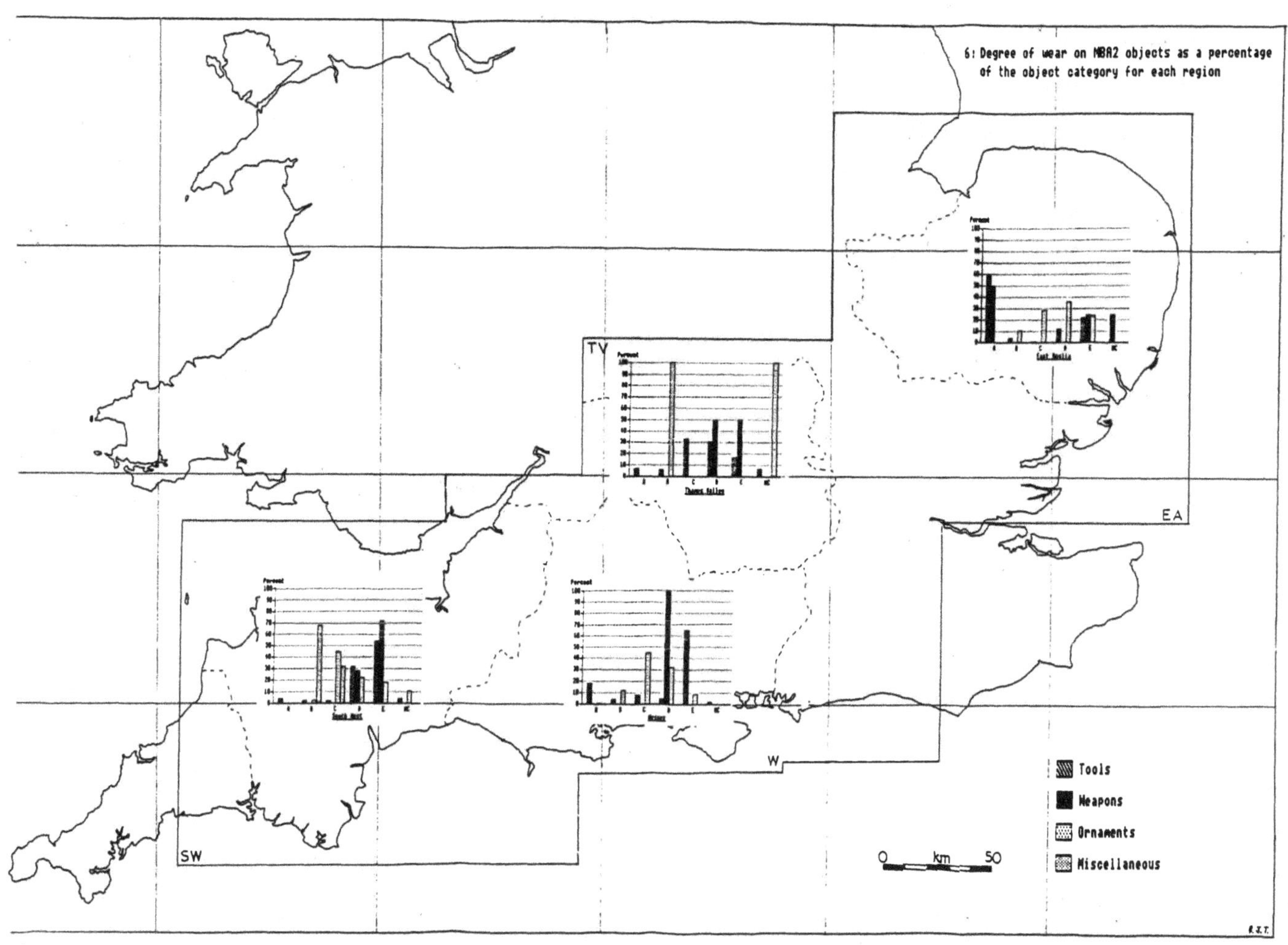
6: Degree of wear on MBA2 objects as a percentage of the object category for each region
TV
EA
SW
W
Tools
Weapons
Ornaments
Miscellaneous
0 km 50

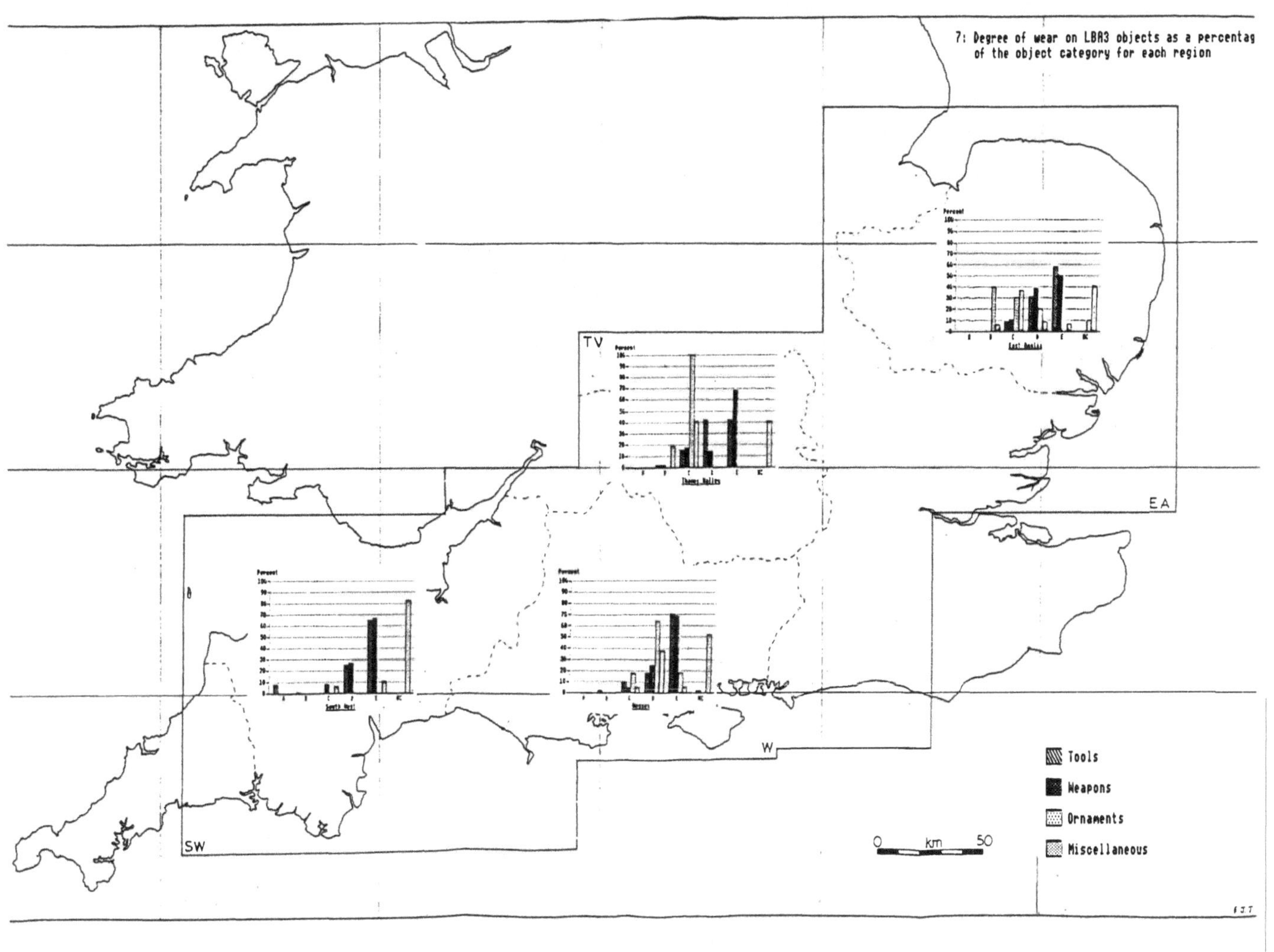

Please view pages in original size at this link: https://doi.org/10.30861/9780860547488_original

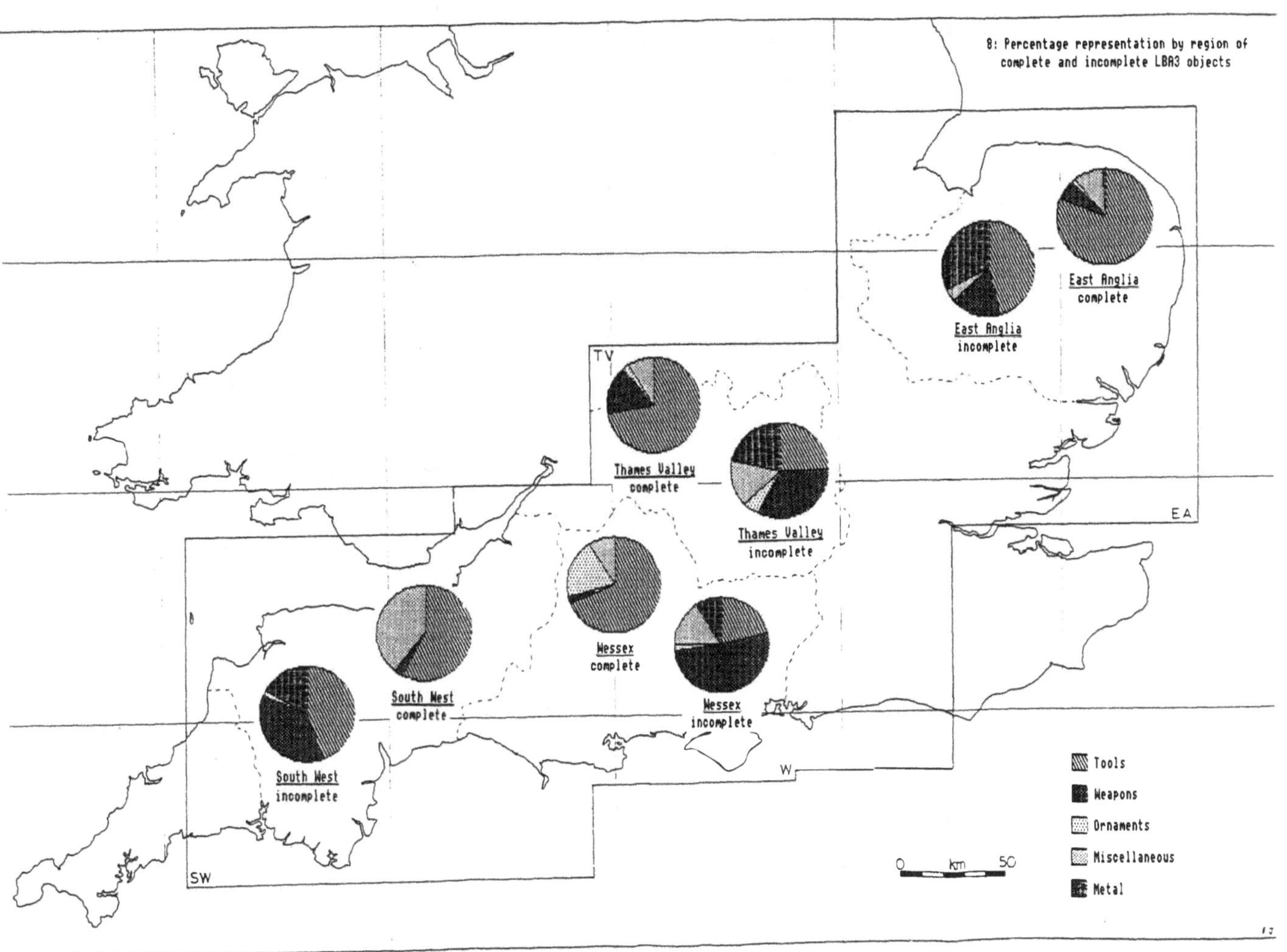
8: Percentage representation by region of complete and incomplete LBA3 objects
East Anglia complete
East Anglia incomplete
TV
Thames Valley complete
Thames Valley incomplete
EA
South West complete
South West incomplete
Wessex complete
Wessex incomplete
W
SW
Tools
Weapons
Ornaments
Miscellaneous
Metal
0 km 50

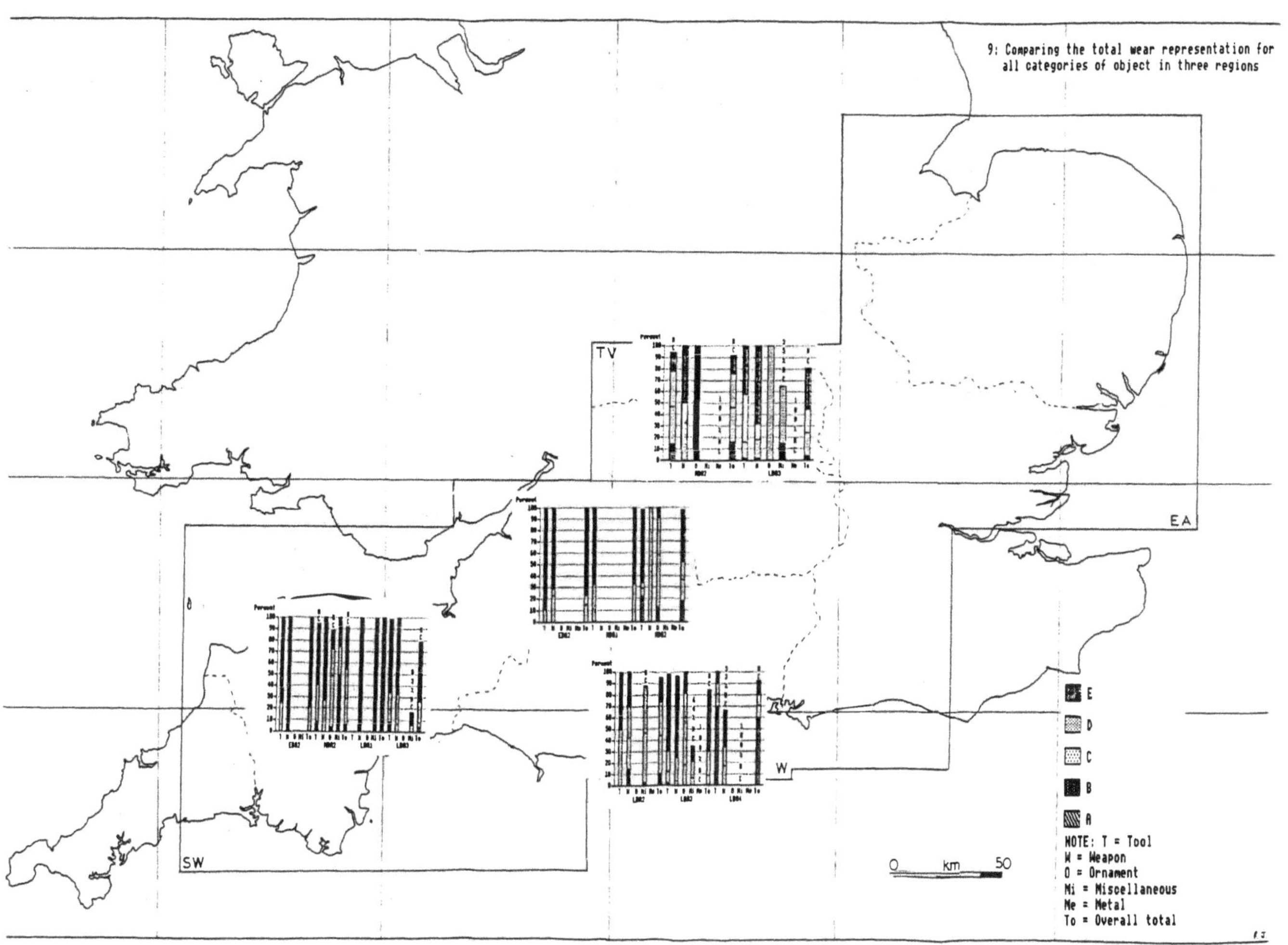

Please view pages in original size at this link: https://doi.org/10.30861/9780860547488_original

www.ingramcontent.com/pod-product-compliance
Lightning Source LLC
Chambersburg PA
CBHW060959030426
42334CB00033B/3298
* 9 7 8 0 8 6 0 5 4 7 4 8 8 *